Routledge Revivals

Footprints in the Snow

First published in 1901 and this English translation in 1970, *Footprints in the Snow* is one of the most popular novels in modern Japan. It is the story of the struggle of a penniless Japanese boy Shintaro Kikuchi, for education and emancipation. Determined to rebuild the family fortunes after his father's bankruptcy, Shintaro runs away from home in a remote corner of Kyushu, in the hope of making his way in the world. Robbed by pickpockets, he nearly dies of hunger and exhaustion, then after slaving for months as a money-lender's boy eventually succeeds in reaching a Christian College in Kyoto. A brilliant student, he accepts Christianity enthusiastically, but is also repelled by the arrogance of the Western missionary teachers towards a Japanese colleague that he walks out in protest. At last, four years after leaving home, Shintaro arrives in Tokyo. Yet even in the city of his dreams his life is far from peaceful- Shintaro has to struggle to keep himself at University, to pursue his career as a writer and journalist and in order to marry the girl he loves. The original Japanese title of Footprints in the Snow is *Omoide no Ki*.

Kenjiro Tokutomi 's novel is still read in Japan today and more than any other novel conveys what it felt like to be young in the days of Japan's great transformation from feudal to modern state. This is an interesting read for students of Japanese literature, Asian literature, and literature in general.

Footprints in the Snow
A Novel of Meiji Japan

Kenjiro Tokutomi
Translated by Kenneth Strong

First published in Japanese as Omoide no Ki by Minyusha, Tokyo in 1901
English Translation by George Allen & Unwin Ltd, 1970

This edition first published in 2024 by Routledge
4 Park Square, Milton Park, Abingdon, Oxon, OX14 4RN

and by Routledge
605 Third Avenue, New York, NY 10017

Routledge is an imprint of the Taylor & Francis Group, an informa business

© English translation © UNESCO 1970

All rights reserved. No part of this book may be reprinted or reproduced or utilised in any form or by any electronic, mechanical, or other means, now known or hereafter invented, including photocopying and recording, or in any information storage or retrieval system, without permission in writing from the publishers.

Publisher's Note
The publisher has gone to great lengths to ensure the quality of this reprint but points out that some imperfections in the original copies may be apparent.

Disclaimer
The publisher has made every effort to trace copyright holders and welcomes correspondence from those they have been unable to contact.

A Library of Congress record exists under LCCN: 72853843

ISBN: 978-1-032-64502-5 (hbk)
ISBN: 978-1-032-64523-0 (ebk)
ISBN: 978-1-032-64516-2 (pbk)

Book DOI 10.4324/9781032645230

Footprints in the Snow

A novel of Meiji Japan

by
KENJIRO TOKUTOMI

TRANSLATED BY KENNETH STRONG

London
GEORGE ALLEN AND UNWIN LTD
RUSKIN HOUSE   MUSEUM STREET

FIRST PUBLISHED IN GREAT BRITAIN IN 1970
This book is copyright under the Berne Convention. All rights reserved. Apart from any fair dealing for the purpose of private study, research, criticism or review, as permitted under the Copyright Act, 1956, no part of this publication may be reproduced, stored in retrieval system, or transmitted, in any form or by any means, electronic, electrical, chemical, mechanical, optical, photocopying, recording or otherwise, without the prior permission of the copyright owner. Enquiries should be addressed to the Publishers.

English translation © UNESCO 1970
SBN 04 895017 3

Translated from
Omoide no Ki, first published in book form Minyusha, Tokyo, 1901

UNESCO COLLECTION OF REPRESENTATIVE WORKS
JAPANESE SERIES

This book
has been accepted
in the Japanese Series
of the Translations Collection
of the United Nations
Educational, Scientific and Cultural Organization
(UNESCO)

PRINTED IN GREAT BRITAIN
in 11 *on* 12 *pt Plantin type*
BY HAZELL WATSON & VINEY LTD
AYLESBURY, BUCKS

Introduction[1]

To many, perhaps most, educated Japanese today the novels of the so-called Meiji era (i.e. the period of the reign of the Emperor Meiji, 1868–1912) seem more remote than the great classics of nineteenth-century French, Russian or English literature, which have been widely and earnestly studied in Japan for the last eighty or ninety years, both in translation and in the original languages. This may seem paradoxical, since Meiji was in many ways a heroic, larger-than-life age, when under the impact of western culture and science enormous changes were put into effect throughout Japanese society and the foundations laid for the emergence of Japan as a dynamic modern state. One would have expected a memorable flowering of literature to record such a dramatic release of a nation's energies. Literature flourished, certainly: in poetry, in drama and more particularly in the novel, valiant efforts were made to portray the changes and to come to terms with the new philosophies flooding in from the west. Yet little was produced that is read today by any but academic students of the period.

There are many reasons for this dearth of enduring literary monuments. The status of serious literature was too low, the literary language inherited from the feudal period too crabbed and inflexible, and above all Meiji society was too authoritarian, to allow the country's many talented writers to express themselves fully and freely. The sheer pace of change, too, was so rapid, the tension between traditional and newly-imported foreign ideas so great, that anything more than a fragmentary response was almost impossible. 'The development that western nations have spread over three centuries, Japan has had to crowd into forty years,' wrote a celebrated novelist and poet not long after the turn of the century—not in pride at his country's nineteenth-century economic and cultural miracle, but rather in anguish at the strain the process had imposed. The tension did not end with Meiji; indeed, it is only since the Second World War that Japan has achieved a combination of political freedom and cultural self-confidence

---

1. For the biographical section of this introduction I rely (apart from brief articles by a number of Japanese critics) on the three volumes by Tokutomi's friend and disciple Koichiro Maedagawa—*Roka Den* (Life of Roka) (editions of 1938 and 1945), *Roka no Geijutsu* (Roka's Art) (1943), and *Owareru Tamashii* (Spirit Obsessed) (1948). Japanese writers invariably refer to Tokutomi by his pen-name of Roka, under which he published much of his better-known work. But in fact he stopped using this pen-name in 1905, and preferred to be known by his given-name of Kenjiro.

strong enough to permit the creation of a literature at once truly modern and truly Japanese.

If most Meiji novels are unreadable today, *Omoide no Ki*, or *Footprints in the Snow*[2], is a notable exception to the rule. First published in book form in May 1901, after being serialized in a newspaper for twelve months, *Footprints in the Snow* was immediately popular, ran through 145 printings in the next twenty-five years, and is now an accepted classic of the period. Though the immediate inspiration of this Japanese 'success story' was a delighted reading by Tokutomi of *David Copperfield*, Shintaro Kikuchi is a genuine native creation. Thousands of young men in the first decade of the century found it easy to identify themselves with him, not merely for his endurance and cheerful energy, but because of more specifically Japanese elements in his story: the ambition to restore the independence and honour of the fallen House of Kikuchi as a filial duty to his widowed mother, the intoxication with western literature and western ideals of freedom, the passionate patriotism and longing to modernize and 'improve' Japan, crystallizing in the romantic vision of a Utopia to be ushered in with the establishment of representative government. To contemporary readers, both western and Japanese—the latter quite as well used as the former to a world of electronics, abstract art and super-trains—*Footprints in the Snow* provides a vivid and truthful picture of what it felt like to grow up in the eventful early years of Japan's modern century. No other novel of the period conveys so readably the freshness in the air, the sense of excitement and liberation that filled the youth of the country for more than a generation after the final ending of the centuries of feudalism and seclusion.

Yet the book has never been without its unkind critics. Some early notices dismissed it as a *komyo shosetsu*, a 'novel of facile optimism', to be taken seriously only by women and other uneducated persons willing to demean themselves by such frivolous reading. The Japanese literary Establishment has never taken kindly to cheerful books, and for most of the modern period has tended to dismiss as 'shallow' novels which could not be discussed in terms of the currently most fashionable European theory. No doubt jealously was behind some of the early criticism, for with his first novel, *Hototogisu* (The Cuckoo), published two years before, Tokutomi had won himself a wider public than any other writer of the time. Nor did it help that he was known to be a Christian. But whatever the motives of the early critics, the defects of *Footprints in the Snow* are real enough. The characters are picturesque but simple; Shintaro's few attempts at self-analysis do not take him very far, nor is there any coherent criticism implied of the society through which he has pushed his way from near-destitution in a remote province to modest success as a journalist in the capital. After the long and convincing story of Shintaro's struggle for

2. The title of the original is simply *Memoirs* (*Omoide no Ki*). The title of the English translation is derived from the Emerson quotation which Tokutomi chose as an epigraph for the novel.

independence and so much earnest talk of the role of 'men of public spirit' in building a New Japan, the sentimentality of the final chapters and epilogue is too lightweight altogether. In part, the immaturity of the Japanese novel at the time was to blame—the lack of an accepted tradition of fiction as a vehicle for serious comment on life.

The weakness of the ending is, however, a pointer to a weightier charge against *Footprints in the Snow*—that its apparent optimism is false and backward-looking, the nostalgia of a man who did not understand the times in which he was writing. The overthrow of feudal rule in 1868, the multifarious changes in economic, political and social institutions, the 'popular rights movement', which reached its peak prior to the establishment of the Diet, had all been dominated by energetic and often idealistic young samurai, very many of them from the more distant provinces—like Shintaro Kikuchi and his creator. But by 1900, when Tokutomi was writing, the world was no longer every young man's oyster. The popular rights movement was little more than a memory, and the Diet it had helped to bring into being singularly ineffective, in spite of the continued lip-service paid by some politicians to democracy. Power lay in the hands of a small self-perpetuating oligarchy at the top, and below them in an army of obedient, office-conscious bureaucrats. Japanese socialism, the inheritor of the defunct popular rights movement, was as yet hardly visible on the horizon. A reaction had set in against the frantic westernization of the second decade of Meiji; the reversion to nationalism, in the name of the 'preservation of the Japanese spirit', was accentuated by victory over China in the war of 1894–5, and by the subsequent intervention of Russia, France and Germany, compelling Japan to surrender Port Arthur and the Liaotung Peninsula. Whatever dreams of fraternal democracy had been fashionable twenty years earlier, Japan at the turn of the century was an authoritarian and increasingly materialist society with an expanding capitalist economy, a nation heavily armed and elated with military victory. Komai Sensei, the 'beloved teacher' in *Footprints in the Snow*, stresses in his last talk with Shintaro before he leaves the country—exiled, in effect, by a repressive government—that the years *after* the establishment of the Diet will be crucial:

'I tell you, Japan won't be able to get by for long on the platitudes they've fed us with till now. The race will go to the swift, not the empty-headed! The real testing-time in politics will come after the Diet gets going in 1890 —and in everything, not only politics: the further Japan advances on to the world stage, the more opportunities for the really able. Now's the time for true patriots to prepare themselves, Kikuchi, without counting the cost: and by "true patriots" I mean every single loyal citizen in every walk of life who has a mind to serve his country!'

Yet what Shintaro himself does in these crucial years, beyond achieving a modest competence, we are not told: the talk is all of domestic bliss. Which is disappointing, when there has been such emphasis throughout on his high ideals and hatred of compromise. There are hints of disillusion. Tokyo Imperial University, which he had so long worshipped from afar as the temple of all wisdom, strikes him very unfavourably:

'A fount of learning, yes: but the waters were far from invigorating. Most of my fellow-students looked on study only as a short cut to worldly success, currying favour with professors, and busily making "contacts" among the wealthy and powerful, while running up debts with all manner of extravagant pastimes. With such undergraduates, and a deal of unsavory intrigue among the professors, the place was more like a "factory for the mass-production of time-serving bureaucrats", as one brave journalist had angrily called it, than a school for true patriots and public men. How disappointed I was! The day of the truly great teacher, whose influence moulds a whole generation, may be past, but I could find neither friend nor teacher worth the name.'

Nicknamed 'Kikuchi the Hermit', he retreats for much of the time into his own private world, and when years afterwards he recalls such former comrades as he had had, it is with a gentle melancholy:

'Of the company that left the University with me to plunge together into society's broad sea, some have disappeared without trace, others have quickly swum through to some island of security. I myself, to be frank, have barely escaped drowning. It's inevitable, I dare say, that a swimmer who ignores the winds and currents should find the going hard, and come in later, maybe, than the rest. Yet we ordinary mortals are so purblind and small in spirit, that we cannot see that our lives are but bubbles on the ocean of eternity, that all things, all creatures, are contained within the Creator's hand as they follow their destined cycle of existence. What looks like "winning" or "losing" is merely an optical illusion.'

It begins to look as if Shintaro's confident idealism is indeed shallow, the rather commonplace optimism natural to a young man who has lived through an exciting period of social change, plus a veneer of vague Christianity. Tokutomi himself, whose family were small capitalists as well as samurai, must have shared in this excitement. In his autobiography *Fuji*, written twenty-four years later, he describes *Footprints in the Snow* as a light-hearted, 'human interest' story, produced in the flush of pride at the success of his first novel; at that time, he says, he had neither the stamina nor the vision to 'walk the Way of God's art'. Whatever the meaning of this curious final phrase, it is true that as an 'inward' account of Meiji life *Footprints in the Snow* was out of date before it was written—less penetrating by far than Futabatei's tortured, unfinished novel *Ukigumo* (Drifting Clouds),[3] published some fourteen years earlier, whose hero, sensitive and

---

3. Translated into English (with a lengthy introduction) by Marleigh Grayer Ryan, under the title *Japan's first Modern Novel: Ukigumo of Futabatei Shimei* (Columbia University Press, New York and London, 1967).

idealistic like Shintaro, clashes directly with the selfish, callous officialdom which was running the country, and at whose existence Tokutomi only hints.

If the underlying theme of *Footprints in the Snow* is a commitment to modernization and reform, it is a commitment supported by a morality that is as yet too ill-digested an assortment of the old and the new values to generate much power for action. Seizan Sensei, the ascetic, lovable old Master of Chinese Studies who tries to inculcate the samurai virtues of simplicity, endurance and manliness without the old samurai arrogance, eventually closes his school in disgust, sensing his own inadequacy in the new world. Shintaro's intoxication with liberty and the novels of Hugo is largely inspired by a very traditional kind of personal devotion to his 'beloved teacher', rather than by any firmly-held principles. His Christianity is of the peculiar samurai brand, much concerned with manliness and personal honour and exerting for the most part no very obvious influence on his own relationships and assumptions: Shintaro's active side, which drives him from penury through all hardships to rebuild the House of Kikuchi, is never satisfactorily fused with his meditative, introspective self, much given to 'repentance', especially when he is ill, and sombre, if trite, reflections on the vanity of human wishes. (For the Japanese, it is perhaps worth pointing out, a due reminder of the evanescence of all things human has long been as necessary and satisfying an ingredient of fiction as romantic love in the west. So it is in *Footprints in the Snow*, with Shintaro's occasional less cheerful meditations, and more especially the three tragic deaths of Michitaro, the idealized Christian, Yabuki, the brilliant but solitary student and Komai Sensei, the 'beloved teacher'.)

Yet if in the end *Footprints in the Snow* pictures a class and a generation which was uncertain of its values and of its place in twentieth-century Japanese society, the vigour and idealism of the novel is not merely naïve or anachronistic. It reflects not only the undoubted upsurge of energy released throughout the country by the Meiji Restoration, but also the special euphoria resulting from the victory over China in 1895, which was popularly regarded as vindicating the upheaval of the Restoration and all that had followed from it. Hence, in the main, the book's success.

But there is another reason for its peculiar vitality—and also for its limitations—which was not fully realized for half a century: its close, but far from simple, relationship to the circumstances of Tokutomi's own life. Although it is usually described as an autobiographical or semi-autobiographical novel, and many of the minor characters are drawn fairly closely from life (Uncle Noda, Shingo, Mr Brown and the moneylender Nishiuchi among them), Shintaro himself is modelled in some important respects on Tokutomi's brother Iichiro, with whom, paradoxically, he was continually and fiercely at odds. More paradoxical still, while Shintaro's struggle is directed solely at re-establishing the House of Kikuchi, the central motif of Kenjiro's[4] life was his long feud—sometimes open, sometimes covert, and patched up occasionally in brief periods of reconciliation, but never wholly healed—with his own House of Tokutomi. *Footprints in the Snow* was written when Kenjiro seemed to be within sight of winning his fight for self-respect and freedom from the authoritarianism of the traditional family system. This is part of the explanation of Shintaro's *élan*, and probably, too, of his relationship with his mother and—at the end of the book—with his young wife: these were relationships which Kenjiro himself had not achieved, but in the possibility of which, at the time of writing, he had come to believe.

In fact, however, the conflict with his family continued for the rest of his life. One source of the peculiar fascination which Kenjiro continues to exercise today for the Japanese is the stand he made, not without much suffering and sacrifice, for the independence of the individual against the near-absolute authority of the head of the family. Seen in the context of Kenjiro's life, therefore, *Footprints in the Snow* is notable not only for the tale itself, the paradigm of a nation bent passionately on self-improvement, but for its indirect testimony to the courage with which its author defied the enormous pressures of a society still feudal and authoritarian at its roots.

Kenjiro Tokutomi was born on October 25, 1868, in the village of Minamata in south-west Kyushu, the seventh child of a prominent samurai family. For several generations a Tokutomi had been village head and local representative of the central government; and after receiving a grant of land at the time of the Restoration, the family substituted agriculture for its hereditary samurai stipend, producing tobacco, malt and saké. During the first five years of the Meiji period, Kenjiro's father Kazutaka held several prominent offices in the new prefectural administration.

Seventh child and third son of an old samurai family in a remote corner of feudal Kyushu, far from the capital and therefore all the more resistant to change—much of Kenjiro's life was determined in advance by the circumstances of his birth. His mother Hisako bore her husband four daughters in succession after their marriage, and Kazutaka grew more and more impatient at the lack of an heir.[5] At long last, however, the all-impor-

---

4. From this point on I refer to the author of *Footprints in the Snow* by his given-name of Kenjiro, to distinguish him from his elder brother Iichiro.

5. In 1863 the marriage nearly ended, in an incident that illustrates vividly the tensions to which Japanese families of this period were subject. During Hisako's fifth pregnancy (with the long-awaited heir, as it turned out), nearly every member of the family, and the servants as well, succumbed to an outbreak of measles, and Hisako wore herself out with nursing them all. When the worst was over, and she took the opportunity to go back to her old home to recuperate, her elder brother, Gensuke Yajima (the original of Uncle Noda in *Footprints in the Snow*) was incensed to hear of the ordeal she had been through, and poured his anger undiluted into a letter to her husband. Incensed in his turn, Kazutaka Tokutomi sent his brother to Yajima's house with a bill of divorcement: but to his surprise the emissary was greeted at Yajima's door by a smiling Hisako, no longer pale and thin—and with a baby boy in her arms. The bill of divorcement never left the emissary's pocket.

tant male child—Kenjiro's elder brother Iichiro—did arrive. Another boy came between Kenjiro and Iichiro, but died while still a baby.

Not surprisingly, Hisako's health had deteriorated by the time Kenjiro was born, and since she could not nurse him, he was fed for the most part —milk-feeding being still unknown—on *amazake*, a sweet drink made from fomented rice. The lack of physical contact with his mother doubtless contributed to the sense of insecurity and inferiority that Kenjiro never wholly overcame all his life.[6] But there was another lack, equally serious. In a real sense Kenjiro was an unwanted child. Iichiro, the future head of the house, was idolized, taught and encouraged by everyone in the big household, and by numerous relatives and visitors. By comparison, Kenjiro was the plaything of the family, brought up as are all Japanese children with indulgent affection, but not with the respect that a child needs just as much: even in childhood, Kenjiro existed only in his brother's shadow. Temperamental differences widened the gap between the two brothers. Iichiro was by nature energetic, practical, sociable and optimistic, Kenjiro introspective and moody, with few friends. Yet by virtue of his position as heir, the elder brother could and did claim a near-absolute authority over the younger, which the latter accepted without questioning throughout their boyhood.

In 1870 the family moved to the town of Kumamoto, where in due course both boys went to school, Kenjiro to the local primary school and Iichiro to the *Yogakko*, or School of Western Learning, which had been founded by the modernizing party within the Kumamoto Clan and employed one Lieutenant Janes, a retired American army officer and earnest Christian, to direct the teaching. There was much that needed modernizing and humanizing in Kumamoto. Kenjiro was often taken by his grandfather to the public executions. Perched on a servant's shoulders, he would watch the hanging, the decapitation of the dead criminal with a stroke of the executioner's sword, the impaling of the head on a bamboo stake for public exhibition, as in Elizabethan England. Tension mounted in the town and surrounding provinces as the *tempo* of change increased. Opposition between the local modernizers and conservatives grew more bitter, many of the former being physically assaulted, till in 1876 the School of Western Learning was forced to close. The ambitious Iichiro—aged thirteen— left Kumamoto at once with the idea of entering a school in Tokyo; but

---

6. Writing not long before his death he recalled the sharpness with which his mother had rebuffed him when at the age of five or six he tried before going to sleep at night to play with her breast, as his nurse had encouraged him to do with her. 'This nurse's hands, in her great love for me,' he says cryptically, 'had early shattered my childish innocence.' But others besides the nurse were responsible. As his mother's health grew worse, his father would bring other women home. Not much can be concealed in a Japanese-style house, and Kenjiro, who had sharp eyes and a photographic memory, remembered everything he saw. At school he suffered much from enormous boils and swellings, and claimed later in life that these were hereditary in origin, his father being syphilitic.

stopped at Kyoto to enrol in Doshisha College, the Christian school founded with eight students by Jo Niijima two years before.[7]

In Kyushu the unrest culminated in the famous Satsuma Rebellion of 1877, in which Takamori Saigo led the clansmen of Satsuma in an attempt to overthrow the central government. Pitched battles took place in and around Kumamoto. The Tokutomi family scattered to avoid the fighting, Kenjiro and his mother spending three months with Hisako's relatives in the country; when they returned, it was to find the house pitted with bullet-holes and Kenjiro's beloved dog Obuchi dead—shot and beheaded, they were told, by marauding samurai. With the death of Saigo, killed at his own request by one of his retainers after his defeat by imperial troops in September, the rebellion ended, but the peace that followed was uneasy. For the Tokutomis, as for many other samurai households, life became increasingly difficult. With the forced commutation of samurai pensions into government bonds in 1876, dissension arose within the various branches of the family as to how best to use their now severely limited resources. Kazutaka now had very little regular income beyond what his wife and elder daughters made by sewing and selling mulberry shoots to the Kumamoto silkworm-breeders: there was little enough money to send to Kyoto to eke out what Iichiro was earning to support himself at Doshisha, and none at all to pay for Kenjiro's education beyond primary school. Kazutaka must have been relieved, therefore, when Iichiro, home on a visit from Doshisha in the spring of 1878, announced that he would take Kenjiro back with him to the College.

Kenjiro accordingly left for Kyoto in his brother's charge. The two had never been close friends. The strict Confucian training[8] which Iichiro had been given from his earliest years, together with his ambitious nature and the awareness that he alone was expected to restore the Tokutomi fortunes, inevitably made him impatient with his dreamy brother, and now that they were on their own together, the differences between the pair must have stood out more sharply than ever. Yet Kenjiro was happy enough at Doshisha, enjoying the discovery of a new world of books, the conversation

---

7. The connection thus begun between Doshisha (Kansei College in *Footprints in the Snow*), now one of Japan's leading private universities, and the Tokutomi family lasted through two generations and took many forms. Hatsuko Tokutomi, one of Kenjiro's sisters, married a close friend of Niijima's, and their son later became President of Doshisha—and subsequently first President of the International Christian University, when it was founded in Tokyo after the Pacific War.

8. In his autobiography Iichiro writes that his parents looked forward so eagerly to his future that they tried 'to make him grow three years in every year'. At the age of four he was reading the Chinese classics with his father; at eight he took his father's place 'lecturing on ethics' to the children of surrounding villages. As punishment when he himself misbehaved, he would be tied to a tree, or locked in a barrel and rolled about the floor in the store-room. His own attitude to Kenjiro while they were at Doshisha he describes as that of 'a sergeant-major to a recruit'.

of American missionaries and an exotic half-western atmosphere.[9] If he had to submit in everything to his brother, he could hardly help admiring him, and profited from Iichiro's popularity with both students and teachers: besides his academic brilliance, Iichiro had made himself prominent by his enthusiastic adoption of Christianity,[10] and by the vigour of his championing of the ideals of freedom and democracy that were discussed with such fervour in the newly-founded Christian schools at that period. For nearly two years life went smoothly by. In May of 1880, however, trouble arose in the College because of the amalgamation of the first- and second-year classes, which would naturally put the second year at a disadvantage.[11] Iichiro and other boys of the senior class (which was due to graduate in the summer) protested, and threatened to leave the school in a body. Alarmed, Principal Niijima[12] addressed the boys after morning worship. Accepting responsibility for the administration's shortcomings, he caned his own hand, broke the cane into three pieces, and finished by reciting an elegant poem of apology. This characteristically Japanese approach, in a school that was often attacked for its westernizing, proved highly effective, and the trouble died down at once. Only Iichiro and two other boys would not accept Niijima's statement: a month before they were due to graduate, all three left to seek their fortunes in Tokyo. Within a few weeks one had returned to Doshisha; the second had found himself a modest job as a private tutor in English; while the third, Iichiro, after knocking vainly on the doors of famous journalists in the hope of persuading them to help him find employment, eventually made his way back, empty-handed but as full as ever of fire and hope, to his native Kyushu.

Unable to stay on at Doshisha without Iichiro, his 'guarantor', Kenjiro too was sent home in June. The family seem to have taken no serious thought for his future. When three months later Iichiro arrived back from the capital and started a small private school in the house, Kenjiro was

9. The food was entirely western. Mrs Niijima, a large, imposing figure, was given to wearing leather shoes and enormous American hats with her kimono, down the front of which she would dangle a long watch-chain.
10. He was baptized in 1877. His Christianity, though, was short-lived, and his democratic convictions likewise without very deep roots, as his subsequent career showed.
11. Other incidents may have contributed to the explosion. The College being avowedly Christian, moral standards were strict. Two boys had recently been expelled for corresponding with girls in the licensed quarters, and a third for homosexual practices—in which he would indulge after conducting a prayer meeting with the boys concerned. (The latter case is not so bizarre as might appear. Many of the students in the early days of Doshisha came from Kyushu where women were often regarded with such contempt that homosexuality was commonly accepted, as in ancient Athens: many of them, therefore, saw it neither as unnatural in itself nor as inconsistent with Christianity.)
12. 'Principal Katayama' in *Footprints in the Snow*. Niijima was much beloved by his students: it was his personality, rather than any doctrinal attractions, which converted Iichiro to Christianity.

enrolled as his brother's pupil. Not surprisingly, he did not make much progress, spending most of his time reading and filling notebooks with copied passages, and sketches and essays of his own.[13] After nearly two years of this desultory home education, his father sent him to learn silkworm-breeding in a nearby household, where he was made to live in. But this project failed, too. Kenjiro seems to have made good friends with the daughter of the family and played a lot of chess with her brother, but done little else, and an appropriate excuse was soon found for returning him to his own home, where he rejoined his brother's school.

The atmosphere in the Tokutomi household was restless and uneasy. Kenjiro lived 'like a snail,' he wrote long afterwards, 'never emerging from my shell,' and letting his brother bully him as he would. Numerous relatives came and went, there was endless discussion of politics and money-making, but the family was still poorly-off, and Kazutaka and Hisako were too incompatible to be able to provide the domestic harmony that might have made poverty less oppressive. Two events, however, soon changed the picture. First, Kenjiro's mother and sisters became Christians —Hisako was finally baptized in 1884—and in January 1883 Iichiro took over the headship of the House of Tokutomi in succession to Kazutaka.[14] The new religion gave Hisako new courage, and some of it seems to have rubbed off on to Kenjiro, who was both attracted to Christianity himself and beginning to doubt the sincerity of his brother's faith. Iichiro's formal assumption of authority was immediately beneficial to the family, since he lost no time in straightening out its financial affairs: but to Kenjiro it meant unwelcome confirmation of his brother's dominance. Trouble was bound to follow. The brothers quarrelled, and fought violently.[15] This was too much for Kazutaka, and he quickly arranged for Kenjiro to be sent

---

13. A domestic incident that took place during this period gives a glimpse of the byways of 'western influence' in provincial Japan. A sister of Kenjiro's had four cats, one of which chanced to urinate over his precious notebooks. She challenged his anger with a reminder that Sir Isaac Newton had kept his temper when his dog Diamond upset a candle and set fire to his notes for *Principia*.

14. This was followed a year later by his marriage. Whatever else in *Footprints in the Snow* is derived from Iichiro's life, it is certainly not the hero's fairy-tale romance with O-Toshi. Iichiro's marriage was arranged for him while he was away on a lecture tour; the wedding ceremony consisted largely of eating a feast of eels caught by the bride's father. Iichiro disliked his wife's given-name, and ordered her to change it, which she obediently did. One night after they were married, Kenjiro heard his brother—through the thin partition wall of a Japanese room—complaining to his bride of her ugliness. But Iichiro, true to the traditions of the Kyushu samurai, was not one to waste time unduly on either beauty or ugliness in a mere woman. The marriage lasted—and was far less stormy than Kenjiro's.

15. This was not the first such quarrel. On a previous occasion when Kazutaka had found Iichiro beating his brother, he told Iichiro to stop abusing his authority —and Kenjiro to commit suicide if he couldn't put up a better resistance. At another time Kenjiro was made by his sisters to apologize to his brother after a quarrel while their parents were away. Kenjiro went secretly to his father's desk and wrote out a vow to the Christian God to 'prove himself a man', sealing his signature with blood pricked from his finger.

away to board with Tokio Yokoi,[16] a Christian pastor living in the town of Imabari, on the island of Shikoku.

The sixteen months Kenjiro spent at Imabari were probably among the happiest of his life. He had been baptized as a Christian before leaving home, and seems to have enjoyed helping the Rev. Yokoi, who found him work translating and teaching English so that he could pay for his own board. Once indeed, the mood of depression that was never far away seems to have got the better of him, and he nearly committed suicide.[17] But for the most part his stay with the Yokois gave Kenjiro both the stability and the stimulus he needed. When in June 1886 the Rev. Yokoi was appointed to teach theology at Doshisha, and suggested that Kenjiro should re-enter the College—perhaps seeing in him a future parson—Kenjiro was very willing to accompany him. In gratitude for the services of their pastor's assistant, the church at Imabari presented him with a pair of fine Osaka clogs.

So Kenjiro went back once more to school.[18] By this time Iichiro was about to move back to Tokyo: his book *Japan and the Future* had created a minor sensation, and he was planning to publish a new journal in the capital from January 1887—with these preoccupations, no doubt he was relieved that his young brother had apparently found something useful to do. On the Rev. Yokoi's recommendation, Kazutaka began to send Kenjiro a small monthly allowance. Kenjiro, for his part, soon attracted his teachers' attention as an outstanding student, with a strong literary bent. Yet he had hardly arrived back in Doshisha before he was laying up fresh trouble for himself—by falling in love with Hisae Yamamoto, a student at the Doshisha Girls' High School and niece of Principal Niijima. His choice was unlucky in the extreme; Hisae was not regarded as a suitable friend for any Doshisha student, let alone a professed Christian.[19]

16. The eldest son of Shonan Yokoi, a famous scholar and patriot who had been tragically assassinated in Kyoto in 1869 after joining the Meiji government. Shonan had married an aunt of Kenjiro's, and Kazutaka had been one of his disciples before the Restoration.

17. The occasion was a curious one. Sogabe, a student who was living with him in the Yokoi household, had been jilted in a love-affair (he is the model for Sone, the love-lorn youth in *Footprints in the Snow*). Kenjiro suggested to him that he should cross over to Kyushu and enter Iichiro's school; and pawned a new kimono of his own to provide Sogabe with the fare, lending him another for the journey. Sogabe gladly took his advice. (Hisako was confronted on her doorstep a day or two later by this young man she had never seen—wearing Kenjiro's clothes.) But Kenjiro had not consulted the Yokois before his quixotic action. They were responsible for Sogabe, and it was Mrs Yokoi's reproach—her husband was away—which brought on Kenjiro's fit of depression.

18. To celebrate Kenjiro's return to Doshisha, Iichiro presented him with a volume of Emerson's *Essays*. Hence, no doubt, the Emersonian epigraph to *Footprints in the Snow*. In his *Shizen to Jinsei* (Nature and Man), Kenjiro likens the evident intimacy of two crocks, crowing harmoniously at dawn, to the friendship of Emerson and Carlyle.

19. The details of this affair are complicated, but some acquaintance with them is necessary for an understanding of the subsequent events, and of the scar they left in Kenjiro's life. Hisae's mother was a geisha whom Yamamoto, Principal Niijima's brother-in-law, had taken into his home to help look after him on his

But while this relationship with Hisae was still developing, Kenjiro's first attempt at launching himself on a career of his own was to be frustrated. Fired with his brother's excitement over the prospects of radical journalism in Tokyo, he telegraphed his father in December 1886 for permission to leave Doshisha, as Iichiro had done before him, and join Iichiro in the capital to help with the journal[20] he was to start the following month. Kazutaka ordered him to stay till graduation.

So he stayed, and continued to meet Hisae in secret. They corresponded too, Kenjiro taking care when he wrote her name and address to make his calligraphy look like a girl's. One of his letters included a vow of life-long faithfulness, 'sworn in the presence of Almighty God, His Son who shed his blood upon the cross, and the Holy Spirit who lives and works eternally.' It was not long before this vow was put to the test. One day in spring when the couple were meeting in a temple compound they were surprised by the Rev. Yokoi—the friend they had posted at the gate having failed to warn them in time. Yokoi had already learnt of their association. Holding himself responsible for Kenjiro, he insisted he should break with Hisae immediately. Reluctantly, Kenjiro gave a written promise not to see her again; and in celebration of his repentance was treated by Yokoi to a dinner at a western-style restaurant. The promise proved impossible to keep, however. Yokoi packed him off to his brother's house in Tokyo as soon as the summer term ended, but the two still kept in touch. Finally Kenjiro was summoned before a tribunal consisting of his brother, his elder sister Hatsuko, now married to Iichiro's deputy Yuasa, and the Rev.

---

wife's death, and had eventually married. Four years before Kenjiro re-entered Doshisha, she had had a child by a young man named Mochizuki, who had been visiting the family as a possible prospective husband for Hisae; and was promptly driven from the house—not at the wish of her husband, who was quite willing to forgive her, out of gratitude for her faithful service, but at the instigation of his other daughter, O-Mine, wife of the Rev. Yokoi, and his sister, Principal Niijima's wife, both of whom were strict and puritanical Christians. One consequence of her mother's expulsion was the assumption in the small circle of serious-minded Christians connected with Doshisha that Hisae, as the daughter of an adulterous geisha, would inevitably turn out to be light-minded, if not worse. Whether these suspicions were justified in any way is hard to tell from such evidence as survives, entangled as it is in the strongly-held beliefs and prejudices of the time. What is certain is that Kenjiro's love for her was genuine. He was only nineteen, of course, and exceedingly immature, but the impact of this first serious love on his volatile, emotional nature, so soon after he had had his first taste of independence at Imabari, was profound. Though he had been married for eight years when he wrote *Footprints in the Snow*, there is almost certainly nothing of his wife in O-Toshi: Shintaro's sweetheart is an amalgam of Dora and Agnes in *David Copperfield*, and Kenjiro's memories of Hisae.

20. This journal, *Kokumin no Tomo* (People's Friend) was an immediate success, and helped to make Iichiro within a few years one of the best-known and most influential journalists in the country. Publication was far from easy in the early days. Iichiro, editor and publisher both, and his deputy Jiro Yuasa would tramp the streets of Tokyo all night before an issue was due to appear, delivering copies of the journal from a handcart.

Yokoi, who had himself just moved to Tokyo. Once again he was ordered to have nothing more to do with the girl.

Again he promised, and this time was more successful. Back at Doshisha in the autumn, he wrote to Hisae telling her of his decision,[21] and asking her to return his letters. The latter request she refused. Crushed and miserable, Kenjiro slipped out of the College dormitory and made his way first to a lodging-house in Kyoto, then to an inn at the foot of Mount Atago, the daughter of whose proprietor was a class-mate of Hisae's. Here, on borrowed money, he stayed for three weeks. At last, torn by feelings of guilt at his 'irresponsible' behaviour towards his family and the Rev. Yokoi, and disgust at the thought of being watched over perpetually as a prodigal son who might at any moment revert to his wicked ways, he decided to leave Doshisha for good. Returning to the College, he sold most of his few belongings to friends, and having earlier sent word to Hisae asking to see her once more before he left, presented himself at her dormitory in the Girls High School compound—to be met by Mrs Niijima, who would only let him see Hisae in the presence of the Principal and herself. The girl was sent for. But the company was too daunting: Kenjiro left without speaking to her, and never saw her again.

To the Niijimas he said merely that he would be leaving at once for Tokyo. But that was impossible: neither his brother nor his father, who had joined Iichiro in the capital, would have had anything but contempt for a Tokutomi who had thrown away his last chance of education for a woman. After writing abject letters of apology for his weakness and failure to Principal Niijima and to Iichiro, he marched out of Doshisha with a bundle and a red blanket[22]—took a train that evening to Osaka, spent the night in a brothel, and went on the next day to Kyushu.

No detailed record of his doings during the next two months survives. He seems to have wandered miserably from village to village, now on foot, now on horseback, borrowing money where he could from unwilling relatives, struggling with his humiliation and shame—which were soon made more painful by the discovery that he had contracted venereal disease. The bitterness must have gone deep indeed. For the Japanese, who through most of their history have felt their very existence to depend

---

21. In a characteristically picturesque way. He sent her two sheets of paper, one entirely blank, one with their two names joined by a dotted line with a drawing of a pair of scissors beneath it, together with a brief poem:

> The butterfly
> Must forsake the flower
> Of which it dreams.

22. 'By a curious twist of circumstance, it happened that of all the foreign articles familiar in Japan at that time almost the only one of use to peasants was the cheap woollen blanket, which they could throw over their shoulders or drape over a wooden bench. It was usually dyed red, and so favoured was it by country folk that the word *akagetto* or "red blanket" was a common name for a rustic among city dwellers.' Sir George Sansom, *The Western World and Japan*, p. 411.

on their retaining their proper place in a network of esteem and obligation, both within and beyond the family, no punishment can hurt so much as the kind of ostracism to which Kenjiro was now driven to subject himself. The rest of his life is in effect the story of his recovery, slow and fitful, of his self-respect.

Thanks to the good offices of a sympathetic aunt and uncle, when he arrived penitent in Kumamoto in February 1888, Kenjiro was able to join the Staff of the Kumamoto English School which had recently been established by a cousin, the editor of the *Kumamoto News*. Teaching there presented a challenge. The school dealt in controversial western ideas as well as language, and was not popular with the conservative-minded burghers: 'the Rev. Ebina,[23] the Principal, walked the streets with a spear-shaft for self-defence, and the services in his church might be interrupted at any time for the congregation to beat off an attack. Besides teaching English, Kenjiro helped with the administration, took morning assembly sometimes, and wrote occasional essays for the school magazine. Under the eye of numerous relatives, he was generally subdued and apologetic, diligently assuring his parents and Iichiro in more letters of the genuineness of his repentance for past errors.

But his powerful, wayward nature still found expression, and in curious ways. One morning at assembly he startled the students—who customarily enjoyed his discourses on stories from the Old Testament, or anecdotes from the lives of great men of the West such as Milton or Galileo—by announcing from the platform that he was 'mad, mad, mad! and therefore no longer fit to teach,' for no more serious reason, apparently, than a mildly sarcastic comment by a fellow-teacher on his eccentricity. For his writing he had a local carpenter construct—after careful study of references and illustrations in Dickens—a table on the pattern of the desk of an English ledger-clerk.

This provincial exile lasted eighteen months, till Iichiro came south-west on a lecture tour in preparation for the inauguration of the Diet. The brothers met in Kumamoto, and it was agreed that Kenjiro should join Iichiro in the capital. At a farewell party given him by his students Kenjiro announced grandiosely that his ambition was to contribute with his pen 'to some great work of charity'. What in fact awaited him in Tokyo was a desk in the editorial room of the Minyusha, Iichiro's publishing company, a desk which he was to occupy, much of the time under his brother's eye, for fourteen years.

The dirt and noise and inhumanity of the capital, however stupefying at first, he soon got used to: his distaste for the work Iichiro gave him, on the other hand, only grew with time. Passionately committed to politics, and

---

23. A leading Meiji Christian and educationist, who later became President of Doshisha. Kenjiro used to go with Ebina to an American missionary's house for the 'Longfellow readings' which appear, in slightly different circumstances, in *Footprints in the Snow*.

already close to some of the leading politicians of the day, Iichiro used his brother's knowledge of English and talent for writing—no doubt with the best of intentions—in the interests of his journal and of the *People's Daily* newspaper he started in 1890. At his instigation Kenjiro translated articles from the *Pall Mall Budget*, the *London Graphic*, *Scribners* and other such British and American magazines, and full-length English biographies of Bright, Cobden and Gladstone; in none of which he could feel any living interest. But the habit of submission and the absence of any obvious alternative work kept him bound to the Minyusha. Only in small things was revolt possible. It was Iichiro's custom, when he could spare the time, to take his small staff at the Minyusha out into the country on Sundays, but Kenjiro would never join them.

When news came that Principal Niijima of Doshisha lay dying at a coastal village forty miles from Tokyo, Iichiro was sitting in a barber's in a frockcoat, having himself groomed for a party to celebrate the launching of his newspaper: properly conscious, as always, of his obligations, he rushed to the station, half-shaven as he was, stayed with Niijima till his death, and attended his funeral at Doshisha. Kenjiro refused to leave Tokyo; he was still very far from forgetting Hisae.

The face of an English actress in a *London Graphic* illustration reminded him so vividly of Hisae that he at once set about rewriting the history of their romance (he had already composed one draft), calling it *Record of a Dream in Spring*. While he was doing so, he was deputed to take to hospital a maid of Iichiro's who was suffering from paratyphoid, and heard by chance from a nurse who turned out to be a relative of the Yamamotos that Hisae was regularly attending a Christian church. In August 1890 he published in Iichiro's paper, in eight instalments, a story based on his experiences with Hisae which ends with the implied suicide of the hero. Nearly a year later, a postcard from Kyoto addressed to Iichiro announced that Hisae Yamamoto had died after a long illness. Kenjiro copied out the formal phrases of the postcard at the end of his manuscript of *Record of a Dream in Spring*, adding the words, 'This is the end of these things'. In fact the spell Hisae exercised over him was not finally broken for another twenty-three years.

Outwardly life proceeded normally enough. In 1894 Kenjiro married Aiko Harada, sister of a journalist friend of Iichiro's. It was not one of the most edifying examples of a parent-planned (or brother-planned) marriage. Ostensibly, with Iichiro doing brilliantly in his profession, and the Haradas owning substantial property near Kumamoto, the match benefited both households, though Iichiro appears to have thought Aiko rather too good for his brother. But as far as the two chief parties were concerned, it was based on complete mutual ignorance. Before the wedding they had seen each other only once, from a distance in a Tokyo square. Aiko was a trained schoolmistress, not likely, on the face of it, to have much in common with Kenjiro's extreme romanticism; and to make matters worse, she was earning more at the Tokyo school where she taught than Kenjiro at the Minyusha. Even the wedding ceremony, such as it was, left the bridegroom feeling insulted. Iichiro wrote out the marriage certificate; Aiko was ordered to make tea for the dozen guests, and her husband was served last. The couple were given as their first home—they moved before long—a single upstairs room in a small house, next door to Iichiro's, that had been built for Kazutaka and Hisako, and out of his Minyusha salary of eleven yen a month Kenjiro had to pay eight yen to his parents for board and lodging.

In such circumstances marriage brought Kenjiro not fulfilment but more tension and bitterness. His wife, he complained, was too cold, too correct; he tortured her with sarcasm and with blows.[24] When, ashamed at his eccentric and shabby clothes, she made him a new kimono, he wore it for a day or two, but tore it into shreds when his mother acidly remarked how 'splendid' he had become. Aiko's wearing of a silver watch when he was too poor to buy such things either for her or for himself struck him as so impertinent that he took it off her wrist and flung it out into the garden.

A little more than a year after the wedding, Aiko's brother suggested a divorce. Somehow the go-betweens who had arranged the marriage managed to smooth things over. Soon, however, Kenjiro had to let her go back to Kyushu to nurse her family through an epidemic of typhus. Her mother and stepbrother died before she could reach Kumamoto, her father shortly afterwards. Kenjiro hurried down from Tokyo for the father's funeral, but before his exhausted wife had had a chance to rest he was taking her on a tour of his own relatives, who were legion. Again her brother Ryohachi proposed divorce. While the relatives on both sides were arguing the matter Aiko herself caught typhus. The shock of this last blow helped to settle the differences: the marriage was patched up, and once more Kenjiro found himself writing letters of apology, to Ryohachi for his treatment of his sister, and to Iichiro—from whom he had had to borrow the money for Aiko's hospital expenses—for this latest bout of irresponsibility on his part.

There is no sign that Iichiro understood his brother very deeply, either at this time or subsequently. To him Kenjiro appeared as an awkward and unstable relative, whom he had generously provided with a livelihood, useful in the office for his knowledge of English and fluent style, but constantly causing difficulties by his moodiness, domestic tantrums and frequent trips into the country to indulge his taste for sketching and fishing when he ought to have been working. While Kenjiro was embroiled with his own and Aiko's relatives in Kyushu, Iichiro, as editor and publisher of the paper which sent more correspondents than any other to cover the

---

24. On one occasion, after being struck repeatedly with a stick, she called out to their cat, in English, 'I am like a drum!' Many such incidents are recorded in the long, remarkably frank autobiography which Kenjiro wrote in his last years.

Sino-Japanese war, had moved for the time being to Hiroshima, where he was attached to the headquarters of the Imperial Army.[25] But to Kenjiro, though he visited his brother in Hiroshima on the way back to Tokyo, his brother's enthusiastic support for the war and increasing intimacy with the great meant little. For some months he found relief in serializing a translation of Gogol's *Taras Bulba*. Iichiro had suggested the book for its epic and martial appeal, which chimed with the popular mood of the moment, and because of his growing interest in Russia, both as a near neighbour and as a possible future threat to Japan; but Kenjiro was attracted to its romantic idealism, into which he could escape for a while from his frustrated longings for independence. With Aiko, since her illness, things had been easier. But in relation to Iichiro and his parents, his position was as weak as ever.[26] The gulf between the brothers widened with Iichiro's departure in 1896 on a trip round the world to study international affairs, and in particular European attitudes to Russian policy.

Iichiro had planned to leave in March, but had fallen ill as a result of overwork during the war. By the middle of May, Kenjiro having helped to nurse him, he was able to sail, with money borrowed from a bank on the strength of his political connections. He had neither suggested taking Kenjiro along with him nor given him any special position of responsibility at the Minyusha during his own absence. Kenjiro's resentment mounted, till one day in a frenzy of accumulated bitterness he slashed at his desk with an inherited samurai sword, and cut to pieces and trampled on two framed Chinese maxims, one a gift from his father, the other in the handwriting of his famous relative, Shonan Yokoi.[27]

The opportunity to pour out some of his discontents to a favourite brother-in-law helped. (Aiko was present at this conversation, and could

---

25. Many of the nation's leaders stayed in Hiroshima for all or part of the war, which lasted from July 1894 to April 1895—the Emperor and Count Ito, the Prime Minister, among them. It is from this period that Iichiro's conversion from a rather vague popular radicalism to militant nationalism began. Visiting Port Arthur after its capture by the Japanese forces, he brought back with him handfuls of Chinese soil to distribute among the Minyusha staff.

26. In January 1896 the family assembled at a coastal resort near Tokyo for the New Year holiday, the time of reunion for all Japanese families. Kenjiro escorted his ageing parents to the inn. When however he took advantage of the beauty of the scenery and the presence in the inn of a young novelist and nature-poet to spend most of the time in painting and talk outside the family circle, his father ordered him to go home, on the ground that if he was going to display such levity he had better get back to the Minyusha office and work. Kenjiro left obediently—but by a roundabout country route that gave him three days of exploring instead of two hours of sitting in a train.

27. Yokoi's maxim read 'Duty to one's family is of greater importance than feeling. The tie of brother to brother comes first, that of husband to wife, second.' It had been given to Kenjiro at his wedding, along with his modest share of the family property.

During this emotional crisis Kenjiro seems, among other outbursts, to have made a half-hearted attempt to rape their maid while his wife was asleep. The maid was living in at the time, and slept inside the same mosquito-net with Kenjiro and Aiko.

thus at last begin to understand her husband: to her he had never spoken of these things.) In his diary for October 25th, his birthday, he wrote:

> Ah, I have been for long years a slave!
> I have been my brother's slave.
> I have been the slave of lust.
> I have been a slave in all things.
> From now I will be a slave no longer.
> Whoever or whatever limits my freedom, shall be my enemy!

With Iichiro several thousand miles away, such defiance was not too difficult, at least in the pages of a diary. In his New Year's poem for 1897 Kenjiro vowed to 'stand firm',[28] and 'Make his own the teachings of the saints/And wise men of old/From this day of the turn of the year.' To celebrate his resolve (which he reported in a polite but firm letter to Iichiro) Kenjiro and Aiko left the house in Tokyo where they had been living and moved to the peaceful seaside inn at Zushi from which Kazutaka had ordered Kenjiro to go back to work a year before. (See above, n. 25.)

One side-trip of Iichiro's during his world tour bore fruit, as it happened, for Kenjiro—his visit to Tolstoy at Yasnaya Polyana. Kenjiro had already read some Tolstoy. Stimulated now by his brother's account of the visit, which appeared in the *People's Friend* in October 1896, after four months of intense work he published in April 1897 his own *Life of Tolstoy*, prefaced with a dedication to his wife ('as a token of the start of their new life') and a lamentation that his own life was so worldly in comparison with that of his subject. But this done, his attendances at the Minyusha grew less frequent, and his trips into the country more numerous, bringing complaints of his idleness from the acting head of the Minyusha. A patronizing letter from Iichiro, written in London in answer to his tentative declaration of independence, gave little prospect of a genuine understanding between them.

After thirteen months abroad, Iichiro came home in the summer of 1897. To celebrate his return he made bonus payments to each member of the staff, raised Kenjiro's salary (which had stayed at 11 yen since he came to Tokyo in 1889) to 20 yen, and gave him 'associate' status, so that he would have more free time. The climax of Iichiro's own career came soon afterwards. On the Prime Minister's direction, he was nominated as a Counsellor to the Minister of the Interior (in theory an Imperial appointment) at a salary of nearly 300 yen a month—a nominal post which gave him direct access to the Prime Minister and Cabinet Office. Even Kenjiro was impressed by his brother's success, by the range of his influence, and by the multitude of clients who came seeking his acquaintance or favour.

Yet in spite of the celebratory gestures Kenjiro's position had not changed.

---

28. As Confucius had done. 'The Master said: "At fifteen I set my mind upon wisdom. At thirty I stood firm. At forty I was free from doubts. At fifty I understood the laws of Heaven. At sixty my ear was docile. At seventy I could follow the desires of my heart without transgressing the right." ' *Analects*, II, 4 (tr. Soothill).

Iichiro had put him to work at once on translating, and transposing into a Japanese setting, a western crime novel, and he was expected to contribute regularly, along lines Iichiro approved, to the *People's Friend* and the *Home Journal*, another of his brother's ventures.[29] A long article of his own on the painter Corot[30] was relegated to the end pages of the *People's Friend*, among the Miscellanea, and printed in small type, without the illustration he had supplied. A trivial enough incident, and the Minyusha at once apologized, claiming it had been merely a mistake. To Kenjiro it was an insult, evidence once more of the inability or refusal of his brother and his minions to accept him for what he was. Iichiro had no feeling for art, so one of the best things Kenjiro had done was ignored, classed with the trivia of unthinking popular journalism. When Aiko expressed her sympathy, Kenjiro struck and kicked her.

Whenever he could he sought consolation, as so many Japanese have done before and since, in escaping into the mountains. A prose-poem, 'Mount Fuji at Dawn', impressed even Iichiro when it appeared in the paper in January 1898. Encouraged, two months later Kenjiro got Iichiro to publish *Green Hills and White Clouds*, his first collection of original essays. Not surprisingly, for it contained mostly youthful unpolished work, it was almost totally ignored. For a time, that spring, the brothers seem to have been close to a reconciliation—made easier, perhaps, by a disappointment of Iichiro's. In February he resigned his Counsellorship, probably because the Prime Minister who had secured his appointment had been succeeded by a less resolutely imperialist rival. Suddenly he found himself out of favour and in debt; the circulation of his newspaper dropped to little over 4,000, and for some weeks both the *People's Friend* and the *Home Journal* ceased to appear altogether. The eclipse was only temporary, however. By October the premiership had changed hands yet again, and the new Cabinet of General Yamagata, whose War Minister, Katsura, was a close personal friend of Iichiro's, welcomed the advocacy in the *People's Friend* of a more expansionist foreign policy, and its warnings of a Russian threat. Within a month the circulation of the *People's Daily* was back to 25,000 and the Minyusha on its feet again.

Kenjiro was interested in none of these things. A spring journey resulted in more of the closely-observed nature idylls he was coming to write with greater economy and skill. But it was in the summer of this year, 1898, that a tale told by a chance acquaintance started a chain of events which led eventually to the decisive break between the Tokutomi brothers.

Kenjiro agreed to give up one of the two rooms which he and Aiko were occupying at the Yanagiya Inn in Zushi to an army widow and her two children, who had been unable to find any cheap summer accom-

---

29. 'A writer of thrillers—is that what I am to sink to?' he complained in his diary.

30. It was in fact based on a similar article in *Scribner's Magazine*, but carried in its style the unmistakable imprint of his own enthusiasm for the subject.

modation elsewhere. Mrs Fuke's husband had been A.D.C. to General Oyama, commander of the Japanese Second Army in the Sino-Japanese War. The two men had been close friends; hence the widow's acquaintance with the tragic story she told Kenjiro and Aiko, of how the general's daughter Nobuko had been divorced by her husband not long after their marriage—at the insistence of the husband's family, without regard to the feelings of the Oyamas and against the wishes of the couple themselves—because she had contracted tuberculosis.[31] Kenjiro was deeply moved. At the time he was engaged on more hack-work for Iichiro. But here was something different—a story that in addition to its romantic character could focus all his resentment at the family system that had conditioned his own upbringing and career. An old saying he was fond of quoting all his life ran *'Mizu itarite kyo naru'*, 'When water flows, a ditch is formed';[32] or, in terms of the condition his temperament imposed upon his ambition to be a writer, 'fall in love with the story, and the book will write itself,' for without a strong emotional commitment to his theme Kenjiro never succeeded in writing anything significant. Nobuko's story fulfilled the condition perfectly. The novel *Hototogisu* (The Cuckoo)[33] began to take shape. Appearing in serial form in the *People's Daily* from November 1898 to May 1899, it was immensely popular. There were troubles on the way: the editor kept altering its place in the paper, and omitted it altogether on some days to make way for more urgent items, which drove Kenjiro to write to Iichiro threatening to stop work on the novel if he wasn't shown more courtesy. For the first time ever, Kenjiro accepted a request to write by someone other than his brother[34]—and angrily turned down a request by Iichiro to translate an article by a foreign ambassador which another staff member of the Minyusha had refused.

Published in book form in January 1900, *The Cuckoo* became a famous best-seller. It is crude and melodramatic by present-day standards, and some of its appeal undoubtedly rested on the easily-made identification of the heroine with General Oyama's daughter—while sales were further boosted when it became known that the Imperial Household had accepted

31. The truth of the story is not undisputed. According to another version (which may have been furnished for public consumption, since the families involved were both prominent in public life) the divorce was not one-sided and arbitrary, but agreed between all the parties.
32. It occurs in *Footprints in the Snow*, p. 224, though the context demands a different rendering: 'let life flow as nature wills.'
33. An English translation entitled *Namiko* (the name of the heroine in the book) was published in England and America in 1904.
There is a curious pathos in the fact that Aiko had long intended to call her daughter, if she had one, Namiko—which besides being an acceptable girl's name is also the word for a certain kind of seashell she and Kenjiro had found while walking on the beach soon after they were married. In fact she never had any children.
34. Seijiro Niwa, the secretary of the then equivalent of the Japanese YMCA, asked him to write a life of General Gordon, as a model for Japanese soldiers, the book to be financed by the balance of contributions collected by Niwa for soldiers' comforts during the Sino-Japanese War. The *Life of Gordon* was published in December 1904.

a copy submitted by Iichiro for the Emperor's personal perusal. Yet its wide success was deserved. It stood recognizably within a long tradition of popular tales of ill-starred lovers crushed by bonds of family and social obligation, and pointed up dramatically, in a society proud of having advanced so rapidly, the inhumanity with which the old values still bore upon the lives of the young, and of young women in particular.[35] By Kenjiro's death a quarter of a century later it had sold half a million copies.

Iichiro, hardly able to credit Kenjiro's sudden fame, remained patronizing. While accompanying Ito (shortly to be Prime Minister for the third time) on a tour of Kyushu, he complained bitterly to relatives, so one of them recalled long afterwards, of the laziness and irresponsibility of his 'parasitic' brother—with some reason, perhaps: in Iichiro's absence, Kenjiro, with his wife, had once again deserted the Minyusha office for the mountain retreat of Ikao,[36] where he was busy reading Ruskin, tramping up and down the valleys, and preparing a new collection of nature sketches and essays. This last was published in August as *Shizen to Jinsei* (Nature and Man), prefaced at Kenjiro's insistence by a short story which Iichiro strongly disliked.[37] It was acclaimed as enthusiastically as *The Cuckoo* had been. Reprinted over 400 times, it eventually sold as many copies as the novel, and may be said to have shaped the sensitivity to nature of a whole generation of Japanese; no small feat in a nation of nature-connoisseurs.

At once Kenjiro began on *Footprints in the Snow* writing, as always with work that was genuinely his own, out of the compelling mood of the moment. 'Inevitably, in the burst of self-confidence that comes with recognition, writers write about themselves. To this rule *Footprints in the Snow* was no exception,' he said himself in later life. Yet as perhaps will now have become clearer, Kenjiro's mood can hardly have been one of self-confidence pure and simple. His own past he was not yet ready to describe: his sense of inadequacy was too deeply ingrained, the scar left by the affair with Hisae still too imperfectly healed, and his relations with Aiko still too turbulent, to allow of any honest reporting. Yet his delight at the prospect of independence that success had brought demanded expression. Since their childhood his relationship with Iichiro had been ambivalent, and never more so than in the years of the latter's public distinction—there is plenty of evidence that Kenjiro admired his brother's energy and abilities,

35. Paradoxically, the best-known sentence in *The Cuckoo*, Namiko's dying cry, 'May I never be born again as a woman!' is omitted from the existing English translation. The point illustrates the difficulties of translation. Without a footnote explaining the common Oriental notion of reincarnation (which the translators presumably wished to avoid in a book that was intended to introduce Japanese fiction to a wide public) the sentence would have sounded either ludicrous or unintelligible.

36. Now a well-known beauty spot, Ikao became Kenjiro's favourite retreat at critical periods in his life. It was there, on his tenth visit in 1927, that he died.

37. It deals with a young man who fought with Saigo in the Rebellion of 1877, and on returning home was ordered by his father and brother to commit suicide for having dishonoured the family by opposing the Emperor's forces. Iichiro, if not the ageing Kazutaka, can hardly have failed to grasp the implication.

even when he most fiercely resented his domination, and took pride in the honour accruing to the name of Tokutomi, even though his own part in earning it seemed until recently to have gone unregarded. So it came about that Iichiro was more of a model for Shintaro Kikuchi than Kenjiro himself. *Footprints in the Snow* derives its peculiar force from three sources: the general dynamism of early Meiji, as both Tokutomis and countless others had experienced it in their youth; admiration for Iichiro's astonishing achievement; and most powerful of all, though with undertones of uncertainty still, the delighted sense of liberation at having emerged at last from under the same Iichiro's wing.

Footprints in the Snow having repeated the success of its predecessors, Kenjiro gave up his modest salary from the Minyusha, the token of his dependence on Iichiro, and moved back to Tokyo to a house of his own choice. There was some bickering over the royalties due from *Footprints in the Snow*, Kenjiro protesting to Iichiro over the latter's continued stinginess; but the basis of a more equal relationship seemed to have been established. Yet the tension between the two was still far from disappearing. The climax of this long fraternal war came when Kenjiro embarked on his next novel, *Kokucho*.[38]

The suggestion for this novel came from Iichiro. The hero was to be a samurai of the mid-Meiji period who inherited from his father a fierce anti-government and reformist spirit, but gradually found himself coming round to sympathy with and support for the regime—such an obvious replica of Iichiro himself, in fact, that at first sight it seems surprising that Kenjiro should have taken up the idea. Iichiro wanted a directly political novel, of the kind that had been popular twenty years before.[39] Kenjiro was eager to try his hand at a serious novel on the western model, dealing from a humanistic viewpoint—deriving in part from his continued attachment to Christianity, which Iichiro had long since abandoned—with the individual in society.[40] But in the enthusiasm of the moment he had not

38. Another reading of the characters for *Kuroshio*, the 'Black Current' that warms the southern shores of Japan.

39. Such as, for example, *Keikoku Bidan* (A Noble Tale of Statesmanship), published in 1883. See Sir George Sansom, *The Western World and Japan*, p. 421.

40. Japanese critics have often lamented the lack in modern Japanese literature of any outstanding novel giving a comprehensive picture of Japanese society. Some have felt that Kenjiro Tokutomi, partly because of the powerful individualism he eventually displayed, and partly because of the greater seriousness of his commitment to humanistic values than many other more 'literary' writers, was better qualified than most to write such a novel. (Others could deal with the psychological subtleties of Japanese private and social life: the humanist and individualist viewpoint was needed to reveal the ramifications of Meiji authoritarianism, and the price which the individual too often had to pay for the national pursuit of modernization and progress.) But for Kenjiro to have done so would have required him to think much more deeply both about novel-writing and about society than he ever showed any sign of doing: to the end of his days he remained essentially preoccupied, in a manner that was partly dictated by his own nature and background but is also characteristically Japanese, with himself and his own close circle of relationships.

thought out the significance of the plot, the implied justification of Iichiro's support for the powers that be and for the *status quo*. Nor was he prepared temperamentally for the solid research that such an ambitious historical novel would entail; nor, perhaps worse still, had he much gift for realistic dialogue, though his narrative and descriptive powers were considerable. Kenjiro wished to write a novel which, in his own words, would 'help to complete the unfinished revolution of Meiji': but if he were to follow the story his brother had suggested, he was setting himself an impossible task. In effect, *Kokucho* became the battleground for the decisive conflict between the brothers.

The new novel began to appear in the *People's Daily* in January 1902. The early chapters describing the hero's father, whose 'liberalism' derived as much from a samurai sense of honour as from any radical intellectual or moral principles, went smoothly enough. But the hero himself was more of a problem. To turn him into a conformist, a mere portrait of Iichiro, was too repugnant. To present him as a continuing 'liberal' and outsider, on the other hand, able to stand firm with the small band of articulate opponents of the Meiji regime—as Kenjiro's inclinations dictated—would have meant equipping him with a system of thought, a clearly-defined political position, which scarcely any of the liberals of the period possessed, certainly not Kenjiro himself. For Kenjiro was never seriously interested in politics. *Kokucho*, therefore, put him to the test on two counts—whether he was finally to accept or reject his brother's authority and attitudes, and whether he himself had it in him to become a novelist in the full (western) sense of the word. Inevitably he ran into trouble with the book. It was planned to appear in several parts: by June 1902 he had finished the first part, but found himself unable to go on.

A crisis was precipitated by the arbitrary censoring of anti-government phrases in an article by Kenjiro in the *People's Daily* dealing with the impeachment of the Navy Minister for having accepted bribes. Kenjiro immediately wrote to the Minyusha threatening not to write another word of *Kokucho* or anything else, if this was how his work was to be treated. A messenger called at his house to apologize, but explained at the same time that any paper was obliged to 'protect its interests'. That night Kenjiro wrote out his *Kokubetsu no Ji*, or 'Parting Message', to his brother. In the form in which it was later published, the Message sets out with dignity the reasons why Kenjiro had decided to end their association—most notably the incompatibility of their basic attitudes: in Iichiro's case, a belief in the supremacy of politics, in 'strong' government at home and imperialism abroad; in Kenjiro's, a humanism akin to that of Hugo and Tolstoy, supported by a temperamental sympathy with the weak and underprivileged.[41]

41. In reality, the quarrel pierced deeper than any differences of ideology. Kenjiro was rationalizing the more personal conflicts, between the two of them and within himself, which I have sketched above. But the weight of feeling behind it makes the Message an impressive document.

The following morning—December 28, 1902—he called on Iichiro, told him he would having nothing more to do with the Minyusha, and laid a copy of the Message on his desk. In the Japanese context, the 'Message' represented a formal and complete severance of one of the most sacred of all relationships, a drastic step indeed. Kenjiro was understandably put out, therefore, when his brother made no move to read the document: in a sudden rage, he threw it on the stove.[42] Later he wrote it out again, and sent it to Iichiro with an undertaking to continue with *Kokucho*, provided that his salary were doubled while he was writing it, and that Iichiro would publish the first part in book form—together with the 'Parting Message'. Iichiro refused. Undeterred, Kenjiro published *Kokucho* at his own expense, with the Parting Message as a preface. With both brothers being now so well known, the book caused something of a sensation: many leading public figures expressed sympathy for Kenjiro, others felt he was lacking humility, and had gone too far. At all events, the breach between the brothers Tokutomi was complete.[43]

Outwardly the second half of Kenjiro's life followed a very different course, but in essence it still consisted of a long struggle for freedom, for emancipation from his family and from the constant imbalance of his own turbulent nature—a struggle which cut him off too often from the society of his fellow-men, and restricted within narrow channels the fulfilment of the literary promise of his early books. For some years after *Kokucho* he produced little. While Iichiro's star continued to rise, with the approach of the war with Russia that he had long warned must come, Kenjiro, now on his own, could as yet find no use for his freedom: restless, irritable, alternately affectionate and violent with his wife, he sought escape in a new passion for music,[44] and in solitary journeys. On one long trip to the southern extremity of Kyushu, he was taken for a Russian spy—always eccentric in dress and manner, he had now taken to wearing dark glasses, to protect others, so he said, from the abnormal brightness of his eyes—and had to appeal to the police for help in getting himself accepted in inns (where he registered his occupation as 'student') as a bona fide traveller. Strangely, the death of a deeply-loved aunt, Junko Takesaki, at her home near Kumamoto while he was visiting the town during this expedition,

---

42. Iichiro, in his address at his brother's funeral in 1927, gave a slightly different account, more favourable to himself, of this incident; but the substance is the same.

43. It is difficult, of course, for Westerners to understand the intensity of the feelings aroused by Kenjiro's public defiance of an ancient code. Everything about the story is so characteristic of Japan, and of Japan at this particular juncture in its history. One more small example, perhaps, is the way in which Hisako reacted to the breach between her sons—by composing a poem:

Though the river has divided into separate streams,
May the waters of each flow clear and strong!

44. He tried to learn the flageolet and the Japanese harp, smashed the latter in a fit of anger, then changed to the harmonium.

seems to have helped him to recover a measure of stability. A remarkable woman by any standard,[45] she was one of the very few relatives who had befriended him during his wanderings in Kyushu after leaving Doshisha as a student in disgrace, and shown him the warmth of understanding he had badly needed but not found elsewhere. Eighteen years later he repaid the debt by writing her biography.

Early in August 1905 Kenjiro and Aiko climbed Mt Fuji with a niece. At the summit Kenjiro fainted, apparently from exhaustion in the rarefied air; and for seventy-two hours he lay unconscious in the stone hut to which the two women had carried him. There were no ill-effects, and the party was able to make its way down safely soon after he regained consciousness. But for Kenjiro this experience, however simple the physical explanation, quickly took on a special meaning. His survival of this death-in-life on the summit of Mt Fuji, with its sacred, almost mystical associations, assumed an awesome significance: he began to think of himself as truly reborn, a Japanese Lazarus. From this dawning vision, or hallucination, proceeded much of the peculiarity of his subsequent actions and writing.

If he had been 'reborn', the effects were not instantly apparent. In September, the *People's Daily* building was stormed by crowds angry at the support the paper was giving to the government's alleged softness in the peace negotiations with Russia; for nearly a month Iichiro was virtually beseiged in his office. Kenjiro made no gesture of sympathy. Because of his advances to their maid, and even to a mentally deficient girl they had promised friends to look after for a period, Aiko was threatening separation. Yet a change was on the way. When Yasukata Cho, an old boyhood friend, and the original of Shingo in *Footprints in the Snow*,[46] urged him to forget the quarrel with his brother, Kenjiro agreed; he called on Iichiro at once to apologize for the trouble over *Kokucho*, and for his silence during the riots. Iichiro paid a return visit the next day. Ostensibly the relationship was restored,[47] at least till the next major clash eight years later; but little communication took place between the two.

At the end of 1905 Kenjiro's rebirth manifested itself in a sudden decision to spend a year in retreat in the mountains. After burning many of his papers—diary, letters, manuscripts—he and Aiko moved to an inn at Ikao kept by a Christian. Together they read the four Christian gospels and Tolstoy's *What Then Must We Do?*, sang hymns and joined happily in gatherings of local Christians; a 'Letter from the Hills' sent to a Tokyo

---

45. Married at sixteen, at eighteen she was tilling the fields to feed her bankrupt husband. Later she became well known as a Christian leader and pioneer of women's education in Kyushu.

46. 'Shingo' is the Japanese pronunciation of Hsin Wu, a noted Chinese scholar of provincial extraction. Kenjiro's father admired Cho and would call him by the Chinese name.

47. As a sign that the conflict was over, Kenjiro bent his samurai sword, and smashed, on a rock in his garden, the pistol he kept for self-defence.

journal tells with thankfulness of an auspicious new start to both their lives. But within three months Kenjiro's plans had changed again. In a growing fascination with Tolstoy's religious and social thought, he conceived the idea of visiting him in Russia as Iichiro had done, though with a different purpose, nine years before. Sending him a copy of the English translation of *The Cuckoo* by way of self-introduction, he at once set about preparing for the journey; and early in April, after a farewell visit to his parents at Zushi, where the family joined in reciting the Lord's Prayer and the fervent singing of hymns, he sailed from Yokohama—Aiko, whom he had persuaded to be baptized before his departure, having been installed at her own wish in the dormitory attached to a well-known mission school in order to learn English. He dined with Iichiro when the ship called at Kobe, and wrote to him shortly afterwards, 'praying for his brother's recovery of faith.'

The trip was planned as a world tour, taking in England and America as well as Russia; but poor health, apparently due in part to an extremely austere diet he had imposed on himself since the Ikao retreat, caused him to return to Japan across Siberia after passing through Egypt, Palestine and European Russia. There is plenty of dramatic incident in his record of the journey. While his ship was crossing the Indian Ocean a young Japanese fellow-passenger produced a copy of *Footprints in the Snow*. Kenjiro promptly tossed it into the sea—perhaps it reminded him too painfully of his former subservience to Iichiro: at Ikao he had come to feel that literally everything he had written till then had been false and worthless, because it reflected his old 'slave' mentality. From Palestine, in a rare gesture of affection for a Japanese husband of his day, he sent to Aiko two petals of a red poppy from the ruins of the house of Mary and Martha, with the message that 'she was more to him than Mary and Martha combined could ever have been'. Jerusalem, whose streets he tramped looking like a beggar pilgrim, disgusted him with its vulgarity, but Nazareth and the Sea of Galilee had more to offer: 'If God wills it,' he wrote in the hotel visitors' book, 'I shall return'—prophetically, as it turned out.

At last, early in the morning of June 30th, Kenjiro reached the Tolstoy estate at Yasnaya Polyana, for what must have been one of the strangest meetings in literary history. No one in the house yet being up, he fell asleep on a bench in the garden—to be woken an hour or two later by Tolstoy himself tapping on his shoulder. The visit was not altogether a success, a classical example, one might say, of the difficulty of achieving serious communication between east and west when mutual goodwill has to contend with mutual ignorance of each other's language and culture. They were soon at odds over the Russo-Japanese War, with Kenjiro contending (and quoting a poem of the Emperor Meiji's to support his argument) that however deplorable war might be, it often brought out the best in men, and that the Japanese leaders, though not Christian, had shown a 'deep seriousness and natural piety'—while Tolstoy dismissed such 'piety' as 'narrow and unthinking', and the Emperor's poem[48] as 'weak and inconsistent'. Though with characteristic honesty he later admitted to himself that Tolstoy's larger view was probably right, at the time Kenjiro was offended. The evident discord between Tolstoy and his wife also disappointed him. With their son Sergei's wedding due to take place shortly, he was given to understand he would not be welcome indefinitely; and it seems that there was not the time for Tolstoy and himself to get sufficiently used to each other and each other's English to be able to have much serious conversation before Kenjiro left for home on July 5th.[49]

Nevertheless, his brief stay at Yasnaya Polyana influenced Kenjiro decisively and permanently. Soon after returning to Japan, he published, besides a book describing the journey, a number of articles far more radical than anything he had written in the past, including one deploring the mood of arrogance to which Japan had succumbed after the victory over Russia, and hinting that a victory so exulted over might prove to be the beginning of her destruction—and another repenting of his own 'cowardice' in supporting the 'animal way' of war. These articles derived less from any reasoned conviction than from the emotional impact, still strong, of the meeting with Tolstoy. More lasting was the effect on Kenjiro's personal way of life. Two of Tolstoy's admonitions—to write nothing but

---

48. The poem in question is as follows:

Kuni no tame
Ada nasu teki wa
Kudaku tomo
Itsukushimubeki
Koto o na wasure so

which might be crudely translated thus:

Though for our country's sake
You crush the enemy
Who would destroy us,
Do not forget that even the enemy
Is to be cherished!

—not exactly the kind of poem one would expect from a Head of State in wartime. One can hardly avoid the feeling that Tolstoy's charge of inconsistency was uncharitable—though how much of the point of the poem got across in Kenjiro's English, and how much of Tolstoy's comment survived *his* English, is debatable.

49. They do, however, seem to have enjoyed each other's company. With his host, Kenjiro tried his hand at scything hay, and marvelled at the Russian's strength and skill. They also went swimming together. On the way to the lake, Tolstoy suddenly stopped to urinate by the roadside. Kenjiro, 'as if challenged' to show similar manly simplicity, immediately followed suit.

It is perhaps worth recording in this connection that there appears to have been another difficulty which led to Kenjiro's leaving so soon, besides Sergei's impending wedding—a difficulty which illustrates the embarrassments to which the Japanese traveller of the day was liable. Kenjiro slept away from the main house, in an annexe without a toilet of its own. Not knowing the use of the chamber-pot under his bed, and having got into severe linguistic complications when asking a manservant in Russian to conduct him to the elaborate toilet in the main house, he had taken to performing at unlikely hours in a remote corner of the garden—and was fearful of being caught in the act if he stayed too long.

what he must, and to live like a peasant if he could—had struck home, appealing directly to his vaguely radical Christianity and Oriental predilection for simplicity and inwardness of living. Within six months he had bought a peasant's cottage and plot of land in the hamlet of Kasuya, some twelve miles from the centre of Tokyo.[50] Here he remained for twenty years, till his death in 1927.

The first five years of this Tolstoyan existence were on the whole settled and happy. The villagers smiled for a while at the sight of a noted writer carrying water to his cottage from a nearby stream (till he managed to redig the old well in his garden) or tramping the dusty road from Tokyo with a pair of newly-purchased 'honey-buckets'[51] slung over his shoulder; but in time they accepted him for what he was, eccentric but genuine, the 'saint of Kasuya', as he later came to be called—a title recognizing in him the (particularly for the Japanese) all-important quality of 'sincerity', rather than any claim to moral grandeur. He continued to write from time to time, producing a successful novel based on a young army officer's association with the celebrated General Nogi,[52] and *Idle Chatter of an Earthworm*, a book of short essays and sketches describing his new life. Early in 1911 events in the political world drew him momentarily and memorably from his retreat. A group of twenty-six anarchists and socialists had been arrested in December of the previous year and tried in secret, on very flimsy evidence, for an alleged plot to murder the Emperor. On January 18th it was announced that all but two had been condemned to death. Aiko's diary records Kenjiro's profound shock at the news: they talked of nothing else, and spent two sleepless nights wondering what, if anything, they as individuals could do to protest. Two days later, however, twelve of the condemned men were reprieved. Kenjiro wrote to Iichiro begging him to use his influence with the Prime Minister, a personal friend, to ensure that the others would be granted a similar reprieve, as he was convinced they would be after a face-saving interval: Iichiro did not reply.[53] Searching for some other means of protest (the report of the first executions had said that the remaining sentences would be carried out at the end of January or early in February), on the morning of January 25th Kenjiro composed a personal appeal to the Emperor, and sent it off before noon by a special messenger to the editor of the influential *Asahi* newspaper

---

50. Tokyo has long since spread far beyond Kasuya, which is now a section of the Setagaya Ward of the city; but Kenjiro's house, containing his library and other possessions, is preserved by the city authorities as a memorial. The small estate is known by the name he gave it, 'Garden of Perpetual Spring'.
51. To be used for distributing night-soil to his fields as manure.
52. Who 'followed his lord in death' by committing suicide, together with his wife, when the Emperor Meiji died in 1912.
53. The atmosphere in which these events took place may be inferred from such incidents as the arrest at Yokohama of a Christian pastor, on the same day that Kenjiro appealed to his brother, for publicly expressing his sympathy with the condemned men.

—a Kumamoto man, like himself—with a letter asking him to publish it immediately.[54] There is no record of any response from the editor, nor could the appeal have served any purpose if it had been published. At three o'clock that afternoon—Kasuya was too remote for a morning delivery—the papers arrived, with the bare announcement that eleven of the twelve had been executed the previous day, the twelfth that very morning.

Again, the shock was severe. Kenjiro and Aiko wept at the news, and talked of fetching the bodies and burying them in their own land, till they found that in this at least they had been anticipated by friends of the dead. But for them the incident was still not yet over. On the 22nd, two students from the First National High School (now incorporated in Tokyo University) came to Kasuya to invite Kenjiro to speak at the big annual meeting of the School's Oratorical Society. When he agreed, they asked him to suggest a subject. One of them, Jotaro Kawakami,[55] recalls his amazement when Kenjiro, with the firetongs from the porcelain brazier around which they were sitting, traced in the charcoal-ash the characters BOHAN-RON, 'On Rebellion'. Such a title being too dangerous to publicize in advance, the subject was given out as 'Not Yet Decided' till the morning of the meeting, when the posting on a notice-board of the explosive words quickly filled the hall to overflowing, with students who were unable to push their way in packing the opened windows from outside. Predictably, Kenjiro's speech[56] dealt with the recent executions. Though emphasizing his love and respect for the Emperor, he deplored the total lack of protest by civil and religious leaders at the arbitrary action taken by the government in the Emperor's name; and pleaded with his audience, backing his argument with three biblical quotations,[57] not merely to lament the past but to learn from it the necessity of living in continual revolt, if the free spirit was to survive. In a hundred years the so-called anarchists, he prophesied, would be national heroes, as Saigo, leader of the Rebellion of 1877, had already become.

The end of the speech was met with total silence, and then with prolonged and enthusiastic applause. There were repercussions, however, which

---

54. An MS of this appeal survives. Influenced, apparently, by Tolstoy's memorial pleading for clemency for the assassin of Alexander II, it is a remarkable document, not revolutionary in the strictly political sense, but displaying a degree of personal courage in opposing the government's action that was very rare at this period, particularly in one who like Kenjiro was never much drawn to political activity as such.

55. Later prominent in Christian and political circles. After the Pacific War he was Chairman of the Japanese Socialist Party.

56. The gist of what he said was not generally known until it could be reconstructed from his notes after the Pacific War. A reporter's verbatim record was confiscated by the police.

57. 'If thy right eye offend thee, pluck it out' (Matt. 5:29); 'Let the dead bury their dead' (Matt. 8:22); 'Fear not them which kill the body, but are not able to kill the soul' (Matt. 10:28).

Kenjiro had not foreseen. When the content of the speech became known, Inazo Nitobe,[58] the School's Principal, who had given formal permission to the students to invite Kenjiro, but without knowing the subject of his lecture, at once offered his resignation to the Ministry of Education. There was a flurry of comings and goings, on and off the campus:[59] students 'apologized' to Nitobe and to the Minister, assuring them both that nobody had been 'influenced' by Kenjiro's dangerous ideas. Kenjiro wrote to the Minister of Education and to the Prime Minister, urging them not to accept Nitobe's resignation. In the event, Nitobe was only censured. No action was taken against Kenjiro himself, perhaps because of his brother's connections: though for a while he was violently attacked, in the press and at public meetings, for 'lack of patriotism', and a Christian College where he had been asked to speak suddenly cancelled the invitation. Kenjiro was unrepentant. He had recently built a small library on to his cottage, and now named it the 'Shusui Room', after the leader of the executed radicals.[60]

Though the uproar over Kenjiro's lecture was not long in subsiding, the peace of Kasuya was soon to be broken again by a reopening of the old feud with Iichiro. In February 1913 angry mobs, rioting against the arbitrary rule of an oligarchic government, attacked once again the offices of the *People's Daily*, denouncing Iichiro Tokutomi as a creature of Katsura (who was now Prime Minister for the third time, and had recently rewarded Iichiro for his political services by appointing him a member of the House of Peers). Shamed by the memory of his own coldness on a similar occasion eight years before, Kenjiro hurried in to Tokyo to urge his brother to keep away from the Minyusha and *People's Daily* buildings till the trouble had died down; but so impressed was he by Iichiro's determination in facing the crowds that he offered there and then to write another novel for the paper, to be called *Junen* (Ten Years), and began to write at once. But he was no longer capable, he found, of writing a mere 'fictitious romance'; if he was to write anything at all, it had to be a direct exploration of the restless years of his own earlier life. And this proved impossible. After only eleven instalments had appeared, the paper's readers were confronted with an announcement that no more would be forthcoming, the writer having decided that the whole work must be 'rewritten from within'. The real reason was reveal-

---

58. The distinguished Japanese Quaker, scholar, administrator and internationalist, later Under-Secretary of the League of Nations.
59. Rumours were rife. It was said, for example, that, on hearing of Kenjiro's proposed lecture, General Nogi, President of the Peers' College, had hurried to Kasuya on horseback to stop him, but had failed to arrive in time.
60. Kenjiro's courage throughout this affair compares favourably with the shocked silence of other and better-known writers, and he surely deserves the posthumous praise he was given when at last it became possible, after the Pacific War, to discuss the events freely. Compare, for example, the attitude of the novelist Kafu, described in Seidensticker's *Kafu the Scribbler* (Stanford, California, 1965), pp. 45–6.

ed in a long and passionate letter Kenjiro wrote to his brother.[61] He was determined, he said, to tell the truth about the Tokutomi family—the full truth, however ugly. This would mean 'a cruel death' for them all; but only that they might live more fully. For himself, he was willing to undergo this death. But for the rest of the family—their father in particular[62]—it would be too cruel, still, to expose *them* to such pain. Hence his refusal to continue with *Ten Years*.

Iichiro replied from Seoul accusing Kenjiro of having for years past undermined all he was trying to achieve in the world, and of having by this latest act of treachery put a weapon into the hands of his enemies. Before this letter reached Kenjiro, however, the latter had set out with Aiko on a journey to west Japan, Manchuria and Korea.[63] The brothers met briefly in Seoul on October 23rd, but the bitterness had gone too deep for another reconciliation. They did not meet again till the day of Kenjiro's death, nearly fifteen years later.

In May the following year their father Kazutaka died. Kenjiro ordered Aiko to prepare *sekihan*, the congratulatory dish of rice and red beans—to celebrate Kazutaka's passing to a better world, or another stage in the progress of his own liberation?—but refused to attend the funeral,[64] which would have implied an admission of his subordination to his brother, the head of the house, who would be in charge of the ceremony.

In his own eyes, Kenjiro was at last free to write openly and truthfully of his past. Ironically, the events he chose to deal with in the first of his series of autobiographical revelations were those which would give most pain to one who had had nothing to do with them—his wife Aiko. She had

61. Immediately he heard of the novel's suspension, Iichiro, who was in Korea at the request of the Governor-General, re-establishing a Japanese newspaper in Seoul, hurried home to visit Kenjiro at Kasuya. He pleaded with him not to disappoint the readers of the *People's Daily*, for whom a new Tokutomi novel was a great attraction. Kenjiro would promise nothing, however. The letter referred to above was written after this visit, when Iichiro had returned to Korea.

62. Kazutaka had been baptized a Christian in 1907, at the age of eighty-five. Kenjiro had always been closer to his father than to his mother; and the fact that Kazutaka had adopted Christianity, though so late in life, may well have been one of the reasons why he found himself unable to write with complete frankness about the past so long as his father was living. He wrote frequently to Kazutaka during the Manchurian journey. (Hisako survived Kazutaka by five years.)

63. The journey is described in Kenjiro's book *Shi no Kage ni* (In Death's Shadow). They had intended to go on to Russia to visit Tolstoy's grave, but ran out of money, and were insufficiently prepared for the cold.

64. When Iichiro sent messengers to urge him to go, he swore he would bring the house down on their heads, like Samson, if they didn't leave. The decision not to attend, and thus to cut himself off publicly from the family once again, was clearly a painful one. Kazutaka, he was told, had called for him three times in his last hours. In his diary he speaks of his need to become strong where before he was weak, whatever it may cost. 'To reach heaven a man must first descend into hell . . . the cross of Christ, not Nogi's suicide, is the Way.' Yet if Kenjiro did love his father, he hated him too, even after Kazutaka's death. After the funeral he tore up a photograph of Kazutaka, and took down the nameplate of 'Tokutomi' from his own gatepost, as if in total rejection of the name he had inherited. Staying in a country inn a fortnight later, he signed himself 'Kenjiro Kasuya'.

some warning of what was coming when he asked her, as he began to write,[65] 'if she could bear to walk naked through the streets of Tokyo?' For the 'novel' was to be the record, not literal but faithful enough for all the characters to be easily recognizable, of Kenjiro's affair with Hisae. Aiko had long known vaguely of the past existence of another woman whom in some obscure way Kenjiro seemed still—after twenty-one years of marriage to Aiko—to regard as his 'real' wife; but she had never been told the full story. Overcome with jealousy and shame on hearing that it was now to be made public, she threatened suicide if he did not give the book up. But Kenjiro wrote on. In five weeks it was finished, freeing him at long last from the trauma of repressed memories. Aiko's ordeal, however, was not yet over. She was ordered by her husband to make a fair copy of his manuscript—or to burn it if her courage failed her. The work was duly done. Aiko's jealousy turned to pity and understanding as she wrote, and miraculously their marriage emerged from this harsh test strengthened and renewed. *Kuroi Me to Chairo no Me* (Black Eyes and Brown Eyes) was published in December 1914. When three months later the strain told, and Aiko fell seriously ill, Kenjiro nursed her with the devotion of a bridegroom.

The rest of the story may be more briefly told. Now that he had made his peace with the past, and the 'family' no longer had the power, as a supposedly hostile and perpetually resented force in the background of his life, to focus his energies, the irrational bias in Kenjiro's thought led him along some strange paths. In *New Spring*, a collection of autobiographical essays and rhapsodic interludes, he wrote ecstatically, at times almost incoherently, of himself and Aiko as the 'Adam and Eve of the new Eden, children of the Sun'—a greying Japanese D. H. Lawrence, he seems sometimes, but lacking the intellectual and imaginative power that might have enabled him to transmute his outpourings into fiction or philosophy. In 1919, or 'Year I', as he called it, of the 'New Era' his 'resurrection' had inaugurated,[66] he set out on a second world tour, this time taking Aiko with him.[67]

65. On an enormous table, 9 feet by 6, which he had had specially made, to celebrate the fuller freedom into which he felt himself to have entered.

66. At times during these final years he gave the impression in his writing that he believed himself to be the Christ of the Second Coming, and has duly been regarded since, by many of his critics, as all but insane. It is not easy, however, given his passionate temperament and peculiar style (with the vagueness of the Japanese language to compound the difficulty) to decide where exuberant imagery and hyperbole end and madness begins. Unbalanced, perhaps, he was, as the result of the tension under which so much his life had been lived; but not mad.

67. When filling in forms at the British Consulate before their departure, he gave as his Object of Journey, 'Messenger of Peace, to cultivate goodwill among nations'; as his Employer, 'Him'—who turned out, on a request for a more specific description from the mystified consular official, to be God—and as his Guarantor 'the Japanese Government', who, needless to say, had not been consulted in the matter. For the crowd of reporters who came to Yokohama to see them off, and asked the Saint of Kasuya for a message, he had only this cryptic remark: 'The Age of the Cross is past: the Jesus of the New Age must take his Bride.'

This journey lasted fourteen months, and took them to Egypt, Palestine, Italy, France, England and the United States, where Kenjiro lectured to the Japanese immigrant community. From Jerusalem, on Easter Day, 1919,[68] he sent a 'personal appeal for true peace', in English, to Woodrow Wilson, Lloyd George and Prince Saionji of Japan at Versailles, and a letter to Lloyd George on the situation in Egypt—two naïve but nonetheless sincere gestures. The Appeal called for a world conference of men and women of all races, a 'world family congress', to plan for human welfare and mutual understanding; the immediate ending of the Christian, Islamic and Chinese and Japanese eras, with 1919 to be Year One of a new World Era; the unconditional abolition of all armies and navies; the establishment of an international currency; the right of all peoples to self-determination; and a 'year of release',[69] with all debts, indemnities, etc. to be cancelled. The letter to Lloyd George is more modest in its demands. Describing his sadness when passing through Egypt at the sight of Egyptians demonstrating against British authority, and of young Englishmen who should have gone home now that the long war was over having to guard, with their rifles and bayonets, the buildings of the occupying Power, Kenjiro claims that there can be no real peace so long as such potentially violent situations are allowed to persist, and pleads in the name of Christ for a more loving way. 'You conquered Germans,' the letter concludes, 'now it is your turn to conquer yourself. To you, one of the chosen servants of humanity at this momentous period, to you I appeal to consider seriously what I propose in this letter. You who are so wide awake and so sagacious should not be ashamed of forgetting yourself for a moment of inspired ecstasy of disinterestedness. Indeed, it is sometimes so necessary and good to be beside oneself, and this is the very time. Don't you think so?'[70]

68. It was just at this time that the delegates to the Peace Conference were discussing the Japanese proposal to include in the Covenant of the League of Nations a clause accepting the principle of racial equality. The proposal was rejected, largely owing to the opposition of the Australian Prime Minister.

69. 'At the end of every seven years thou shalt make a release. And this is the manner of the release: Every creditor that lendeth ought unto his neighbour shall release it; he shall not exact it of his neighbour, or of his brother; because it is called the Lord's release.' Deuteronomy, c.15.

70. Two weeks later Kenjiro wrote yet another Appeal, this time to General Allenby in Cairo. First proclaiming the need for a New Era after two thousand years of war and suffering ('Away with the Cross! No more of the bleeding Christ! Let death with it's [sic] pain perish and Life with it's joy shine in its glory') he then expresses the hope that 'Egypt will find not merely a friend but the very father in you—father who would be glad to bestow anything needful for the growth of his child and who take [sic] delight in making his child a man'. But the real occasion of the letter is explained in a PS, where Kenjiro asks Allenby to arrange for the return from a PoW camp at Heliopolis of the two sons of an elderly German couple living in Nazareth. Enclosing a personal message from the couple, he ends the letter as follows: 'So they asked me to write a line to you to somewhat lighten the heavy burdens ... I persuaded them to write ... the letter here enclosed. There is no need of adding any word of mine. You know how to deal with. Only I assure you that even a cup of fresh water given to them will make me glad and grateful as given unto me.'

Back at Kasuya in March 1920, Kenjiro at once started his second long travelogue, *From Japan to Japan*, but found time to invite sixty local farmers to his house to tell them of his experiences and present them with a variety of western vegetable seeds that he had brought back with him from abroad. On a holiday journey to celebrate the book's completion in the spring of 1921, Kenjiro and Aiko visited together for the first time the grave of Hisae Yamamoto in the cemetery of Nyakuoji Temple in Kyoto. Aiko records in a letter her joy at finding herself truly reconciled at last to the rival she had never met, and whose story she had heard only after her death.[71] Another journey followed—to Kumamoto,[72] to collect material for a biography of Junko Takesaki. His debt of affection to the aunt who had befriended him after the Doshisha crisis was well and truly paid. Of the thirteen thousand copies of the first printing of this biography, Kenjiro bought three thousand himself, sending two thousand to the girls' school with which his aunt has been associated, three hundred to relatives and friends, and one each to six hundred and eight girls' schools throughout the Japanese empire. If it seems in retrospect an exaggerated gesture of respect to her memory, the mass distribution underlines his gratitude for one from whom, as from no other woman in his life, he had known nothing but sympathy. It was her example, no doubt, that led him to show particular interest in these last years in women's education and women's rights.[73]

The great earthquake of 1923 damaged the Kasuya house, now much enlarged, but not seriously. More important was the destruction in the fires resulting from the earthquake of the stereo plates of several of his books, which made reprinting impossible for the time being and consequently brought about a sudden drop in his income. Iichiro, who was ill at the time, suffered more severely: his son was killed, and his offices burned to the ground. Within a few weeks the *People's Daily* was up for sale. The tragedy did not bring them together, however.[74] Kenjiro was meditating a ten-year plan, so he wrote to a friend, for a multi-volume autobiography, on the completion of which he would rebuild his house—with a flat roof,

71. The letter ends: 'Kenjiro, I know, longed for this moment to come much earlier; but come it has at last—the reward for respecting (each other's?) freedom.'
72. By now Kenjiro's reputation was considerable. When he was invited to give a public lecture in this conservative provincial town, an audience of 3,500 came to hear him speak on 'My Gift to My Native Town'. What they thought of the gift—his new philosophy of individualism and sexual harmony—is not recorded, though he is said to have remarked later that there was some restiveness at the gathering, 'no doubt because his ideas didn't appeal to the extreme nationalism of Kumamoto people—or perhaps because they didn't approve of Aiko's western clothes.'
73. He and Aiko had made contact with American women's organizations when passing through New York in 1920.
74. How little had changed, at least on Kenjiro's part, is suggested by an incident that had occurred the previous year when he was travelling in Kyushu. A newspaper editor, visiting him in his inn at Beppu, noticed a scroll with a poem by Iichiro hanging on the wall, and asked him—either from ignorance or a singular lack of tact—whether he carried his brother's work around with him in his baggage. Kenjiro replied angrily that the innkeeper had produced the scroll on his arrival, thinking to please him; and ended the interview forthwith.

from which he could contemplate the stars—and invite all his relatives to a grand reconciliation: he considered offering it to Iichiro to help him over his difficulties, but thought better of it. Perhaps wisely: the four volumes which Kenjiro managed to write before his death would in all probability have widened the gulf between them if Iichiro had been directly involved with their publication. As it is, there is no sign that he ever read them, though he survived his brother for thirty years.

These four books of the autobiography *Fuji* occupied most of his time from the end of 1923 onwards. In the intervals of writing, he still followed the second of Tolstoy's two injunctions, rising at 4.30 a.m. in the summer to hoe and manure his fields. Occasionally there were interruptions to this placid routine. Early in 1924 he drew up a second appeal to the Emperor— a different Emperor now—this time for clemency for Daisuke Nanta, who was charged with having attempted to assassinate his Majesty when he was on his way to open the Diet in December 1923, and sent it to the Crown Prince's steward. The passage by the U.S. Congress, in April of the same year, took him away from autobiography to edit a volume of protest, *The Ocean Between Us*, to which he himself contributed seventeen short essays on American-Japanese themes and an Open Letter to American Missionaries, the latter in English.[75]

Towards the end of 1926 his health deteriorated so rapidly that at least one Tokyo paper had the report of his death already written. Alarmed, Iichiro hurried to Kasuya. But Kenjiro would still not see him: a maid was sent to the door with the brief message 'Too soon!' Slowly he recovered, and by July was able to make his tenth and last journey, accompanied by a doctor and nurses, to his favourite mountain retreat of Ikao. For a while the improvement continued, and he talked of spending the winter at Ikao too. But in August and the first half of September he grew weaker.

75. The Letter is compounded in equal parts of affection for American culture and disgust for American policies. Its appeal is if anything enhanced by the occasional quaintness of the English in which Kenjiro strove to express to the English-speaking world, as he had in his appeals to western statesmen, an Oriental point of view. Some of it has scarcely dated after forty-five years. A few brief extracts: '... it is high time you go home. Your country now most needs you. Gardeners sent to look after the neighbour's garden now return to find their own full of weeds. Dear America! What a naughty boy you have turned into! Too much prosperity must have spoiled you. You got too much flesh that your delicacy is well nigh benumbed. Too much momentum you have got that you can hardly restrain yourselves. You dream of overrunning the world. You think you are entitled to force anything to anyone. You want to patronize, to meddle in another's business everywhere. No doubt you mean good, for naturally you are a good boy and I cannot but love you ... Dear friends, it is time you hurry back to America, to wake up the slumbering Jesus there, to pacify your countrymen, and to warn them of the danger they are fast provoking. You shall teach them to be more humble. You shall remind them that it was not the giant armed to the teeth, but the shepherd lad with only a sling and some pebbles, who won the laurel. You shall admonish them that envy is cowardice, and that pressing for gratitude is not better than ingratitude. You shall teach them that it was a shame for a nation to slight his brother on account of his swarthy colour, or short stature, or small area of his dominion, or his seeming poverty ...'

On September 17th, agreeing suddenly to the doctor's suggestion that he should be moved for the colder months to the coastal resort of Zushi, where Iichiro now spent much of his time, he asked that Iichiro should be sent for. Iichiro was telephoned immediately, and promised to come next day with his family. As if impatient, Kenjiro ordered a telegram to be sent to his brother, saying only 'Waiting—Kenjiro'—and the moment it had been sent, cursed and cried out to his wife, 'He has won!'

The following morning Iichiro and his family duly arrived. The brothers shook hands; Kenjiro apologized once more for the trouble he had caused. In an atmosphere of harmony it was agreed that Kenjiro should be moved, not to Sushi, but to the warmer Atami; arrangements were made at once, a room in an Atami inn booked for the 20th onwards.[76]

That evening, after more talk with Iichiro and an apology to Aiko for some earlier irritability, Kenjiro went quietly to sleep, and died during the night.

In an hour-long address at the Christian funeral service in Tokyo, which was attended by a congregation of 2,000, Iichiro played down the breach between them. According to him, from the beginning it had been unnecessary. Some of his hearers believed him; some were indignant that even now the elder brother could not take his share of responsibility for the estrangement. So a question-mark hangs over the final reconciliation that took place on Kenjiro's death-bed; at his funeral, ironically, the elder brother occupied the centre of the stage, as he had twenty-seven years before when Kenjiro was writing *Footprints in the Snow* in the confident but premature hope that he had freed himself from Iichiro's control.

A final word on Kenjiro's Christianity may be in place. It has given Japanese critics peculiar difficulty. Many Japanese literary men of the modern period have taken up with Christianity, but Kenjiro Tokutomi alone remained a Christian till he died a natural death:[77] all the others either abandoned the western religion in their maturity or clung to it more or less fervently till they were driven to commit suicide. A 'Japanese

---

76. After the mid-day meal Iichiro's daughter Tsuru, who had to leave early, said goodbye to her uncle, 'till we meet again in Atami in two days' time.' 'No,' replied Kenjiro, 'I shall be visiting Bankuma then.' Bankuma was Iichiro's son who had died in the great earthquake four years before.

77. It is true that one of the last entries in his diary reads, 'I'd like the Ishikawas, the Asamuras, and the Maedagawas to bury me. No Christian nonsense!' (*Yaso-kyo wa peke da*); but this meant only that he wanted no ceremony, no sermonizing. After reading a newspaper report of the address given by the Rev. Ebina at Kazutaka's funeral in 1914 in which Ebina had spoken of Kazutaka's two sons, the elder a 'paragon of filial piety, the younger a literary genius,' Kenjiro had writtten, also in his diary, 'So he had a genius of a son, as well as a paragon of filial piety? No genius, but a fool, a self-willed fool; a criminal . . . Two thousand mourners, all the big names you can think of, led by the paragon, and a buffoon of a priest to preach at them! "Let the dead bury their dead"—that's how it should be!' But however unorthodox, he never abandoned his allegiance to Christianity as he interpreted it.

Christian writer' seems to many, one may suspect, a contradiction in terms: and indeed the kind of Christianity that was preached in Japan in the late nineteenth and early twentieth centuries, while appealing powerfully in some respects to the samurai character, was often so overlaid with western habits of thought and cultural attitudes that anyone who embraced it would inevitably have to abandon much that was good and representative, as well as much that was bad, in his own tradition. According to one authority,[78] Kenjiro's Christianity was so eccentric that it cannot even be called a Christian heresy. Another critic[79] sees him as a 'true Protestant', if unorthodox, with a highly personal faith and strong social conscience, influenced perhaps by the Methodism of the church where he was baptized. Others have criticized as un-Christian his samurai 'élitism', his unconscious clinging to the values of an out-of-date, authoritarian morality, even while claiming to reject them,[80] the 'pseudo-Tolstoyan pose' of his life at Kasuya—indeed, at times one is driven to suspect that any stick is good enough with which to beat a man whose persistent and powerful individuality, manifested in a crucial area of Japanese life, has, at least until recently, shamed the conformity of the majority. Many of the discussions are weakened also by a rather rigid conception of what constitutes Christianity—for which the Japanese are perhaps not entirely to be blamed.

But the argument as to whether Kenjiro was in any meaningful sense a Christian is likely to be inconclusive, and not very profitable. If an answer to the question must be given, the most satisfactory is that suggested by Sasabuchi,[81] that in its many-sided character—including missionary-inspired evangelistic faith, a pantheistic element, aspirations toward liberty and social justice, combined with a nationalism that saw in Japan the vehicle of a Christianity purified of its materialism, and an everpresent tendency to lose touch with mundane realities[82]—Kenjiro's religion followed a pattern typical of much of Meiji Christianity, inconsistent perhaps from a western point of view, but sincerely held, and perfectly understandable in its historical context. This would explain why a considerable proportion of Kenjiro's most faithful readers have always been Christians.

78. Seiichiro Katsumoto, 'Roka to Kirisuto-kyo' in *Bungaku*, Aug. 1956. Katsumoto finds the nearest parallel to Kenjiro's religion in Omoto-kyo, one of the more optimistic and syncretistic of the Japanese so-called 'new religions,' which was launched in 1892.

79. Mantaro Kubota, 'Roka to Kirisuto-kyo' in *Nihon Bungaku*, Dec. 1957.

80. In *Footprints in the Snow*, for instance, it is not without irony that Shintaro's wedding to O-Toshi, the start of his new life in which his prime desire is to be 'truly free', takes place on the birthday of the Emperor, the summit and symbol of the hierarchical family system Kenjiro himself fought against all his life.

81. In his articles 'Roka Bungaku no Tokuisei' (*Bungaku*, Aug. 1956) and 'Roka to Kirisuto-kyo' (*Meiji Taisho Bungaku Kenkyu*, Oct. 1957).

82. In Japan, with its long Buddhist tradition, the Protestant Christianity of Meiji shied away from the firm recognition of the material world that had been characteristic of its European counterpart. Hence in part the split, about the time that Kenjiro was writing *Footprints in the Snow* and *Kokucho*, between Christianity and incipient Japanese socialism.

More important, however, in the final analysis, is the quality of 'sincerity' which all agree he possessed in outstanding measure, and which in Japanese eyes more than makes up for his intellectual or doctrinal deficiencies. In Japan, as elsewhere, the majority give up the pretence of continuing their youthful search for 'truth' as soon as they reach 'maturity'. Kenjiro persisted rather longer, which has led one critic,[83] at least, to describe him as a lifelong *shugyoso*, a 'priest practising austerities in search of enlightenment'.

For their help in preparing the translation that follows, my grateful thanks are due to Mr A. Owada, Temporary Lecturer in Japanese at the School of Oriental and African Studies, University of London; to Mr K. Nomoto, of the National Institute of Language Research in Tokyo, and formerly himself a Temporary Lecturer at the School; and to my wife, Sonoko Strong. Its inadequacies are of course my responsibility alone. I should also like to thank Daniel L. Milton and the Literature Division of UNESCO, for their constant and welcome encouragement.

Kenneth Strong
London, 1968

83. Umenosuke Bessho, quoted by Sasabuchi in his article 'Roka to Kirisutokyo'.

Note on the pronunciation of Japanese names

The consonants are pronounced as in English (but with the g always hard), the vowels as in Italian. There are no silent letters. Thus 'Tsumagome' is pronounced 'Tsoo-mah-go-may', and 'Suzue', 'Soo-zoo-ay'.

Dedication
to the author's father

To my Father
on his eightieth birthday
who thirty years ago would take me on
his knee and delight me with stories
of Momotaro, the Peach-Boy, and of
Kachi-Kachi Mountain, or The Badger
Who Got What He Deserved: who urges
me still—as he strokes a beard long
since turned silver—to uphold what
is right and respect the feelings of
men.

Kenjiro Tokutomi

All things are engaged in writing their history.
The planet, the pebble, goes attended by its
shadow. The rolling rock leaves its scratches
on the mountain; the river, its channel in the
soil; the animal, its bones in the stratum;
the fern and leaf, their modest epitaph in the coal.
The falling drop makes its sculpture in the sand
or the stone. Not a foot steps into the snow,
or along the ground, but prints, in characters
more or less lasting, a map of its march.

Emerson

Part I

The 'superior men' of ancient China commonly showed their qualities very early in life. 'At ten,' we are told of one such prodigy, 'he had already decided he was to rule a province'; another 'had mastered characters by the time he was three'; of a third it is recorded that 'hardly had the young plant grown its first leaf when men caught the fragrance of the blossom-to-be'. Commonplace persons like myself, unhappily, have no such early marks of genius with which to embellish the opening chapter of their life-story. A vague awareness of 'myself' as a distinct entity by the name of Shintaro Kikuchi did not begin to take shape in my very ordinary mind till the year I turned eleven. If I were a politician, I should have a lot to say about that year, 1878, for it was then that Toshimichi Okubo, Home Minister in the Meiji government, was assassinated. But politician I am not, so it is pointless to recall events such as these. The year was memorable enough for me, though: my father went bankrupt that spring, and by the autumn he was dead.

The place where I was born is remote indeed. A valley in central Kyushu, about two and a half miles wide by seven and a half miles long, and curving upwards from the bottom like a housewife's scales—this was my cradle. A screen of thickly-wooded hills guarded the valley, topped all round by a fringe of distant peaks that turned from a brilliant blue to white as spring and summer wore on to winter. The highest of these peaks, Mount Takakura, towered above all others to the east. A solitary cloud would be clinging about its summit whenever rain was on the way, like a great white saddle dropped carelessly on the mountain's back; and however violently it might be pouring in the valley, as soon as the mountain came clear of cloud we knew the rain would quickly stop. Always the first to catch both cloud and returning sunshine, Mount Takakura served as our weather station.

The clear waters of innumerable rivulets tumbling down from the hills merged into two streams—Big Stream and Little Stream, we called them—which provided ample moisture for the soil. The valley itself was a long patchwork of fields, with here and there, squeezed in among the squares of paddy, a tiny hamlet or a line of twenty or thirty straggling cottages. Up in the northernmost corner lay the 'capital' of our valley, Tsumagome Village, or Town, as some preferred to call it, though it contained less than a thousand households.

Two things I still cannot forget, though they may seem too slight to deserve a mention. One is the purity of the water, the other the sheer beauty of the rice-plants. A lot of our rice still finds its way to Tokyo, I believe, for use in *sushi* dishes. But those fields of shining green, those rows of healthy, straight-growing stalks—that's a sight I should like the gentlemen of Tokyo to see! And the cheerful bustle when all the village goes out together to transplant the young seedlings, wading in the mud to a chorus of croaking frogs; the girls' white headbands fluttering in the wind, the lilt of the old planting-songs flowing from field to field across the valley! And in the burning height of summer, when the long task of weeding the paddy is painful even to watch—the evening rain! Just when the heat seems beyond bearing, thunder rolls, and there is a sudden chill upon the air. You glance up. A black giant of a cloud has all but swallowed Mount Takakura; a moment later its inky mass has seeped into every corner of the sky. A single flash of lightning, two or three fierce cracks of thunder, a sharp thrust of wind, a few thick drops of rain ... Farmer Taro, his hands over his ears, has hardly run fifty yards when the storm breaks—thunder, lightning, rain and wind, raging around him all at once as if the world itself were dying in agony. Then, just as suddenly, the blackness fades—it's stopping, thinks Taro, and peers out of his shelter at the few threads of rain, white-tinted now with the returning light, that mark the squall's passing. By the time he has pulled off his straw rain-hat and stepped outside again, the storm is over the next village, half-hiding it like a gigantic bamboo screen. The sky is nearly split in two, the east blacked out still and echoing to the thunder's drumroll, the west glowing in the mellow evening sun; a perfect rainbow reaches down across the valley from near the summit of Mount Takakura. How cool it is now! And look at those rice-plants, that you thought had wilted under the storm—greener than ever now, and spilling their raindrops as they wave and rustle in the breeze, an inch or two taller, you would think, for their buffeting! In the paddies the churned and muddied water swirls and overflows; tiny roach and mudfish thresh about on the footpath ridges dividing field from field.

Some weeks later, when the farmers have held their annual torchlight processions through the fields to frighten away the pests, and the rice-plants sway gently in the first breath of autumn, the nights shake off the thundery closeness of the rainy season—and how beautiful then the ripening ears, scented in the fresh morning sunlight! The autumn 'storm days' pass—no typhoons this year; the valley's green carpet turns to shining gold, and everywhere there is frantic activity; soon the harvest reaches its peak—nobody will be at home now, no matter who you want to see. With the coming of the autumn showers, the sound of hulling is to be heard on every side late into the night, and by the time you catch your first glimpse of snow on Mount Takakura, the wavy gold of scarcely a month before has turned into rows of bales neatly stacked in shed and barn, while every village in the valley smacks its lips over new-brewed saké, in honour of another lucky year.

And the water! If Tokyo had a few such streams criss-crossing its crowded wards, there would have been no need to spend vast sums on a City Waterworks, and none of the criminal speculation such grandiose schemes engender, either. In our town we hardly needed any wells. Big Stream and Little Stream—which were alive with darting sweetfish—and the mountain rivulets that fed them, carried their music everywhere.

> What need of flute or harp
> Where mountain streams make music?

as the Chinese poet says. And on a moonlit summer evening, if you stilled your senses to listen, the sound was magical. Kyoto is famous for its water, but ours was better. You could find it literally everywhere, bubbling up anywhere you cared to dig, and always of the same perfect purity. Everywhere—in the ditches by the roads that served instead of horse-troughs, in the rills running in front of the cottages, where the women would kneel and do their washing, even in the irrigation channels, in spite of churning waterwheels—the water was ice-cold and clear as a jewel. Even now, summer makes me specially homesick.

Perfect rice and perfect water. With this combination, saké-brewers abounded. Brewing was the hereditary business of our family, too; and we were among the most prosperous households in the valley.

I.2

We were of good warrior stock, the family tree going back five hundred years to the retainer of a senior samurai who served the Emperor of the Southern Court. Hence the swords which lined the walls of the inner rooms, while the shop in the front of the house was filled with kegs of saké. Every New Year till I was about six, I myself used to go with a servant to worship at the shrine of Hachiman, God of War, in formal dress with a pair of wooden swords stuck in my sash; and on the day of the Boys' Festival there would be a regular canopy of pennants and huge cotton carp overshadowing the entrance to the house. I was not a little proud of my samurai rank.

Such is the cruel trickery of time, a man is forced to forget the things he would best like to recall, and remember only the trivial: the massive thickness of the timber columns around which our house was built, the shadowy half-light of its rooms, the carved pigeons projecting from the gable-ends, the store-sheds in the big yard at the back, one of them always packed to the roof with rice-bales; visits from Kan, the local idiot, who used to sponge on all the big houses in turn, moving on somewhere else as soon as he sensed the larder on one house was getting empty—a couple of days here, four or five days there, mostly, but with us, as often as not, it was a month or two that he would 'humbly accept our gracious hospitality'; another of the sheds, full of great vats like giant bathtubs, itself half-hidden under a huge lotus-tree, so that in summer you could mistake the chanting of the innumerable cicadas among its branches for raindrops pattering on the roof; the score or more of young men and girls, dancing in the garden by moonlight, on the night of the Bon Festival—odd fragments like these I remember, but I could not give you a complete picture of our life at home, even if you were to ask me. Going out into the fields by torchlight on a summer evening, mounted on a servant's shoulders, and tinkling a tiny bell to help scare away the insects; Father and I oversleeping—no more of that when I began school!—and coming down after nine on a winter morning to find the big fireplace in the centre of the eight-mat living-room uncovered and a young servant unloading burning charcoal from an enormous pan, the size of a paving-stone; my great-uncle, imposing in formal dress, shouting 'In with good fortune! Out with evil demons!' as he scattered beans from the doorway in the old ceremony of *setsubun*; the bedtime stories this same great-uncle would tell me—he would doze off sometimes in the middle of a story, the smell of saké on his lips, and infuriate his little hearer, for even though I shook him awake, the words would soon fade into a mumble once more, and the stories get mixed up with each other till I could not understand a word; my nurse carrying me on her back when she went out and boasting wherever she went of how marvellously clever the little gentleman was ... fragments, no more, dimly recalled. I can give no ordered account of those earliest years. My life was no different, shall we say, from that of any other only child of a well-to-do countryman.

But in this world of ours one cannot for ever enjoy the beauty of the flowers and the gentle breezes of spring: and our family, by repute the richest in the valley, came as I said to face bankruptcy. I do not know the details, nor would I want to discuss them if I did. But it was my father's excessive kindliness, I fancy, that was the real cause of our downfall. There was not the tiniest trace of guile or suspicion in my father's nature: he was incapable alike of doubting others and of refusing any request. When my grandfather died, for instance, and the family had to divide into two households, my uncle—not my great-uncle, the story-teller, but my uncle proper, whom I loathed—was so insistent in his demands that Father not only gave him half the entire estate but built him a house into the bargain. No one who wanted money from us was ever turned away, whether relative or stranger; nor did Father ever decline to buy when a pedlar called. What with all these private transactions, contributions to the school, and signing huge promissory notes for relatives who begged him to help them in their business projects—which had a strange way of never turning out as well as had been expected, so that Father always had to pay in the end—and on top of all this, the spoiling of his saké two seasons in succession, even Father's substantial fortune began to wear thin, like a bamboo shoot after peeling. Strange people began to call on business: slimy, cringing fellows. My mother was shocked at this, and tried to remonstrate with him about the way things were going. A Buddhist priest we were friendly with came to offer his advice. People of our town and others from villages down the valley began to stare about them warily whenever they visited our house, as if it were a rotten tree that might fall on them at any moment. Seeing and hearing such things, vague nightmarish fears pressed on my childish mind; and at last the catastrophe came. Father sold everything—our land up in the hills, paddy-fields, all our tools and equipment—gave up his brewing business, dismissed most of his men. Finally, a silk-spinning venture on which he had staked his last remaining capital collapsed. In the spring of my eleventh year he sold up the house and everything in it, and the three of us—Father, Mother and I—moved into a tiny cottage my grandfather had built for himself on his retirement.

Troubles never come singly. From that day on Father gave way to melancholy and drink. In the autumn of the same year, murmuring apologies to Mother and me, he passed into the silence of the tomb.

1.3

Ever since the defeat in 1873 of the 'Subjugate Korea' party, Japan had been unsettled in the extreme, and the series of political disturbances that rocked the main centres had their repercussions even in our far-off rural world. The villagers trembled at the news of the storming of Saga Castle in February 1874, the rising of the Akizuki clansmen and the murder of the commander of the Kumamoto garrison by the 'Divine Wind' plotters in 1876, and most terrible of all, Saigo's full-scale rebellion in 1877. But to a small boy living happily with his parents in a well-to-do home these crises were no more frightening than stormy seas watched from the safety of a hilltop. All kinds of stories were passed from house to house—that Issei Maebara, a former Councillor of State, had been beheaded for rebellion, but not before crying out with his last breath, 'the gods of heaven and earth know I am innocent'; that a provincial governor had been disembowelled; that a battle had been going on for eighteen days in Tawara in Bingo Province, and a force of sword-swinging samurai had swarmed over the earthworks thrown up by the government forces, massacring everyone who stood in their way. Once a rumour that units of the Lord of Satsuma's army were about to invade our valley flung the whole town into a panic. Such talk had thrilled me, like a succession of good ghost stories. Lying between my father and mother at night, holding their hands while storm winds whistled round the house, I would think of all I had heard during the day. *I* was safe whatever happened, I knew; but what of the government soldiers and rebel samurai, fighting that horrid war out there in the wind and rain?

No warm bed for them, no mother and father . . . safe here anyway . . . poor soldiers . . . safe . . . till thought faded into sleep.

But now even those happy nights seemed no more than a dream. The three of us had always slept side by side, like the three strokes of the character for river 川 : now one of the strokes was missing, and Mother and I were alone. I loved my father, and respected my mother. It was Father I had always wanted to rock me to sleep in his arms, Mother's hand I would hold when I was sick; Father who took me flower-viewing each spring, Mother I would cling to when burglars broke into the house, hiding under the deep sleeves of her kimono. Mother's name was O-Setsu. She was a capable woman—though I am not the one to say so—with a natural dignity, and a mind of her own, for which my father had the greatest respect. After the catastrophe he behaved towards her with an apologetic deference that outsiders must have found pitiful. Sometimes they quarrelled. 'Better a dry morsel with quiet than a house full of feasting with strife'—true; but alas, even a dry morsel can lead to strife, the more easily in a family that has sunk in a matter of days from comfort and prosperity to poverty so severe that it cannot afford even rice, and has to grate its teeth on millet-gruel. Usually Mother got the best of these arguments. 'It's all been my fault,' Father would say gloomily, whereupon Mother would burst into tears, and I with her. There were scenes like this several times a month. But now even these tragic clashes had ceased. I should no more see those gentle eyes of Father's, his boyish smile, the dignified figure he had once been at family councils, sitting at the head of the gathering in his formal clothes picked out with the family crest; no more feel that air of weary sadness that clung to him as he sat against a pillar in the tiny house we moved to after the disaster. With both parents to care for it, the poorest child is a millionaire, we say: and that evening, when Mother and I came home after following Father's coffin to the cemetery and sat facing each other, even I, for all my boyish innocence, sensed the isolation, the desperate loneliness that 'ruin' can bring.

Can there be any calamity so painful as the sudden downfall of one's family? When a man is on his way up in the world, he may have to tread a path of thorns, and sweat for every step he takes; but there is always hope ahead, beckoning him to the heights. But for one who must bear a double burden, the dreamlike memories of a prosperous yesterday and the terror of a dark tomorrow, the descent into obscurity is the cruellest agony. It is easier in Tokyo or Osaka, where people jostle each other like potatoes in a bucket. Rich or poor, you can do as you please in the big cities: it is nothing unusual for a man to lose his millions one day and be calmly selling matches at a back-street stall on the next—but not in the country. A countryman come down in the world is like a gibbeted head stuck on a pole for all to see—only worse, since he is still alive to feel the pain. Not a face but is familiar; tormentors surround you wherever you turn. Everyone knows your story, the history of your happier days; for you, even their closed lips carry hints of mockery and sneer. You take a walk, and there by the roadside, waiting to humiliate you, is property your family used to own —a house, a plot of land, fields. Village elders who till lately would bow when you passed no longer recognize you. The neighbour who used to be so obsequious when he caught you in his garden reaching for a sprig of plum blossom—'Mind you don't hurt yourself, young master! Let me break it off for you, shall I?'—has changed his tone: 'Where've you sprung from,' he shouts, 'you little rat! trespassing on other people's property!' Twist and squirm as you may, it is no use: country attitudes are like a deep well, and once you have fallen in, there is little chance of climbing out.

Into this well Mother and I had fallen. If the truth be told, our family was one of the oldest and best-known in the valley, with a long record of unostentatious service to the community. There must be somebody, one might have thought, who would throw us a lifeline. But no one came forward. We were left to our fate—and for a good reason: the hostility of my uncle.

This uncle, Kengo Kikuchi, was my father's younger brother. I had never managed to like him. Even Father, for all his natural tolerance, called him ungrateful, while Mother spoke caustically of his 'inhuman' ways. Not content with half of Grandfather's money, he still grumbled even when Father built him a new house. Even to me, a small and ignorant boy, the very sight of him was like a sudden exchanging of sunlight for cold, dark shadows. His soya-sauce business prospering, he went in for charcoal and made a success of that; everything he touched made money, for he certainly had a better head than Father for managing his affairs. But when his brother went bankrupt, he would not lend him a single sen. What is more, he bought up our house and furniture, under another name—and moved in with his own family. So now he had grabbed all the Kikuchi property for himself. Even Father was angry when he heard what had happened: he wrote to Uncle at once informing him that they were no longer brothers. Money is stronger than blood, and Uncle showed not the slightest sympathy for Father in his troubles. Even when Father died he only paid a brief formal call, which so infuriated Mother that she did not tell him the date of the funeral. To this day I don't know why he should have persecuted us like that, though I have heard that Grandfather didn't like him much, Father being always the favourite of the two. Then there was Mother, still in her twenties, and the beauty of the valley: she had always hated him. I can see her now, disappearing abruptly whenever she saw him coming.

After having cold-shouldered us as the family fortunes declined, and finally driven us out of our home, this callous uncle of mine still would not leave us alone, not even after Father died. We had lots of relatives—most of the solid families in Tsumagome were connected in some way with the Kikuchi. There was Kinzo Kikuchi, for instance, a meticulous old gentleman for ever sweeping and dusting. There was the elderly lady with a passion for cats—ten of them she kept, black, white, tortoiseshell, and tabby; 'How can you possibly eat such *vermin*, my *darlings*!' she would exclaim whenever they caught a mouse, and bring them a plate of fresh-cooked tunny-fish instead. Then there was the haiku poet, a self-styled 'expert' at peeling-persimmons-without-tearing-the-skin; and the master chess-player, whose skill at the game was so nicely offset by his mediocrity in everything else. But not one of these could stand up to my uncle, whose boycott of Mother and me carried the near-absolute authority of his position as new head of the family.

There were some in the town, I dare say, outside the family, who pitied us in secret. But even they dared not risk offending Uncle, reputed as he was to be the wealthiest, the smartest and most hard-headed man in all the valley. The good in us is but a feeble growth. 'Give way to the strong, use the weak as you will'—that's how life goes; and Mother and I had to face the persecution of indifference as well as that of active hostility. I can't blame them, though. Human nature is like that. Only the foolish ancients 'helped the weak and crushed the strong' Nowadays it is the 'survival of the fittest' that people accept as the Law of Heaven. Reverence for cash is a quicker way to the top than reverence for the Emperor. Some time in the future things may be different, but that is a long way off, and in the meantime—get on the wrong side of a man with money, and it won't be long before you feel the pinch where it hurts. As Japan prospers, the rich grow richer, the poor poorer, for 'to them that have shall more be given, and from them that have not shall be taken away even that which they have.' The railways provide fat cushions and hot-water bottles for their first and second class passengers, smart young men who keep themselves delicately warm with seal-skin collars to their overcoats and plush rugs spread over their knees, while in the third class cars—haven't you seen them?—old peasants worn out with years and work sit snivelling on wooden boards.

But I have been wandering. The upshot was that Mother and I, though surrounded by any number of relatives and friends, were yet left friendless and alone.

1.4

As I said before, Mother was a woman of spirit. Financial ruin, and then her husband's death—with most women a double shock of this kind would be fatal, but Mother hit back at disaster: there was a brightness still in her eyes, the sign of a stubborn resolve to hold her own with the world. Though her life had never been extravagant or luxurious, she was the daughter of wealthy parents and had married into a wealthy family. Now our circumstances had changed, she cut off all her rich black hair without a murmur of regret, dressed in a cotton kimono with a crude camlet apron, and worked herself to the bone spinning, weaving and dress-making till late every night—she and the maid. I said before that we were completely ostracized, but this isn't quite fair: there were a few exceptions. This maid of ours, for instance—she deserved the Green Ribbon Medal, if ever anyone did. O-Ju, her name was. She must have been about five feet five inches tall, and as strong as two men, with pockmarks all over her face— a plebeian Amazon, if you like. It was twenty years since she had come to work for the family, long before my father's marriage, and never once, so I was told, had she been ill, or even irritable, or caused us trouble of any kind. When the crash came, O-Ju was the only one of our many servants who refused to leave. Father thanked her for her loyalty, but told her he simply could not afford to pay the wages she had been getting—whereupon for the first and only time in her life Mistress O-Ju flew into a temper. 'S-i-i-r!—What d'you take me for—one of your animals?' she demanded to know, all but coming to blows in the vehemence of her refusal to abandon us. Since then she had been one of the family in all but name. Father's death had only made her work the harder. Whether it was hoeing in the fields, hulling rice, chopping wood, mending the big stove, or needlework; in everything she was Mother's untiring helper. She had known me all my life, and still thought of me as a baby, though by now I was nearly eleven; she would fondle me like an old cow licking her calf. Everywhere she went, no matter who she was talking to, she would sing 'her boy's' praises. Absurd, really; but I loved her.

I loved her father, too. Old Katsusuke had been a village headman and tax-collector when my grandfather was superintendent of the district, so in all he served our family for three generations, a humble Sukune Takenouchi.[1] Not that he could boast of a snowy beard like Takenouchi's; but with the cheerful ruddy glow of his complexion, stretching from the crown of his bald head to the last wrinkle of his chin, his perpetual smile, and the delightful warmth in his eyes and the set of his lips, he could have passed for the god of happiness himself, humanized with a topknot. Coming into the room in his unhurried, ponderous way, he would sit himself down by the charcoal fire. 'We-e-ll, Master Shintaro, eh?' he would begin expansively. Then a slow feeling in the fold of his kimono for his old tobaccopouch; the tiny Japanese pipe lit, two or three very deliberate puffs, a knocking out of the ash on to the palm of his hand, another placid puff, followed by a slow tossing of the ash, still smouldering in his hand, into the fire (there must be some magic about that hand of his, I used to think—I scorched my own hand a choice black once, trying to imitate him); and then at last he would be free to talk. He was specially fond of *kabutsuke*,

---

1. A famous courtier, said to have served five successive emperors in the third and fourth centuries A.D. His bearded head appeared on some pre-war currency notes.

pickled turnips, which made an easy pun on his name. Hey, *Kabutsuke*, how about some *katsusuke*? I was never tired of calling out.

The world's a strange place, though. A man may bring you a splendid present, carefully tied with the proper red and white string, and hand it over to you politely with all the appropriate phrases, without your feeling the least bit grateful; yet if someone quietly deposits on your doorstep a bunch of radishes straight from the field, and comes in and sits down without mentioning anything about it, then you are really grateful, and so glad to be released from the tiresome formality of 'acknowledging his quite extraordinary kindness, etc. etc.' Truly, silence is golden, and eloquence is silver. In this gold Katsusuke was rich indeed, though of the kind the world values he had none. But even he could be eloquent on occasion. 'See how the blessed sun be shining, lady,' I remember him saying to Mother one day. 'When things go well with a man, 'e gets through life easy—like them snowballs of Master Shintaro's....' (Snow had fallen the day before, and O-Ju and I had been busy making big round boulders of snow) '... set 'em rolling, and they put on weight all right—fatten up all the way with bits o' mud and snow. But let there be a bit of sunshine, and they'll be melting pretty quick, and the mud and rubbish dropping off, till there's nought left of your fine big ball, so it might just as well never 'ave been. That's it, lady; it won't be long now, you'll see. The New House up there' (by which he meant Uncle Kengo and his family)'—'e'll be no better off than them snowballs, come the good sunshine, that 'e won't! Patience, lady, patience, that's what counts!' Exactly what he meant I was too small to understand, but the words stuck.

Then there was Shingo, a charcoal-burner of twenty-two or three who lived deep in the mountains, eight miles or thereabouts from our valley, and came down to Tsumagone three or four times a month, leading his horse with a load of charcoal. We were firm friends. Shingo fascinated me: he was a huge man, with a voice to match, but oddly narrow eyes, which looked the smaller for his gigantic nose, this latter so massive that at first sight you got the impression there was nothing to his face but one solid block of nose. He never gambled, and drank little. Any spare evenings he would spend practising calligraphy, with the help of a copy-book the priest had given him; and on his trips to Tsumagome he would always carry a copy of the Analects, repeating over and over 'the Master said, "Is it not a pleasure to acquire knowledge and constantly to exercise oneself therein?"' as he guided his horse along the mountain tracks. And always there would be a present for us tied on top of the bales of charcoal—a huge yam, maybe, nearly six feet long, or some mountain peaches, or a big bunch of fresh mushrooms he had dug out of the bamboo grass, or a bundle of bracken shoots. 'You make yourself famous one day, eh, boy?' he would boom at me whenever we met. 'Make a name for y'self, never mind other folk and what they say; you'll have 'em all bowing and scraping one day!'

There was somebody else I was fond of. Who do you think it was? My cousin—the daughter of that horrible Uncle Kengo. Not O-Fuji—she was as bad as her father—but her younger sister. O-Fuji was a year older than me, and quite pretty, but she had already started giving herself airs, smearing herself with makeup, staring endlessly in the mirror as if she were stuck to the floor in front of it, and for ever grumbling about her clothes. I had always hated her. Her sister Yoshi—she was two years younger—was an intelligent girl, dark, but with neat, clear-cut features. Before we had to move she had been in and out of our house every day to play. Afterwards, she did come once, without telling her parents; but it cost her a beating when Uncle Kengo found out where she had been, and that was the end of our playing together. When I met her sometimes on the way to school, as often as not she looked so unhappy, tearful almost, as if she were ashamed. Mother hated even to speak of 'the New House' (though Yoshi's mother, she admitted, was not really to blame). Yoshi was the only member of Uncle's family she had any use for. 'Poor child,' she would say sometimes, tears in her eyes, 'she'll have to suffer one day. It isn't only us.'

Every desert has its oases. Lonely as we were, living like unheeded strangers in our native place, these few friends remained for our comfort and support.

1.5

I went on attending primary school as before. The school was a small thatched building, standing among paddy-fields about half a mile from our cottage. It was not much different from the old temple-schools of feudal times, our valley being so out of the way; though we did have slates, along with old-fashioned fixed ink-slabs. In summer we went to school while it was still dark and practised writing by candle-light—Morning Penmanship, it was called—while in winter, as there was no heating in the school building, at the beginning of term each of us would carry his own tiny charcoal brazier with him to school, and keep it there till the holidays. That's how primitive things were then. Not only were we remote from the capital; the walls of our valley rose steeply on every side, as if we were living on the bottom of a giant stone bowl. If it was to reach us at all, modern civilization had to sweat its way over the mountain passes in straw sandals—so it was pretty slow in coming, like the doctor who doesn't hurry to a poor patient. As for the Tokyo newspapers, only one copy penetrated to our town, one single paper for the whole community. The thirty or forty citizens who formed the local 'intelligentsia' passed it round among themselves from house to house, with the result that this globe of ours had rolled round sixty times or more before it reached the last reader—long enough for quick-tempered Frenchmen to stage half-a-dozen revolutions, or throw out twice that number of cabinets. Consequently we were not very well up in the way things were going on in the country as a whole.

But such was the constant stream of reforms and changes of all kinds in those early years of the Emperor Meiji's reign that even with us there was always a feeling of instability in the air.

At school we were first divided into ten graded classes, then into six, then finally into three—upper, middle and lower. As a result we found ourselves taking the same examinations over and over again—even in some cases graduating several times over from the same school. We would start off with a Wordbook and a First Geography Reader, but the textbooks would change abruptly two or three times a year, and some of the poorer children had to give up school altogether because they couldn't afford so many books. I hated arithmetic and calligraphy, but got on splendidly with history, composition, geography, not to mention general mischief, managing to keep at the top of the class in spite of losing marks on my sums and copy-writing. Looking back from this distance, I can see the teacher must have let me off lightly now and then (he was a fine old fellow, short-sighted and devoted to his pipe; he could not have been kinder to me, though everything he taught was wrong. Lenience was his creed, and Masumi, I think, his name—Teacher Masumi, that's it). I can't have done too badly, though. An Inspector from Tokyo who was visiting schools all over the country praised me when he came to our school (you can't imagine what a heroic figure this visitor from the capital seemed in our eyes—and how Teacher Masumi must have trembled as he took him around!). I was clever, they said, as well as being a rich man's son; and at school I gave myself airs accordingly.

Then came our bankruptcy, and Father's death. Suddenly I was stripped of the status I had acquired at school. Hitherto even the humblest peasant's son had shown his respect: 'Master Shin' or 'young sir' they called me. Now I was 'Shin' or 'Kikuchi' to them all. The other well-to-do children looked down on me, as if they had grown taller all of a sudden, and kept me out of their games. It was hard enough to bear when the tiny boys asked in all innocence why I'd moved to 'such a small house', but the bigger ones were more cruel: they took every chance to sneer at my misfortune, imagining their own importance to increase with every word of insult or mockery they spoke. I couldn't stomach this, the more so as I was the sort of boy who always wanted to be on top, and had in fact been the acknowledged leader of my school group. So I announced I wasn't going to school any more. Mother wouldn't hear of it. Whatever else happened, she said, she would never let me give up studying. She must have guessed what I was going through, though. She had determined, I think, that however poor we might be I should never go short of anything I needed at school; that I need never feel ashamed of my family, or lose my self-respect. She saw to it, too, that I still wore good clothes, smart little cotton kimonos as good as, if not better than, anything I had had in the old days. Every morning she would tie my sash herself, help me shoulder my satchelful of books, and watch me from our door till I disappeared behind the school gate. So to school I still went, willy-nilly. I went—but no more to a place of joy: I was more like a convict being led to forced labour than a schoolboy on his way to school. Nothing to look forward to there, nothing to work for. So I grew lazy, and soon began to run wild. 'Prodigy' they had called me, but already the blight had caught my little bud of fame.

I was sore for a while, as I have said, at the way the children of the 'better' families in this little world of ours had decided to treat me as beneath them. But there is nothing so painful for a child as complete isolation, so it wasn't long before I began to make friends with poor boys I had been too proud to know till then. It wasn't pleasant at first. But gradually, without my noticing it, I changed. My language grew coarse, my pranks less innocent; I began to lie. Nothing is easier than to sink to the level of the company one keeps, and before long I was less interested in schoolwork than in playing the careless, slovenly idler. For all this I was punished—I, who had never once been punished since I started school. The only effect was to make me more unruly still, till finally the time came for the winter examination, and I disgraced myself for the first time in my life. The little prodigy's brilliant career seemed at an end already.

Not unnaturally, I was ashamed—and angry, miserable, and terrified, too. When I came home with the bad news, flushed with the humiliation of it, O-Ju could only think it was the teacher's fault—'Gone too far, 'e 'as!' she shouted when I told her. (Mr Masumi, I should say, had left. We had a younger man now, who parted his hair with great precision, and whose sole idea of education was that the Dignity of the Profession must be Maintained—a principle he lost no opportunity of impressing on us.) Mother said nothing, only looking at me steadily as I spoke. She had warned me now and then to work harder instead of wasting time with those vulgar low-born boys, and I had come home ready to face her anger. Yet nothing happened that day: she just seemed to be thinking, very quiet and still, though there was something ominous about her silence. Night fell; still no scolding.

Next morning it hurt me somehow to hear my friends shouting outside the cottage for me to come and play. Mother got O-Ju to tell them I was busy today—I had no idea what she meant—then changed into her best remaining kimono, dressed me in my special cotton *haori* coat, dyed with the family crest, and went out into the road, calling to me to follow.

1.6

The morning wore a wintry look, sullen to the edge of tears: nature withered everywhere, in a silence broken only by the dry *suzudama* stalks tapping against the stone blocks of the well in the wind, under a cold sky heavy with snow. We had hardly walked twenty or thirty paces when we met Yuji, a pale-complexioned boy from a family as well-to-do as we had been.

> The father failed
> Because he'd nothing left
> His debts to pay:
> The son he failed
> —the stupid!—
> On examination day!

he jeered as we passed. I wanted to knock him down, but Mother looked down at me so sharply, I could only follow quietly after her. A few moments later we ran into Kanjiro, one of my new friends, one side of his face dark and swollen from some fight or other. 'Hey, Shin-chan!' he called out, 'What yer all dressed up for? Off to Teacher to complain?' Cheeks burning, I walked on behind Mother as before.

Neither of us speaking a word, we made our way along a raised path between paddy-fields up towards an oak-covered ridge, enveloped in the desolate, eery silence that precedes a snowstorm. So we're going to Father's grave, I thought. All my ancestors lay in the same burial-place, the far side of the ridge. But if that was it, why had we brought no flowers, no incense? Still without speaking, Mother hurried on up the hillside, where the narrow track disappeared under a carpet of fallen leaves.

Behind the ridge, the ground rose further to a modest hill, thickly covered with oaks and cryptomerias. A clearing of about half-an-acre some way up its slopes was the hereditary burial-ground of the Kikuchis. A low stone wall enclosed the clearing, topped with long flat stones. Here and there stood small stone pagodas, overgrown with moss, and tombstones engraved with our family crest, the bellflower. A beautiful old pinetree on one side and a huge cherry on the other threw a canopy over part of the clearing, but now, late in December, the cherry was bare, and every niche among the stones lining the top of the wall stuffed with pine needles. When we brought my father's coffin here, in the autumn, a few reddish-brown cherry leaves had fluttered gently to the ground with every breath of wind. Now only the tree's harsh outline remained. Nor was there any sound to be heard but the faint rustling of bamboo grass; no birds came here now to sing, no human visitor to disturb this bleak solitude.

Slipping off her clogs at the entrance, Mother walked straight into the enclosure without looking round, and sat down on a rock in front of Father's grave—there was no tombstone yet, only a temporary wooden stake inscribed with his posthumous name. I kicked off my sandals and followed. For a while neither of us spoke.

'Shintaro.'

I looked up at her. In her left hand she was holding a tiny dagger in a black sheath.

'How old are you?'

I hung my head.

'You never listened all those times I told you at home, did you?

Mother is struggling like this all alone, in spite of everything being so difficult, for one thing and one thing only—to restore the name of Kikuchi to what it used to be . . . You are only a child still—but this one longing of Mother's all through our trouble, can't you understand that? With your father wasting away and dying like he did, and the house given away to strangers, we ought to have died with the shame of it . . . How do you think I could bear this kind of life, if it weren't for the hope of bringing you up to lift your family out of the mud—you're the only Kikuchi left now—so that one day we shall hear them say in the town "The Kikuchis are back where they belong"? What d'you mean by playing about like that with those snivelling peasant boys all these weeks? Maybe you want to be a peasant yourself, do you, and spend the rest of your life as a miserable shiftless good-for-nothing? It doesn't matter to you, I suppose, that you're dragging the family still lower, as if it hadn't fallen low enough already! Can't you feel the humiliation? Shintaro! What's come over you? Why don't you speak? I'm ashamed, I can tell you, today of all days—when I've been scraping and slaving in the hope of bringing you up to be somebody people could respect! But it's no use, I can see. I've given up that hope now, do you hear? I'll kill you, and then myself . . . or is there any shame left in you after all? There isn't? Then take your mother's dagger and kill yourself, boy! Oh, but you're a coward, are you—afraid to die?'

The dagger gleamed like ice as Mother unsheathed it from its black lacquered case and thrust it close to my chest. After more than twenty years I can still see her face, the light in her staring eyes. All through my journeyings those eyes have followed me, to flash a warning at the first sign of discouragement or temptation.

Big beads of sweat dripped from my forehead. My skin seemed wrapped in ice, yet inwardly I burned, as if I had swallowed red-hot iron; there was a buzzing in my ears, a giddiness knocking at my eyes, my heart hammered like an alarm-bell . . . No longer seeing or hearing Mother, I put out my hand as if in a dream, till it closed round the handle of the dagger—when she wrenched it out of my grasp and flung it away.

'Coward!'

Shivering, I clenched my fists. Suddenly a tear fell, and the next thing I knew, I was sobbing, whether out of shame or relief or sheer misery I could not tell. I cried and cried and cried, as if my very being would dissolve and merge with the dew upon the tombstones.

Twenty minutes later, after washing my face in the rainwater that had collected in the incense-burner, I knelt with Mother before Father's grave and the tombs of our ancestors. Still sobbing, though less violently, I murmured a prayer through my tears.

1.7

It began to snow. Sheathing the dagger and putting it back in her sash, Mother took my hand and led me out of the cemetery. Neither of us spoke.

A little way down the hill, nestling under a huge oak-tree, there was a tiny shrine of the Goddess Kishimo, where we sat down to rest for a while. It was just above the ridge we had crossed on the way up, and the view was magnificent. We could see two-thirds of the whole valley—our town, and the school, and the two streams, and the road running to the castle-town, the capital of the old feudal province, and the crows stalking in innumerable fields: all the scenes to which our family was heir, spread out before us in the desolate winter light. Soon the snow was falling less heavily, though now and then the bamboo clumps around us rustled in a sudden violent gust of wind.

Still with my hand in hers, Mother began to tell me stories of the Kikuchis: how Great-grandfather had planted that cluster of cryptomerias to prevent floods, how Grandfather had built up that river-bank at his own expense for the benefit of the village nearby; how all that hill—look! where the kites are flying—had belonged to us; how Father had given the land for the school; how the Kikuchis had once been the first family in all the valley, and how for generation after generation they had been upright men who had thought always of the good of their town or village, so that some had been rewarded by the Lord of the Province himself, while others had fought fearlessly for the just treatment of wrongdoers. Such was often my lot in those days, to hear from Mother of the past glories of our family, while I saw before my eyes its present ruin. And now, as I listened intently, and looked out over the Kikuchi houses, their fields and forests, that were now in other hands, the tears flooded to my eyes once more. Yet even then, young as I was, ambition had taken deep root within me.

There is a well-known passage in Macaulay's *Life of Warren Hastings*:

> 'On one bright summer day, the boy, then just seven years old, lay on the bank of the rivulet which flows through the old domain of his house to join the Isis. There, as three-score and ten years later he told the tale, rose in his mind a scheme which, through all the turns of his eventful career, was never abandoned. He would recover the estate which had belonged to his fathers. He would be Hastings of Daylesford. This purpose, formed in infancy and poverty, grew stronger as his intellect expanded and his fortune rose. He pursued his plan with that calm but indomitable force of will which was the most striking peculiarity of his character. When under a tropical sun, he ruled fifty millions of Asiatics, his hopes, amidst all the cares of war, finance and legislation, still pointed to Daylesford. And when his long public life, so singularly chequered with good and evil, with glory and obloquy, had at length closed for ever, it was to Daylesford that he retired to die.'

Do not misunderstand me—I am not trying to pose as a Japanese Hastings. I am not forty yet, for one thing. It's hardly likely that mine will be a soldier's grave, I suppose, but unlike most people I haven't any idea where I shall end my days. I love my native place, yes—but that doesn't mean it is unique, the only possible place for me. But when I read Macaulay's account of young Hastings and think back to my own state of mind at the time I am describing, I can't help being aware of a deep fellow-feeling for the Englishman. I still remember how moved I was when some teacher lent me the *Life* to read; all of a sudden I found myself crying, and when I hurriedly wiped the book dry, the printer's ink came off on my hands and there were black smears left all over the page.

About this time, then, the fierce determination began to burn within me not to waste my life for want of a purpose; and Mother's anger it was, of course, that had kindled the fire. But for her, what would have become of me? So I worship her still—and more: it is because of what she did for me that I have become such an ardent advocate of education for women.

1.8

It was the first lonely New Year I had ever known. A year earlier the decline of the Kikuchi had already started, no doubt, but then we could still find more than five bushels of rice for the servants to pound and make into New Year buns—the cakes we laid before the family shrine were as big as bathtub lids, and an endless succession of visitors from town and village came to pay their respects and grow merry on our special New Year saké. This year, by contrast, it was a melancholy festival indeed.

But even brambles don't lack flowers, and so it is with this world of ours. Even in our downfall we were not left altogether without delight. The cottage had three rooms, an eight-mat, a six-mat, and a two-mat, the six-mat room[2] with a sunken fireplace in the middle—a change from our former mansion. My grandfather (it was he who had built the cottage for himself when he retired, as I mentioned earlier) had chosen a site in the fields outside the town, away from the noise and distractions of the main house. I had visited him here sometimes—I was very small then, but I remember how he had a phobia of flies and mosquitoes, and in summer would spend all day lying in his bed under a green mosquito-net in the eight-mat room. Mother and my nurse would take me to the cottage. 'Grandpa!' I'd call out as we went in. 'It's you, is it, you little rascal?' would sound from somewhere inside the net, and presently we would see a white head moving, and the tiny red gleam of his pipe, like a firefly in a cage. In winter he loved to sit by the fire sipping his favourite dish of boiled rice steeped in citron and bean paste. A lively old fellow he could be, too. He kept his gun and spear hanging from a ceiling-beam, and even when past eighty would startle us on occasion by grabbing the spear and

2. The size of a Japanese room is always referred to in terms of the number of floor-mats it contains. These mats, which are made of compressed straw, measure about six feet long by three feet wide by two inches thick; they are laid from wall to wall, like a fitted carpet.

bawling out he'd 'take on any ten burglars single-handed, and flatten 'em all!' But now that too was but a dream of the past, Grandfather and Father too—only their memorial tablets remained, watching us from the family shrine. Only Mother and I and O-Ju lived on, alone, in Grandfather's cottage.

And yet, as I've said, there were flowers as well as thorns. For all our poverty and loneliness the life we lived was not to be pitied. Mother was so brave. She and I kept alive within ourselves a great hope for our future, shadowy and ungrounded though it was; and if you had taken pity on me then for the way I had to work, I'd have been angry, I daresay, rather than grateful. When I saw how chapped Mother's beautiful hands had become, or heard some village nobody jeering at her, I couldn't help feeling sad and angry, but for myself I was aware of no real hardship, not even in winter, when I had to break the ice in the early morning to draw myself water to wash, and hurry off to school in my cotton kimono after swallowing a breakfast of rice soaked in *miso* soup. At night the family, all three of us, would gather round the wood fire in the six-mat room, with a single paper-covered oil-lamp between us; Mother to weave cloth from bits and pieces of waste silk, O-Ju to prepare cotton yarn and slice white radishes for pickling, and myself to go over my history lessons. In stormy weather the wind would howl frighteningly and the snow beat against the windows, but inside the cottage our wood fire and oil-lamp gave us warmth and light enough. My murmuring as I learnt sentences by heart from *A Shorter History of Japan*, mingling with the crackling of faggots and the creaking of the old spinning-wheel, would continue far into the night. Mother had had as much education as women ever got in those days. Her calligraphy in particular was outstanding. She was highly intelligent, and would take great pains, by asking all sorts of questions, to ensure that I understood the passages I would memorize so mechanically. By the time I had got through my homework, the sweet potatoes that had been cooking in the ashes at the edge of the fire would be done; I would clear away the ashes, scorching my hands and cheeks more often than not—and how good they tasted then!

So the days and months slipped by, till the willow-tree behind our cottage put forth new shoots, and a white cloud of blossom descended upon the mountain cherries on the hill opposite. Lonely we might be, but spring did not desert our valley.

One day, when I came home from school, I found the priest of Ennenji Temple visiting Mother. The Reverend Saicho, we called him; he was about seventy by then, a priest of the Pure Land Sect. Our family had always been pillars of Ennenji, and Grandfather in particular had been a close friend of the Reverend Saicho, who would often come round for a chat or a game of checkers; so I knew him too. His health was none too good—he suffered so severely from piles, he had to keep his bedding always laid in his room, even receiving visitors in bed, and going straight from bed to preach—but his cheerful, lively manner made up for his physical weakness. 'Reverend Octopus' I called him whenever I spoke to him—boiled octopus being a great favourite of his—at which he would pat me on the head and tell me I was quite a little wit. Priest though he was, he loved to talk of the world and its doings; and knew more of what was going on than any of the teachers we had at school. He could explain exactly how it was that Saigo had come to start his rebellion, could tell us knowingly how timid Kido[3] was, how tough and stubborn 'that Okubo[3] fellow'—there's a character for you, he would explain triumphantly—not that any of us had much idea of what he was talking about. He was the only one in our valley who regularly took a Tokyo newspaper, and read it too.

The Reverend Saicho, a letter-scroll open on his lap, was urging something on Mother when I entered the room. What it was I couldn't make out very well; all I heard him say was, 'Better do it, ma'am, better do it! Better a beggar, even, in the big world, than rot your life away in these backwoods. And this lad of yours', patting my head, 'you can't be content, the way things are changing in Japan now, to have him brought up on those "Elementary Chinese Classics" which is all they can teach him here. Young trees don't grow in worn-out soil. Better make up your mind, ma'am, and do as she says! Better do as she says!' Still repeating 'Better do as she says!' the Reverend Saicho took his leave.

That evening Mother told me for the first time of her sister's letter—the letter I had seen unrolled on the priest's lap—with its proposal that we should leave the valley for good.

1.9

There's as much freedom in the country as in a prison, believe me. Drop a pebble in a bowl and you set up a tidal wave. Stretch your arms in the country, and you bump into old Tagobei's front door—your legs, and they get caught in Gonsuke's back gate. If your daughter so much as changes the neckband of her kimono, the whole village must be talking about it. A hermit can hide in the middle of any town, and in the capital nobody bothers about anything—but in the country you can't even sneeze without wondering what people will say. It wasn't so bad when we were the richest family in Tsumagome, but as soon as we came down in the world the strain of it became unbearable. I suppose Mother insisted so stubbornly on staying on in the valley after Father's death because she was incapable of running away from disaster. And then there were the Kikuchi graves—it would not have been easy for her, I'm sure, to leave them uncared-for. What is more, we had nowhere to go. 'If only I still had a family of my own worth the name, at least there'd have been people to talk things over with at a time like this,' she said sadly once—the only occasion I ever

3. Leading figures in the central government of the day. For Okubo, see also n. 2, p. 75.

heard her complain about anything before or since. She had come from a village forty miles or more away to marry Father. Her family, the Kawakamis, had been every bit as prominent as our own, but had died out some years before, the only surviving member apart from Mother being her one sister. This much, I remembered hazily, she had once told me. At any rate she seemed to have given up all hope of advice or assistance from that quarter.

But it happened that my aunt's husband had recently returned with his family from Tokyo to the castle-town not very far away from our valley—that much we had known already—and had been so shocked to learn of our misfortunes that he had told my aunt to write to us suggesting that we go to live with them. Aunt would have liked to visit us the very moment she heard the news, so she wrote, but had been unwell after coming home, and Uncle was so occupied with putting up new buildings on their property and all kinds of other business that he couldn't spare even a day. So we were to be sure and move as soon as we possibly could. Oh, and as luck would have it, she added in a postscript, there was a school nearby that would be just right for Shintaro...

After consulting the Reverend Saicho, Mother decided to accept. The preparations began at once. There wasn't a great deal to get ready; the few clothes we possessed were always kept clean and pressed. The cottage had to be cleaned and tidied up, that was all. The pots and pans, and what little furniture there was we gave to O-Ju, who had served us so loyally over the years. When all the packing was done our baggage only amounted to two leather cases, a wicker box, and a few bundles: all the wealth of the Kikuchis, reduced to barely two horse-loads. The Reverend Saicho, old Katsusuke, and Shingo the charcoal-burner all came to help. Only O-Ju kept grumbling. With us moving, she protested, there'd be nothing left for her but to 'go for a nun.' But Shingo was all encouragement: 'Off you go, Master Shintaro, and get you on in the world. 'Tain't right for a man to throw himself away down here, miles from nowhere. Shingo'll be following you soon, you'll see!' 'Get on in the world' was an exhortation Shingo never tired of, slipping it in as a refrain between whatever else he had to say.

We were soon ready. I had stopped school four or five days before, and to all the excited questions as to where we were going and why, had responded only with a superior smile. I didn't regret having to part from my schoolfellows, or even from the teacher: the respect I had once had for his authority had begun to fade. But my cousin Yoshi—what would she think about our going, I wondered. The direst threats would not have made me set foot inside that hateful Uncle Kengo's house, so I would not meet Yoshi again—I couldn't, I thought sadly. As the news of our leaving got about, old friends we had not seen for months began to drop in to say goodbye: the house-proud old man, the lady with the cats, the persimmon-peeling poet, the master chess-player—all of them apologizing awkwardly for not having called before. Ashamed of themselves for neglecting us, I daresay. Mother wasn't in the least put out, though, merely remarking with some sarcasm that at least they had saved us the trouble of making the customary round of formal farewell calls. From Uncle himself, not a word. We heard however that my aunt had meant to come with Yoshi, but Uncle had been furious when she told him, and forbidden the visit. Was there no limit to his subtle cruelty?

The day before our departure, Mother and I made our way once again over the ridge to the Kikuchi burial-ground, every step bringing back more vividly the memory of that last visit at the dying end of the year. We were nearly halfway through April now, and the ground was strewn with fallen cherry-blossom; but here and there small patches of snow still hid among the brownish leaves, some disintegrating with each puff of wind. Along the foot of the cliff that rose sheer behind the graves, the early irises had begun to flower, their pale white blossoms peeping out like quietly smiling faces from a mass of rich green. Oppressed by the thought that after we left next day there would be no one to care for the graves—even my inhuman uncle might visit the cemetery occasionally, since those who lay there were his ancestors as well as ours, and Katsusuke and O-Ju would no doubt come up now and then to pay their respects; but who would remember to bring the flowers or burn the incense that signify our loving regard for the dead?—Mother and I stood sadly for a while in the fading light, as if the very stones that marked the graves were friends we could not bear to leave.

Life never seems so serious as on the evening before one sets out on a long journey. Boxes packed and set out in order in the living-room, the small bundles stacked in a corner, even the clogs and sandals we were to wear lined up neatly in the porch—how to describe with my poor pen our feelings as we sat down at last around the oil-lamp, poised between past and future, and wondering, wondering . . . Our friends gathered with us in good number that night: old Katsusuké, O-Ju, and Shingo, to name no others, and the little room was busy with talk. But little by little as the night deepened the speeches grew shorter, less lively. At first I listened to everything, the voices mingling oddly with visions of Father and Grandfather, of my failure in the examination last year, Yoshi's face, cicadas singing in the lotus-tree overhanging the shed in the garden of the old house, till the whirl of sounds and images proved too much for my small tired head, and—protesting wakefulness to the last—I fell asleep with Mother's lap for a pillow.

I.10

Some hours later our great day dawned—April 10, 1879, for Mother and me the day of our 'passage into Egypt', or rather of our setting out from Abraham's tent, a latter-day Hagar and her Ishmael. We breakfasted by lamplight. To help us do what little justice we could to the occasion, O-Ju had boiled red beans with the rice, and cooked some sweetfish whole—a dish I loved, but found little appetite for this morning. O-Ju herself was weeping as she served us; even old Katsusuke had to sniffle as he scolded her, 'What's them tears for, girl, just when they're leavin'? Bring 'em bad luck, it will!' The spring night was already fading when we went outside. Here and there a cock crew. Shingo was waiting for us at the gate with three horses, newly-shod and with guide-bells tinkling at their necks. He insisted he would escort us to the castle-town. Two of the horses were loaded with our belongings, a blue striped quilt thrown over the third for Mother and me. Taking the reins in one hand, Shingo glanced up at the sky. 'Fine weather—that's a good sign!'

As we ambled out on to the road, I was more excited at the thought of this journey to a new world—and in Mother's company, too—than sad at leaving my native place. Shingo's words echoed this mood; following his glance, I looked east, to where broad banks of cloud were breaking up before the sun. So we set out, the two travellers and their escort in front, with O-Ju and old Katsusuké walking behind to see us on our way. But we had not gone many paces when we noticed a figure dashing after us from the village, waving furiously. 'Don't get down—don't trouble yourself!' panted the Reverend Saicho—it was he—as Mother hurriedly started to dismount, '—perfect day for journey—not to worry—shan't forget promise!' (Mother must have asked him to care for Father's grave, I suppose, and recite the sutras in his memory on the anniversaries of his death)—take care of yourselves—will come and see you—Shin, little gentleman, come back when you're famous—mustn't die till then, eh—ha, ha, ha!—off with you now, goodbye!' A comical priest, if ever there was one: having said his say, he ran off as abruptly as he had come, before we could reply.

Our horses moved off once more, to the tinkling of their bells. A cool morning breeze stroked our faces; all trace of night had vanished. A white mist hung about the village, now noisy with the clucking of hens, but above us larks were already singing. 'Goodbye, little Shintaro—goodbye!' a tiny stream seemed to murmur as it pushed its way through tangled vetch, between cornfields. Most of the farmers' cottages scattered about the valley had still not taken down their shutters, but here and there a woman washing her face at a well would look up suddenly and mutter in astonishment as we passed. Soon we had put behind us the last of the cottages, the road running now through broad fields. As we approached a teahouse a little farther on where they sold candy, sandals and the like, a girl hurried out to meet us, followed by a maid with a bundle. It was Yoshi, with one of the family servants. They must have come even earlier, to be sure of catching us.

What happened next I don't remember very clearly. Shingo hoisting Cousin Yoshi up on to our horse, Yoshi throwing her arms around Mother and bursting into tears; the maid offering Mother the bundle again and again;

Mother listening silently at first, then at last accepting; Mother taking the comb from her hair, wrapping it up and slipping it into Yoshi's pocket—'for when you're grown up'; her telling Yoshi to greet her mother from us all; weeping herself and stroking Yoshi's hair before helping to put her down. Nor can I recall what Yoshi said to me, or I to her. All that remains with me is that last sight of her standing by the hibiscus outside the teahouse in her gaily-striped kimono, staring after us through her tears. In spite of the joy and thrill of riding high on horseback like a victorious general, my eyes too grew misty.

Some way beyond the teahouse the road leaves the plain and begins to wind up the long spiral of Seven Bend Hill. Old Katsusuke and O-Ju showed no sign of leaving us, so Mother ordered them to turn back—at which there were more tears on both sides.

'Take care of yourself, ma'am! Goodbye, Master Shintaro.'

'We'll never forget your kindness.'

'You've been so good to us, ma'am.'

'Look after yourselves!'

'You too, ma'am!'

'Write to us now and then, won't you?'

'We will—and we'll hope to hear from you too, if we may!'

After several such farewells, mistress and servant, both victims of the same misfortune, had finally to part, and the horses started up the hill. '*Hai! Hai!*' Shingo urged them on, shortening the reins. Sad voices still called behind us, 'Goodbye, ma'am! Goodbye, Master Shintaro!' though O-Ju and her father had disappeared behind a bend in the road. Neighing in the crisp morning air, our horses pushed on briskly up the hill.

Three-quarters of the way up we came to Sugi-no-Taira, a stretch of level ground with a small roadside Jizo[4] shrine standing in the shade of a huge cedar tree. All travellers stop here, whether coming or going, for the view of the valley below; and Mother and I dismounted as Shingo adjusted the saddle-girths. Indifferent to our last farewells, our valley had taken on the unchanging beauty of a spring morning. Here and there smoke rose slowly as fires were lit to cook the morning rice. The town—*my* town, for ten years—the school I had grown so used to, and hill where Grandfather and Father lay, the gold squares of rape-blossom, the streams, the fields of vetch, the water-wheels, the shrines: a vast canvas of spring itself stretched before us. On the road we had come by, not far from where it began to climb, I could make out a little group of two or three travellers—no, they must be old Katsusuke and O-Ju on their way home. They were waving, they'd seen us—the small figure with them, surely that was Yoshi. A mist of tears blurred the valley.

'There's no telling how life will go,' Mother was murmuring. 'How could I ever have dreamt I would be standing here like this one day? Thirteen years ago I stopped here to rest, a bride on her way to her new

4. A Buddhist deity, protector of travellers.

home—in a chair, with servants, quite a procession we made that time . . .'
I couldn't bear her talking like this. Pressing my tear-wet face to her breast, I mumbled, in words I can't remember, pleading with her to forgive me, and promising I would study and study and study, till I could bring her home again in style, just as she had come that first time. Mother hugged me tightly.

'That's the way, young Master Shintaro!' Shingo boomed out suddenly. 'But what a day for you. Look at our mountain now!' I looked eastwards to where Mount Takakura rose triumphant into the morning sky, diminishing all other peaks of the range. Itself a richer blue than indigo, a white belt of cloud hanging lightly about its waist and the bright sunlight at its back, the mountain faced us, calmly smiling. Once again the horses' bells set up their tinkling. A bend in the road, and our valley vanished like a scene in a picture scroll. What etched itself most vividly on my youthful memory was not the town and the smoke from its morning fires, nor the small weeping figures on the road below; but the mountain, a massive, tranquil eminence in the bright sky.

Part II

After a night at a mountain post-station, on the afternoon of the next day we saw below us the provincial capital with its castle—my Promised Land. By early evening, after skirting halfway round the town, we had dismounted at the foot of a small hill on its western edge, the lowest of a chain of hills rising to the blue peaks behind. My uncle's property covered most of its southern slopes. At our first view of the town from horseback, before coming down from the mountains, Mother and I had been as scared as minnows tossed into the sea, wondering whatever would become of us in such a vast expanse of buildings. Now, as we stood before Uncle's gate, and Mother straightening my kimono, it was still more terrifying; I seemed to feel myself shrinking.

Once through the gate, we made our way up the hillside along a track littered with small stones, past a group of men busily engaged in digging up rocks and carrying earth—all wearing brown uniforms, and chained together in pairs; and all with grim, fierce faces. They were 'bad men', Mother told me in reply to my whispered question, working at something called 'penal servitude' as a punishment for their crimes. I was shocked. What a terrible fellow Uncle must be, to employ such wicked men! Higher up still we came across a lot more workmen, not in uniform this time, some planting trees, some erecting stone walls, while others, with much din of axe and hammer, were busy putting up a new outbuilding.

Suddenly a voice bawled a rebuke. Turning, I saw a huge man standing under a persimmon tree, scolding a workman in a cotton uniform coat with a carpenter's square in his hand. The scolder looked about fifty, balding a little above the forehead, the lower half of his swarthy face covered in a thick beard already showing streaks of white; both shoulders lifted in exasperation, he towered above us, a veritable giant. Kimono tucked up into his sash, feet in big Satsuma clogs, sweat-rag at his waist, he was leaning on a branch of mountain-cherry for a stick. Hearing our footsteps, he turned towards us, the anger still blazing—yet somehow not altogether disagreeably—in his eyes, and stared at us suspiciously for a while before ejaculating, 'Ha! So it's you.' He came down to the path where we were standing. 'Well! We weren't expecting you so soon,' Uncle continued—I guessed at once who it was. (I had seen him once or twice before, but not since I was about four, so I didn't remember his face.) Without waiting for

Mother to finish her bow, let alone greet him formally, 'This'll be young Shintaro—a lot bigger than he used to be!' he fired off again. 'Walked all the way, did you? Oh, horses—' he was going on, with much nodding and patting of my shoulder, when a fair-complexioned girl of about my age came running down the hill.

'Suzue!' Uncle called to her. 'Tell your mother your aunt's come.' The girl bowed, and ran back.

'Miss Suzue—how she's grown! And how pretty!' Mother exclaimed, looking after her.

'Ha, ha! More of a tomboy than a beauty, though. But you get up to the house now—I've a bit of a job to finish here, then I'll be along too.'

So we started off again up the path, leaving Uncle to bawl away as before at the workman with the square, who had been gaping all the while at his master's strange visitors.

The house stood on the hillside, on a specially levelled stretch of ground nearly a quarter of a mile from the gate. While we were still some way from the door a woman of about forty, very like Mother, hurried out into the porch, waving. 'We've been waiting—!' Just the one short phrase; but that must be Aunt, I thought. Thus far every detail stands out, but of what followed only hazy memories remain: of the three of us being bundled into the house and pushed along to the best room; of Aunt's tears when she saw Mother's hair, cut short since Father's death; of her praise for my good behaviour, and Mother's asking her not to be severe on an ignorant country boy; of Mother's admiring the way Cousin Suzue served the tea and cakes, and pointing her out to me as an example, while I told myself indignantly that Yoshi back home could do just as well . . . Soon it was dark. We bathed and sat down to supper, by the light of several of the new wick-lamps that in our valley were still the height of luxury, and not at the tiny individual tray-tables that were all we ever used in the country, but all of us, Uncle included, at one big table, like a huge desk. And then—there was the astonishing sight of Uncle eating, eating endlessly and snorting all the time like a boar; and the din from the kitchen when Shingo made too free with the saké—you could hear his booming all over the house, and Mother had to apologize: all kinds of unlikely things happened that evening, but more than that I can't remember, except that my first day in this new world ended in a jostle of strange and marvellous impressions.

II.2

Uncle Noda came of an old samurai family of the district. In his youth he had been one of the brightest pupils of the most distinguished teacher in the clan. After the Restoration he had held a number of official posts, some in Tokyo, some in the provinces. Everything about him was big, as his first name, Taisaku, suggested[1]: his body, his ideas, his courage, his talk, the meals he ate—all in the heroic mould. Yet heaven's attention must have wandered for a moment when this masterpiece was near completion, for it had some fatal flaws. A four-hundred gallon barrel is a useless piece of lumber if its hoops are loose; no matter how impressive its size, it won't hold bath-water, let alone saké. Yet one quality in Uncle redeemed even his weaknesses—a passionate love of Japan and his native province that gave his hopes a scope and a dignity beyond the reach of the bright young men of our day. The outbreak of the Saigo rebellion in 1877 (Uncle was then a prefectural official in Kyushu) filled him with patriotic anger. Condemning 'Ichi and Kichi'[2] for 'a pair of ignorant fools,' who thought of nothing but private feuds in the hour of their country's need, he announced his intention of 'giving them a talking to', and rode off alone into Higo Province to force 'Ichi and Kichi' to a reconciliation by castigating the one for his obstinacy and persuading the other to demobilize his army. Unfortunately he was captured by a party of Saigo's rebels on the way, and taken to their stronghold in the mountains. When they met on the road, the rebels had held him up at swordpoint while they debated among themselves whether they should take him prisoner or save themselves trouble by killing him on the spot—but turned instead to praising his bravery when they noticed how nonchalantly he was listening. Up in their camp that night, he kept them all awake with his snoring; and when morning came, calmly proffered a five-yen note and ordered boiled eels for breakfast. The rebels were so taken aback at Uncle's demeanour that after three days they gave him back his horse and let him go, though without having seen Saigo. So far, so good, one might say; but it seems he fell asleep in the saddle on the way home, and his horse carried him back again to the rebel camp. The rebel captain had a sense of humour, though. 'You be off home, Noda old fellow, and leave us in peace!' he said with a laugh, and dismissed Uncle again, this time providing him with an escort who rode with him for eight or nine miles. Incredible, perhaps, but true.

This being the kind of man he was, it wasn't to be expected that he would survive long in the bureaucracy, which is supposed to be a meeting-place for the country's sharpest intellects. In one prefecture Uncle flew into a rage with a departmental chief, swearing he had used his office for private gain—knocked him down with a sudden blow from one of those massive arms, and beat him up to his heart's content. He was sacked, of course—by telegram. It was after a quarrel with his superiors, too, that he had been dismissed—or resigned, for it was as much of one as of the other —from his latest post, in the central government. Now he had come home, his idea was to lead the local notables in a campaign for the development of

---

1. Taisaku = great achievement, monumental work.
2. Ichizo Okubo and Kichinosuke (or Takamori) Saigo. The former was Home Minister at the time of the latter's rebellion, and played a prominent part in its suppression.

agriculture in the district. With this in mind he bought the house on the hill from its owner, a man of taste and refinement, built cowsheds, hog-pens, and rooms for rearing silkworms, laid out poultry-runs, planted scores of fruit trees, mulberry trees and tea-bushes, and set up in general as a pioneer of modern civilization and enlightened enterprise.

Aunt's name was O-Jitsu. I mentioned earlier that she looked like Mother; but she was ten years older, bigger both in face and build, and of a calmer, more easy-going temperament. Though she could not have been much over forty, streaks of white in her hair were already noticeable, and wrinkles on her forehead, too; her husband being what he was, she no doubt suffered a good deal in secret. She had a curious habit of repeating, 'yes, that's right, that's right,' rather mournfully, as if she were going to cry any minute. At first sight her features seemed masculine—another look, and you thought only 'what a gentle, kindly soul she must be'—a third, and you sensed the dignity and strength behind the gentleness. If Mother was an unpolished crystal, a mass of jagged edges, Aunt was pure agate, filed to perfect symmetry. It was the day after our arrival, I remember, that I heard them talking softly in a small room as I passed along the corridor. I stopped to listen.

'You're young still,' Aunt was saying to Mother, 'and just as obstinate as that day you threw your copybook in the river to show how much you hated the writing lessons. But that sort of thing won't do in the wide world, you know: one has to cultivate a little more humility. It's the proud swimmer that drowns; too much confidence in yourself only leads to trouble.' The voice was caressing, protective. From that day my heart went out to Aunt Noda: there was a curiously intense delight in getting to know her, as if I had acquired a new granny.

Besides their daughter Suzue, Uncle and Aunt Noda had a son of fourteen, Daiichiro, who was at school in Tokyo, lodging with his aunt, Uncle's younger sister. Suzue was the same age as me. She had inherited her father's openhearted, generous nature. The day after we arrived, Aunt noticed me wandering about with nothing to do—Uncle had gone out, Mother was talking with Aunt—and told Suzue to show me over the house and land. Without the slightest shyness, Suzue took me round, explaining everything. The first place we visited, our feet shuffling through shavings and sawdust, was the silkworm room. It was nearly finished—which was just as well, for the first worms were just beginning to hatch. Other workmen were busy with the new stone wall or trimming the fruit trees—everything was going on at once: this was Uncle's way.

'I wonder why Uncle has bad men working for him?' I couldn't help saying when we passed the convicts digging and carrying loads of stones.

'Father tells us we're not to call them bad—they're just unfortunate, he says. That's why they get such good meals—fancy rice-balls and fish slices and dumplings; we give them all kinds of good things.'

I gaped. There were so many new sights and sounds: some exciting—

the turkeys and Canton ducks; some dirty—the pigsties; some charming—the calves; some terrifying—the mooing of a great cow (watching the milking was interesting enough, but that evening, for the first time in my life, I drank some of this milk they talked so much about—and instantly vomited all over the living-room); some exotic—the eucalyptus, acacia and catalpa trees, which Suzue explained were to be used for 'sleepers'. I hadn't the courage to admit I didn't know what a 'railway' was . . .

Miss Suzue still had more to show off to her young yokel of a cousin, to his continuous delight and astonishment. Finally she announced that we should climb to the highest point of the property, and we began to make our way up a narrow stony path the previous owner must have made. In the terraced fields on either side dense-packed ears of wheat shone in the sunlight, but here and there the ground had been mercilessly torn up and new trees planted—plum, peach, damson, apricot, almond, Japanese pear, persimmon and mandarin orange. Higher up, the fields gave way to uncultivated ground, enough to have made two or three more fields, where wild violets, dandelions and vetch peeped out above the bright green carpet of spring grass, with a few scattered clumps of bamboo and in the centre, a huge rock, as big as a small house. Up this rock my guide and I now scrambled, till we could sit down and look at the view. And what a view it was—dwarfing our valley at home! A hill to our left obscured the town and its castle; but the vast, calm beauty of the plain before us, bordered all round by misty peaks fifteen, twenty, twenty-five miles away, and patterned with yellow rape-blossom and already whitening corn, its villages half-hidden in the haze, its streams transmuted into threads of flashing silver! Looking southwards across the great expanse, listening now to the singing of larks, now to the clang and thud of hammer and axe below us, we boasted to each other, the raw boy straight from the mountains and the polished girl of the castle-town, where water ran in pipes . . . Mount Takakura, Big Stream, Ennenji Temple, the fun we had in the fields at the torchlight procession to drive away the pests—I brought out everything I knew: but it was useless. Suzue had seen—Tokyo . . . Tokyo! The Emperor, Mount Fuji, the Kannon Temple at Asakusa, the Ryogoku Fireworks, the Kanda Festival; a 'fire-wagon', or 'train', as she called it, a 'ship', a kind of boat that belched smoke and could cover twenty-five miles in an hour—stories of these and other marvels, decked in the clear, refined sounds of Tokyo speech, poured upon my country ears, and I was made to feel, as I had felt the day before when I had first set eyes upon the town, what an ignorant insignificant little boy I was. Suzue astounded me with her great learning; to me she was a figure of awe, even to the mole on her smiling upper lip.

I learnt more in that day than in all the eleven years of my life. It left me dizzy, as if I had been staring into a huge revolving stereoscope; so dizzy that I couldn't even say goodbye properly to Shingo when he left later on that day. What is more I forgot to send a message to Yoshi—Yoshi, who when she came to see us off had given me that charming little box, of the kind I had always longed to possess, its sides painted with vines in tiny panels, like the old picture scrolls, and inside, a beautiful brocade purse...

That evening Uncle and Aunt and Mother and I gathered to discuss my schooling. Mother seemed unhappy at the idea of packing me off to a *juku*[3] school; but I myself, out of a silly wish to impress Suzue, who was also there, announced immediately that a *juku* was the school for me—and so it was decided. The *juku* in question, a one-man school nothing like the modern primary school where Suzue went, was run by Seizan Nakanishi Sensei,[4] a friend of Uncle's.

II.3

Seizan Sensei's school was about two miles from Uncle's house, some way out of the town, and close to the mountains. On the way there with Uncle next morning, in a special kimono with the family crest on it, I was thinking: if the primary school back home was that big, how about this famous *juku*? What a great master Seizan Sensei must be! But one surprise followed another that day. Not only that day, either: for ten days or more after leaving home I was in a state of such continuous bewilderment and fright that I wonder now how I came through. The first thing that astounded me on this particular morning was the sight of two men, looking very much like *eta*[5], who hurried past us carrying a big basket slung from a pole. I managed to peep inside; it was full of bones, to which tiny lumps of raw meat still clung.

'What's that for, Uncle?' I asked in disgust.

Uncle laughed. 'Tomorrow's dinner—yours too.'

'Cows' bones, Uncle?'

'We boil 'em, of course, and drink the stock.'

I felt suddenly sick, and nearly cried. The cruelty of it! There didn't seem much point in study, if all it led to was sucking the juice out of cows' bones. How terrible! But I trudged on silently after Uncle, afraid to question him further.

A narrow valley came into view as we rounded the hill. A tiny village nestled in a corner of the valley, facing a network of paddy-fields and with the mountain at its back; and tucked away in a corner of the village two thatched roofs were to be seen, one large and one small, separated by plum trees and thickets of bamboo. Making our way along the footpaths between the paddy-fields, crossing a water-channel by a stone bridge, we climbed a stony track to the gate of the smaller of the two thatched buildings. A small man of about forty-five or so, lame and wearing straw

3. A boarding-school of the old Confucian type, where the students live in the house of the master or 'sage' and are taught by him alone as his disciples.
4. Sensei = Teacher, a title of respect.
5. The name given in feudal times to the 'outcast' class, principally those engaged in slaughtering animals, curing leather, etc. See also n. 1, p. 207.

sandals, was sawing withered branches off a plum tree. Surely *this* was not Seizan Sensei... We were shown to a six-mat room—the mats were of coarse Ryukyu fibre—and served tea by a thin, middle-aged lady, presumably the Sensei's wife. After some minutes Sensei himself came in from the garden, wiping his hands; and a long discussion followed between Sensei and Uncle on the care of plum trees. At last, Uncle introduced me.

'How old are you? Eleven? Small for your age, eh? Never mind; I'll train you up. You'll find it a bit hard at first, though.'

A moment later two boys wearing tight and unbelievably short kimonos came in from the verandah. 'Time, Sensei!' they announced with a bow. One picked up Sensei's tobacco-box, the other his book and portable desk; and we all marched off, Uncle and I trailing behind Sensei. So I came to my first sight of Seizan School.

Leaving Sensei's house, we stepped through a mass of rotting camellia leaves to the back gate. A hum of voices could be heard now, like bees buzzing round a hive; and soon the big thatched building appeared through the trees. Probably it had not been built as a school, but converted from a farmer's house. Passing a heap of swept-up plumstones, sardine heads, bits of bamboo and the like, a porch with lines of jostling clogs and straw sandals of every shape and size, and paper windows black with scribbles, through a hole in which I glimpsed a row of wooden name-tags, we entered by a separate door, to find ourselves at once in a twelve-mat room, the mats reddish-brown with age and split open in places, showing their insides—with the thirty or forty pupils of the school seated around the walls, and all staring at me, as if I were too small to be credible... I sat down, feeling smaller still. Sensei nodded; the pupils bowed. All the boys' faces were dirty, yet I admired the way every one of them, even the smallest, sat stiffly upright in the formal posture.

The lesson began—the text, if I remember rightly, was 'The Prose Writings of Han Yü.' The boy nearest Sensei bowed, and started to read in a loud voice, explaining the meaning as he went along. I hung my head, more and more aware of my insignificance; how many years, how many decades would it take me, I wondered miserably, before I could read difficult Chinese books like that—so easily, like running water... But by now Sensei had finished questioning the first reader. Calling the senior boy, he introduced me. I bowed. Uncle asked them all to look after me; I bowed again; they all bowed back; Ueda wrote 'Shintaro Kikuchi' on a blank wooden tag and hung it on a hook at the end of the row. No application form to fill in, no examination to pass—I was already a student of Seizan School.

Next morning, after much heartfelt advice from Mother about how to behave towards the other boys, Uncle and I left the house, followed by a servant carrying my bedding, a small desk and a wicker box. I felt miserable and desperately lonely—in all of my eleven years I had never spent a single day away from home. But I could not cry in front of Mother and Aunt, let alone Miss Suzue, who were all standing at the gate to see me off: so I squared my shoulders and walked away without so much as a look round—as bold as a lion for the first hundred yards, like a mincing girl for the second; all the rest of the way, like a lamb on its way to be butchered. . . .

A child quickly gets used to different ways. For all my comfortable upbringing, by the time we had changed our lined *awase* kimonos for the unlined *hitoe* of summer, and back again to *awase* when winter came again, I was clumping round happily in high student's clogs, wrapped in a short, tight-sleeved student's kimono. Outside the school, with a waxed umbrella at my waist and an enormous bag slung over my shoulders, I swaggered along in all the conscious pride of a student—a meat-eating student—of Seizan Sensei's Private School.

II.4

Count not the trials of those days so far from home;
What richer fount of friendship than the life we shared,
When from the brushwood gate we ran up frosted paths,
You to draw water from the stream, I for firewood—at dawn?

So Tanso Hirose describes what it felt like to be a student at a single-teacher private school of the old type. There are very few of these left now. The world has progressed: our teachers ride to brick-built schools in private rickshaws, students line up for military-style physical training, wear uniforms, caps—every activity is becoming splendidly organized, or regimented, to put it bluntly. Inevitably, therefore, the old-fashioned type of home school that depended entirely on the personality of one man is disappearing—and with it, unhappily, many of the qualities it fostered: the deep tie between teacher and student, the peculiar enthusiasm for moral and intellectual improvement, the sense of honour and integrity, the characteristic gaiety, that grew naturally out of the life of such a small community.

Our teacher, Seizan Sensei, was the second son of a samurai of low rank. As a boy he had studied at the same school as Uncle, but had taken no part in public life after the Restoration, preferring to start a school of his own. I have no detailed knowledge of his personal history, but he does seem to have been extremely poor from very early in life, and to have suffered accordingly. Looking back, for all his eccentricity one did sense in him a certain toughness, as of one who knew by experience the hard realities of life. He was lame—but in body only. At a time when even the strongest, in every sense of the word, found it hard to keep up with all the changes that were sweeping over Japan, and many samurai, on the other hand, were still strutting about with two swords in their sashes as if the Restoration had never happened, Seizan Sensei was often to be seen leading his horse into town with a load of firewood or sweet potatoes to sell. Of course he no longer did anything of that kind by the time I entered his school; but he still loved farming. We would often notice such books as *The Three Elements of Agriculture*, or the *New Agricultural Journal* on his desk along with the *Analects of Confucius* and the *T'ung Chien Annals*. Anyone who disliked the smell of dung, he was fond of saying, wasn't worth talking to. His own pet dislikes were laziness and priests. An original himself, who had cut off his samurai topknot while still a boy and sold his swords within three or four years of the Restoration, he would urinate defiantly in the precinct of a Shinto shrine, and fire angry abuse at any mendicant bonze he happened to see: to a countryman, an eccentric indeed. It was just these qualities that endeared him to Uncle. They would quarrel vigorously from time to time, Sensei castigating Uncle for his recklessness and Uncle jeering at Sensei for an obstinate old fool; but at least they understood each other, thanks to the very eccentricity—the touch of madness, if you prefer it—that they had in common.

Such being Sensei's character, his way of teaching was peculiar, to say the least. I don't know how to describe it, except to say it was something like the methods of Sparta, Pestalozzi, and the old-style Oriental 'master', all rolled into one. First of all he tried to develop in his students physical strength, and the capacity to endure hardship and poverty. Secondly, I think, he wanted to give each of us the habit of determining his life by his own efforts, which meant rooting out the old samurai attitudes we had inherited. Time after time, since the official abolition of the feudal 'clans' and their domains, formerly arrogant samurai had failed in enterprises they had started, and sunk very low in the world: you even heard of once-wealthy ones being reduced to knocking on strangers' doors and begging for help. Sensei only laughed at such dismal stories—according to him, a samurai who couldn't make a living just because he had given up his samurai swords was a nerveless good-for-nothing. Nine out of ten of his pupils were sons of samurai, some from noble families who had once had an income of I don't know how many *koku* of rice; but to Sensei wealth made not the slightest difference. He was quite happy for boys of fourteen or fifteen to go on wearing the same old kimono they had worn for years, though by then the skirt would have climbed half-way up their legs and the sleeves be barely covering their elbows. We were never allowed to wear socks, even in mid-winter. Even our 'rice' was a Spartan mixture of one part of rice and two parts of the cheaper millet—and we always had to cook it ourselves, three of us taking it in turns to prepare each meal.

I was the youngest boy in the school, but the rules were applied to me as strictly as to anyone else, and I don't like to think how many times they stared at me in disgust because I'd undercooked the rice ('comrades' rice', a student riddle calls it: comrades' hearts 'stand firm together', and so with the heart—the hard core!—of each grain of rice), or how often I cried on my knees in front of the range, when the kindling just would not burn, not for all my coaxing it with lighted spills. But it was not only the cooking we had to do. As in Tanso's poem, we collected firewood from the mountain slopes, drew water from the well for Sensei's bath, and were even made, most trying of all, to manure the plum-trees with our own night-soil. In short, there was no heavy work to be done that we did not do, so that we wondered sometimes whether we were students or coolies.

'When from the brushwood gate we ran down frosted paths, you to draw water from the stream, I for firewood—at dawn' . . . Fine lines to recite when you're sitting with your feet roasting over a charcoal footwarmer, but in the operation itself there's more pain than poetry. Our school was enclosed in front by paddy-fields and at the back by thickets of bamboo, with the mountain rising directly behind, which made it ideal for mortifying the flesh—mosquitoes in summer, in winter bitter winds unrelieved by sunshine. The winters were hard indeed. Our quilts were so light and thin, we often used to cover them with a layer of stones or firewood, just for the weight. Men may 'go through fire and water', as we say, to achieve their ambitions, but I wonder whether we were not the first to sleep with stones and firewood for bedclothes. And when at dawn one or two of us tossed aside our wafer-thin quilts after dreams of climbing mountains covered with ice, and ran outside, our breath hanging around us like smoke, to strip the ice from the well-rope before letting the bucket down—the frost as white and thick everywhere as if it had snowed all night, onions and tall radishes drooping in the vegetable patch, stalks of rice-straw lying locked in ice where they had fallen in the ditch beside the house, a bitter wind rasping our ears and noses like a razor—it wasn't easy, even for young would-be imitators of Old Woman Masaoka.[6]

On the rare occasions when I went home to Uncle's, Mother and Aunt and Suzue would glance anxiously at my chapped and frostbitten hands and feet. Occasionally boys from aristocratic families who had only joined the school in the autumn would leave as soon as winter began. I myself sometimes thought our life was made unbearably hard. But in retrospect I can see that while it may have seemed rather excessive at the time, it is thanks to the training in endurance we were given during those years at Seizan Sensei's that I find it easy now to wear the same kind of clothes almost all the year round, and can cross Siberia—as I have done—with only the thinnest lining to my kimono.

Why did we submit so readily, though, to the severity of the training Sensei inflicted upon us? Because he loved us: that was his secret. He led us himself in everything by example. At Seizan School there was no selfish puffing at a 40 or 50 sen cigar while the students were forbidden to smoke, no lining his own pockets with an easy income from hastily-written

---

6. Wet-nurse to the family of Date, Lord of Sendai, in the Kabuki play *Meiboku Sendai Hagi*, and apparently a historical figure. During family squabbles over the succession, Masaoka sacrificed her own child in order to protect her lord's son; and every morning at dawn would pour well-water over herself, as an act of purification before praying for the safety and future welfare of the boy she was trying to save.

textbooks while preaching frugality in the classroom; no expounding of ethics while a sick relative lay neglected at home. Seizan Sensei made bone-soup for us, caught roach and catfish in the ditches between paddy-fields as we did, sipped with us the stew we made with his catch and ours. When we had all been up the mountain to dig for yams, he would get us to steady the big stone bowl and mash and season the yams himself, till all was ready and we could sit down together, master and students, to a common meal of juicy *tororo*. Yes, there was hardship, but plenty of fun too. The only complaint I had was that from all the hundreds of plum-trees he had planted he would never let us have a single plum. Even to wander about—for too long—under his trees was to ask for trouble. But they were the only property he possessed: and besides, if once he had let us have the run of them, there wouldn't have been much fruit by the time it was ripe and ready to sell, so it was only reasonable for him to be strict. But the prohibition had one unexpected consequence.

Three-quarters of a mile to the north there was a small village set among a mass of almond-trees. The pale-pink mist of blossom that draped these trees in spring gave way in summer to a bountiful crop of downy purple stone-fruit that fell everywhere in heaps and was left to rot—you could tell when you were nearing the village because of the smell, which was just like saké. I'm sorry to say we slipped out in the middle of the night sometimes, to prowl about among this treasure. There were not a few restive spirits among us. But in general we obeyed Seizan Sensei, as I've said, because of the way he 'led' us; like the Russian general Sukovelev who always wore a white uniform without decorations and led every charge in person, shouting 'Follow me!' Sukovelev-style—that's the word for Seizan Sensei's plan of education.

II.5

I left my native valley at a time when that part of Japan was still in medieval darkness as far as learning was concerned. Till five or six years before there had been in the castle-town some sort of a 'school for western learning' where English was taught after a fashion, but then for some reason it had been closed down, and the students of English had moved to Tokyo or Osaka or Nagasaki; so that now there was literally no one who could read, let alone translate, the English-language letters the Prefectural office occasionally received. Unfortunately Seizan Sensei wouldn't have anything to do with western languages. Nine-tenths of our time we spent on old Chinese literary texts, the remaining tenth on Japanese translations of foreign books. I remember that once when we were reading together a recently translated *New World History* we came across the Japanese word *seiki*. Not one of us could make head or tail of this, from Sensei himself down to the lowest in the class. But then as we stared at each other, scratching our heads, a boy who had picked up a few fragments of foreign learning in Nagasaki explained that *seiki* meant 'a century' or 'a hundred years', a western expression used in counting long periods of time; and the clouds of our bewilderment were dispelled.

Besides Seizan Sensei, our master proper, we were taught sometimes by the correct and conscientious Matsushima Sensei, who invariably came to school in a formal, crested coat of greenish-blue, and by Ueda, head boy of the school, who used to take the smallest boys for rote-reading of Chinese texts and other such elementary work. I began with Ueda on Rai's *History of Japan*, but was soon promoted to Seizan Sensei's classes on the 'Tso Commentary on the Spring and Autumn Annals', the 'Nine Classics of Confucianism', and the 'Eight Poetical Sages of T'ang and Sung'. Sensei seemed to take a liking to me. He would often call on me in the class, and was fond of saying in front of everyone that Kikuchi was like a flea, small but quick—which made some of the bigger boys jealous. Not that I was specially intelligent. But my memory had always been good, for one thing; and I hated being outdone. And then, if ever I felt lazy, my mother's bright eyes would flash before me, driving me to greater efforts. But if the truth be told, it wasn't altogether unpleasant for a tiny fellow like me who till the year before had been squirming in a cramped little village school to find himself among these great hulking boys—who if it came to a bout of *sumo*[7] could throw him with their little fingers—and have them ask him shamefacedly, 'Tell me, Kikuchi, how *do* you read this character?'

The school building had originally been an ordinary farmer's house, as I have said, so there was no division into classrooms, dining-room, and dormitory, only one large all-purpose room. Our 'classroom' was simply the area where the floormats were a little cleaner than elsewhere, our 'dining-room' the noticeably dirtier part, while we slept anywhere out of the way of desks and tables. At the shout of 'Class-time!' we would jump up from wherever we had been relaxing, under the windows, or in the quiet light by the sliding half-transparent paper doors, or in one or other of the shadowy corners of the room, to sit in a big circle—and there was our 'classroom'. Outside lesson times you might find anything going on: one boy declaiming sonorously from the *T'ung Chien Annals*, another silently marking difficult passages in the *Intrigues of the Warring States*; the head boy helping a newcomer with his first texts; a group of intermediate students reading their *History of Japan* in turns, correcting one another's mistakes; a dayboy with a fan stuck in the sash of his hemp kimono (if it were summer), gingerly peeling the cloth wrapper off the rice-balls he had brought from home and grilling sardines over a tiny brazier. Next to some fastidious calligrapher working at his characters, with brushes neatly stacked on his desk and bookbox to his right, a latter-day Wang Mang[8]

7. Japanese wrestling.
8. A Chinese recluse of the 4th century A.D., remembered for the nonchalance and vigour with which he scratched himself for lice while discussing politics with a visiting warlord.

would be scratching himself with one hand, pinching in two any lice his grimy finger-nails collected on the way, as he pored over the poem set for homework. In winter we would sit reading, wrapped from head to foot in our bedclothes, only our eyes and noses showing. At night there might be a burst of angry abuse from someone who had woken up suddenly just after dropping off—to find a stick of twisted paper stuck in his nose; others would furtively munch jam buns they had kept hidden in a desk drawer, or make up for inattention in class by conning the popular version of the Chinese *History of the Three Kingdoms*. And the confusion at mealtimes—your imagination will picture it to you better than any description I could give.

This being the way our school was run, we didn't get much of an intellectual education, apart from the simple learning of characters. What we did get, and in good measure, was a training in sheer perseverance, the will to endure, along with a process of physical toughening. There was none of the organized 'physical education' or sport customary in modern schools, but plenty of other energetic activities—digging for yams, the drawing of water, fishing and exploring trips, swimming parties in summer. Most exciting of all were the rabbit-hunts, though we didn't use guns or dogs, only long nets, which we would draw round any spot up in the hills where it looked as though there might be a warren.

Harvest is over—the first frosts have arrived—the maple-trees on the hillside behind our school take on the red dye of autumn: all reminders that the rabbit-hunting season will soon be here. The nets we sent out for repair are delivered. And then one day, a big notice on the board— RABBIT-HUNT TOMORROW. Instantly there is a rush to get sandals and leggings ready. Everyone is too excited to settle to anything now. The duty-cooks get up in the middle of the night to make rice-balls. By the time we have turned out and assembled in the garden it must be half-past three; the moon is white and clear, awaiting dawn. Three mighty cheers, and we step off through the moonlight. Which way will the hunt take us, and how far—who knows? The senior boys march in front with the nets on their shoulders, singing a Chinese song for all they are worth; we smaller ones follow in silence, but with hearts leaping. We pass through a village as the cocks are starting fitfully to crow, still half-asleep; through another, where a dog barks noisily out of the dusk as we approach; out into the open country, stretching endlessly away under the pale light—and on and on, till gradually drowsiness returns, heads grow misty, we sway dizzily back and forth, some of us; only our legs walk on mechanically. Suddenly we hear a murmuring sound ... the wind in the pines? No, look! a shallow stream, whispering to the moon. We dash past the bridge-warden's hut, shouting, and over the bridge. Four miles we've come already! The moon is much lower now; the moors sink back into darkness to await the sunrise—I can hardly see the boys in front.

A huge black mass looms straight in front of us ... the mountain we have been heading for. Plenty of time still. We run in all directions, picking up armfuls of millet-husks, and light a fire to warm ourselves till dawn. Some who can't wait for breakfast are scratching at the ground like moles a little way off: next minute they are back with a load of sweet potatoes, bake them in the ashes, and are munching away, chattering merrily. 'Hey, Kikuchi, here's for you!' They offer me one, but I am too sleepy. I lie down on some straw—the fire roasts my face and stomach, though my back is still cold; the row of faces round the fire, flickering in the dancing light, grows gradually dim, and finally I doze off—but already a voice is shouting, 'Up you get, it's morning! They're off to set the nets!' I rub my eyes. It's true, the sky is white now in the east, my face is smarting in the dawn wind. Frost lies everywhere, except for a black circle where our fire has burnt itself out. We form up again, ready for the mountain, a senior shouts the order 'Advance!', a cheer from our little army—and we are off. By the time the hunt is over the first two ridges the sun is well up in the autumn sky.

Those joys live still in memory. The thrill of climbing up the mountainside, shouting as we push our way through the branches in their autumn splendour of yellow, gold, red, purple, brown; the moment of expectancy when we know we have driven the rabbit near the net—and the whoop of triumph, the frantic waving of your stick, at the cry 'Caught him!' from some beater hidden among the trees; the disappointment when your quarry vanishes utterly—then a sudden rustling in a thicket, the flash of a light-brown shadow under your very nose as you peer after the sound—and he's jumped—jumped straight into the net! You rush forward from the tree where you were hiding to grab him as he rolls over, tangling himself in the net... what exaltation in that moment! You come suddenly on a badger, only to let him slip through your clasped hands—to a mocking cry of 'Look! Kikuchi's praying... praying to Old Man Badger!'[9]

Can it be midday already? A hen is clucking from some tiny mountain farm. Pushing aside the floating leaves, we sip water from a valley stream; and thirst quenched, tuck into a dinner of rice-balls, legs outstretched among the undergrowth... how delightful to lie, all hunger satisfied, on a bed of flowers and gaze up at an azure sky, with the cool breeze to dry the sweat from your face! 'Up with you now!' comes the cry... Off once more, legs a shade heavier now; over two more hills, over three. A sudden glimpse, through a tangle of creepers, of purple damson flowers; the delectable but deceptive redness of wild persimmons—one bite, and the foolish faces we make! So many memories stand out, past counting.

The autumn day is short, though. We have caught only three or four rabbits when the crows begin to caw; and far below us a lake and its river gleam with gold in the evening sun. Tying the rabbits up by the feet with creepers, and slinging them over their shoulders with the nets, the older boys are the first to step out for home; we juniors saunter along behind, armed with branches of maple. By the time we reach the moor again, the sun has disappeared behind the zelkova forest to the west. The smoke of evening

9. The badger is credited in Japanese folklore with supernatural powers.

fires throws a mist over the scattered villages, and above the rim of the moor, tinged with purple in the twilight, a huge moon rises, slow and stately ... so perfect is the beauty of the scene, I long to make a poem—'The Huntsman's Life', shall I call it ... Little by little the moon mounts higher, shrinking as it climbs; our shadows contract—and already we are home. At last we can kick off our sandals; a quick wash, and all are sitting cross-legged on the schoolroom floor, from Seizan Sensei down to little Kikuchi, each one with a bowl of real rabbit-soup to go with his rice. Not that there is so very much rabbit about it, with so many of us to be served—it reminds you of the 'crane soup' old Hikozaemon Okubo[10] used to trick his friends with—better call it a concoction of radish, carrot, burdock, broiled beans and devil's tongues; but the taste—the taste of that soup! Or better still, the after-feeling, when we've emptied every bowl and lie on the floor in our clothes, soon to drift into sleep too deep for dreams; motionless as corpses till nine o'clock or more next morning ...

People still hunt nowadays—for comfortable jobs in the bureaucracy; such untroubled sleep as ours they will never know.

11.6

We had few rules in Seizan Sensei's school, most matters being left to the students themselves to decide. Some 'punishments' there were, from caning with a bamboo stick, or confinement to the school building, to the cleaning of the toilets; but their purpose was not so much to restrain the unruly as to discourage cowardice, meanness and impertinence. To preserve in us a sense of honour, while eradicating the arrogance that had become second nature to the samurai class after generations of living on the tribute of peasants; to retain all the traditional authority over his students, yet ensure that they would not grow into obsequious yes-men—these, I believe, were Sensei's aims.

One unusual feature of the school was 'Hearing', as we called it, a kind of Court of Complaints. One day each week after classes, when we had gathered in a big circle in the schoolroom, Seizan Sensei would make a solemn entry together with Matsushima Sensei, and take his seat at the head of the circle. 'Any charges to bring forward?' he would say, after a slow stare round the room. Whereupon anyone with a complaint would point to the boy he wished to accuse; the two of them would then come before Sensei, and the plaintiff prefer his charge, other boys being called out sometimes to give evidence. His questioning completed, Sensei would at once pronounce judgement. No counsel for the defence, no preliminary examination; and of course no appeal. The charges brought were of all kinds and degrees, from the childish 'Sensei! X hit me with a broom!' or

---

10. Tadataka or Hikozaemon Okubo (1560-1636), a retainer of the Shogun Ieyasu noted for his eccentricity.

'Y said my nose points upwards!' or 'Z stuck his tongue out at me!' to a variety of more serious complaints. Sensei's judgements ranged equally wide. 'Stuck your tongue out at him, did you? What d'you think he is—a doctor? Apologize!' 'So you said his nose sticks up? It does. Better keep that kind of knowledge to yourself, though—why make a noise about it? Apologize!' 'What—with a broom? Right! He can sweep round your desk every day for a month—with the same broom!' To be accused in public in this way was a serious humiliation, so that the words 'I'll tell at Hearing' were a dreaded threat.

But if men were content with no more than the regular courts of justice and the penalties they prescribe, America would have had no need of lynching. A greater terror than caning or being kept in, or even than the disgrace of being accused at Hearing, were our own unofficial punishments. First the whole school would stare at the victim; then he would be for it. 'Cheeky brat! We hate the sight of him! Hit him, everybody!' someone would shout, the injunction being instantly obeyed . . . 'Softy! Toss him, boys!' and the next thing the criminal knew, he had been thrown up to within an inch or two of the ceiling. Worst of all were 'ducking'—when we went swimming in summer—and 'stifling' in bed-quilts. A boy might find himself unpopular for some reason; 'Who's for stifling X, the poisonous blot!'—the words aren't spoken, but it is just as though they had been, and everybody has agreed what to do. You can imagine what happens. A boy goes up to where the victim is sitting reading. 'Hey, come over here a moment, will you?' he says. The poor fellow gets up—a quilt is flung over him from behind. Shouting angrily, he tries to wriggle out, but boys rush at him from all directions with more quilts, big boys, small boys, all shouting 'Stop your noise!'; they knock him over, smother him with quilts, pile on more, till he's buried under a mountain of bedding. As if that wasn't enough, the biggest boys of the school, still bawling abuse at the invisible criminal, clamber up the heaving pile, roll off it heavily, climb up again and caper round the summit in a crazy torturers' ballet. By the time the recipient of all this punishment, pummelled to jelly-fish flabbiness, has crawled gasping out into the air, the dancers of a moment ago are sitting primly at their desks, coughing oddly at intervals and looking maddeningly innocent: he can't know who started it. Nothing to do but smart in silence.

I myself was lucky enough never to have to undergo any of these horrors; and once I managed to help a friend to avoid a stifling he had been condemned to. Seima Matsumura was two years my senior, though he had entered the school six months or more after me. He came from a well-to-do family in a very remote country district, we gathered, which no doubt explained why on his first arrival at Seizan School he presented all of us, master and students alike, with the boxes of 'red rice' and bean-jam buns that new pupils were expected to bring with them in the days of the old temple-school. But he was unusually quiet and reserved—and it was this that the other boys objected to. All of them 'country' boys themselves, they sneered at him for a 'country boy who didn't know his place', a snob, a conceited upstart, till finally it was agreed that he should be 'dealt with' on such-and-such a night, the signal for the start of the treatment being the snuffing out of the oil-lamp in the schoolroom. On the afternoon of the day appointed, I was sharpening a knife on the stone edge of the well behind the school when Matsumura came by, silent as always, and smiled at me. That smile—I felt so sorry for him, I decided I would play the traitor, whatever the risk, and told him what they had planned for that night. Then I went to Mrs Nakanishi to ask her help. Seizan Sensei's wife had always been specially kind to me, I suppose because I was the youngest boy in the school, mending the tears in my kimono and slipping plums into my sleeve when Sensei wasn't looking. She hid Matsumura in Sensei's house that night—and that was how he escaped stifling. We became close friends as a result. Truly man is a shallow creature, so ready to judge his fellows by outward seeming. The 'snob' Matsumura turned out on acquaintance to be a shy, quiet boy with much to him that you would never have guessed from the silence with which he usually confronted the world. Our friendship grew with time. When in the spring of my second year (I think it was) the school had to close for a month on account of Sensei's illness, and Matsumura asked me if I would go and stay with him in his village, I lost no time in asking Uncle's permission, and coaxing Mother into parting with me for a while.

II.7

We were three for the journey—Matsumura, myself, and a servant of the Matsumuras who had been sent to fetch him. First we walked about twelve miles, then took a boat down the coast, a small Japanese-style junk with a single sail. This, I had to confess, was my first real sight of the sea. Born and bred in the mountains, till now I had seen it only in pictures, or as a distant horizon glimpsed occasionally on climbing expeditions. Once when somebody brought some live prawns to school I had made myself ridiculous by bursting out, 'But they're so white—they can't have grown properly yet!' Never having seen anything but the dried kind, I imagined all prawns must be red. But that wasn't my only gaffe where the sea was concerned. There wasn't a wave to be seen when our boat put out to sea, so at first I was happy enough, joking with Matsumura to pass the time. But before long she began to rock a bit—and then! instantly I was seasick, and raving at them to 'stop the boat' . . . Matsumura, the servant, and the boatman, the three of them couldn't calm me down. Eventually I collapsed into some sort of sleep. Which would have been fine, if I hadn't woken up in the middle of the night with a burning thirst. No tea left, it seemed. Wait a moment, though—wasn't that perfectly good water all round the boat—and there's a nice bowl, that's handy—down she goes; I dipped it over the side, and leant back to pour the nectar down—how I coughed and choked and spluttered! I can still taste that salty mouthful. Fortunately Matsumura was asleep, and the boatman was out of sight behind the sail; but even the memory of such stupidity makes me squirm.

I spoke of 'the sea', but 'inland sea' would be a better description, bordered as it was by a chain of islands on one side and on the other by mountains piled one behind the other in suspended waves. From a distance these mountains resembled a long screen like those we divide our rooms with, rising so sheer, by the look of it, from the water's edge that you found it hard to believe a boat could put in anywhere along such a coast; but there was more to be seen as we drew in closer: tiny scattered islands, here and there an inlet, half-hidden between steep mountain walls, with a village perched along its narrow beach. Going overland to the same destination involves crossing a whole series of notoriously difficult passes; taking the sea route, you can sit back and enjoy the same mountains without effort, putting in at any little harbour you please. Halfway through the afternoon of the second day, we tied up at a village in one of the larger inlets, and stepped out over the pebbles and oyster-shells, a little dazed and unsteady, for Matsumura's home.

Facing the sea and walled on three sides by mountains, Matsumura's 'village' covered a much smaller area than Tsumagome, though it numbered three or four times as many households. A river divided it into two. Fishermen's cottages predominated along the right bank, but behind them, at the foot of the mountain, I caught a glimpse of ornamental tiles, white walls, and the curved roof of a big temple. More cottages lined the left bank, interspersed with some ricefields and salt ponds. Matsumura took me first to a big house surrounded by a white mud wall on a stone base, not far from the beach and near the centre of the village.

The Matsumuras were tobacco merchants, to judge by the bales stacked in the courtyard, and the long mats in the garden strewn with newcut leaf drying in the sun. A man in this thirties, evidently the master of the house, but not resembling Matsumura very closely, smiled as he saw us coming. He's got a young father, I was thinking—but learnt a moment later that it was his brother, not his father. His parents had retired already, and handed over the family property to the eldest son, who thus became the present head of the family. So having paid our respects at the 'main house', we walked another hundred yards or so down the road, crossed a small bridge over a creek running into the estuary, reaching at last the little house overlooking the sea where the parents now lived in retirement. A duck quacked noisily outside the gate. Inside, a path led between a mass of aronia trees in full flower and a two-storied house, from which we could hear the sound of a loom, to a smaller house of one storey, with a luxuriant zamboa tree overshadowing the porch—and shading a crowd of sleepy white hens from the hot sun. The servant must have brought the news of our arrival already—a lady of almost forty, with strikingly beautiful eyes, was standing in the doorway; she smiled at Matsumura and then at me, greeting me politely as her son's guest.

'Where's Father?' At Matsumura's question, a pleasant-looking man of fifty or so came round from the back garden, a pair of scissors in one hand and some chrysanthemum seedlings in in the other. Tea was served. The taciturn Matsumura chattered unceasingly. For some reason the cheerful bustle all around me made me sad; I could not talk, and was almost in tears. Matsumura's mother noticed. 'Not feeling well, Shintaro?' she asked.

'I'm all right.'

'He was sick on the boat, Mother.'

'So that's it! You'd better lie down for a while then.'

'That's the boy—bit of rest 'll put you right,' chimed in Matsumura's father.

Soon I was fast asleep on some quilts Matsumura's mother laid specially for me, and saw no more of the family reunion. When they called me, it was evening; my sea-sickness had worn off. They had put a long bench outside on the white sand (it is so warm down there in the south, especially along the coast); and here we sat down to a special supper of sea-bream—Matsumura, his father and mother, myself, and a pretty little girl of about eight I hadn't seen before who I guessed must be Matsumura's sister, for she too had those beautiful eyes I had noticed in his mother—watching the craggy islands in the bay darkening from purple to indigo.

II.8

This house to which Mr Matsumura senior had moved on his retirement occupied a superb position on a spit of land jutting out into the estuary, so that it was surrounded by water on three sides, with a clump of wax-trees and a wheatfield adjoining the garden at the back. At high tide the whole house seemed to be afloat on the river. You could fish from the walls, and watch the white sails of passing fishing-boats without leaving the living-room.

The goodwill and affection of the villagers surrounded the Matsumuras as the river did their house. The family resembled a fine old tree, loved equally for its strength and beauty: the house of Matsumura was prosperous, its members upright. Yahyoe, the old gentleman was called. Past fifty now, he had given up all authority to his eldest son, to settle down the more completely to his retirement. He neither drank nor smoked, nor played checkers with his friends, even; growing chrysanthemums was his pastime and joy. Chrysanthemums and fir-trees—the taller the tree, and the straighter the branches, the better—these were his loves. 'Shodo', he liked to call himself: The Pine-Tree Man. So there were plenty of trees in his garden, as you'd expect; and not one of them but was perfectly straight.

Nor was his passion for straightness confined to trees. Anything twisted he hated as unnatural, and as there is nothing so natural as nature herself, men being mostly twisted in some way or other, old Mr Matsumura, like Byron, really loved nature more than his fellow human-beings. Once he had travelled by sea up to Tokyo. A violent storm blew up while they were off the coast of Shizuoka, it seems, and kept all the passengers in their cabins, alternately retching and praying to Lord Buddha for mercy—all except for old Yahyoe, who stayed on deck, clinging to the rail and calmly watching the mountainous waves, till finally the captain had to order him below. When he returned from this trip and everyone asked him what he thought of the capital, all he would say was 'Tokyo? People—people, everywhere, swarms of 'em. Three fires every night. Plaguey place!'

Another story concerned his visit to a relative whose daughter, it had been arranged, was to marry his son. Yahyoe found the girl's parents had had three or four enormous chests of drawers made, all of the finest pawlonia wood, and had even sent for a sempstress from the town to prepare a huge trousseau of expensive brocade kimonos. Nothing could have angered the old man more. 'Such extravagance—can't have anything to do with that sort of foolishness! The marriage is off!' he told them sternly, and that was the end of his son's engagement. Not that he said or did anything much out of the ordinary while I was staying with them, though. Matsumura did complain to his father once about how all the boys at school would boast about their fathers having such-and-such an income or such-and-such a position in the government, or whatever. 'All right,' smiled the old man, 'suppose you tell them your father's a tobacco-man. How'll that do?'

On another occasion, a disagreeable old man who lived in the neighbourhood, wealthy but looking exactly the vulgar boor he was, called for a talk one evening and overstayed his welcome. Calling his wife from the next room, and asking her pointedly what the time was, Mr Matsumura ordered her to put up the shutters and get to bed, with the rest of the family. So much for the 'entertainment' the caller was no doubt expecting. And such being the old man's ways, it is no wonder he was nicknamed Mr Peculiar by the humbler villagers, who looked upon him with a mixture of amusement and awe.

If Mr Matsumura had been on his own, the strictness of the standards he set himself might have prevented close and easy relationships within the rest of his family, and with their relatives and friends; but Matsumura's mother (I found out, by the way, why Matsumura and his elder brother were so unlike—the brother was the son of a former wife) was always there to smooth things over. Her name suited her perfectly—Mutsu, the Friendly One. She could make herself agreeable to anybody, whoever he or she might be. Or rather, it would be truer to say, others invariably found themselves behaving with particular courtesy to her simply because she herself was so pleasant with everybody. She was fond of doing things for other people, helping them out in little ways, though I don't believe these good works of hers were necessarily a deliberate attempt to win friends: people naturally grew attached to her.

Somehow she had learnt how to write traditional Japanese poetry—self-taught, no doubt, for there can hardly have been anybody to teach her in a fishing village so far off the beaten track—was a skilled calligrapher, and a painter too, not to mention all kinds of other interests. You couldn't be in the house long without noticing the black lustre to which the long fire-box in the living-room was polished, or the gleaming copper of the kettle sitting on the ashes. Waxed paper umbrellas shut away in cases, daggers in their ornamental sheaths, paper pipe-cleaners arranged in little bundles in the desk-drawer—wherever you looked, no speck of dust from one end of the room to the other: such order, such invigorating tidiness, as if the lady of the house were a beloved general, and every object in it her loyal soldier, to be called out for a brief spell of duty and then return of itself to its position in the line. But among her qualities there was a grace of feeling, a sensitivity to beauty, as well as mere tidiness. A tear in the panel of a sliding partition would be covered over with paper cut to a pattern of maple or cherry leaves, a slit in a cupboard door hidden with a painting of a morning-glory or a Chinese bellflower. Once I happened to see Matsumura's mother cleaning a huge pile of old clogs by the well. What a ridiculous waste of time, I thought. For all Seizan Sensei's training in austerity, evidently I was still the young Master Kikuchi, used to servants and the best of everything. Matsumura told me afterwards, to my shame, that his mother always washed their discarded clogs, sewed in new thongs herself and gave them to poor families or beggars in the village.

Apart from the old couple themselves, the household consisted of Matsumura's young sister, O-Toshi; Mankichi, the servant who had come to fetch him from school, and his wife; one dog, fifteen or so ducks, a similar number of hens, and (I nearly forgot to mention it) one sweet-voiced nightingale. It wasn't surprising that at school Matsumura was always homesick: his home was such a refreshing place. As for O-Toshi, his sister, she was a simple open-hearted little girl, without a trace of affectation—a single glance at her smiling, flower-like face was enough to tell you that. Families differ so much. In some the atmosphere is close, stifling; others freeze you to the marrow; others burn aloes in the living-room to hide the smell from the kitchen. It is grown-ups who are deceived. A child's sense of smell is more acute: one sniff, and he can classify the air each family breathes. From the start I fell in love with the Matsumura family.

Maybe it was just that I was their son's friend, or maybe they might have heard of my family's misfortunes, I don't know; but whatever the reason, the old man and his wife treated me very kindly. ' "Adversity is youth's opportunity" ' Matsumura's father was fond of quoting. 'A man who's not trained to endure when he's a boy will never be any good for anything when he's a man. That goes for you too, Seima. Study for all you're worth

—never spare yourself!' Matsumura's mother asked me all kinds of questions about my mother and the difficulties we had been through. She did not say much, besides asking the questions; but often there were tears in her eyes.

With the change from school, and so many excitings things to do and see, the time passed without our noticing it. Some days we would go shell-gathering at low-tide. I learnt how to squash gobies underfoot, and catch prawns; my hands would get caught in crabs' claws, and my face turn red and sore when I rubbed a cheek with one hand after picking up a jellyfish—in short, it wasn't long before I became quite an expert on the sea and its creatures. On rainy days we took down a great heap of books from the bookcases upstairs in the main house, and skimmed through them, munching crackers and exchanging our lordly, childish comments on what we read; or we might wander down to see how the fishermen and their families in the village were doing, to be met with friendly astonishment—'How big Master Matsumura had grow'd now, ain't he?'—and welcoming smiles that left a faint sad shadow in the mind of the said young master's friend. Another day we painted grotesque pictures, breaking every rule of drawing, and solemnly presented them to O-Toshi, till we tired of art and terrified O-Toshi by turning ourselves into ghosts; or walked arm-in-arm past the primary school with our noses in the air, as if to say to these ignorant country folk, 'Have the goodness to note, if you please, that you are in the presence of students of the Master of Chinese Studies, Seizan Sensei . . .' But when a neighbour brought some western letters that he had somehow got hold of (word having got about that two young scholars were home on holiday from the town) and asked us to read and translate them, we could only blush and scratch our heads. That night we made a solemn vow that we would start learning English as soon as school began again.

II.9

A highlight of my stay was the trip Matsumura's father sent us on (Matsumura, Mankichi, myself, and their dog Kuma) to inspect the pine-woods he owned up in the mountains. Mankichi and I were great friends. He was a male version of our former maid, O-Ju, slow of speech but quick-moving: he could walk the thirty-five or more miles, half of them up a steep mountain-track, from Matsumura's village to the nearest town in one day with ease. He had been in the Matsumuras' service since boyhood, and kept every detail of the woods in his head: the number of trees of each size, their location and trunk measurements, how many had been felled and when, how many planted to replace them. A few preparations and we were off, Matsumura and I in trousers and straw shoes, Mankichi in flat sandals with a hatchet stuck in his sash, a bagful of rice-balls over his shoulder and a measuring-rope in his kimono-sleeve; Kuma in the good suit he was born with, his tail wagging furiously as he led the way.

The Matsumura woods consisted of several small plots, some by the sea, some up in the mountains, the furthest being some seven or eight miles up the coast to the north. To wander through those mountain forests in spring was sheer joy. It was warm already, but there was little undergrowth to get in our way, and no snakes to worry about—nor, in those days, that just as deadly species, the amateur hunter. The thrill of entering the shadowy solemnity of a grove of cryptomerias, treading under strawshod feet the tufts of new grass and spring plants peeping out from among last year's leaves; of wandering deep in a pine-forest heavy with the scent of resin, kicking aside the fallen cones; of pushing a way through a tangle of lesser trees and bushes, alive with leaf-buds as pretty as flowers! We shout for Mankichi to cut us lengths of camellia or oak for sticks; collect bracken, suddenly eager to take home specimens; toss it aside, as suddenly forgotten; break off camellias, to wonder at their beauty . . . The wild mountain-cherries have lost almost all their flowers, but here and there, half-hidden among the leaves, a gleam of white still lingers, like the last streak of snow in May. A growl from Kuma—a pheasant starts up from our feet, blossoms tumble in a whirring of wings. Kuma stares disconsolately after his lost prey, nostrils twitching—we stop, too, listen—to silence; no sound now, the bird vanished, but the faint thud of a woodman's axe. Abruptly a shadow strikes down among the trees. We stare up at the white flossy cloud sailing among the treetops. It is gone, the azure returns; light enfolds us once more. We wipe off the sweat, start to climb. In seconds, the ridge-top—and the sea, a vast and placid mirror, edged with jagged, misty islands. We sit on old tree-stumps, and gaze down, yawning, eyes contracting at first in the glare; limbs and spirit fuse slowly in a muted, drowsy harmony . . .

Refreshed with tea at a ranger's hut, we wandered on over two more hills, till at last, weariness beginning to make itself felt, we broke out of the forest above a tiny bay and harbour. A harbour, here of all places, tucked away amongst such steep green walls—who could have imagined it? Twenty or thirty thatched cottages lined the further shore; smoke rose from some, and we could catch the faint clucking of hens. At one of the cottages, which Mankichi pointed out to us, we were to have dinner. Half-sliding down the steep slope, we were soon at the water's edge. Small though the bay had looked from the top of the hill, it must have been about three quarters of a mile across, and a good two miles round by the shore. But who could call that stretch of sea a 'bay' merely; that smooth, still, gemlike surface, picturing at its edge the young foliage of the mountain, the blue sky sparkling at its heart; that flawless, jewel-bright mirror rimmed with green?

In a small boat that lay at rest a little way out from where we stood, a fisherman sat mending his nets, legs stretched lazily across the transom. Could he ferry us across, we called. Very deliberately he brought his boat in. Kuma, his eyes flashing understanding, jumped in at once, followed by the three of us. Below the gunwale the water was crystal, barely tinged with blue; through it rays of sunlight darted down, to wave like gold threads over the shallow pebbled floor. 'Sea-slugs! Mr Boatman, Sea-slugs!' The fisherman speared us several; Mankichi washed and ate them there and then. To the creaking of its scull the boat moved across the broad smooth water of the bay, trailing a white ribbon at its stern, till too soon we were standing on the opposite shore, looking back to the beach we had left. The reflected hills, unsettled by our passage, still swayed gently.

Thanking the boatman, we threaded our way through fishermen's cottages to where the big thatched house we had seen from the hilltop stood in a long garden aflame with azaleas. From a bamboo thicket behind the house a nightingale sang incessantly. 'It's Master Seima!' a homely country-woman who came out to greet us exclaimed in astonishment. She wouldn't hear of our eating the cold rice-balls we had brought—we were famished by now—and cooked us a hot meal of boiled rice and beanshoots.

Three days we spent tramping over the hills, sleeping at the thatched house and setting off again at dawn, so that we covered practically all the land the Matsumuras owned. Our clothes absorbed the scents of spring, our hearts the freedom and peace of the hills. Once, though, we did have something like a quarrel. I was to blame, really. Ever since I had come to stay with Matsumura, every fresh excitement and delight had brought back vividly the misfortunes of my own family, which I had practically forgotten while I was living with the others at school. Once my home had been like this; and now. . . . Discontent stirred vaguely within me—you couldn't call it jealousy—and this it was that erupted suddenly between us.

The cause of the quarrel was nothing more than the simple question whether we should go home by boat or overland. Matsumura chose the boat: he had blisters on his feet: I was for the walk, for the boat would make my sick. Neither of us would give way. I was the guest, I insisted—oh yes, I was a wilful little piece of goods, I can tell you—so I had a perfect right to choose.

This was more than even the gentle Matsumura could take. 'I invited you,' he said. 'You're my guest, and a guest obeys his host!'

Finally we lost our tempers.

'Think you can sit on me just because we're poor and my father's dead, do you?' I burst out. 'All right—I'm going to walk back now—and I'll go back to school—alone!' Even as I said it, I knew it wasn't true; but I wouldn't give way, not an inch.

Disaster was averted, however, when Mankichi, the Prince Bismarck to our tottering alliance,[11] suggested we should go half-way on foot and half-way by boat. Prince Gorchakov-Matsumura was a mild, gentle fellow. His 'Sorry!' was not long in coming, and was echoed instantly by a Beaconsfield no longer stubborn . . . Five minutes later, the two small statesmen were laughing together as before.

11. The reference is to the Congress of Berlin in 1878, at which Russia was forced to modify the terms of the Treaty of San Stefano.

In short, the four weeks I spent with Matsumura made us much closer friends than before; and to crown it all, when I left, Matsumura's mother gave me a parcel of salted bream to take home as a special present from her to my mother.

So we returned to Seizan School. But not for long, as it turned out. Seizan Sensei must have done a good deal of thinking during his illness. One day—the first of July, 1881, I remember the date very clearly—Sensei gathered us all together and made a speech. Things were changing so rapidly in Japan, he told us, that for an old-style teacher like himself to have charge of our education might prejudice our future. So he had decided to turn farmer again in his old age. As for us, we must find ourselves proper teachers, study foreign languages, and make ourselves useful in the world.

We were dumbfounded by the suddenness of Sensei's announcement. Some boys wept—I among them. That evening Sensei invited us all to a farewell supper of rice and fish and vegetables; next morning, after a commemorative photograph had been taken, the Seizan School of Chinese Studies ceased to exist.

II.10

The other day when I was tidying my study I came across that photograph. It is old and faded now; the faces look like ghosts, for it is nearly twenty years since it was taken, and photography was not up to much in those days. Between forty and fifty of us posed in every sort of attitude: some standing, some squatting, some with their shoulders squared and folded arms, some wearing a faint sardonic smile of superiority. Nostalgia swept over me. And that tiny fellow peeping out from between those giants on the right (you can almost hear him pleading, 'Squeeze me in too, if you please!')—yes, that's me: mouth tightly shut, just a trace of a smile on those small cheeks. So that was how you looked twenty years back. Even you have aged a bit since then, Kikuchi! The baby of the school, you were called, the inevitable simile for anything small, a diminutive figure in your absurdly short kimono (your mother used to make two from a single length, remember?), yet never without your pride . . . Can twenty years have passed since you flaunted your little dignity as a student of Seizan School, though it seems but yesterday?

Water flows; days and months pass by and are gone. I was gazing wistfully at the boy in the photograph, as if he were my own son, when my real son (who will be nine this year) came into the study and asked me what I was staring at.

'An old photograph of Father and his classmates.'

'Which one's you?'

'This one, here at the end.'

'This one you? Were you as small as that?' Laughing, he snatched the photograph and ran off to show it to his sister, aged four. 'Look how tiny Daddy was!'

I haven't the photograph before me now, but if I shut my eyes I can see every one of those faces still, across the gap of twenty years. That long smooth beard, those high cheekbones; the whole face so strong, yet shrewd—who but Seizan Sensei? That smiling fellow on his left, the would-be gentleman with the dignified little moustache—Matsumura, surely? And there's Komatsu, so poor he wore the selfsame kimono all the year round: 'Master Wang Mang' we nicknamed him, so plentifully was he always supplied with lice—and that kimono of his, how unbearably it stank of sweat and cooking-oil and sauce! Hence the celebrated 'Komatsu's knockout blow'—the whiff that struck you if you were anywhere near when he stood up. And Yamaga, whose nose was always running (though he was a year older than me, even), the sleeve he wiped it with as stiff and shiny as if it had been starched; Kanai, the clever, ambitious youth, who took delight in tearing his perfectly respectable kimono, pulling off the strings of his *haori* coat and substituting a belt of twisted paper (this last, I must say, being no more than I did myself); Kawakita the Giant, as strong as a bull, and as intelligent, so tall you had to crane your neck to look at him, for ever making me furtive presents of cake and buns in return for the 'private lessons' I gave him in how to read the text of the *Eight Poetical Sages*; the brothers Shikata, who spent so much of their time quarrelling that once, when their father gave them a pheasant to give to Seizan Sensei at the beginning of term, it was seven or eight days before they finished arguing which of them should present it—in the end they went together to Sensei's house, with a pheasant that by that time fairly stank. Arai is there too, 'charcoal' Arai was his nickname, because of his temper—he would flare up so easily and cool off as quickly, but only to sulk for three or four days on end. Wake all these sleeping memories and it wouldn't be hard to make a book of biographies.

Twenty years: long enough for a seedling, even, to grow into solid timber. What have I done with these years, that I can sit here now so satisfied, so revoltingly smug? How unfathomable our destiny is! How various the later fortunes of those comrades who daily shared the rice we cooked in the huge, soot-blackened communal pot! Of the students of Seizan School who gathered for that single photograph so long ago, there are some who before their forties have etched a name for themselves on the scroll of lasting fame; another is headman of a village; another sits in his prefectural assembly; another, so brilliant in boyhood, has lost everything and pulls a cart for hire; another, alas, straying from the Way, has turned burglar; others again disappeared into obscurity on the day we parted, like drops of water let fall upon the sea. Look at those faces: so lively, so innocent—no genius here, you would say, but no baseness either; yet destiny has drawn these lives along such strange and diverse paths. Truly the very thought of life's uncertainty is cause for tears.

Part III

Look closely at the rings of any pine or zelkova tree, and you will see how much the gaps between the rings vary in thickness. Some rings are so close, you wonder whether the tree can have grown at all that year; while others show an extraordinarily rapid maturing. Time moves forward in arithmetical progression, Time's creatures in geometrical. So it is with the history of nations and of individuals: a single year may hold the promise of a century, while days may pass as little noticed as seconds on a clock.

 Between July of 1877 and April of 1879 I changed so much that I could hardly imagine I was that same little boy who had come down from the mountains on horseback with his mother two years before. My old home was only two years away in time, a mere two days' journey: yet already its outlines had begun to blur in my memory. Youth is a carthorse in this at least, that it looks ever ahead as it walks the road; which is as it should be, for the young have no time for backward glances. One step forward in the spring of life, and instantly the past dissolves. Nor, in truth, did we hear much news of Tsumagome. The priest of Ennenji did not keep his promise to pay us a visit. Katsusuke and O-Ju, unhappily, could neither read nor write; it was all they could do to find a friend a little less illiterate than themselves to write to us a few barely legible lines enquiring after our health and reporting that they themselves were well. But real news did come—once. A few days before the school closed, I think it was, I was sitting at my desk copying out a text when a schoolfellow called to me. 'Visitor for you, Kikuchi!' I ran out just as I was, in my tight-sleeved apology for a kimono. A huge figure was standing in the entrance—Shingo! Where else would you find a nose as massive, such narrow eyes?

 'Shingo!' 'Master Shintaro!' we both exclaimed at once, as Shingo stood there staring at me and I stared back, fascinated by the way his nostrils kept expanding and contracting—a sure sign with Shingo of quite exceptional delight. Not till moments later did I notice that for once he was without his horse, and how dressed up! a dark-blue striped kimono, if you please, worn but highly respectable, with a stiff sash of duck-cloth, leggings and straw sandals, and even a pencase stuck in the sash. There was of course no parlour at the school where guests could be received, so I took Shingo to the shade of the bamboo grove behind the building, and there we talked and talked, to make up for two years' silence. The old priest's piles had got worse: he rarely left his bed now, but was as talkative and lively as ever, though he had given up eating octopus. Katsusuke, still bright and cheerful, never missed his monthly visit to Father's grave; a marriage had been arranged for O-Ju, who was now the wife of Bunji, son of an honest farmer—though still she talked of nothing but Mrs Kikuchi and little Master Kikuchi, and prayed every morning at the family shrine for our safe return to Tsumagome. Not much had changed at Uncle Kengo's, except that Aunt had been terribly upset when Uncle took up with some slut of a woman who had appeared in the valley from no one knew where and made her his mistress. Cousin O-Fuji was 'dressing herself up something terrible these days', and spent her time plucking out love songs on the samisen; while her little sister Yoshi was still at primary school, where she always did well, but looked weighed down somehow, things not being happy at home. And Shingo himself? Still working away at his books in spare moments; reading, practising arithmetic and calligraphy. Last month he had started to work for a big charcoal-burner as his clerk, and it was on business for his new boss that he had made the trip down from the mountains. He had called on Mother first at Uncle's house, and then come straight on to see me. And how pleased he was to find me 'grow'd so big, so full of life'. All this in a torrent from those usually slow-moving lips, then the inevitable exhortation I had not heard for so long, 'You work your best, and make your way in the world, Master Shintaro!' Finally he produced from the sleeve of his kimono, apologizing all the while for *not* having brought a present, a bundle of something wrapped up in an enormous hand-towel. I untied it, to find a pile of the wild peaches I loved. Shingo must have brought them specially all the way from home.

Our news exchanged, I took charge of my guest and marched him triumphantly round the school, telling him on the way (to his particular delight) how we cooked every meal ourselves. His joy mounted when I gave him a couple of books I no longer needed from my box, together with a few pages of my calligraphy practice-work which he wanted to show to the priest of Ennenji and the others back home. But the climax came when I told him I would take him to see Seizan Sensei. Entranced, he could only repeat, 'Oh please, young Master Shintaro, if you could be so kind . . .' It was not often that Seizan Sensei agreed to talk to such visitors; but Shingo he welcomed, sparing him the sharper edge of his sardonic humour. 'Don't worry, Mr Shingo,' he nodded, 'I've taken a liking to the boy. He shall be properly trained, I promise you'—at which Shingo beamed in ecstasy. 'Wonderful teacher, wonderful, wonderful!' he went on murmuring to himself after we had left Sensei's room.

It is hard sometimes to be a child. There was nothing but greetings I could send back to Yoshi and Katsusuke and the others, but at least I made sure I gave plenty of those for Shingo to convey. So he went on his way. But the memory of his visit remained, like the stones of the peaches he had brought me; my schoolmates teased me richly about the strange ways of 'Kikuchi's uncle', as they chose to call Shingo. One day Sensei overheard them at it. 'So you think Kikuchi's friend is just a stupid country know-nothing, do you? Then wait a while—you'll learn!'

III.2

For a while after the school was closed I stayed at Uncle's. While at school I had been back there once in eight weeks or so, to deliver a load of washing and enjoy my mother's dumpling soup and *gomoku* rice; but I rarely stayed overnight, and since in those days there were no summer and winter 'holidays' as there are now, this was in effect my first real stay at Uncle's house.

Two or three men were still hard at work building the stone wall and breaking up ground for cultivation, but the renovations to the house and outbuildings had been completed. Nature's growth, never pausing for so much as a second, astonishes by its speed. The young fruit trees that had barely been planted when Mother and I first arrived two years before were already beginning to bear; the vines, then so harshly pruned and tied, now covered their trellises with long tentacles of green, from which the milder green of innumerable thickly-clustering grapes made a pattern of faint shadows on the ground below. In fan- and crescent-shaped flowerbeds all kinds of western flowers (Aunt had brought the seeds from Tokyo) displayed in the summer sunlight their brilliant tapestry of reds and purples and yellows and blues, a daylong feast for the bees; near the compost shed at the corner of the garden, alongside a tangled mass of morning-glory, balsam-pear and several kinds of gourd-plant, two more of Uncle's importations lay snugly under a canopy of leaves—water-melons and pumpkins. Here and there a western cabbage, that Benkei[1] of vegetables, its coarse outer leaves hiding a soft and succulent heart, sat weightily among the lesser breeds; there were rows of Indian corn, too, tall and straight, each with its tasselled head, like a regiment on parade.

Uncle's attempt at breeding goats and pigs had failed, but he did have one more cow than before, so that there was more fresh milk now than the family needed, and Aunt was constantly trying her hand at butter-making, though without the slightest success so far. Uncle had done well with his fowls, too; the imported ones as well as the Japanese. Every morning when Suzue came out to feed them they would swarm round her in a dense black mass, clucking furiously, like soldiers charging the enemy. Uncle stuffed himself with eggs—and with hens. So many of the latter did he eat, in fact, that eventually Aunt announced a 'constitution' for the birds, and laid down (to Uncle's dismay) that except on festival days or when we had visitors, he was not to go beyond one chicken a month.

1. A hero of the twelfth century, famed for his strength.

Then there were the silkworms. When I came to stay they had just finished with the summer batch. The droppings had been collected for manure, the remains of the mulberry branches they had been feeding on swept up and tied into bundles for firewood, and the egg-cards for the second hatching hung from the ceiling in an airy room in the house; all day long you could hear the creaking of the reeling-machine in the newly-built silkworm shed. Suzue liked to take a turn at the reeling when the machine was free, more for the fun of it than anything else, and pretty knotty thread it was she turned out. But that didn't stop her boasting each time: the silk she produced, she would say airily, would easily buy ten pounds or more of rice. Tea was another of Uncle's enthusiasms. He hadn't had his bushes planted long enough to get much of a crop, but already in the living-room there were two enormous canisters of his home-grown leaf, packed in paper specially tanned with persimmon juice. Considering it was only two years since he had started them, all these schemes of Uncle's were doing remarkably well.

Mother's coming to join them turned out to be a great help to both Uncle and Aunt, though it was purely for our sakes, no doubt, that they had sent for Mother and me in the first place. Uncle was always full of enterprising ideas. He had both the intellectual ability to translate his visions into concrete plans and the courage to put them into practice. But with his temperamental fondness for dwelling on the spectacular effect of the whole, he was very apt to miscalculate in details; on top of which his lack of patience—first qualification for any businessman—meant that he would often tire of admirable schemes as soon as he had devised them, or explode in anger if they couldn't immediately be put into operation. He was a truly public-spirited man, more concerned to help others than further any personal ends of his own—yet the combination of inattention to detail with an irascible temper tended to whittle away his influence and popularity.

The modernization of Japan could only start with individuals, men of spirit and resource acting in the local communities to which they belonged: this was Uncle's constant theme. Often he would invite heads of households and others of particular influence in the locality and lecture them on the subject. If a lecture or two were enough to pull a nation up to date, there would have been no need for the tears and sweat of history's heroes, no shedding of martyrs' blood; but that's not the way of the world. I don't know where Uncle got the idea, but he was convinced that only by the practice of eugenics could Japan hope to reach the level of the western nations, and that the first step was to persuade people to eat meat; as he already did himself, to point the way. To this end he urged everybody in the village to keep poultry and pigs, importing chicks of foreign breeds and breeding them up to distribute in twos and threes to the more respected households; but it wasn't long before Farmer A was explaining how the cat had got his chicks, while at Farmer B's they'd fallen down the drain and Farmer C had killed his pig and eaten it because of the mess it made of his field—and so on, every kind of mishap you can think of. Cabbages were the next thing. Uncle had leaflets on cabbage cultivation printed in the *kana* script, without any difficult characters, which he then distributed together with the seeds. The birds took most of the seeds though, and the leaflets probably ended up as handkerchiefs for the farmers' children.

But Uncle's enthusiasm was still not exhausted. We must educate the grown-ups no less than the children, he declared, and promptly started a kind of night-school in the village, paying the teacher himself. The farmers turned up all right, out of respect for Uncle, to scratch their heads as they pored over the first pages of the reader their grandchildren were half-way through at the primary. After a while one dropped out, then two ... till the teacher was protesting he couldn't teach students who never came. This was too much for Uncle. Furious, he summoned the villagers to a meeting, and flayed them for their backwardness. Mere anger, however, doesn't much help the cause of reform. The villagers apologized very humbly, but their very apologies were a kind of passive resistance against which Uncle was powerless.

So his great scheme for meat production came to nothing. 'The fools!' he would burst out sometimes at supper, whereupon Aunt would remind him soothingly that even with his own children things didn't always go the way he wanted, and that he must treat these countryfolk too as children: roar at them, and they would only gape in terror. Indeed, if it hadn't been for his two helpers—Aunt on one side with her common sense, and Mother with her flair for organizing and strength of will on the other—Uncle's affairs would as likely as not have been in a pretty shaky state. Mother worked herself to the bone on his behalf. Sometimes on my brief visits home in the summer, when they were at their busiest with the silkworms and getting in the tea-crop, I would find her in a short-sleeved kimono in the silkworm-shed, directing a whole crowd of men and women employed by Uncle for the season—herself working hardest of all, black with dust and sweat. The servants and gardeners went more in awe of her than of Aunt. Her combination of energy and obstinacy was more than a match even for Uncle, and there were collisions again and again, but Aunt wasn't the only one in the family who realized how valuable Mother's contribution was to the Noda household.

III.3

Suzue was just fourteen, only a few months older than I. She was big—I was small for my age, of course, but even so there was more difference between us than you would have expected. Just about the time Mother and I first arrived she had given up the Tenjin hairstyle and taken to the more grown-up 'butterfly' style. Since moving from Tokyo she had picked up the local dialect: her brother, she told me quite naturally, would be 'coomin' hoam' next year; but there was a touch of refinement about her speech still; you could feel she hadn't been living all her life where water came out of a well. Of a placid and open disposition, she took everything easily, too easily for her mother and aunt, who seemed to want her to cultivate more of a 'feminine' concern for the subtle and the delicate; but any deficiency in this respect only endeared her all the more to Uncle.

My friends and I despised girls, or at any rate behaved as if we did. We were at that brutal age when boys delight, as we did, in chopping up snakes, roasting frogs alive, and generally torturing any living creature they can lay their hands on; and we had inherited the samurai assumption that to boast to all and sundry of your own strength and superiority was the proper way to show yourself a man. 'Strong', 'hardy' and 'straightforward' were the most coveted words of commendation, 'soft', 'girlish', the most bitterly insulting. A man of honour and standing, we thought, could not bear even for a moment to be put on the same level as woman, the very personification of weakness. The best thing was not to speak to women at all, or if speech was unavoidable, to be as short and sharp as possible, with your chest stuck out and elbows folded square, so as to display beyond doubt your contempt for the insignificant creature thus disturbing you. Such was our unwritten code at school. The sneer of 'girly! girly!' reserved for those who offended against it being a punishment more terrifying than the worst 'stifling', even a boy who really loved his mother and sisters was afraid to show it, pretending not to know them if they met by chance on the street; and the merest attempt on Mother's part to mend a tear in his kimono when he was home for a visit would send him dashing back to school.

I was no exception. Two years before, when I first set eyes on Suzue, she had struck me as a kind of goddess; then I started lording it over her, glaring at her contemptuously as an inferior being. But now that I was home for longer, I couldn't keep the glaring up all the time, and before long we became close friends. I liked her for her easy ways, her inability, oddly unfeminine, to worry over trivial things. She was intelligent, too, though I gathered she herself thought I was the cleverer of the two at some things. She would put me in my place with complicated sums, which I loathed; whereupon I, by way of counter-attack, would overawe her with weighty talk of Japanese and Chinese history, in particular with tales from the History of the Three Kingdoms.

One thing at least we had in common—a passion for fruit. I remember how once (the story is not exactly to our credit, I fear) Suzue and I had a pear-eating match: I won with thirteen, but she managed to put away twelve. And how we were scolded, she by her mother and I by mine! Uncle only laughed, though. As I said earlier, the new trees were already beginning to bear. The persimmons especially, though planted only a year before, were heavy with fruit. Cousin Suzue was marvellously well behaved, but one perverse habit she did have, that of snatching a bite out of fruit while it was still on the branch, to see whether it was ripe. As often as not, when you happened to be strolling in the garden you would notice toothmarks in pears or persimmons on the lower branches, just about as high as a child could reach; and aha! you knew at once the young lady of the house had taken the air that way not long before.

Suzue's elder brother Daiichiro, as I have said, was studying in Tokyo under the watchful eye of an aunt. He often wrote saying he would like to come home, and Aunt badly wanted to see him; but Uncle always insisted he must stay in Tokyo till he had graduated. I had never met this cousin of mine, but the sight of his photograph (in western clothes, looking positively heroic) and his letters (though even I could see these were full of mistakes—he was obviously as heedless of detail as his father) filled me with unbearable envy. *Tokyo*—the writer of these letters was studying in the Great City! I wrote to him secretly, stringing together all the most ceremonious phrases I could think of: 'May I respectfully request your guidance', 'I should be humbly grateful for the honour of your acquaintance', etc. Daiichiro did not deign to reply. Maybe he despised me as an ignorant country boy—I don't know, but I was furious.

I began now to be of some small service to Uncle, though not of course to anything like the extent that Mother was helping Aunt. As might have been expected from his reputation in the locality, Uncle had been elected two years earlier to the prefectural assembly, and so far had managed to maintain his position, in spite of occasional clashes with the Governor. A lot of paper work came his way as a result. Now Uncle was not businesslike at the best of times, least of all in correspondence. His way of dealing with it was to commandeer any literate youngster who happened to be around at the time and get him to write whatever letters needed to be written—and to make up his accounts for him, come to that. There can hardly have been any of the young men of Uncle's acquaintance who had not been pressed into service as his temporary secretary. Even Suzue, I suspect, had had a good deal of calligraphy practice in writing her father's letters. Directly after I came home for good from Seizan School, Uncle had sent for me. 'Answer this letter for me, will you, Shintaro, there's a good fellow!' This was the beginning. From then on I was kept busy every day. 'Copy this out, Shin boy', 'Just read this through, will you?'—the calls came thick and fast. But I enjoyed the work: it gave me a grown-up feeling to have Uncle depending on me, and Uncle was so pleased to find how conscientiously I carried out his instructions, he treated me with as much affection as if I had been his own son.

The new Private Secretary was accommodated in a small four-mat room next to the Minister's office, divided from it by two sliding screen-walls. A veranda running round the other two sides of the room faced a jungle of bamboo, which rustled pleasantly in the breeze and provided a shady refuge from the heat of the early afternoon, when I would sit out on the veranda in my wicker chair, tapping my feet on the wooden floor as I read my book or a Tokyo newspaper, while the dull thunder of Uncle's snoring sounded from beyond the screens.

Inevitably, given Uncle's standing in the community and his own hospitable nature, his visitors were many and various. As he received them all in his study, I couldn't help hearing everything that was said, there being only the sliding screens between us; though as far as Uncle was concerned, *his* voice carried about a quarter of a mile anyway. But it wasn't all like that. Uncle had an odd habit of interrupting himself in the middle of one of his own booming speeches, fixing his eyes abruptly on his visitor and whispering—whispering something entirely trivial as if it were a secret of the most profound significance. Even these whisperings were perfectly audible to me at my desk in the 'secretary's' room. I don't know how many times I peeped through the chink between the screens. If only I had known photography or shorthand, to record the voices, the gestures and expressions of my eccentric Minister and his visitors!

For those were exciting times. After a pause in 1877 as a result of the Civil War, political feeling among the people at large had flared up again, feeding on the agitation for a national parliament; public opinion all over the country had been roused by the issue of the selling of government property by the Land Reclamation Agency, and waves of controversy surged out from the capital to engulf the entire country, so that even in our remote prefecture there was a spate of passionate argument in newspapers and on public platforms. A constant stream of politicians invaded Uncle's house to discuss the situation, the sheer din of Uncle's booming voice merging with those of the visitors, as they fired off their wordy bursts of indignation, conveying forcibly the impression that the far-off fortress of the Meiji government itself must be in danger.

At Seizan School we had not heard much of politics. Seizan Sensei himself was a moderate progressive, like Uncle; but he never spoke to us directly of his own political opinions, and would roundly scold us for the mere possession of a newspaper, even—no doubt because he hated the idea of boys hardly off their mother's milk skimping their studies to run after the cloudy notions of politics. On the very rare occasions when he did refer to public affairs he would castigate both the government and the 'popular' opposition with such impartiality of satirical wit, that we were left with the feeling that our Seizan Sensei believed in letting fly at every politician in sight, so to speak, as a matter of principle.

But then I came home; and those first two months in Uncle's household opened before me a new world, vaster than anything I had imagined in my two years at Seizan School. The tiny four-mat room next to Uncle's study, it's not too much to say, became for me a hothouse of political ideas, a true school, however indirect, of current affairs. I read bits here and there in the Tokyo newspapers and our own, I picked up fragments of the talk in the next room; and gradually, as words like 'parliament', 'popular rights', 'rights and duties', and 'political parties' came to sound more familiar, I too developed a passion for 'freedom', and grew impatient, in my childish way, for the setting up of a parliament in our country. With no experience of life's harsh side, and ignorant, alas, of the truth that both our sixty centuries of history as a people and one man's seventy years' span of life are alike no more than the laborious climbing of an endless mountain-range—the 'last' peak no sooner conquered than another reveals itself beyond, and then another, and another—I saw in 'parliament' a magic wand, one wave of which would bring us peace and happiness for ever and make a paradise of our stormy uncertain world. Absurd, when you think of it; but the illusion was not mine alone.

III.4

When Seizan Sensei closed his school all of us were scattered about the country, and I lost touch with my old comrades for the most part; but Seima Matsumura, my special friend, and I did exchange letters now and then. About the end of August a letter came from Matsumura with a tremendous piece of news. 'Tremendous news'—for us boys, in those days, these words could have only one meaning: Matsumura was leaving next month, to study in the capital—in Tokyo! You could feel his excitement in the hardly legible scrawl; his handwriting was none too firm at the best of times, but this! the characters fairly danced their way down the page in a kind of dishevelled ecstasy.

Tokyo! How the two characters of the city's name set my heart throbbing! Tokyo nowadays is a battlefield of more than a million souls, jostling each other, trampling each other down, straining to raise themselves above their fellows; for the ten in every hundred who grow fat on the blood and sweat of their ninety fellow-citizens, a mirage inspiring fugitive dreams of glory—ask yourself what our capital is today, and you find yourself cursing the place. But in those days Tokyo was our Promised Land. Just as the idea of parliament shone for us as a symbol of the loftiest political ideal, so was Tokyo the focus of all our curiosity, all our ambition, all our aspiration. The very word was precious; paradoxically, the thought that my cousin Daiichiro was studying *there*, of all places, made him almost hateful to me. Tokyo! The Imperial Capital, the bridge of our ship of state, the great repository of learning and knowledge; its invigorating streets swirling with opportunities for success and fame more plentiful than the motes of dust kicked up from horses' hooves; city of splendid houses, of delicious foods, of citizens at once shrewd and noble-hearted, their very speech endowed with a clarity and force unknown elsewhere; city of ease and convenience of living, of inexhaustible fascination—it was to this city that Matsumura was now going—Matsumura, till recently my classmate and closest friend. And I—what of *my* future? Suddenly I was crying over Matsumura's letter. If only Father were alive still, and our family what it had once been, the most prosperous in Tsumagome, they would have let me go, sent me after him directly, once Matsumura said he was going. But what were such thoughts but dreams, of a past that could never return? As it was, I felt as if for the first time how low we had sunk, Mother and I, and how humiliating was our position as 'hangers-on' in Uncle's house. I glared resentfully at Matsumura's letter.

A few days later Matsumura himself, beaming and resplendent in new kimono, new *hakama*,[2] new clogs, and new straw hat, called with his father to say goodbye. His letter alone had kept me awake for four or five nights, and the shock of seeing him now, already on his way, was so great that I could take in neither his father's kindly words (like the sensitive man he was, he saw what I was going through) nor Matsumura's own promises of continued friendship. Even the 'thank you' for the box of dried prawns (my favourite) that Matsumura's mother had sent stuck in my throat. I still tried to look brave, but at the last moment, when Matsumura called from his rickshaw just as they were moving off, 'Goodbye! Join me soon!' I burst out crying like a weakling. Standing there miserably by the cumquat tree outside Uncle's gate, staring after the Matsumuras, father and son, as their rickshaws rattled farther and farther into the distance, I must have looked the very picture of hopelessness.

Suzue was in the garden picking mulberry leaves for the autumn silkworms when I walked back from the gate, wiping the tears from my face; I can see her still. She came over when she saw me, wonder in her frank, cheerful face.

'What's the matter, Shintaro-san?'

'Nothing!' barked the small would-be politician and seeker after glory, in a fierce burst of anger very much out of character—then ran off, leaving Miss Suzue to gape.

III.5

Matsumura's departure for Tokyo reminded me sharply that it would be stupid to neglect my own studies. Working as Uncle's secretary was all very well, but the days and months were speeding; I couldn't go on indefinitely without any schooling—do we not say, 'Youth fades quickly into age, and difficult indeed is learning to acquire'? Truly the frustration was hard to bear. Mother too prayed daily that we might hear of some reputable school.

Three new schools had been set up not long before in our prefecture: a Medical School, a Teachers' College, and a Middle School. I had no wish to be a doctor, and the most one could expect after graduating from the College was a teaching job in some miserable country school, which would never do for the one-time prodigy of Tsumagome (admittedly the prodigy had failed his examinations once, but not entirely, perhaps,

2. A kind of skirt, worn over the lower part of the kimono on special occasions.

through his own fault), let alone the young man who had won even Seizan Sensei's praise. No: only Middle School would satisfy me. Middle School, and eventually the University, seat of the highest learning—it must be that or nothing, I pleaded with Mother and Uncle. But Uncle told me to wait a while, as he and his political friends were planning to start an entirely new school on their own.

Uncle's 'political friends' were in general terms the moderate progressives of our prefecture. There were three 'parties', or factions, in our part of the world at that time. First, the conservatives, who themselves had been through three phases. Before the Restoration they had been supporters of the feudal administration; ten years later they were mildly opposed to the new government; by now they had become its firm supporters. Then there were the 'radicals', much given to patriotic denunciation of Japan's backwardness, men who had early breathed the air of freedom. Between the radicals and conservatives came Uncle's moderates, sober, experienced men mostly, who had formerly served in responsible posts in the central or provincial governments, but were now in opposition, regarding themselves as the true 'men of public spirit' in our provincial community. As far as politics were concerned, they believed in gradual change, most of them having been brought up originally on a kind of reformist Confucianism; sometimes, though, on the pretext of 'seeking for new knowledge', four or five of them would meet to study the latest translated books on modern theories of liberty, citizens' rights, and morality. To this group of moderates Uncle belonged. Inevitably his eccentric ways and dislike of discipline kept him somewhat on the fringe of the group as a whole. But both they and he felt strongly the need for a new school where a new generation could be taught their own reformist ideas. If 'she who rocks the cradle rules behind the throne', they who control the schools are society's real masters. Already Tokyo Imperial University had developed into little more than a bastion of the Meiji Government, and Fukuzawa's[3] new School at Mita[4] was spreading his more liberal influence throughout Japan; but quite apart from national developments such as these, Uncle and his friends had long seen the need for public schools that would serve the community in more practical ways.

By virtue of his own background and outlook, Seizan Sensei should have belonged to Uncle's group; but his powerful individuality made him so disinclined to work with others that Seizan School had to the end remained Seizan Sensei's private academy. Even when the possibility of starting a new public school was being discussed, he brusquely refused to have anything to do with it. 'Education, schools—bah! No more of that for me. I'm a peasant now, and nothing else besides. You start up a school if you want to: I'll send you a sack of potatoes for the opening!' But

3. Yukichi Fukuzawa (1835–1903), the great pioneer of the Japanese 'Enlightenment'.
4. Now Keio University.

enthusiasm for the project grew nonetheless. Land was bought on the edge of the town, official permission obtained; a landowner gave the timber; even a teacher of English was found (the hardest part of the whole business, this), a former student of the Engineering College in Tokyo who had had to give up his studies before graduation; and in October 1881, just five days after the promulgation of the Imperial Rescript promising the establishment of a National Diet, the flag of the New School fluttered out for the first time in the autumn breeze.

Whereupon Uncle lost his secretary. Released at my own request from official duties, I returned once more to dormitory life.

III.6

Coming to the New School from Seizan Sensei's was like climbing out of the dark depths of a valley to a forest of tall straight trees on a mountainside. The building, for instance. For all the spaciousness of its one big room, Seizan School was no more than a converted farmhouse, and an old-fashioned one at that. The New School wasn't luxurious, but at least it was new, and built from the start as a school, with a second storey (what did it matter if it had no ceiling?) and windows all round, which made the rooms almost dazzlingly bright, a playground, imposing black gates, with the school's name inscribed on the posts, and a flagpole. It *looked* like a school. Drawbacks there were, of course: the cold when the north wind blew, rattling the sliding windows (the school stood by itself among fields, just outside the town); a pretty sight the building certainly made in summer, surrounded by acres of waving corn, with its smart tiled roof, its white plaster walls gleaming in the sun, and bravely fluttering flag—but the smell! (pardon the intrusion of such low matters!) the smell of nightsoil riding in at every window on the sultry summer breezes—the very memory makes me choke.

One can't have everything, though. No more getting up at dawn, rubbing sleepy eyes in summer and chapped hands in winter, to cook our own rice; a one-eyed cook employed for the purpose provided us with three hot meals a day, which was a lot to be thankful for, even if his rice did sometimes taste more of bran than anything else, and bits of charcoal, small stones and pieces of straw find their way into the soup. Seizan Sensei the Strict was a hard taskmaster: he was always sending us off to sweep the garden or draw water from the well, as if we were merely youthful servants. Here at the New School we had only to fold away our bedding when we got up, wash ourselves and sweep round our desks, and then we were free to study as much as we liked. Then again, at Seizan Sensei's we had only one real teacher, with one assistant, and only one subject—Chinese Classics, whereas now our teachers numbered thirteen in all, more than the students at first, and included one who held the senior grade of the fifth Court Rank, not to mention another who was a master spearsman of the Hozoin Style (though it wasn't javelin-throwing but 'Specimens of Model Prose' he taught at school); and the curriculum consisted of Chinese and Japanese Classics, western books in translation, arithmetic, both abacus and written, and English—this latter taught us by the mild young ex-student from Tokyo out of an incredibly difficult book called *Spelling*, with much toil and sweat on his part, faced as he was with our barbarous southern dialect.

But things rarely turn out as men foresee. In spite of the great hopes with which it had been started, in a mere three months the New School was already falling apart. 'Too many sailors will run the ship aground,' we say; nor is it only the English who (as Disraeli remarked) dislike coalition Cabinets. A piece of marquetry, after all, doesn't take much knocking apart. The administration of the School was organized on republican lines, and for a little while things went smoothly, with one Komorita Sensei acting as a kind of President. But before long the mania for organizing political parties that was sweeping the entire country about that time infected two or three of the older teachers, including the 'President'. When this new-found political zeal began to keep them away from school, trouble broke out among some of the younger masters; they quarrelled, the ones who got the worst of it enlisted others on their side, and discipline started to collapse. A kind of lethargy, probably heralding the break-up of the whole experiment, lay over the whole school.

Seizan Sensei's regime, with all its severity, would have been easier to bear. At Seizan School, you could feel Sensei's character and influence everywhere, right to the obscurest corner of the communal toilet. Granted he hardly exemplified the Confucian 'Golden Mean', his uncompromising personality and intensely individual views permeated his little community with an extraordinary clarity, leaving no room for the slightest uncertainty or vagueness about anything whatever. None of us ever felt he didn't know what to do next, if I can put it like that. If the discipline was irksome, which it was, there was satisfaction to be derived from it too: however biting the cold on a frosty morning, it helped to develop a fine manly contempt for physical sensations—a pride in taut muscles, in blood no longer sluggish. The atmosphere at Seizan Sensei's excluded the slack, the mean, the lethargic, the wavering; alertness was constantly forced upon us. Better an open enemy than a doubtful ally, remarked the great Corsican. No one likes the man who won't commit himself, the political party that sits on the fence, the colourless government; and what the young hate most is tepidity.

The New School had been founded by progressives. Its teachers were all stalwarts of the party, pleasant and reliable men, yet there was too much of a sameness about them all—a 'fine team', if you looked on the good side, 'not a real mind among the lot of them' if you didn't: the admirable qualities each of them possessed harmonizing into a corporate dullness, on the same principle as colours lose themselves in a prism, and hydrogen and oxygen combine to form nothing more exciting than water. The School lacked the distinctive 'aroma' that boys need. Coming from Seizan Sensei's, which was so remarkable in this very respect, I was much upset by the difference—as were all those of my old schoolmates who moved with me. Still, depressing though this obvious difference in atmosphere was, I didn't at the time attempt to discover the reasons for it, but only worked away as hard as I could, thankful at least for the chance of learning English.

Things went from bad to worse, however. With the trouble among the teachers that I have mentioned, some of the senior ones missing classes and the younger ones falling out among themselves as a result, the students lost all interest, and soon they became so uncontrollable that even our quiet, conscientious English teacher was shouting at us, red in the face—till suddenly he gave out that he was sick, and stopped coming. As if this wasn't bad enough, some of the boys transferred to a school which the conservatives had set up at about the same time as ours, and which, as luck would have it, was now flourishing. For all its promising start, after less than a year the New School was on the verge of collapse.

Finally life became so impossible that one day I cut school and walked the three miles home to talk things over with Uncle. Just as I reached the gate of Uncle's house, a man in a worn but neat kimono, handsome and rather slight of build, like a girl, was on his way out. Two jet-black eyes were raised to look closely at me for a moment as we met, but without a smile: then he hurried past and was gone.

III.7

Who could he have been, I wondered?

I found Uncle relaxing in a rocking-chair, stroking his beard—evidently he had been busy till a moment before with the young man I had just met.

'Hallo, Shin boy! How's school?'

I described the troubles as clearly as I could, adding that I wanted to move to another school, as with things as they were it had become all but impossible to study properly. Although he was not directly connected in any way with the running of the New School, Uncle obviously knew already what had been happening, even without my report; in fact, he hardly seemed to be listening. But suddenly 'He'd do it!' he burst out, 'Marvellous fellow!'—with a vigorous shake of the head, followed by a confirmatory nod.

Bolts from the blue were a habit with Uncle. I thought at once of the young man I had seen at the gate.

'Do you mean the visitor who just left, Uncle?'

Uncle stared at me, as if mystified by my apparent reading of his thoughts; then broke into a smile.

'Oh—ran into him, did you, Shin boy? Marvellous fellow, you know. Truly, a marvellous fellow!'

Some people see only the worst in others, some only the best. Uncle belonged to the latter category. Once he took a liking to somebody, there was no limit to his admiration. Sometimes he would swallow the most outrageous deceits, till one stuck in his throat and he had to cough them all up in a hurry; he could meet a man for the first time in the morning, be his fervent admirer by lunchtime, and have broken with him for ever before dinner. Maybe this is just Uncle's soft spot again, I thought . . . He began to praise the handsome young man, his enthusiasm rising as he talked. Tetsutaro Komai was the visitor's name: of Tosa extraction, he was now in his early twenties and already well versed in both English and French. Until recently he had worked as a journalist in Tokyo, writing anti-government articles for the daily and weekly press, but then for some reason had washed his hands of the capital and made his way, armed with several letters of introduction, down here to the wilds of Kyushu. Highly educated, possessed of a forceful personality and excellent judgement, yet without a trace of vanity or showiness—not many about like *him* nowadays, Uncle insisted.

Even allowing for Uncle's susceptibility, I could see he must have been pretty deeply impressed; but I still doubted whether all these qualities could really belong to that slender, almost dandyish figure I had passed at the gate. But Uncle hadn't finished yet. The arrival of such an outstanding man in our country parts was providential, not a doubt of it. 'If only we can get *him* to take charge of the School, all the trouble will be over in no time,' he exclaimed triumphantly. 'Don't you think so, Shin boy?'—insistently—as if *I* knew anything about it! By the time he had done I wasn't sure whether I had come home to tell Uncle about the School or simply to provide an audience for his panegyric; Uncle's wordy enthusiasm wrapped me round like a mist, in which I completely lost my way. But truth is stranger than fiction. Less than two weeks later Uncle's scheme was realized.

III.8

A great number of ex-samurai would-be politicians were wandering up and down Japan at about the time I am writing of, driven this way and that by the stress of change, like the great masses of seaweed that our Pacific typhoons prise from the rocks along the seashore and blow far and wide, to toss upon the ocean's surface. Of these, it seems, Komai Sensei was one. A good many people, including some of the moderate progressives, were very hesitant about his taking over the New School; but two or three of the group, including Uncle, backed him so enthusiastically, and the School itself was so obviously in need of drastic change if it was to survive at all, that the rest agreed to the appointment as a necessary leap in the dark. Komai Sensei in turn only accepted on condition he was to be given complete authority to run the School without interference, so that the step was a radical one for both sides. This was 1882: all the world was running around organizing political associations and parties, and here was a man of talent like Komai Sensei refusing the most pressing invitations—as we gathered he had—to join the radicals' newspaper in order to take on a tottering school like ours. The whim of an eccentric, indeed.

We students greeted our new headmaster in a mood of suspicion, or at best of chilly indifference. From our point of view he had several unforgivable faults. First, he was a 'foreigner', not a Kyushu man. The old prejudice that had driven our grandfathers to proclaim so passionately the slogan 'Close the country, drive out the foreigner' still lived in us deep down, to flare up instantly at the mere sight of an unfamiliar face. Komai Sensei, the foreigner—that was all we could think of. To ears like ours, believing our own staccato squawk to be the most melodious of music, his smooth Shikoku speech sounded absurdly weak, the voice of a detestable insincerity. Again, to be great in our eyes a man had to be massive both in body and in mind, swarthy of skin, with a voice as deep and sonorous as a temple bell, and strength enough to 'lift a cauldron', in the old Chinese phrase; such men had heroes always been, we knew, from Ousu-no-Mikoto[5] to Takamori Saigo[6]: 'great souls in great bodies' was nature's law. But here was this Komai Sensei, womanishly neat and refined-looking, whiteskinned and red-lipped, come to trample, if you please, on our precious image of all that was noble!

Hence the coldness, the hostility of our welcome. We sat in silence, deceptively well-behaved, as he began to address us on his first day. We could be as nasty as cats with strangers at the best of times; all the more so now, with all discipline gone and the whole student body reduced to a mob—and almost at once a stir ran though the room, someone started coughing, in no time the entire school was overcome with catarrh; coughing here, coughing there, turning in the end to a gale of laughter, raucous enough to make the most heroic of headmasters flinch. For Komai Sensei this was the first battle-cry from the enemy blocking his way.

But we were wrong, all of us. Even Confucius had to admit his mistake in judging Tan-t'ai Mieh-ming[7] merely by his unprepossessing appearance; and who could have guessed that this diminutive, gentle-looking teacher would turn out to be a volcano—one of our Japanese volcanoes, the perfect beauty of its snow-covered outline capped with the whitest of white clouds, but hiding in its depths a furnace ready to pierce the sky with its

---

5. Third son of the Emperor Keiko (A.D. 70–130), and a famous warrior.
6. Leader of the rebellion of 1877.
7. Because of his extreme ugliness, Confucius was at first unwilling to accept Tan-t'ai Mieh-ming as a disciple, but soon had reason to regret the superficiality of his judgement. Tan-t'ai Mieh-ming later acquired 300 disciples of his own.

flames? History tells us of such men, certainly: there was the delicate, smoothskinned Chang Liang who plotted to have the Emperor Shih Huang Ti murdered at Po Lang Sha, or, from our own recent history, that Sanai Hashimoto[8] whom even the great Saigo revered. Uncle had been right all along; but alas, we students were blind—it was more than two months before we realized we might as well wrestle with a rock as make a butt of Komai Sensei.

Man is a foolish creature. It isn't only the Jews who, having crucified the true Christ, calmly go on praying for His coming: we ourselves are always re-enacting the same drama. We reverence the heroes of the past in our shrines, depict them in paintings, celebrate their memory with monuments and poetry, write their biographies in letters of gilt, and still do not tire of doing them honour, yet the great men of our own time we do not even notice when we pass them in the street; what is worse, we persecute anybody a little different from ourselves as if he were a monster. And still we clamour for more great men, more geniuses. Who can know how many of these geniuses our unthinking cruelty has withered before their flowering! You cannot see the top of Mount Fuji from its foothills, nor can you get the feeling of its immense height unless you are standing many miles away. By the same token it is only now, when I shut my eyes and recreate the past in memory, that I can see how remarkable a man Komai Sensei was. I have met every kind of man in my lifetime, but never another like him—and it is not just a sentimental wish to make amends for our hostility now that he is out of the way (he is already dead) that makes me say this. Unhappily he died very young, before he had a chance to achieve any great work; his name won't be written in the history books. But the man himself, in my humble opinion, was cast in the same heroic mould as Sanai Hashimoto and other outstanding figures of our Restoration period.

An old man of wide experience once remarked that if he could find a man who knew how to run his kitchen for him, he would recommend him as Finance Minister. I would say rather, find me the man who has it in him to take over an enterprise that others have let go to ruin and put it on its feet again, though he himself be an outsider, penniless and totally unknown —and I will recommend him for Prime Minister of the land. Komai Sensei did just this. Our language was strange to him, as were our customs and way of life. Two or three teachers may have been sympathetic, but to the majority of the staff, not to mention the students, he was an impudent upstart. For some months incidents continued that would have taxed the patience of the Buddha . . . I won't go into all the details. After a few days of behaving with a sneering, exaggerated politeness the 'keep-the-foreigner-out' rowdies showed their true colours: the jokers among them mimicking

---

8. A noted scholar of western learning in the years immediately preceding the Meiji Restoration.

9. See note 6, p. 114.

him to his face, the brawny ones bombarding him triumphantly with nonsensical questions, some of the extremists even proposing we should boycott classes without notice, then grab hold of Komai Sensei and chair him out of the building (though we didn't in fact go that far). In imagination, if not physically, the students practised every kind of violence on their new principal.

All this daunting treatment Komai Sensei stood up to with the patience, a cynic might say, of a bird of passage, a wanderer inured to such things. But I could fill a book with the story of how with a blend of self-possession, cool obstinacy and cunning he fought against and overcame every obstacle, never tiring and never forcing any issue, till all hostility was dissipated and he could build up the school in the way he wanted—but that's a book I'll have to write some other day. All I want to do now is confess my own stupidity in not recognizing Komai Sensei for the man he was; I wasn't one of the ringleaders of the campaign against him, but I shared the general distrust of him just the same. We Japanese are said to be weak-willed, but when one comes across someone like Komai Sensei, one has to admit there is a hidden strength in us too, behind the façade.

III.9

An army thrills at the approach of its general; the master actor's entry brings the stage to life; the magic of a great personality never fails. Whatever names we called Komai Sensei—Vagabond, Mr. Dandy, Tosa Fish—it was astonishing how the moribund School began to revive as soon as he had taken control. Taking as his headquarters a tiny groundfloor room in the north corner of the dormitory, he ate with us and shared our life in every way. The room itself had a tranquil, austere air—its only furniture a single oil lamp, a charcoal brazier littered with tobacco ash, a bamboo clothes-stand, and a shelf with a few Chinese and western books—but Komai Sensei's life was far from tranquil. Up in the morning before any of us, he taught without a break the whole day; and at night, if you peeped through the holes in the paper-panelled door you could see him studying still, reading foreign books by lamp-light. There is nothing more difficult than managing a crowd of boys—or easier, if you know how, as Komai Sensei certainly did. The young toughs among us despised this foreigner with the face so meek and mild—though his eyes were bright enough, piercingly so—that you would have said he was a natural for an *onnagata* actor, the kind that plays only women's parts. When Komai Sensei took no notice of them, they would crowd into the room next to his and bawl out the song:

> 'If muskets fail to mow the invader down,
> We'll greet him—with our swords upon his crown!'

or leap about in the room directly above, till the ceiling threatened to collapse. He didn't turn a hair, but sat quietly reading, as calm as any Po Yi or Liu-hsia Hui.[10]

They tried other tactics: boycotting classes, turning up late, ostentatiously bowing twice whenever they spoke, asking the simplest questions with servile politeness. Still no effect. The students grew more furious than ever. This was when they began to talk of throwing him out by force, but it never came to anything: they could sense too clearly the forbidding core of strength in this gentle man. No attempt to dislodge him upset Komai Sensei. Nor was it that he was insensitive: I'm certain nothing we said escaped him, not even soliloquies mumbled in the privy. No, it was just that he understood our mood so exactly. He knew that the slightest loss of temper or sign of weakness on his part would only infuriate us all the more; once used, the big stick would be useless. Through every disturbance he stood firm, coolly inviting attack, and in fact for some time it was just as though our headmaster's firmness were a physical object, an obstacle that every boy in the School was competing to demolish.

But Komai Sensei remained undefeated. As in Japanese *sumo* wrestling a contender will patiently tire his opponent out in order to be able to throw him when the moment comes with a sudden twist, so our long bout with our principal ended with a quite trivial incident that occurred when we students were beginning to tire of the struggle. It was like this. Some three months after Komai Sensei's arrival there was a holiday of some kind, I forget exactly what the reason for it was, and the whole school went off on a walking tour for four days. Poor Komai Sensei, whose legs weren't very strong in the first place, soon developed a mass of blisters on both feet; Lin Ch'ung[11] himself can scarcely have suffered as much. He said nothing, not a word, though it was obvious from his drawn face how great the pain must have been. The moment we got back to the School, after four days of walking in the mountains, he fainted. The doctor was sent for. He was amazed when he examined Sensei's feet—a man *couldn't* have walked a hundred yards with his feet like *that*, he kept repeating . . .

In no time we had heard of this, and marvelled, not for the first time, at Komai Sensei's endurance. Next morning, when he came crawling into class with both feet wrapped in bandages and began the lesson as if nothing had happened, with his face still as pale as it had been the day before, none of us so much as whispered. For about a month after this he still could not stand properly; but there was nothing shaky about his authority now.

    10. Ancient worthies mentioned frequently in Mencius as examples of virtue, modesty and integrity; e.g. 'Mencius said Po Yi's eyes would not look on an evil face, his ears would not listen to an evil sound . . . Liu-hsia Hui was not ashamed of a foul lord, and did not refuse a small post . . . neglected and idle, he did not grumble; straitened and poor, he did not mope . . . So hearing the ways of Liu-hsia Hui, the narrow man grows broad, and the mean man grows free.' (Menc. XI, trans. Lyall, in *Mencius*, London, Longmans, 1932.)

    11. Hero of a Chinese romance, forced by his guards to walk day and night till he reached his place of banishment.

I myself had tried to keep out of the battle: I didn't abuse Komai Sensei, as most of the others did, nor join in the rowdy attempts to upset him. But I wasn't on his side, either. I stood by, watching my schoolmates, without every trying to check them in their antics—a pretty cowardly part to have played, and one of which I am still ashamed.

III.10

The New School changed out of all recognition under Komai Sensei. The curriculum, for one thing. Nakamura's translation of Smiles' *Self-Help* took the place of Confucius and Mencius, the history of European civilization that of China and Japan. English, which had barely survived under the previous regime, now took up most of our time. Komai Sensei's own English was far from grammatically perfect; but under his guidance we made big strides, from spelling, the *First English Reader* and a modicum of grammar to the reading of Parley's *History of England*, Swinton's *Universal History*, and Guizot's *History of Civilization*. Classes in Chinese prose and verse composition were replaced by Japanese Composition and Public-Speaking, solemn discourses on ethics by venerable Confucian scholars gave way to Komai Sensei's lectures on his beloved *Plutarch's Lives*. These were radical changes indeed—too radical for some of the old teachers, who resigned in protest; but Komai Sensei forged ahead, undeterred by such minor obstacles.

But a bigger change than any in the curriculum was the transformation in the spirit and atmosphere of the School. Looking back, I would say now that Komai Sensei's political ideas were a blend of the sober British approach with more characteristically French ideals. Already old in learning, he was as young as his years in spirit. The lessons he gave us on the history of the British Constitution were far from dull, but it was Greece and Rome, the Greece and Rome of Plutarch, and eighteenth-century France that set the spark to his enthusiasm: at his lectures on the French Revolution we might have been listening to a reincarnation of Buzot or St Just, those heroes of the Gironde, so strongly was he fired with the ideals of freedom and equality. These ideals spread rapidly throughout the School, dyeing a deeper colour the pink banner of the moderate reformism it had been founded to promote.

For our part we welcomed the change. Youth wants its standards drawn in black and white: life in the tropics or life at the poles is youth's peculiar dream. I had missed Seizan School for its clearly-defined eccentricity, for its atmosphere so charged with an oxygen suited to our young lungs, and contrasting vividly with the lukewarmness and lack of purpose that we found so disheartening when the New School was going through its worst period. No matter if some of the older teachers seemed to think Komai Sensei was leading us into strange and dangerous places, we followed him joyfully, marching forward to a future shining with the glorious light of Liberty and Equality.

Whereas Seizan School had created its own little world, private and aloof, the New School under its new principal opened itself freely to society's turbulent winds. Newspapers, Seizan Sensei's great bugbear, found their way in. Politicians and other public figures passing through the neighbourhood stopped by to visit us. One dropped in casually, and stayed with us in the dormitory for six months, lecturing on the Social Contract; others came in groups of three or four, in the evening, more often than not, to bring us news of the capital. We welcomed them all. Once, in honour of a rather well-known visitor, we held a mock parliament. How wildly we applauded, I remember, when one bright youth denounced his opponent: 'That kind of shallow talk might have done for a schoolboy at that school at the back of beyond you've all read of—the "New School" they call it, I believe—where they played at parliaments ten years or more ago; but from the mouth of an honourable member of our National Diet— what absurd, what *childish* nonsense!'

To sum up, in the two years that Komai Sensei was our headmaster practically everything about the New School changed except its name. The older teachers gave him little help, but neither were they inclined to interfere, having suffered enough before he came; and besides, even they were by now sufficiently infected by the intoxicating atmosphere of change in the world at large to be willing to give him a chance. So Komai Sensei was able, after all, to run the School the way he wanted.

III.11

They were happy years, and still stand out as memorable. Ignorant of the world, of the pitfalls that await any who try to walk a straight path through life, of the price of progress for both individual and community; childish disciples of a youthful master, we moved confidently forward, as we thought, towards the shining kingdom of our ideals. Our hearts leapt at the word 'freedom', our eyes flashed at the tales of the heroes of history. An unsullied hope surged within us as we watched the world outside, yet with one eye on our books, like young recruits listening eagerly to reports from the battlefield.

Change followed change, like the waves of an incoming tide. Two years before we had been deep in the *History of the Three Kingdoms*, thrilling to the tale of how Chang Fei destroyed the bridge of Chang Pau 'with a single shout': now we pored as eagerly over up-to-date novels like *Brief Carnage in the West*[12] and *Song of Freedom*.[13] A boy of seventeen, Asai by name, used to answer jeers about his size—he was so small, you would have

12 and 13. Titles of Japanese translations of extracts from *Ange Pitou* and *Mémoires d'un médecin*, both by Alexandre Dumas (père).

taken him for no more than twelve or thirteen at the most—by saying an oppressive government was sitting on his head and stopping him growing; 'Wait five years,[14] and see how I'll shoot up then!' He had a wonderfully clear and musical voice, though, in spite of his size. The instant the Freedom Weekly arrived with the latest instalment of the 'Song of Freedom', a crowd gathered on the playground shouting for Asai, who would then station himself by a dormitory window and declaim the instalment in ringing tones, interrupted now and then by great waves of applause. Then there was Fumio Yano's *A Noble Tale of Statesmanship*.[15] I don't know how many nights we wore our eyes out on the exploits of Epaminondas and the fortunes of Thebes.

Nothing we saw or heard in those days but brought its own excitement. At night, rolled up in our biscuit-thin quilts in the dormitory upstairs, we dreamed of joining with Lafayette in helping the American colonists to win their independence; of mounting the guillotine with Madame Roland, of shouting with Patrick Henry, 'Give me liberty or give me death!'—of talking with the poet Milton; of Komai Sensei miraculously appointed Prime Minister, the Gladstone of Japan, and bringing forward to one short year from now the opening of our National Parliament ... Hectic times they were, but happy! Now, alas, even the dreams have gone.

Quite apart from textbooks and classroom lessons, a succession of dramatic events occurred in the world outside to widen our horizons still further—and to make our blood boil, each time we read of them. During the outcry over the Fukushima Incident,[16] we fought with each other for a sight of the Tokyo paper carrying the report of the trial, tearing the paper to shreds in the process, and wept at the sufferings of the victims. If only we could fly to their side, to kiss their wrists where the chains had bitten and stroke their backs where the police had struck them with their scabbards! How we longed to kick and thrash and trample under our avenging feet the magistrates of Fukushima and their defenders, the brutish government in Tokyo! When we read of how the prisoners had been dragged barefoot through the snow, we went walking barefoot in the snow ourselves to test our strength of will, in case we had to follow in their footsteps.

Talking of snow, we had many other such winter tests of endurance to train us to stand up to any future trials: cold baths, dawn bouts of fencing and judo, racing each other up craggy hills in the middle of the night, not to mention hunting expeditions and marathon walks. With two years of

---

14. i.e. until near the time set for the establishment of a Parliament. An Imperial Edict of 1881 announced that a Diet would be convened in 1890.
15. A historical romance based on Plutarch's *Life of Epaminondas*. It was published in 1883, with the subtitle *Young Politicians of Thebes*.
16. The reference is to the arrest in 1882, on charges of 'fomenting unrest', of several members of the Fukushima Prefectural Assembly who had been opposing certain measures planned by the Governor of the Prefecture. They were executed in the following year.

Seizan Sensei's regimen behind me, I myself took easily to such Spartan training; but some found it pretty hard.

One of the more exciting tests was supposed to be specially good for the timid. It involved walking—at night and alone—about ten miles to an old graveyard, then making your way through the close-packed ranks of upright tombstones, some of them quite new, to stick your namecard on to one of two cryptomeria trees in the middle. A cemetery is never a cheerful place to visit: but at night, in drizzling rain, or under a pale, melancholy moon . . . This was one test, at least, that did not depend on how big and beefy you were. Even if I could never win at *sumo* wrestling, I thought nothing of the trip to the cemetery and back (it's true I always approached it very warily, brandishing a borrowed dagger to cut down any wandering spirits, and ran home at top speed afterwards, but I don't think I was any the less brave for that).

One of the brawniest of us, whose apparent stolidity quite made up for his lack of any scholastic pretensions, would invariably complain of a headache or a pain in his legs on nights when the graveyard test was announced. Others were more subtle. One such was Okamoto (known to all and sundry by his English nickname 'Eastlake'—originally it had been 'Lake',[17] but then a new boy, Yamanoe, turned out to be equally cunning and sly, so we called them both Lakes, East for Okamoto and West for Yamanoe). Okamoto used to give the cook five sen to go to the cemetery with his namecard, while he himself would sleep comfortably in the cook's room and turn up smiling at the dormitory next morning as if he had enjoyed the walk. But secrets will out. When a boy guessed what was happening, Okamoto promised him a bag of bean-jam to keep his mouth shut; but 'Eastlake' defaulted on the contract, the truth was told, and for a while all the rest of us boiled with the righteous anger of youth.

III.12

My life at the New School flowed on undisturbed until a melancholy event occurred in the Noda family which was to affect my future very greatly. Just before the beginning of the summer holidays in 1883, not having seen Mother for some time, I walked back after school one day to Uncle's. The house struck me as unusually quiet. To my astonishment, I found the whole family gathered in the big living-room at the back: Uncle sitting brokenly in an easy chair on the veranda, Aunt weeping over a piece of paper she was holding, a travelling-bag at her side, Mother and Cousin Suzue weeping with her. The news they gave me was startling indeed: Cousin Daiichiro was dead. That morning a telegram saying he had suddenly fallen ill had come from Tokyo; to be followed by another—

---

17. An untranslatable pun is involved. The (Japanese) word used here for *lake* can also mean *cunning*—if written with a different ideograph.

just as Aunt was getting ready to leave—announcing his death. It had been cholera, apparently: his body was to be cremated immediately, and only the hair would be sent to the family.

Truly man's life is beyond all understanding. When Uncle and Aunt had left Tokyo in 1879, Daiichiro had stayed behind, and this summer he was due to come home for the first time in nearly five years. Only four or five days ago he had written to say he would be leaving in two weeks; he promised to bring lots of presents for Suzue, and added special greetings to me, even, all with a warmth unusual for him, so that to us the letter read strangely like a leave-taking. Uncle had been more than usually cheerful of late in anticipation of seeing his beloved son again, while Aunt, in the intervals of broadcasting to all the neighbourhood that 'Daiichiro was coming,' had been making *yukata*,[18] tidying all the rooms, even sending to a river mill three miles or more away for specially-ground flour, because Daiichiro had always liked wheat-cakes. Suzue had been telling me whenever we met how Elder Brother was coming home, and how much bigger he would surely have grown; and she was jealously guarding all the juiciest-looking peaches in the garden, insisting to anyone who tried to pick them that 'these are reserved for Elder Brother!' I, for my part, was thrilled at the prospect of meeting for the first time this cousin of mine, and hearing about Tokyo and all the learning he had acquired there. How sad the transience of life, that before I could speak to him he should have passed already into the darkness, no more to me than a face in a photograph!

'Cholera, indeed—a poor, spiritless way to die!' said Uncle, clearing his throat several times. 'Better take it quietly, O-Jitsu: tears won't help.'

'Yes, dear, I'll not weep any more,' said Aunt, wiping her eyes as she spoke. 'Tears won't bring him back, I know . . . I can still see him standing on the pier at Yokohama when we sailed, holding his aunt's hand. Every year he wrote how he longed to come home, but always put it off—always put it off—and then just when he really was coming . . . undutiful boy . . .' Aunt burst into tears once more. Finding no words to comfort her, Mother wept too, and soon Suzue was sobbing again.

'Fools!' said Uncle angrily to no one in particular. 'Come, Shin boy: you and I'll take a walk.' Outside he marched me round the garden, but aimlessly and without speaking. I followed as silently, not knowing what to say.

Ten days later there was fresh weeping over the arrival from Tokyo of Daiichiro's hair and some photographs, together with a letter giving the details of his death. Because of the nature of the illness, there was no question of sending the ashes; so only the hair could be buried. For the 'grave' Uncle chose a piece of high ground not far from the big rock where I had sat with Suzue on the day Mother and I arrived and listened to her stories of Tokyo and of Daiichiro. There, sheltered by a Japanese cherry-

---

18. A light cotton kimono, much used in summer.

tree and a pine, my cousin's tombstone stands guard over the land and house he never saw. Uncle would climb the little hill sometimes to pull up the weeds; Aunt went often, alone and telling no one, to weep at the grave. Suzue took up armfuls of wild and garden flowers every morning, smothering the tombstone in blossoms.

From this time Aunt started to cry whenever she looked at me. I felt somehow guilty, and tried as hard as I could to avoid her face when I was home from school.

III.13

The summer holidays that year were the gloomiest I had ever known. At any time Uncle's depression was liable to explode in a kind of hopeless fury on anyone he happened to be with. Aunt was perpetually sad, so was Suzue, and even my beloved Mother, who was usually so bright; the only cheerful sound left in the house was the chiming of the wall-clock. And on top of all this melancholy I acquired a marvellous companion—marvellously unwanted, that is. It must have been due to karma, I suppose, his being forced on me in place of the cousin I had so eagerly awaited, who was now beyond hope of homecoming. But to explain.

Inevitably, several relatives the family had normally kept at arm's length turned up for the funeral. Among them I noticed a fat, pockmarked woman of about forty with bobbed hair, running round chattering busily to everybody. She was Mrs Kasamatsu, Mother told me, the widow of a cousin of Uncle's. So this was the widow Kasamatsu. I remembered hearing talk of a woman who had brought up five or six children after her husband's death without touching the quite considerable property he had left her, and who was somehow related to Uncle. Uncle's relatives had scattered all over the country after the Restoration; of the few who stayed on in our part of Kyushu, most were too daunted by Uncle's eccentric personality to want to have much to do with him—so that in all the five years Mother and I had lived in his house I had scarcely met one of them. Most of the time, of course, I was away at school. But the coolness between Uncle and his relatives was obvious, and with Uncle regarding the relatives as vulgar nonentities and the relatives convinced Uncle was slightly mad, the gap between them had grown too wide to be easily bridged.

Worst of all in Uncle's eyes had been 'that squalid boorish pigmy of a man,' his cousin Kasamatsu. They had quarrelled once, and Uncle had struck him on the forehead, leaving a scar he carried for the rest of his life. Nor did Uncle's feelings soften on his cousin's death. 'Like marries like,' he would say of the widow whenever her name was mentioned. 'Look at her—she proves it, if ever anyone did. People say she's thrifty, a hard worker, but look at the rotten stinking humility she puts on whenever there's a chance of making up to anyone with money or power! She's a shameless, unscrupulous woman. If she once gets it into her head that there's something to be got out of me, you'll see how soon she'll come bowing and scraping on my doorstep!' So naturally I took a good look at the widow Kasamatsu when she came for Daiichiro's funeral. It was true: there was something unspeakably revolting in the sharp stare of her eyes, in the peculiar twist of her mouth every time she smiled.

The widow went home, after peering into every room in the house and pouring out a stream of condolences, apologies for having neglected us, and compliments for Miss Suzue. But sure enough, four or five days later she suddenly reappeared, this time with a present. Stationing herself in the living-room she rattled on for the best part of half a day—trumpet-blowing most of the time, two thirds of it a panegyric of her own son Sanjiro, a genius, model of filial affection, etc., etc. Why, when his mother was sick in bed he hadn't undressed for three days and nights; and at the Gentlemen's Academy, where he attended as a dayboy, his papers were marked EXCELLENT in every exam. How he loved his Uncle Noda, to be sure—wasn't he always saying he wished he could have a chance of learning from *him*! The trouble was, his health had suffered from too much study . . . with all his brothers and sisters about the house it was difficult for him to get his strength back. 'Now in a quiet, roomy place like this . . .' After a number of hints of this kind, she finally came out with it more bluntly. 'If he won't be troubling you, then, just for the summer holidays . . .' Uncle was out at the time. Aunt had always been concerned at Uncle's estrangement from his relations, wondering anxiously whether she herself were in any way to blame. Remembering no doubt how fortunate her own Daiichiro's school years had been, she agreed to take the widow Kasamatsu's boy, 'for a while, at any rate.'

Mother smiled sardonically.

Two days later the ailing genius and paragon of filial virtue, Sanjiro Kasamatsu, arrived in person. Convalescing, she had said—I was on the lookout for a pale, thin, pitifully listless boy. The reality was startlingly different. The boy the widow brought was a great, brawny, brown-skinned youth, with a flat nose and bulbous cheeks, already growing his first moustache; at least three inches taller than Suzue, and three or four stone heavier than I, though he was only a year older, I had been told. I looked him over pretty carefully, but couldn't spot anything a layman's eye could take for after-effects of an illness: only a singularly heavy look about the eyes, and whiteish sores at each side of his mouth—overeating, probably.

'Why isn't he sick?' I whispered to Mother.

'Sanjiro? Oh, he's . . .' she said, and stopped, smiling.

III.14

'The boys had better be together. Shintaro won't be so lonely.' I was painfully conscious, very painfully, of Aunt's kind thought in suggesting that Sanjiro should share the four-mat room with me. Still, perhaps it would be as well to be friendly. After showing him where to stow his box, finding him a desk, and generally helping him to settle in, I thought we'd better talk a bit.

'Where's your school?' I asked him.

'School? What school?' The genius looked puzzled.

'The Middle School you go to. It is a Middle School, isn't it?'

'*Middle School*—who'd have anything to do with a stupid place like that? Gentlemen's Academy, that's what I go to.' The 'Gentlemen's Academy' was run by the conservatives, on principles the exact opposite of those of the New School. '*You're* at a Middle School, aren't you?'

His Excellency having honoured me with a question, I replied politely, 'No—the New School.'

'The New—huh!' I could have struck him for the sneer on his face. 'The poor boys' school—where they teach you treason!' The conservatives must have taught him that 'freedom' = disloyalty = treason. I was furious, but said nothing, fighting back the temptation to tell him straight out how stupidly wrong he was. It would hardly do to fight when we'd only just met.

Mandarin trees bear different fruit when moved from south of the Yangtse to the northern provinces, we are told; and it wasn't hard to believe when I saw the change in the widow Kasamatsu's prodigy after a move of two miles from his home to Uncle's. Every morning the overworking student we had heard so much of slept on past breakfast. The clearing of our room was left strictly to me—no sign of him then; he would be sitting cross-legged under a tree in the orchard, nibbling at a persimmon. Most of the day he spent like a good disciple of Tsai Yü,[19] asleep on a mat under the camphor tree behind the house. But by eight o'clock in the evening he would start nodding again, as if he hadn't slept enough already—it may have been his stomach, I daresay; he displayed such ability in putting away his food three times a day as to astonish even Uncle, who was not notably abstemious. Even when he fell asleep at night he would snore (*snort* would be a better word) and mumble and click his teeth. This I wouldn't have minded if he hadn't kept kicking me every five minutes in his sleep, as if I were the Emperor Kuang Wu himself.[20]

As for his passion for learning, he never sat at his desk for an hour together. If Uncle gave him a document to copy, the characters would get all mixed

---

19. Confucius *Analects*, V, 9: 'Tsai Yü used to sleep during the day. The Master said, "Rotten wood cannot be carved, nor a wall of dried dung be trowelled. What use is there in my scolding him any more?"' (*The Analects of Confucius*, tr. Arthur Waley. London, 1938.)

20. Kuang Wu (c. 6 B.C.–A.D. 57), first Emperor of the Later Han dynasty, sent for his old school friend Yen Kuang to come and stay with him. The night Yen arrived, the two friends slept side by side—Yen with his feet on the Emperor's stomach. Next morning, astrologers reported to the Emperor that the untoward movement of Yen's feet had caused a corresponding commotion in the heavens, shooting stars having impiously disturbed the Emperor's own constellation.

up; he would misread the simplest words in the newspaper; if he tried to bring out a proverb to make his talk sound wise, it would be sure to come out as 'Better the tail of a horse than the head of an ass' instead of the other way round. The good grades he was supposed to be getting were a mystery—I didn't know then, though, how many presents the widow showered on the teachers at the Academy. Change the house and you change the man, we say; but not so much as this! Before he had been in the house three days, even Aunt was frowning occasionally.

Now that she had deposited her son with us, the widow Kasamatsu insisted on calling every few days, making a point of visiting Daiichiro's grave and always bringing some favourite dish of Uncle's. Invariably, too, there would be sweet words and a present for Suzue. 'Sanjiro,' she would say, producing a packet of crackers or a box of jam-cakes, 'give this to dear Miss Suzue. You'll share them with Sanjiro, won't you dear?' As for me, it didn't matter if I was sitting right in front of her; she'd pretend I was invisible. When she did notice Mother and me, it was only with glances of contempt, while from the way she spoke, as often as not, she might have been on the point of ordering us out of the house for a couple of useless parasites.

I felt as if something precious deep within me were being trampled on. Often, when we were subjected to her impudent stare and innuendo-laden speeches, I wanted to scream with anger. Mother would only smile; but she was still a proud woman, after all, and more than once I noticed a tell-tale flicker of her eyelids.

I had given up trying to understand why the widow ignored Mother and me and made such a fuss of Uncle and Suzue, till one day Shozo, an old servant of Uncle's I was very friendly with, spoke to me about Sanjiro.

'Listen, Master Shin, sir! That fool boy Sanjiro told me he'd be master here afore long—when that day came, he said, he'd raise me wages —that upstart pig of a boy! "What'll be the good to anyone of *your* being master, I'd like to know," I told him. Look sharp, Master Shin, look sharp!'

III.15

So that was what they were after? That was why the widow always pretended we didn't, or ought not to, exist, why Sanjiro would speak to Suzue without the least reserve, and challenge me ostentatiously in her presence to arm-wrestling or sumo. 'They're like flies, that sort; any juicy smell, and they'll be there. Humble, too, you'll see. Bow themselves flat, if they think it'll pay them'—it was exactly as Uncle had prophesied. With Daiichiro dead and no other child in the family but Suzue, the widow's motive in pushing her son was transparent.

But did Uncle and Aunt and Suzue see through her so clearly? Dazed with grief at his son's death, Uncle had lived in a kind of coma ever since.

His old temper would flare up sometimes for no apparent reason, like thunder out of storm-clouds; such momentary explosions apart, he looked very weary, and slept much of the day. It was while he was in this melancholy state that Master Sanjiro had insinuated himself into the family. Aunt was the kind of person who can love and care for anybody, even this good-for-nothing Sanjiro, to whom she never spoke but with her usual gentle politeness. As for Suzue, with her simple, open nature, it did not seem to have occurred to her that there was anything odd about the behaviour of the widow and her son, or that she herself might be involved; laughing at his jokes, answering his questions, she was as cool and natural as ever. All in all, the family seemed to have no particular objection to harbouring this creature that was sucking at their lifeblood.

Was this really the best attitude for them to take? I, Shintaro Kikuchi—though maybe a boy not yet out of his teens shouldn't have had such a conceit of himself—I couldn't dream of that kind of meanness, sleeping all day long in somebody else's house and thinking of getting at his money. To be frank, Mother and I were unhappy even about our own dependence on the Nodas. Uncle and Aunt showed us nothing but kindness, and the work Mother did for them more than paid for our keep; but if often came home to me, even then, that we couldn't go on accepting their help for ever. Mother, I am sure, thought of nothing else. She said little, but every time she looked at me I could read an unspoken 'Not yet—too young, too young!' in her eyes. With this longing for independence, we couldn't possibly object to any reasonable addition to the Noda family. But for the widow, of all people, to ingratiate herself—this disgusted us both, just because we owed them so much. I hated the way they treated a dunce like Sanjiro no differently from me; and when even Suzue began to show herself less friendly, I couldn't help feeling that Uncle couldn't be so fond of me now as he had been.

On the afternoon of the day old Shozo spoke to me of Sanjiro's ambitions, I was sitting under a cherry-tree reading a book. The first leaves had just started to fall, and the music of autumn insects filled the air. Not being able, alas, to join my more fortunate classmates, who had gone off on a tour of Kyushu with our beloved Komai Sensei, I was determined to work at my English during the holiday; and at this particular moment I was battling my way with the aid of a dictionary through the chapter on the French Revolution in Swinton's *History of England*. I had just started on the guillotining of the king, when a hand tugged sharply at my right ear.

'Hey!' It was Sanjiro. A casting-net thrown over his shoulder, he was holding out a creel.

'Come on, we're going fishing. Up you get, creel-boy!'—knocking the creel against my head. Just then I caught a glimpse of a white patterned kimono with a red sash at the kitchen window—Cousin Suzue, surely. My right fist struck at the creel he was dangling.

'Told you I wasn't coming, didn't I?' The sudden shrillness of my voice astonished me. Sanjiro looked thunderstruck, which was not surprising: there being no chance of my beating a boy his size in a fight, discretion had kept me patient till now, and several times already I had carried his creel for him, however reluctantly. But gradually the expression of amazement on his loutish face gave way to a bullying smile.

'When I say come, you'll come! Don't you ever obey your elders?'

'I needn't go if I don't like.' My ears burned.

'You won't come, huh?' Closing in suddenly, he grabbed my arm. Suzue appeared at the kitchen door; I thought she looked frightened.

'No!'

'Oh, yes, you—' He threw me on my face. Picking myself up, I flung myself at his heavy frame. The Bastille itself was not more solidly built than Master Sanjiro.

III.16

A Transvaal is no match for an England in this world of ours. The older as well as the bigger boy, Sanjiro threw me again and again. Black in the face, I made a frantic grab at his feet; we rolled together on the stony, uneven ground—gravel in my eyes, a girl's scream in my ears, blood streaming into my mouth from my nose. Eventually, to my chagrin, he managed to straddle my stomach, so that I couldn't move, and started punching my head. Unable to hit back, I bit savagely at the nearest flesh—arm or thigh, I don't know which it was—my teeth crunched into his soft skin.

'A—a—a—a—!' He jerked his head back, bellowing with pain. Even my half-blinded eyes caught the new fury in his face—and then the storm broke in a mad cascade of blows on my face, arms, body. This I couldn't survive. Clenching my teeth, I waited: 'Shintaro Kikuchi, died in battle, aged 16 . . .'

'A—ah!' Sanjiro had rolled off me, screaming. I jumped up, rubbing my eyes. It was Uncle. Beside himself with anger, he had brought down his cherry-wood stick on Sanjiro's back. Instantly Sanjiro threw himself at Uncle. The shock must have made him lose his head.

'Raise your hand against me, would you—you fool!' Uncle thundered, as if he were charging an enemy army. Past fifty he might be, but it wasn't for nothing he had once shown his disapproval of the provincial governor, a muscular giant of a man, by kicking him down a corridor. He had scarcely lifted his foot when Sanjiro was rolling away like a football.

'What on earth—' Aunt had come running out before he could repeat the dose. 'Do *you* have to join in when the boys quarrel? Shintaro—your nose! Fetch a bowl of water, Suzue—quickly, no dawdling! But where's Master Sanjiro?' We looked round in surprise—but he had vanished; Uncle might have kicked Sanjiro to kingdom come for all we could see of him. After washing my face and stuffing paper up my nose to stop the bleeding, I walked, not very steadily, back to the living-room, where the family were discussing where he could have gone. Aunt was anxious. There was no knowing what he might do after such a humiliation, she insisted, ordering the servants to search the bamboo thickets and look down the well. Uncle smacked his lips contemptuously. 'Don't be silly—he hasn't the guts to kill himself. He's hiding somewhere—or maybe he's run home. We're well rid of a pesty nuisance. Any damage, Shin boy?' If I was hurt, it wasn't serious. But there was no trace of Sanjiro, and we agreed he must have gone home, as Uncle had said. Aunt was quite upset. Perhaps she should go to the widow's to enquire? Uncle only laughed, and told her to forget it.

Mother was out that afternoon. She didn't scold me when she heard what had happened. In fact I think she was hoping that Sanjiro's mother might call, so that she could give her, at last, a piece of her mind; but the widow didn't show up. Not in person, that is: a letter came, though, a most extraordinary document. After thanking Uncle ceremoniously for having looked after her Dear Son for so long, she described how on a certain day the said Dear Son had come home in tears, minus his sandals and wearing only a singlet and pants (his fishing outfit); and finished by assuring Uncle her Dear Son would treasure the tooth-marks on his forearm and the bruises on his back as proof of the family's kindness, etc., etc. There was an old saying, was there not, she added in a postscript, about 'letting the wife's relatives have their way,/Sure recipe for a family's decay'—but she was sure *she*, at least, wished for nothing but prosperity for the Noda family all their days ... We couldn't help laughing at the thought of that big baby of seventeen arriving home in tears, barefoot and half-undressed, though we were sorry for him too. I didn't feel any hate or envy for Sanjiro now. But it was not altogether unpleasant to find out after this upheaval that Uncle's affection for me was as strong as it had ever been.

Obviously I could not fill the void Daiichiro's death had left in Uncle's heart. Nor could Suzue. Daiichiro apart, though, it was I he liked best, after his daughter. But the dead are beyond recall; and gradually, as time softened his grief, I felt his love for me increase. 'Don't work too hard, Shin boy! What good will all that study do you if you kill yourself with learning, eh?' he would say when he found me deep in a book, and drag me off for a walk; father and son, a stranger seeing us out together might have thought.

As Uncle showed himself more openly affectionate, so a shadow fell across Mother's face.

III.17

Soon after I had gone back to school for the autumn term of 1883, I had some very distressing news. Uncle had been arrested. Alarmed, I went home at once and was told the details. Among Uncle's fellow-members of the Prefectural Assembly was a certain Kuroki, whom he had long detested. At a recent dinner party attended by the Governor and most of the Assemblymen, the two of them had fallen into an argument which grew more and more heated, till Uncle, completely losing his temper, flew at Kuroki and kicked him out of his seat, battering him savagely with feet and fists, while the company were still rubbing their eyes in astonishment. When the Governor tried to restrain him, Uncle had angrily accused him of partiality—and punched him in the face ... Pandemonium followed; it was an hour or more, I gathered, before order was restored. The Governor, very sensibly, had decided to overlook this violence of Uncle's, but Kuroki, a spiteful, scheming individual of the kind Uncle loathed, was taking the matter to court.

Fortunately, as a result of the good offices of Uncle's friends, including Komai Sensei and other teachers of the New School, and a tactful visit by Aunt and Mother to Kuroki's wife, a letter of apology was sent (without Uncle's knowledge) to Kuroki, who then withdrew his charges. I went with a rickshaw to fetch Uncle from the jail, where he had been detained for a week pending trial. At first, so we heard afterwards, he had stormed around his cell, still in the same blazing temper, but after a day or two, he had quietened down and slept most of the time, ordering delicacies from outside when he woke up with the same grand manner with which he had demanded boiled eels when a prisoner in the camp of the Satsuma rebels, guarded by the naked swords of samurai.

His release without even a magistrate's hearing, when he had been convinced he would have to face imprisonment or at least a fine, aroused Uncle's suspicions.

'Have you been meeting Kuroki?' he asked Aunt and Mother as soon as he got home.

'No,' replied Aunt.

'You haven't, of course', ominously, 'sent him an apology?'

'Certainly not!' Mother declared emphatically.

'Hard to see why the scoundrel didn't proceed, though,' he said, half to himself, while staring distrustfully at the two women.

'The Governor and everybody else have been very helpful,' Aunt interposed.

'What about the Governor?' said Uncle sharply, his temper rising.

'It's quite simple. When the Governor heard Mr Kuroki was going to court, he sent for him and told him not to be so silly—who on earth would be so stupid as to start a court case just because he'd been struck once or twice by a distinguished public figure like Mr Noda? He'd much better drop the charge, and apologize to Mr Noda into the bargain—that was the Governor's advice,' Mother lied brazenly. It was laughable, really—but there was something oddly pathetic too about Uncle's worn, anxious face, reminding one of Lien P'o[21] when he was finally rejected by the ambassador of Chao.

Uncle was silent for a moment. Then with a smack of the lips, 'The Governor's an interfering fool!' he burst out. 'If he hadn't butted in, I'd have trampled the life out of that miserable Kuroki, and good riddance too!'

Soon afterwards Uncle resigned from the Assembly, so that now his time was all his own. Saying he'd better 'study a bit', now that he was at leisure, he consulted with Komai Sensei, and ordered a lot of translations of foreign works from Tokyo, but men of his heroic mould don't take easily to books: Lieber's *Self-government*, Spenser's *Principles of Ethics* and other tomes remained untouched on Uncle's desk.

Not long after Uncle's affair with Kuroki, which was painful enough even to me, in spite of my tender years, my schoolfellows and I were startled to hear that Komai Sensei was to leave us.

III.18

Not that we had ever imagined he would stay permanently at the New School; but no one had dreamed of his going so soon. Surely our Komai Sensei, whom we so loved and respected as teacher and a second father to us all, would share our lives for some years yet, guiding us, staying at our side until at least our wings were a little stronger: so we had believed, with the faith of the young. Our disappointment was the greater, therefore, when it got about that he had resigned, and would soon be returning to his native town. It wasn't because he had wearied of the School, or that the School had wearied of him; he was worried about his aged father, whom he had left behind at the family home in Tosa. His elder brother was there to look after him, but Komai Sensei himself must have been the favourite son; and when letters began to come from the elder brother describing in detail how the old man (who was in poor health now and could not have much longer to live) had been asking urgently for his younger son, Komai Sensei decided he must pack his bag and leave as soon as possible. He would come back, he assured us, once he had seen for himself how his father was, and join us again in study, for we were as dear to him as brothers, or as children of his own. But we knew somehow, all of us, that this parting was to be final.

The evening before he left we gave a supper party for him, not a formal farewell party, but just a small sign of our gratitude for all he had meant to us. Besides the guest of honour, we invited my Uncle, and all the staff of

---

21. A Chinese general of the 3rd century B.C. To prove to an envoy of the State of Chao that old age had not rendered him unfit for campaigning, Lien P'o is said to have consumed twenty pounds of rice and ten pounds of meat at one sitting, in the presence of the envoy. But impressive though this demonstration of prowess must have been, he was prevented by the intrigues of an old enemy from being chosen by Chao to lead the campaign in question.

the School too. Having agreed to Komai Sensei's appointment only under pressure, the other teachers had been suspicious at first, watching anxiously the changes he introduced: but in time his enthusiasm touched even their rigid, crusty minds, turning them into surprisingly fervent advocates of freedom, so that now they were truly sorry to see him go. Uncle Noda was the most disappointed of all; Komai Sensei's success had been a source of personal pride, a vindication of his first favourable judgement.

After opening remarks from Kitagawa Sensei, a short-sighted, bespectacled teacher of no great presence who had been chosen as Acting Principal in succession to Komai Sensei, the party continued with speeches of thanks from a number of students. When it came to the turn of the juniors, Asai spoke first; then I read out from a Grateful Address I had composed: 'To Komai Sensei, our honoured and beloved teacher and father . . .'—no sooner had I begun than my voice faltered, my eyes grew misty; for some moments I couldn't go on. Normally, I suppose, an audience would merely laugh at such a display of weakness. But not on this occasion: the only reaction was a still deeper silence, so completely did every boy share the emotion I was feeling. More speeches followed from the staff, till finally Komai Sensei himself rose to reply.

He began by thanking the staff for having entrusted him, an outsider from a distant province, with the great responsibility of Principal, and for having given him also complete freedom to put his ideas into practice. He was grateful to the students, too, who had accepted him so readily in spite of his youth and lack of experience and unfamiliarity with their part of the world, and followed so loyally his poor attempt to guide them in their studies. For the time being, at least, he was forced to leave—but with the resolve to return one day, if ever it were possible, to serve once more the School he had grown to love. Truly, he went on, he had found himself among kindred spirits. 'Heart is won by heart,' the proverb says; we had surely won his, and for his part, wherever life might take him, he would never for a single day cease to treasure the memory of each one of us, his friends—indeed, he would die for us, if death were the best service he could give. Komai Sensei broke down as he spoke these words. An electric current seemed to strike through every listening student. Some wept openly, some gritted their teeth and hid their faces, some hurriedly brushed tears away with a clenched fist: not one head but was bent with the shock and sadness of losing such a Sensei.

Wiping his own tears, Komai Sensei resumed on a different note. Each of us must go forward, he urged us solemnly, as a soldier of truth, resolved upon reform, never yielding to temptation, never succumbing to the commonplace, the conventional; preserving as long as we lived the eager student spirit and a true concern for the welfare of society, so that all about us would recognize us as worthy graduates of this School . . . We straightened up again, pride in our School and ourselves renewed.

After the speeches, the feast—a stew of our own cooking—a performance of the sword-dance, and finally, the triumphal entry of enormous basketfuls of steamed potatoes, a gift, apparently, from Uncle. So for a while we made merry, and forgot the pain of parting.

Next morning, Komai Sensei started out on his journey home, escorted by a crowd of students. Yet as the Chinese poem says, 'Though I go with you a thousand li, the moment of parting must surely come,' and between two and three miles from the School, where two huge nettle-trees overhang the road, one on either side, he climbed into the rickshaw he had ordered, wished us godspeed, and waved his hat in a last farewell.

I turned away, a sudden lump in my throat. They were all shouting something, I didn't hear clearly what. When I looked down the road a moment later, the rickshaw was a hundred yards or more away, but Komai Sensei was still looking round and waving. We waved back like madmen. The rickshaw gradually grew smaller, till it turned with the road and disappeared.

III.19

Komai Sensei's departure left the New School with no more life than the cinders of a burnt-out fire. We had always admired him, but even so it was a shock to find how empty the School seemed now that he had gone. Classes went on as usual, in the same subjects; the wheels of the machine turned as smoothly as before. But the place was a dead shell. Kitagawa Sensei (Mr Myope, we called him) struggled valiantly on, alternately scolding and exhorting; he was bitterly ashamed, on his own and the School's behalf, that things had deteriorated so quickly—but it was useless. Before the week was out we were yawning openly in class. Any hopes we may have had of Komai Sensei's early return were shown to be wishful thinking by a letter that came from Sensei himself about a month later, in which he told us sadly that there seemed to be little chance of his rejoining us in the near future—he would never come back, in other words. Every self-respecting young man must stand on his own feet, he reminded us at the end of his letter. Only the small-minded would depend on others for achievement. That we should develop and keep the true spirit of self-respect and independence—this was his earnest wish for all of us at the New School: on the analogy, I suppose, of the lion abandoning its cubs to test their power of survival. If so, we certainly didn't thank Komai Sensei for choosing this method of training.

Not long afterwards I had a letter from my old schoolfriend, Seima Matsumura, who was now studying in Tokyo. Most of the boys I had known at Seizan Sensei's I hadn't kept up with; but Matsumura was different. For three years we had never stopped writing to each other, though there were 750 miles between us now. I would send him glowing descriptions of how exciting a place the New School had become under Komai

Sensei; he would pour scorn on schools 'out there in the backwoods', urging me to come to Tokyo as quickly as possible; I would work up a passionate defence, he would renew the attack as passionately—and so on, the arguments flying back and forth so furiously that sometimes one of us would lose his temper and announce that he wasn't writing any more, this was the end of our friendship, etc., etc. But friends who really suit each other don't give up so easily, and after a few weeks' silence we would be at it again. So we had gone on for three years, patching up every quarrel, as close friends now as ever we had been before Matsumura left home.

In the letter I was speaking of he wrote that he had graduated from Middle School and expected soon to start the preparatory course for entering the University. As usual, he asked why I was still 'mooching about down there in the country': if only I'd make up my mind and come to Tokyo, school-fees would be no problem—he himself would be glad to help me out, he added, sounding suddenly grown-up and protective. All of which he had said many times before, but this time, coming as it did when Komai Sensei's departure had drained the life out of the New School, the invitation read like a gospel direct from heaven. To Tokyo—why, of course! Now that there was no prospect of Komai Sensei's returning, what could be more absurd than to waste one's precious youth in a school as dead as any corpse? A man must make his own way in the world—make up his own mind and not depend on others—had not Komai Sensei told us just that? Hadn't he himself worked as a school cleaner to help pay for his own fees? Fees didn't amount to much, anyway, less than five yen a month ... I must, I *must* go to Tokyo! I couldn't wait any longer, so I cut my afternoon classes the day after I got the letter from Matsumura and went home to talk it over with Mother.

She listened in silence while I poured out my plan, breathless with excitement.

'How do you propose to pay your school fees?'

'School fees? Oh, I'll work—as a cleaner, or houseboy, or something.'

Mother looked thoughtfully at my diminutive figure, a faint shadow crossing her face.

'I haven't told you before, but I've managed to put away a little, for emergencies and the like—if only we were back in the old days, though!'

Mother wept a little; a woman still, for all her courage and resilience.

'No, Mother, I've decided I won't depend on anybody. I'm sure to find some way of paying.'

Mother looked me in the face; relieved, seemingly, by the determination in my voice.

'If your mind is made up, I can give you the money for the journey, and enough to keep you for two or three months after you get to Tokyo. After that—you're sure you'll not be a burden to anybody?'

'I'm a man, Mother.'

'Not even to your Uncle?'

'Not to anybody, Mother.'

She nodded, for the first time. 'Come with me, then. We must talk it over with your Uncle.'

Just then Suzue came out of a room at the back of the house. She looked after us, surprised, as we walked together down the corridor to Uncle's room.

III.20

Uncle seemed to sense there was something unusual in the air the moment we entered the room. Putting down his paper and taking off his glasses, the enormous glasses he had taken to wearing in the last year, he looked up at us enquiringly.

'I was wondering if I might have a talk with you about Shintaro . . .' Mother began.

'About Shin, is it? H'm.' Uncle stared at me.

'It would be a pity to keep him here in the country all through his school years; and it's wrong, too, that we should go on depending on you like this. I think it's time I sent him to Tokyo to study.'

Instead of rejecting the idea there and then, as I had expected, Uncle nodded vigorously. 'You're quite right. I've been thinking of it myself. No point in his staying at school here now Komai's gone. Let's see, the boy's sixteen, isn't he—the same age as Suzue? Time he went off now. But what does he propose to do in Tokyo? What do you want to be, eh, Shin boy?'

I wanted to study politics, I said, and become a politician. Not that I really knew what politics was, or what a politician was, for that matter: having a vague notion, inspired by Komai Sensei, of doing some great work for the country, I assumed that to serve one's country one *had* to become a politician. And how did one become a politician if not by studying politics?

Uncle was silent for a while. If the proposal was vague, precision had never been Uncle's strong point, either, but years count for something: he must have been considering the practical details, I suppose.

'I'm inclined to think Hokkaido Agricultural College would suit you. How would that be?' he said, to both Mother and me.

That summer, Uncle had had a visit from a student, or he may have been a graduate, of the Hokkaido College, an eloquent young man with a loud, confident voice, by whom he had obviously been impressed. But the idea of *my* going there was so sudden, I didn't know what to say.

'Don't you like the idea of an Agricultural College? No reason to turn up your nose at it, you know. You say you want to be a politician, but if every boy like you went in for politics, Japan would starve. Much better get a good training in agriculture, then start up a farm or business on your own; there's no telling how much good you'd be doing that way. Japan's a farming country, after all. Agricultural College—that's the place for you, Shin boy, that's the place.' Warming rapidly to the theme, Uncle launched into a harangue on the importance of agriculture as the foundation of the nation's prosperity, till it began to sound as if the future of Japanese farming depended solely on Shintaro Kikuchi. But why I should have to go all the way to Hokkaido, and just to learn farming at that, I could not see. I glanced at Mother; it was obvious she disliked the scheme. A woman with her fierce pride could never be content to let her only son end up as a mere Bachelor of Agriculture.

For a few moments after Uncle had finished, none of us spoke. Uncle seemed to be thinking still.

'As a matter of fact, there's something else,' he said at last. 'Something I've been wanting to talk over with O-Setsu; and now that Shin is here too—Suzue! are you there, Suzue?' Her pale face appeared instantly in the doorway. Had she been waiting there?

'Where's your mother?'

'In the kitchen.'

'Ask her to come here a minute—and then go into the other room and stay there.'

Mother's expression altered slightly.

III.21

'What do you think, O-Jitsu? Shin here says he wants to go and study in Tokyo,' said Uncle as soon as Aunt appeared. She was wiping her hands on her apron.

'To study in Tokyo?' said Aunt, looking anxiously at Mother and me. Since Daiichiro's death she had been easily upset, and was often in tears. My going to Tokyo, she seemed to imagine, meant going to my death.

'To Tokyo. And now that he's had this idea, I'm wondering whether it mightn't be a good time to mention that matter you and I were talking of, O-Jitsu. What d'you think?' Uncle went on, taking no notice of her distress.

'By all means,' replied Aunt, her eyes on my mother.

'Well, then,' Uncle began, straightening up in his chair, 'I'd like you to hear the plan I've been thinking of, O-Setsu-san and Shintaro. Now that Daiichiro has gone, there's only Suzue left, and that means we're bound to adopt a boy to take Daiichiro's place. But who? That's the question, and a big question it is. Much better settle on a boy we've had in our home since he was twelve and know so well, he's like a son to us already, than waste time looking around outside. If we can leave the house and property to Shintaro when the time comes, and he's willing to take Suzue for his wife, it'll all be settled inside the family, and O-Jitsu and I will have no more to worry about. What'd'you think of that, O-Setsu-san? And you too, Shintaro?'

My heart was thumping violently, and my ears tingled. Mother looked pale but determined, as if confronted suddenly by a quagmire whose existence she had long suspected. For a moment she said nothing. Then, clearing her throat,

'Is it your intention that Shintaro should take the name of Noda?' she asked in a rather formal way.

'That doesn't matter so much. We want him to keep the family going, and that's the main thing, isn't it, O-Jitsu?' said Uncle, turning to Aunt for confirmation.

'It may seem strange to you, O-Setsu-san, that we should talk of adopting Shintaro when he is your only son,' Aunt said more diplomatically, 'but since we are both in the same position, with just the one child each, wouldn't it be better for both families to combine, instead of our adopting someone we'd know nothing about? And fortunately Suzue and Shintaro are such good friends.' The more my ears burned, the paler Mother grew.

'You do us a great honour in suggesting that Shintaro should be your heir,' Mother began slowly, each word taut and hard, like the teeth of a hacksaw. 'And we both owe you so much for your kindness in giving us a home here that no doubt we ought to accept at once. But this boy is the last of the Kikuchis . . . you know the ruin that came to us under the last holder of the name. His father begged me just before he died that if I did nothing else I should bring this boy up to restore the Kikuchis to what they once were.' Mother wept a little, but only for a moment, and went on as before: 'So I want him to keep his father's name, and give the family a home again—a hovel or a shack, anything, if it can only be our own.'

'But how would it be if Shintaro were to inherit this property, and have a child of *his* take the name of Kikuchi, when the time came? You wouldn't object to that?'

Mother was silent for a while. 'There's no telling how boy-and girl friendships will develop. Whatever we decide now, these two may feel quite differently when they're grown up; and it'll be ten years before we know what Shintaro's future is going to be. But what does he think himself?'

I understood Mother's expression perfectly. She didn't dislike Suzue, but nor was she especially fond of her: inevitably her brisk, alert temperament clashed with Suzue's easy-going nature. Nor was she unappreciative of the kindness behind the proposal; but she did loathe the idea of having her only child depend so absolutely on Uncle's goodwill.

'Well, what about it, Shin boy?' I could see the anger in Uncle's eyes. Komai Sensei's plea flashed into my mind—*only the small-minded would depend on others for achievement* . . . Till then I had said nothing: suddenly the words came of themselves, unasked—

'I love Uncle. I love Aunt. I like Suzue-san very much. *But I would hate to be Uncle's heir!*'

III.22

Years afterwards I attended lectures on rhetoric and learnt how even the simplest inversion of a phrase or two, or the most insignificant-seeming alteration in the wording, can drastically alter the effect of a statement. 'You may have a good point there, but this—this is really bad' makes quite a different impression from 'You may be mistaken there, but this—this is really good.' But a child doesn't make such distinctions. As far as I was concerned, I had merely said truthfully what I thought; so I was startled when I saw the effect my words had on Uncle. Already irritated by Mother's refusal, he lost his temper altogether when I added my own flat rejection, unwrapped in any of the customary polite verbiage grown-ups use.

'Who do you think you're talking to, the pair of you? Taisaku Noda is Taisaku Noda still, I can tell you, for all he's had to go through! I'm gentle with you, out of respect to a widow and her child; and you have the impudence, do you, to stand up and say you'd hate to be my heir! What right do you have to talk like that, when you'd have starved but for me these five years?'

Mother smiled bitterly. 'We have much to thank you for. We know that. When Shintaro comes of age he will repay you for your kindness; and all these years I have been trying to repay what little I could.' Uncle knew very well how much Mother had done for his household ever since we arrived. But the knowledge only infuriated him the more.

'Silence! Just because you've helped a bit you're trying to make out you owe me nothing—never heard of such insolence!' His rage finding no outlet, for some moments his mouth jerked violently behind his beard.

'Get out!' he roared suddenly, to a rattling of the sliding door and windows.

Mother smiled—so placidly, that but for the gleam in her eyes she might have been enjoying Uncle's outburst as if it were a delectable fragment of melody on the harp or flute.

'If we are a burden to you, we are ready to leave at any time.'

'Insolence!' Trembling with anger, Uncle stood up—but Aunt forestalled him.

'Need you be quite so—hard?'

'Hard? What d'you mean, hard?' Uncle towered over Aunt, glaring down at her like one of those awesome-looking statues you find on guard outside Buddhist temples.

'Can't you be a little more gentle with them? And weren't you perhaps a little too abrupt, O-Setsu? Surely we need to think more carefully about the whole idea. Why don't we let it be for a while, and talk it over again later when we've had time to consider?' With a restraining hand on Uncle's shoulder, and soothing glances at Mother, Aunt did her best to lower the temperature. Uncle stood without speaking for a moment; then strode out of the room.

A melancholy silence. Aunt sighed. 'It was my fault, O-Setsu-san. I'd been meaning to speak to you about it, just the two of us together, but I put it off and put it off. It's not the kind of decision you can make all at once, though. Shintaro, you'd better get back to school for today, anyway, and we'll see about having another talk later. Stay a moment: that tear in your sleeve—' She mended the tear herself before she would let me go.

After saying goodbye to a silent Mother and a worried Aunt, I left the house, but hadn't gone more than fifty yards when I heard hands clapping behind me. It was Aunt. She beckoned to me to come back. When I came up with her she drew me to one side of the road, and said in a low voice,

'Shintaro! Uncle and Aunt really are as fond of you as we were of Daiichiro—you know that, don't you? Don't be upset because Uncle was so angry just now. He's keen for you to go away to study. Let's have a talk about that soon, shall we? Don't get wild because of what's happened, will you? Promise?' With quick fingers she tightened my sash where it had come loose.

Respectfully I said goodbye.

III.23

My goodbye was respectful enough, but inside the threads were well and truly tangled. 'Uncle', 'Aunt', 'Suzue', 'Noda family', 'the Kikuchis', 'inheritance', 'adoption', 'Agricultural College', 'Tokyo', 'so much to thank you for', 'don't be upset'—a host of such words and names jostling in my mind, I was angry, thrilled, sad, indignant, and hopeless all at once. My feet were carrying me steadily along the road back to school; my mind stumbled, caught in a matted growth of feelings I could not clearly understand. One thing stood out: I had come to a turning-point in my life. If I agreed to what Uncle wanted, it was simple: I had only to say 'yes', and the future would be smooth and easy. But that would be the end of Shintaro Kikuchi; the name Kikuchi would simply not exist any more. And wasn't that as much as to say he would have thrown away his honour, his title to respect as a man? That was why (though shyness may have had something to do with it too, I suppose) I had rejected Uncle's proposal to his face. Should I stick to what I had said? Uncle had been furious: probably he would be just as mad if I held out against him the next time he spoke about it. But supposing he didn't get angry, which was hard to believe—suppose he and Aunt didn't take it so badly; even then, if Mother and I were going to go against his wishes, we couldn't stay on in his house, accepting his hospitality. 'Let's talk it over again later,' Aunt had said. But what difference would two or three days make?

Whatever should I do? Suddenly those words of Komai Sensei's, 'the strong man does not depend on others,' took on new meaning, and with them Aunt's plea 'not to get mad'. 'To get mad'—what might that mean? Maybe that was the only way out after all . . . I began to think of running away.

If I stayed, there would only be more confusion, and with Uncle so angry life would be very awkward for Mother. If on the other hand I were to slip quietly away—the whole question of adoption would soon be forgotten, Uncle and Aunt would come to see things differently, and Mother's position would be less embarrassing. What better way of achieving my own ambition—to study in Tokyo—while at the same time breaking free of dependence on Uncle and his family? 'I'll go, I *will* go,' I muttered to myself. When? 'Swift movement was ever a grand principle of strategy'[22] —so the sooner I went the better, before the complications began. Tomorrow morning! My mind was made up. I'd need to go home, then, to say a quick goodbye to Mother, though not to the Nodas. I turned and walked back five or six paces. But supposing she wouldn't let me go? Much better carry it through without telling either her or Uncle, then Uncle wouldn't suspect her of having anything to do with my 'escape'. 'Strong men have their tears, but shed them not at parting': painful though it was to have to abandon Mother without even a goodbye, I turned my back resolutely on Uncle's house.

The winter light had faded into evening by the time I got back to School. Money for the journey was my first problem. All the way to Tokyo —I should need ten yen, at least. Mother would surely have let me have that much, if I had asked her, but now I was running away, without leave or warning, it wouldn't be so simple. Fortunately I had in my desk nearly four yen, which I had been saving up to buy an English-Japanese dictionary, and a few old books and clothes. As inconspicuously as I could, I called to the cook, who was a good friend of mine, and asked him to take the books and clothes down to the shops and get what he could for them—I needed money in a hurry, I told him, to pay back a debt that was due that night. He agreed, and came back in two hours with just over two yen. He'd pawned the things, he said: it would be such a pity to sell them. If only he *had* sold them, I thought. But I couldn't tell him the real reason I needed the money, besides which two yen was a lot better than nothing, so I took it gratefully. Just under six yen in all. Walk to the coast, though, instead of riding a rickshaw, bottom class on the boat, eat nothing but rice all the way, sleep in the cheapest inns, or in the open if necessary—and six yen, I reckoned, should get me to the capital.

Thus provided with money, I began to think of the messages I should leave behind. I looked round the dormitory. It was well into the night by now; most of my comrades were fast asleep and snoring, though here and there a few desk-lamps still burned, like the last stars left in a dawn sky.

22. The maxim appears in this form in the *San Kuo Chih Yen I*, or *The Romance of the Three Kingdoms*, the cycle of stories dealing with the anarchic years following the collapse of the Han Empire in A.D. 189.

First I wrote to Mother, apologizing for my unfilial conduct in leaving her without a word, explaining why it had to be so, and begging her to take great care of herself till the day when I had accomplished what I was now about to begin, and came home to fetch her . . . I cried a good deal as I was writing, in spite of myself, but managed to finish the letter and seal it. Just as I was starting a note to Uncle, 'Kikuchi!' a voice called suddenly. I looked up, startled. It was Asai, peering down over the bookcase to the right of my desk.

'What are you writing, Kikuchi? Show me. What d'you need to hide it for, huh? Been crying, haven't you? Your eyes are all red!'

To fend him off, I told him I was replying to a letter from a friend in Tokyo inviting me to join him there, adding for good measure that I'd been crying because it made me so miserable having to say no.

'Truly, I'd like to go to Tokyo, too. Precious lot of inspiration any of us are ever likely to get from old Myope, curse him. Oh yes, I wish *I* could shift to Tokyo. If only Komai Sensei would come back, though . . . "Cold whistles the wind across the River Yi/And bleak indeed are our country's fortunes;/But steadfast yet my spirit breasts the wind/As now I leave you—never to return!"'[23] he intoned in his most musical voice, and—to my relief—went off to bed. Lowering the wick of my lamp, I went on writing to Uncle. ' "The gentleman will never speak ill of others, even of those from whom he must part", and I too, though in small measure, have studied the Way of the gentleman,' I began ceremoniously, aping Yüeh I,[24] and went on, in a hurried jumble of phrases, to assure him of my gratitude, declare my longing for independence, and plead that Mother should not suffer because of my action. Lastly I addressed a short note to 'all my schoolfriends', explaining that I had been compelled to leave in secret for the capital and asking them to deliver the other letter to Mr Noda. Mother's letter I put in with Uncle's, and left the two envelopes in my desk drawer.

Everyone was asleep now. Stealthily I tied up my bundle, then crawled into bed, thinking it best not to leave till nearer dawn—but not to sleep, of course; I lay there quietly, wideawake and with heart racing, listening to the snoring and clacking of teeth all round me, and thinking . . .

An hour or so later a cock crew in the next village beyond the School. Creeping out of bed, I shouldered my bundle and picked my way by the faint glimmer of my oil-lamp, over a confusion of sprawling limbs, my legs trembling at every step. A yard or two from the top of the staircase—I

23. From the 'Farewell Song' sung by Ching K'o (?–227 B.C.) before setting out on an unsuccessful attempt to assassinate the King of Ch'in, afterwards first ruler of the centralized Chinese empire.

24. A Chinese general and statesman of the 3rd century B.C. After serving Chao, King of Yen, loyally for many years, Yüeh was dismissed by Hui, Chao's successor, and left the country—only to receive a letter from Hui some time later begging him to return and rescue Yen from its enemies. It is from Yüeh's courteous letter of refusal that Shintaro is borrowing his ceremonial phrases.

must have grown careless, I suppose, thinking I was safe already—I trod on a leg.

'Ouch!' The owner of the leg jumped out of bed, but too late to see me: streaking down the stairs, I had hidden in a corner at the bottom.

'Who was that—clumsy idiot!' a voice growled sleepily from upstairs. But there was no sign of his coming down. Breathing again, I slipped on my clogs and stepped outside.

It was still quite dark. Over the roof of the school building hung the dull golden bow of a dying moon. I ran across the school grounds, the frost crackling under my feet, and for half a mile or so down the road without looking round, terrified that they were after me already. Then I slowed down a bit; and felt in my face the rasping cold of the dawn wind. Suddenly I remembered I had left behind the umbrella I had put out ready, and the bag of riceballs the cook had made for my supper . . . I stopped; shook my head, and walked on.

By the time I reached the big nettle-trees where we had seen Komai Sensei off a month before, the eastern sky was beginning to lighten. I tightened my cloth belt, a last preparation for the long walk ahead; though come to that, I wasn't particularly well prepared for any kind of journey. The lined kimono I was wearing, a *haori* coat, a cheap white cotton belt for a sash, a pair of Satsuma clogs, an old black cap, a towel stuck in my belt; the six precious yen that were to take me to Tokyo wrapped in an old sash and wound round my stomach under my kimono, the purse my mother had given me with fifty sen in copper coins, in my sleeve; another old sash slung over my shoulder with a dark blue kimono Mother had made me for New Year tied on one end, and on the other, to balance the kimono, an odd volume of Macaulay's *Essays* (a present from Komai Sensei) together with one or two other books; a piece of bamboo picked up on the road to serve as a stick in place of the umbrella I'd left behind—such was the grand inventory of my equipment.

I stopped as I was passing the nettle-trees. What would be the upshot of Shintaro Kikuchi's great expedition? Success or disaster? Would he achieve his goal, or come home in rags and shame? Supposing I can land a stone on that great wen on the tree trunk over there, I thought—that would prophesy success, or failure if I missed. I picked up a stone, aimed carefully, and threw it. It didn't even graze the tree. I tried again from two or three steps nearer, with a bigger stone. Result as before. Furious, I marched up to the tree, grabbed a piece of rock as big as my head, and dashed it against the wen I'd been aiming at. No mistake this time: a gash across the wen, and three inches of bark torn off. Feeling better, I wiped the dirt off my hands and continued my journey.

The sun would be up any minute now. I walked on briskly towards the golden glow in the east, resolved to make my way to Tokyo, the Eastern Capital—to the sun itself, if need be, given but a road beneath my feet!

Part IV

It was on December 23, 1883 that I ran away from my second home in the Kyushu castle-town and set out on the road to Tokyo. My plan was to walk to the port of Beppu in Bungo Province, cross by boat to Osaka, and on from there to Yokohama either by boat again if my money lasted, or else by Shanks's mare. Beppu first, at all events.

I was miserable enough the first day, thinking of Mother left all alone. I couldn't stop worrying either about whether they would send anyone after me. Every clip-clop of a pack-horse in the distance behind me made me shiver, and at the little post-inn in the mountains where I slept that night I wrote a false name in the register, carefully disguising my handwriting. But from the second day I took more calmly to the prospect of my long journey. There seemed no chance of being overtaken now, for one thing, and my straw sandals were easier on my feet. I had started out in big Satsuma clogs, but the thongs snapped after six or seven miles, so I changed to sandals at a roadside tea-stall, and left the clogs with the old woman who kept them in payment for my tea. It was a solitary road I took, running among mountains and bare wintry moors; but with so many—too many—thoughts for company, I did not feel lonely. When I recalled that Komai Sensei had been this way, even the stony road seemed somehow familiar and friendly.

I imagined how astonished Matsumura would be when I dropped in at his lodgings in Tokyo and clapped him on the shoulder with a 'Here I am—I've made it!' What of Uncle and Aunt and Cousin Suzue—it was just about now they would be learning of my disappearance? And Mother: the news would be a shock to her at first, but secretly she would be pleased, I knew. What a noise my schoolmates would make! 'How's that for daring!' they'd be saying to each other admiringly. What was that line from a western poet Komai Sensei had quoted to us once, something about 'while others sleep, the hero to the summit crawls'? Hadn't I too stolen away when all the school was sleeping? Hardly a hero, maybe, but I couldn't help feeling proud of what I had done. The names of all the famous men of times gone by who had run away from home rose in my memory like stars; and smiling to myself, I recited as loud as I could the poem[1] beginning,

---

1. Written (in Chinese) on the wall of his home by Priest (as he afterwards became) Gessho (1817–1858) when he ran away from home at the age of fifteen to study in the capital.

'My purpose firm, I turn my back on native home and village'. Fortunately the weather was kind. Nothing held me up, and on the third day a little after four o'clock, without even a blister to my feet, I reached a place called Kanzaki, from which (I was told) it was only a step to Beppu. I was trudging on, weary but in high spirits now that I knew I hadn't far to go, when a man of thirty-five or thereabouts in silk trousers, a merchant by the look of him, came up with me from behind.

'Bound for Beppu are you?' he said, looking me up and down.

'Yes.'

'Catching a boat?'

'Yes.'

'Where for—Tokyo? Osaka?'

'Somewhere up that way.'

'First time in these parts, I suppose? Where are you from?'

I didn't answer. His tone was patronizing, and I didn't take kindly to such familiarity from a stranger.

'I'm heading for Osaka too. Take you along, shall I—risky for a young boy like you, you know, travelling all alone. Too many sesame flies[2] about,' he went on, staring at me still. *Sesame fly*—what kind of fly might that be, I wondered.

'Where'll you spend the night at Beppu?'

I mumbled something about having no particular plans.

'All right, you just come along with me: I'll take you to my inn. There's a little place I stay at every time I'm passing through. The boat don't leave till tomorrow sundown, anyway.'

Knowing very well that you shouldn't be too friendly with people you meet casually on the road, I took a good look at him. All his clothes were of silk; he wore expensive lined clogs, and carried a small travelling-bag—nothing if not respectable. He was a rice-merchant of Oita, he told me, on his way to Osaka on business. My suspicion began to fade.

Coming down into Beppu just as the sun was setting, we made our way along streets where everyone was busy preparing for New Year—some pounding steamed rice in big wooden tubs in the garden,[3] some disposing of basketfuls of soot swept from kitchen ceilings—till my companion turned abruptly into a building with the words 'Shipping Agents/Travellers' Inn' inscribed in thick black characters on a flag flying from a pole above the entrance.

2. It is hardly surprising Shintaro was mystified. In feudal times unscrupulous pedlars did good business by selling to the more superstitious of their fellow-citizens what they claimed to be *goma no hai*, 'ashes of exorcizing fire', guaranteed to clear a house of demons. *Goma no hai* thus came to mean 'trickster', and was then corrupted to *goma* (written with different ideographs) *no hae*, 'sesame flies', with the sense of 'pick-pocket'.

3. After being pounded into a glutinous mass, the rice is used to make special New Year rice-cakes.

'This way. This way. What are you waiting for?' he called. I followed him in.

IV.2

We were to share a room, it seemed. At first, I still couldn't help feeling uneasy; but then he happened to drop his purse while we were undressing for the bath—it fell with a comforting thud, as if to demonstrate his solid merchant's honesty. Calling the innkeeper, he asked him to take care of the purse, adding with a glance at me, 'Best give him yours too—there's all sorts here tonight, and you can't be too careful.' The innkeeper offering the same advice, I went to a corner, away from prying eyes, took off the belt in which I had tucked away my little fortune of nearly six yen (sixty thousand, it might have been to me!), slipped five yen in a book, wrapped the book in a towel and handed it over. Now there *can't* be any need to worry, I thought. My companion made himself at home, calling for saké when the meal came and joking with the maid; but for my part three days of walking had left me so exhausted that I fell into a deep sleep directly after supper.

Next morning he suggested he should take me out for a look at the town, as the boat didn't sail till late afternoon. After strolling along some shabby waterfront streets for a while, we stopped at a store dealing in foreign goods for my companion to buy a woollen scarf. Suddenly, his hand in his pocket, he burst out laughing.

'Odd thing now—I've forgotten my purse. Hold on a moment!' So saying, he strode off the way we had come.

I started walking up and down in front of the shop. Ten minutes passed, twenty—and still no sign of my merchant friend, though our inn was not more than a few hundred yards away. Growing suspicious, I hurried back to the inn myself. The innkeeper was sitting in his office.

'Back already, sir? And the other gentleman . . .?'

'He said he was coming to pick up his purse—'

'Ah yes, he came back for it a few moments ago, then went out again—had some more shopping to do, he said.'

A horrible suspicion flickered at the back of my mind.

'And *my* money?'

'I gave it to the other gentleman, sir, along with his.'

'*You gave it to him?*' I shouted, white-faced, or so at least I felt. The innkeeper was flabbergasted. He was bald-headed old fellow of sixty or so, with a not unkindly look.

'Then you didn't know—? He said when he came in that the two of you were going shopping together, so could he have your money as well as his own . . . You weren't with him after all?'

Shock in his face, tears on mine . . . We were still staring at each other when a maid rushed in.

'One of the guests upstairs, sir —'
'What about him?'
'— missing his watch, sir!'
'His watch! Then that fellow *was* a thief!'

Uproar broke out. A policeman appeared, angry guests kept discovering new losses, a wallet had disappeared from this room, another watch from that. Come to think of it, those eyes of his, said the innkeeper: something shifty there all right. And wasn't he carrying a bag when he went out? added one of the maids. But hindsight couldn't find him nor the bawling of the victims; nor the policeman, feverishly searching for clues, nor the inn boys, dashing excitedly in all directions.

Midday came, and still the hullabullo hadn't subsided. But by then the steamer was getting ready to sail, so a grumbling crowd of guests began to pour out of the inn, minus their valuables, many of them, and having to make do instead with an endless stream of apologies and bows from the innkeeper. I alone had to stay behind, like Priest Shunkan[4] left solitary in his island exile. To me too the innkeeper was humbly apologetic: the fault was his entirely, and would I be so good as to wait till evening, as the police thought they had a clue? I had no choice but to wait, whether he asked me to or not. Now that that 'sesame fly' (the phrase needed no explanation now!) had swallowed all my journey-money, all I had left was twenty or thirty sen, out of the fifty I had kept back the night before. At least he hadn't made off with my bundle; but what could I do with a cotton kimono and a couple of books?

The steamer sounded its siren. Leaning on the wooden rail of the balcony upstairs, I watched it sail slowly out of Beppu Bay, trailing a thickening line of black smoke—with what feelings I leave the reader to surmise.

IV.3

The painful thought kept rounding on me that this disaster only three days out, even if it was strictly speaking not my own fault, might be a punishment for my having run away without telling Mother or Uncle or any of my friends. Hope receded steadily. Where now was the heroic mood of that secret flight from school? Suddenly I was nothing but a child again, longing only to cry. But this was no time for tears. Time hadn't stood still, my bill was mounting: whatever I was going to do, I had better make up my mind and do it quickly.

Should I go home? No, never; I should never hold up my head again. What if I wrote to Mother or sent her a telegram—told her what had

---

4. A prominent priest who was exiled to one of the remote Kikaigashima islands off the south-west coast of Japan in 1177, together with others who had plotted the murder of Kiyomori, leader of the great Taira clan. With the pardon of his fellow-conspirators shortly afterwards, Shunkan was left alone on his island, where he died the following year.

happened and asked for money for the journey? No, again; having come so far, how could I sink to such a weakly, womanish plea for help? The catastrophe was of my own making; I must find my own way out. Suppose I just pushed blindly on. If I spent my last sen, I'd never get even half-way to Osaka, let alone further: nor, on the other hand, would staying on here in Beppu solve any of my problems. Where could I—where *could* I go? To Komai Sensei? He was the nearest source of help I could think of. I had his address—His home was in Suzaki, in Tosa Province over in Shikoku, south-west of Kochi; steamers put in there, I had heard. Right—next stop Suzaki! If I had to live on dirt and salt water, I would find Komai Sensei. I sent for the innkeeper. He came in scratching his bald head and looking very sympathetic.

'Most unfortunate—I'm very sorry, sir, but they've had to give up—found nothing at all, nothing at all.'

Which was as I had expected. So I told him all my story (except for the running away) and asked him how I might make my way to Suzaki. He thought for a moment.

'There's no boat to anywhere in Tosa for some time. The Uwajima boat goes back this evening, though. You'd best take that, I daresay, and get another on from there to Tosa.'

I asked him to get me the cheapest possible passage on the Uwajima boat—as a ship's boy, if that would help. But before he left I got out the new lined kimono Mother had made (I had meant to keep it to wear by way of celebration on the day I arrived in Tokyo), my cap and kerchief, even my old belt—all these I handed over to the innkeeper, telling him to get the best price he could for them, take out what I owed him and give me the rest. Another string of apologetic bows, and he went off to see what he could do.

Some time later he reappeared, scratching his head as before in embarrassment.

'Sorry to have kept you waiting, sir. Your passage is arranged—the boat will be leaving very soon. Then there was the other matter—it's not the best time of year, I'm afraid, for disposing of such things . . .' He handed me one yen and thirty sen—and gave me back my cap and kerchief into the bargain. 'If you will get ready at once for the boat, sir, I will send up the maid with a meal.'

'And your bill?' I put in hurriedly, as he was leaving.

'It is paid already, sir,' he said—meaning he had taken it out of what he had got for the clothes—and slipped out of the room. A lie, of course; the kimono couldn't have fetched all that much—he had probably provided half the money out of his own pocket. I don't know which upset me more, the sudden shock of pleasure at such kindness, or the shame of having to accept it, but at any rate I couldn't get a single bowlful of rice down when supper came. It was time to leave, anyway. Waiting till I could be sure there was no one about, I slipped three ten-sen coins under a plate on my tray, ran out of the inn like an escaping thief, and boarded the boat for Uwajima.

The said boat couldn't have been more than fifty feet long, depressingly small when you realized it was in her you would be breasting the rough waters of the Hoyo Strait, between Kyushu and Shikoku. The crew was the 'captain', his wife—and their baby. They had taken on a cargo of some kind of dried fish; I could tell by the smell the moment I stepped on board. A favourable wind having just blown up from the north-west (as they told me), with much shouting and mutual abuse the good captain and his lady hauled in the anchor and hoisted the sail. Soon we put the bright lights of the harbour behind us, and were making good speed out of Beppu Bay.

I emerged from my refuge among the bales of dried fish to talk with the captain for a while, but lay down again before long, with an old patchwork quilt his wife had given me. Sleep would not come, though. The sun had gone down long before and left a trail of cold—in the sky, bright with the cold gleaming of the stars; in the night wind, playing softly on the sail; in the cold plash of waves breaking under our bow. The boatman was singing as he steered:

> Hard is life for the boatman
> On the Inland Sea,
> Whose racing currents bend
> His strongest oar.

The voice floated over the water, melancholy and quavering, as if close to tears.

IV.4

Sleep must have come eventually, I suppose, for I opened my eyes on a sea glittering with jewels scattered by the morning sun, and away to port a line of mountains stretched out across the waves like an enormous russet dragon.

'Where's that?'

'Sada,' grunted the boatman, his pipe between his teeth.

'Have we come far?'

' 'Bout halfway.'

'When shall we get to Uwajima?'

'Best not ask, lad.' To be sure, at sea one doesn't ask such questions, it would be unlucky. But if we kept our present speed we ought to be in Uwajima by afternoon at the latest, which was comforting. Fortunately I wasn't seasick, and once I had gargled with sea-water over the gunwale (with memories of my famous blunder on another boat on the way to Matsumura's three years before) and swallowed some of the piping hot rice and potatoes which the boatman's lady, her baby on her back, had been cooking, I began to feel pretty cheerful. After the cold of last night, the winter sun shone with a gentle warmth, in which even the boatman's wheezy singing sounded peaceful and springlike. His wife was full of womanly sympathy for this boy passenger of hers, travelling all alone, and eager curiosity about his identity. Where did I come from, she asked; were my parents living, how old was I, where was I going and why, who was going to look after me when I got there, every question you can think of. On top of which she fried some rice-cake for me. A friend had given it her in Beppu, or so she said. I remembered the story of Han Hsin[5] and the washerwoman of Huai Yin; it set me dreaming of the day when I would shower the boatman's wife with rice-cakes in payment of this debt of kindness. As it was, I had nothing with which to show my thanks; so I did my best to help a little by playing with her baby while she was mending quilts and getting the next meal ready.

About midday the wind dropped suddenly. The boatman had been watching the east uneasily for some time: now, shouting something I couldn't catch to his wife, he hurriedly took down the sail and began to work the scull. His wife got out the side oars, leaving the baby to me. An hour or so later we entered a cove off a tiny island called Okinoshima. The boatman worked frantically to lower the anchor and put out mooring lines to the shore.

'What are you going to do?'

'Proper storm blowing up', was all he would say, as he made fast the rush covering over the cargo and working space. Nothing, assuredly, is so uncertain as sea-weather. Jewel-bright that morning, the sky had darkened suddenly in the east, the wind had backed right round and risen to a gale, till in minutes after we had arrived the boat was rolling and pitching madly for all its two anchors and four mooring ropes. Fortunately we were lying right at the head of the cove, so the full force of the storm didn't hit us directly; but even so we shot up and down with every wave like a trapeze. For the boatman and his wife this was nothing new. They got out the rice-box and sat down to a meal, unperturbed. But for me—I couldn't eat a mouthful: listening in terror to the splashing of the rain, the roaring of the wind, the crash of waves on the sides and bilge, choking with the stench of dried and salted fish, I lay stretched out under the covering like a sea-slug.

It didn't make things any easier when the boatman and his wife chose to start a quarrel right in the middle of the storm. What with the noise of the wind and the waves, and the dialect they spoke, which I couldn't make much of anyway, I had no idea what it was they were arguing about; but the quarrel kept getting fiercer, along with the gale, till they came to blows,

---

5. The general whose military skill enabled Liu Pang (see note 11, p. 164) to defeat his rival Hsiang Yü after the collapse of the Ch'in dynasty in 207 B.C. In his youth, when he was friendless and extremely poor, Han Hsin was once cared for by a washerwoman: he did not forget her kindness, and rewarded her suitably on achieving fame. Many stories are told of his extraordinary patience and powers of endurance.

and I couldn't bear it any longer. I couldn't stand—I was too seasick by then, and the boat was rolling too violently—but I managed to crawl over and separate them. So the storm inside the boat subsided, though not the storm outside. Not long before dawn next day, the wind abating a little, I fell asleep at last, utterly exhausted.

The next thing I knew was a hand vigorously shaking my shoulder. I opened my eyes. The sun was already high in the sky; we had arrived safely at Uwajima.

IV.5

Tucking away in my sleeve the sixty sen or so that was all I had left after paying the boatman for my fare and food, I stepped up unsteadily on to the jetty, my head still reeling from the tossing of the boat. It was December 28th. The new calendar was in force here too, by the look of things: the little port was extra busy, with a great number of boats making their last call of the old year. Boats discharging, cartloads of fish arriving for shipment, everywhere boatmen shouting the strangest dialect—in the midst of all this din I stood alone, quite as much of a castaway as Robinson Crusoe. My legs refusing to carry me, I sat down on the nearest bollard.

Instantly an arm pushed me off.

'Get off there—*chibo*[6] !' screeched a hoarse voice. I looked round, startled, to find a man standing just behind me, a thin, sneering fellow. I jumped up and made off in the direction of the town as fast as my still weak legs would take me. Before long I came to a little eating-shop. Thinking I had better get something inside me before deciding what to do next, I slipped in as unobtrusively as I could and took a seat under a shelf with a statue of the god Kompira on it, and sucked away, rubbing my sleepy eyes, at a bowl of noddles as thin as worms. How should I make the rest of the journey? Going by boat saved your feet all right, but suppose you had to face more of those storms—no, it was overland for me, whatever the hardships. I asked the way of the old woman who kept the shop. An old fellow who was sitting the other side of the room swilling raw saké and a stinking mess of boiled fish chipped in before she could answer.

'Be you for Susaki, lad, down Tosa way?' There were two routes, he told me: the main road, and a short cut. The main road was much the easier going, but the journey took twice as long that way. The short cut, on the other hand, meant crossing right through the mountains, which was hard enough even without the snow, which might have started by now, he thought. The short cut for me, snow or no snow, I decided: my money would not hold out much longer. How much were the noodles, I asked the old woman, and felt in my sleeve. My purse was gone! Horrified, I shook both sleeves, undid my sash: no money anywhere. What on earth – I was certain I had the put the change in my left sleeve after paying the boatman,

6. A dialect word for 'pickpocket'.

so where could it have gone, that sixty sen—little enough, but all I had in the world. I was stupefied. This, I supposed, was what they meant by 'it never rains but it pours'! I dashed out of the shop, to the old woman's consternation, and ran down to the jetty, asking everywhere if anyone had picked up a purse; but without success.

'One of them *chibo* boys got it off you, most like,' said somebody. 'Chibo', he explained, was the local word for pickpocket. So that was it—that pale, sneering fellow who knocked me off the bollard had been announcing his own profession. No use crying my eyes out now, though. Not once but twice, to my shame, I had left myself be hooked. I walked back crestfallen to the noodle-shop. The old woman was all sympathy, and the old saké-swiller urged me to call the police; but there couldn't be much hope of getting my purse back that day—if I did, well and good, but if not, I'd only have a bill to pay: stopping the night would cost me as much as a whole day's journey. Despair gave me courage. There was nothing for it now but to push on, I decided, even if it meant begging.

Leaving my cloth wrapper in payment for the noodles, I ran out of the shop. Further down the street I stopped outside an old clothes stores, where after a moment's thought I took off my *haori* coat (it was only cotton, needless to say) and cap and persuaded the crusty old dealer to take them for twenty sen. At a bookseller's nearby I managed, after a deal of tearful pleading, to sell my last two books (not the Macaulay—the 'sesame fly' had got that already, together with the five yen I had slipped between its pages) for another eight sen. Goodbye to my bundles and coat and cap! and only twenty-eight sen in my pocket. Twenty-eight sen to take me to Komai Sensei's, at Susaki in Tosa Province.

A clock in a shop on the edge of the town said two o'clock. It was quite a way to Yoshino, the next village (so they had told me in the noodle-shop), and a mountain road at that. I had to get there that day, however late. Thick grey clouds swirled across the sky, dimming the sun. Just as I left the last buildings of Uwajima behind, it began to snow.

IV.6

Snow buries the road
Over plain and hill:
Blinding the traveller
Grey skies fall!

The old poem[7] came home to me now with a vengeance. The further I went, the more thickly the snow fell, collecting on my head and sleeves, no matter how often I shook it off, and working its way down my back and into my eyes and nose till I could bear it no longer. If only I hadn't sold

7. By Saigyo (1118-1190).

my cap, at least! Not much use repenting now. But what was to be done, when I hadn't even the money to buy a peasant's straw cape and hat? I struggled on, keeping my eyes open in the hope of picking up something to keep off the worst of the snow—till I noticed a scarecrow a farmer had left standing after the harvest. The coat wasn't much use—all rags, and soaking wet—but the bamboo hat, an ancient affair with a torn strap and noticeable holes: that might still serve. I tied it round my head with bits of straw, trying hard to pretend it was a silk umbrella. A bit of rush matting for a coat, and I'd be all right. All I could find anywhere near was a big sheaf of straw lying on a path between two fields; but that was better than nothing, so I humped it up over my shoulders, and trudged off up the road once more.

Still the snow thickened. I could hardly have come five miles from Uwajima when dusk fell, as it does so quickly under a snowy sky; soon only the white line of the road stood out against the enveloping dark. A heavy grey sky hung low overhead, showering down an endless succession of tiny snowflakes, monster snowflakes, snowflakes without end. Worn out from days of travelling, worry, and the buffetings of the day and night at sea, I walked on still, but exhaustion was beginning to tell: except for that one bowl of noodles at Uwajima, I had eaten nothing since the morning of the previous day, and the cold was knifing through me from fingertips to stomach. I couldn't stand it much longer. If there was a cottage somewhere where they'd let me sleep with the horses, or in the cattle shed, and maybe give me a sip of left-over barley-and-rice, I'd give half my precious twenty-eight sen for such a feast and such a bed. I had plodded on another two or three hundred yards when a tiny light glimmered through the snow.

It turned out to be a thatched hut with the words SAKÉ, REFRESHMENTS painted on the door and lit up from within. Inside, a woman was scolding someone angrily. Half-paralysed with cold, I blew on my hands and knocked.

'Anyone there, if you please?'

The door opened. A woman's face, eyebrow-less, hard and brutal-looking, peered round the edge. Behind her stood a girl of about ten, who stopped crying suddenly to stare at me, wide-eyed. The woman looked me up and down.

'Nothing for you!'

Nothing! So she takes me for a beggar? I was furious, till I looked down at myself. Who could have taken me for anything else, with my torn old mockery of a hat and bits of straw sticking all over me?

'I'm not begging! I'll pay, if you'll give me shelter for the night—'

'This isn't an inn! Look at him, scattering snow everywhere. Get out, will you!' she snarled.

'Will you sell me something to eat then? I'll pay—'

'No food here. Shut the door and get out—get out, when I tell you to, will you!'

I stepped quickly half outside the door, she looked so threatening—as if she were ready to pounce on me if I didn't move.

'How far is it to Yoshino, then?'

'Don't know!'

'Isn't there anywhere near 'd put me up? I'll pay —'

'Stop your gab and GET OUT, beggar!' She slammed the door in my face. I stood there, staring at it for a moment, then started off again up the road, which now began to climb up into the hills. Behind me I could still hear for some time the woman's harsh, angry voice and the child's crying, till they too faded into silence behind a wall of driving snow. Suddenly my foot slipped. I fell forward, and made the best of it by swallowing a couple of mouthfuls of snow to quench my thirst. Better get your courage up with a song, I told myself. Straining weary muscles in an effort to breathe deeply, I started off on 'At the banquet's height, the young man rose —'[8] But my voice gave out before I could sing any more, and I was streaming tears instead, weakling's tears. Teeth locked into shivering lips, I stumbled on another hundred yards.

IV.7

I could see nothing. The snow blew thicker and faster still, driving into my face no matter how low I pulled my hat, soaking through my kimono and numbing my fingers to the bone. Gradually the cold, hunger and the pain of walking faded into a pleasant drowsy weariness. Dreams swirled around me . . . My running away was a dream, and Beppu, and the sea-voyage to Shikoku; the noodle-shop at Uwajima, this dragging up the mountain road alone through the night and snow—all dreams. . . . I stumbled, and fell again. I must get up, I knew, I must get up . . . suddenly the road disappeared—falling in the snow, that too was a dream—I was back in Uncle's house, no, in the burial-ground on the hill at home, kneeling before Mother, pleading her forgiveness . . .

'Mother!' I called aloud; then every memory and sensation vanished but that of trudging, trudging mechanically and endlessly over a vast white moor.

'Hi the-re. . . .!'

Very faintly, far behind, a voice called over the snow. Who would be calling me back, I wondered, when I had got so far—but pushed on without looking round, till I noticed a tiny point of light ahead, like a fire-fly. Slowly it grew bigger, though whether I was hurrying towards it or it towards me I couldn't make out—and the voice with it, repeating 'Hi there—hullo—hullo—'

8. From a poem by the celebrated Chinese poet Tu Fu (712–770), describing how a friend of the poet's who had been appointed to a post in the remote provinces rose in the middle of his farewell party to sing of his sadness in leaving the capital.

'He's all right then,' said the voice abruptly into my ear. I opened my eyes. Moor and mountain road faded. I was lying on my side in some kind of dwelling, a place I seemed to know. In front of me a fire was burning merrily. On a bench near it sat a thickly-whiskered man of forty or more, wrapped in a heavy overcoat like a policeman's and grasping with both hands an enormous singlestick he had planted on the floor before him; next to me, a rough-looking, red-faced fellow with a top-knot, a peasant by the look of him, was squatting on the floor. I tried to get up—and fell back, dazed. At Whiskers' orders, Topknot brought me a bowl of thick pungent liquid, warmed up, and poured it down my throat, nearly choking me in the process, though that didn't seem to worry him in the least. It was crude saké, I found out afterwards.

'You'd better thank the gentleman 'ere for that. Brought you in on 'is back, 'e did,' said a woman's voice behind me. The voice was familiar. I looked round—there she was right enough, the termagant who had driven me away so harshly from her door. Then this must be the cottage. Whiskers must have found me lying in the road halfway up the pass and carried me down here . . . and the girl who had been crying, while her mother shouted abuse at her, she was asleep somewhere, no doubt. Topknot would be the woman's husband, though I hadn't seen him when I knocked at their door.

'A noble act of charity it was you did, sir, a blessed deed and no mistake,' said Topknot.

'You call me a devil; but even a devil has a heart, you'll be surprised to know. I take what's due to me, no more,' said Whiskers, pulling at a tuft on his cheek.

Warmed by the saké and the fire, the stiffness began gradually to thaw out of my limbs and tongue, till I managed to sit up and thank Whiskers, and tell him briefly who I was and how I came to be on the road that night.

'Better come and stay with me awhile. Wait, though, you can't walk yet. Carry him, Jisa, will you?'

Scratching his head, Topknot, alias Jisa, glanced at his wife. The look she gave him settled his doubts. Muttering something in answer he hoisted me up on his back (my kimono had dried by now, more or less), threw a straw coat over us both and stepped out into a blinding rush of snow. Singlestick in one hand and lantern in the other, thick straw sandals on his feet, Whiskers led the way. I seemed to be dreaming still—a dream within a dream . . .

A mile or so down the Uwajima road we turned off into a track, and came after two or three hundreds yards to a single house standing by itself in a hollow, the hills rising steeply behind. Three dogs, growling angrily, rushed out at us as we approached. 'Down, you fools, it's only me!' shouted Whiskers. Instantly the growling gave way to barks of delight as they danced round their master. The door opened; an old woman with a lantern peered out at us.

'Be't you, sir?'

'Aye, it's me all right.' Whiskers pushed past her, stood his single-stick in a corner by the door, shook out his coat on to the earthen floor, flung it over a bamboo clothes-pole to dry, knocked the snow off his sandals, and settled down to wash his feet. This finished, he turned to Topknot.

'All right, Jisa.—Get that old lined kimono of mine out, will you'—this to the old woman, who kept glancing suspiciously at the strange load Jisa had slipped off his back. 'Change the boy and put him to bed in the two-mat room. And give him some blankets; the green ones 'll do.' I hardly had time to thank him before I was wrapped up in a grimy old kimono and bundled off to bed in a tiny pitch-dark room. Through the flimsy sliding-door I could hear Whiskers talking.

'Now, Jisa, that bit of business of ours. Two more days you've got, and no more. I can't wait any longer.' Jisa mumbled something I couldn't catch; then there was a clattering of the door; he must have gone home. After that there were sounds of Whiskers drinking, but I was so comfortable under the blankets that it wasn't long till exhaustion and relief at meeting with such kindness from a stranger and knowing I was safe, at least for the time being, carried me off into a dreamless sleep.

IV.8

Next morning I was so tired, and the cold so severe, that I just could not stir from my blankets. The following day too I spent in bed. When finally I did get up it was on the morning of New Year's Day, 1884, so that I found myself combining the season's greetings to my host with heartfelt thanks for his having saved my life. He was kept constantly occupied while I was in bed. A visitor would come—click-click from Whiskers' abacus—the visitor would go; another visitor would take his place—more clicking—and he make way for a third—and so on all day, with hardly a break; he might have forgotten about me entirely. But the old woman looked after me kindly enough, bringing a bowl of gruel now and then, and asking me how I did—besides which, old age not having deprived her of her woman's love of chatter, I picked up a great deal of information without having to ask for it.

Heizaburo Nishiuchi, for that was her master's name, was the third son of a minor samurai family of the Uwajima clan. Now forty-two, he had experienced much poverty and hardship, she told me, in his youth. After the Restoration he had joined the army and risen to the rank of captain; but then he had suddenly left the service—whether by resignation or dismissal wasn't clear—and come back here to Uwajima. That was the year after the Civil War of 1877. It was then that he had started his money lending business, from a rented room in the house of a farmer he knew.

Things had gone so well with him that in four years he had got together quite a little fortune; two years ago he had built this house, on a plot of land he had been able to buy cheaply because the owner had defaulted on his mortgage.

But success has envy for its shadow, no matter where you go, and so he wasn't much liked in the district, particularly as it was money-lending he had done so well out of. Not that he always charged high rates: but he was cruelly rigid in all his dealings, insisting that just as he kept his side of every contract, so must the borrowers keep theirs, and pursuing them mercilessly if they lagged with their payments, whatever the cause. Consequently he was busy from one year's end to the next with distraints and the like, all of which aroused much bitter hostility. Three men, big strong fellows, had lain in wait for him one night as he was on his way home from dunning someone, but he hadn't been a samurai for nothing, so the old woman said: he drove them helter-skelter with a stick no bigger than a poker, and came home without so much as a bruise himself. Since then, there had been no more ambushes. All the same, he was more careful now, and never went out at night without his enormous stick of medlar-wood. A regular demon, some people called him, but in fact he wasn't all that fierce—on the contrary, once you understood his ways he was easy to get on with, otherwise how could she herself have gone on working for him for so long?

Particular he certainly was. Let him find a single grain of rice spilt in the sink, or a scrap of paper in the garden, and he'd be scowling for the rest of the day. 'Old Niggard' was one of the names they gave him down in the village, she'd heard; 'His Honour the Ogre' was another. She knew how to deal with him, though—took such care with all his things, never wasting the smallest flake of dried bonito, even, that he trusted her completely, and was quite content to leave her to look after the house when he was away. And talking of bonito, he had divorced his second wife—what had happened to his first, she didn't know—for not grating this same bonito finely enough. 'Ruin me in no time, a woman like this', he had complained when he sent her back to her family with a letter of divorcement. 'Little sparks start big fires' was his watchword.

Whenever he wasn't too busy, he loved to recount—after a nightcap or two of saké—the miseries he'd had to endure as the third son of a decayed samurai; and how when he joined the army he wasn't stupid like all the other officers, who would not merely spend every sen they possessed on pleasure but piled up endless debts: he starved himself, very nearly, so that he could actually save, with the result that while most of them, when they had done their time, had had nothing to fall back on and had been driven nearly mad with despair in consequence, he had been able to use his savings and set himself up here, till now it was Your Honour, Your Honour for miles around.

All this I heard from the old woman while I was still in bed, so that though

I had as yet seen little of her master, I had a pretty good idea of his character and circumstances. On New Year's Day, when I did manage to leave my bed, we had our first real conversation, and I was able to thank him properly for having rescued me. Sipping *toso*[9]—today, for once, he was at leisure—he questioned me closely about my family, what had happened on my journey so far, why I was travelling alone, and whether I could write a good clear hand and use an abacus. Finally he asked me straight out if I would stay with him for a while at least, as his clerk or assistant, to help him with his books, in return for board and clothes; he couldn't pay me a salary. I thought hard. I had no money, and was still far from fit. If I tried to go on right away, I couldn't expect anything but trouble; besides which, I did owe him something for his kindness so I decided that for the time being I would stay. Time enough to think about my next move when I had written to Komai Sensei and asked his advice. It wasn't exactly what I'd expected—setting off so bravely to study in the capital, and ending up as a moneylender's clerk down here in darkest Shikoku—but at least it was one better than dying on the road.

So from that day I became book-keeper to 'His Honour the Ogre'. Uncle Noda's secretary, I had been not so long ago; now I was a moneylender's clerk. Secretary, clerk—was I ever to be anything else?

IV.9

There's nothing more incalculable than the suddenness with which our human fortunes change. Ten days ago a proud student of the famous New School, now a usurer's runabout in a corner of Shikoku . . . it would sound too abrupt even in a novel. My duties were many and various. Opening all the shutters was my first job, at dawn each morning. Then outside to draw water and sweep the garden with a bamboo broom, its long handle frozen like an icicle—I had to wrap it round with cloth sometimes before I could touch it. After breakfast (I did get three meals a day, but only gruel each time—nothing else, at least at first) I'd sit at a tiny desk making up my master's books, checking on an abacus the sums he called out, writing out tickets for borrowers who came with something to pawn. Sometimes I would take messages down to the village office, or accompany the moneylender when he went dunning. Two or three times we called on Jisa, who had carried me through the snow that night. Much more of an ordeal, though, were my first visits to other houses, where they glared down at me, as much as to say, 'Who's *this*—the big devil breeding up a little 'un, is 'e?' But most painful of all was having to listen to my master in the shacks of the poorest peasants, calm, unhurried and relentless, demanding his money from emaciated men and women till the sweat ran down their skinny foreheads and their eyes filled with tears. I swore I would never be a

9. A thick, sweet form of saké, drunk in every home on New Year's Day.

moneylender, no matter how low I fell. Nor get into debt, either, after seeing the pitiful way the borrowers prostrated themselves in our porch (though they would be paying good interest on what they had borrowed, and providing security into the bargain), bowing repeatedly even to me when I opened the door, and mouthing servile compliments. In his youth, it seemed, Mr Nishiuchi had suffered so much from physical hardship and humiliation as a result of poverty that he had come to the conclusion poverty was life's greatest misery, from which nothing could save a man in time of need, certainly not parents, nor brothers and sisters, let alone gods or Buddhas—nothing, that is, except money. Consequently all his life was now devoted to the twin aims of making money and keeping it—the keeping looming as large as the making.

Fire and burglary were the two great bogeys of his life. Even in the middle of winter he wouldn't allow a charcoal footwarmer; at ten o'clock each night, he himself went round putting out every light in the house (they were old-style Japanese lanterns, for he wouldn't have anything to do with kerosene); every bit of left-over charcoal from the living-room had to be soaked in water for twenty-four hours and dried out before we lit it a second time; and sometimes, in spite of his trust in his old housekeeper, he would make a visit of inspection to the kitchen, to add some water to the porcelain charcoal-extinguisher, just in case, and take up the floorboards over the charcoal-store to make sure no smouldering splinters from the cooking brazier had found their way down there between the planks. But more than half his mind, I reckon, was given up to the devising of ways and means of protecting the house and himself from burglars. Visitors were confronted first of all by a massive gate and a hedge of prickly citrus all round the house, as solid as a wall and bristling with thorns that looked as if they'd stab you if you took a step nearer. That was formidable enough, but you were hardly through the gate when three huge and ferocious dogs would leap out at you from nowhere, growling ominously, a sight and sound to put to flight the boldest thief.

As for the house itself, the door and shutters were lined with tinplate, with a stout wooden bar to reinforce the metal door-latch, double locks on every shutter, and even bolts on the sliding partition-doors. Buckets would be left in strategic positions to clang when knocked by the unwary burglar, boxes and stools ranged along the partitions to trip him up if ever he succeeded in opening one. My master kept candles and matches by his pillow, with a sword two and a half feet long stuck in his bedclothes, and a loaded revolver within easy reach. He would let no one but himself lock up at night. Even then, when he'd had his drink and was ready to go to bed, he could not sleep unless he did his rounds once more, outside and in. On his instructions, the housekeeper slept with a carving-knife at her bedside—even I was supplied with a 'night-dagger', which I kept under the mattress. Once every night at least I would be woken with a bawled 'Kikuchi! Kikuchi!' to go round with my master checking the locks. On stormy nights, what with his shouting and the constant clattering of the shutters, I hardly had time to doze. Lying under siege every night must have been like this, I suppose. In short, 'every man a thief, every day a storm' was my master's philosophy. This being so (and his housekeeper being a special case) it was surely very favoured treatment that I was getting—I, a mere wanderer, picked up penniless off the road one day, and made into his confidential clerk the next, with a room in his house, and even knowing where he kept his money.

He's not a bad man, I often found myself thinking—and not just because he had saved my life, either. Then why, I wondered, did he spend all his time and energy on making money this way, so wearing himself out with worry about fire and thieves that he couldn't even shut his eyes in peace at night, when he'd nothing to spend the money on, no one to leave it to (as far as I knew), and his only reward the curse of every peasant in the district? I was still a child, you see. When I saw him late at night, a little drowsy after his saké, looking round placidly at the little fortress of a house he'd built himself, or sitting, chin on hand, with his collection of title-deeds spread out on the floor all round him, right up to the walls, as if he were playing some queer grown-up version of the New Year game of poem-cards, he didn't look the least bit the devil he was supposed to be—more like a human copy of the good-natured, beaming Ebisu, god of wealth. Only put aside the troublesome questions of how it was come by and what to use it for, and money has a strange magic power, it seems, that will make men smile no matter how long they fix their eyes upon its golden charms.

IV.10

Indeed both my master and his housekeeper showed me much kindness. Once when I praised her sardine salad the old woman made nothing else for three days, and kept summoning me (unbeknown, needless to say, to Mr Nishiuchi) to the kitchen for more helpings between meals, till I was ready to cry at the very sight of fish. The moneylender, for his part, commended me for honesty and diligence, and a steadiness beyond my years. Of course there were grumbles too now and again: I had written these characters too big, I must pick up those scraps of waste paper and put them to use again, I must hold the broom more lightly, or I'd sweep all the soil away, etc., etc. But 'devil'—no, he wasn't that. What the peasants thought about my staying with him, I don't know. But at least I neither starved nor froze under his roof; for a clerk-cum-houseboy, in fact, I was pretty comfortable.

But was I content, you say. How can you ask? Was I not Shintaro Kikuchi still, however young and foolish? Had I not studied under Seizan Sensei and Komai Sensei? Had I not run away and left my mother alone, out of a simple determination to study and study till I could restore the fortunes of our house by my own efforts—slaving as a menial in some humble school, if need be, rather than sell my independence? Did I not know what Freedom was? Had I not listened to lectures on the shining lights of history? Was it not my secret ambition to serve society and my fellow-men? I would never forget what I owed Mr Nishiuchi. I could never think of him as a monster, as the villagers did; only pity him for the extent to which the hardships of his youth had drained him of the power of feeling. But to live day in, day out with this man whose fate had turned him into a money-making automaton, shut up in his little house like a chrysalis squirming in a cocoon, looking at nothing, talking of nothing all day but money, money, money—to be at such a man's beck and call was galling indeed. The blood ran hot in my veins still, the light of my hopes still shone before my eyes, so distant, yet seeming close, too, by its very brilliance.

Unknown to my master or his housekeeper, I wrote to Komai Sensei, describing all that had happened and asking his advice. I was ready to leave instantly if he sent for me—and even if he didn't, I planned to go just the same. But alas, my letter was returned, marked 'Gone away—address unknown'. Another shock, and a painful one. So it was no use looking to Komai Sensei. Probably his father had died after all, and he himself had gone back to Tokyo. Where else could I turn? Should I write and explain the situation to Mother and Uncle and Aunt, relying on them to help me on my journey? Several times already I had started such a letter, only to change my mind. I looked on myself as a child still, but I was sixteen this year, for all my physical smallness, and suppose I were to go begging ignominiously for help now—just because I'd run out of money for my fare—after having thrown Uncle's offer in his face and run away from home and school: what sort of filial duty would that be? To turn to Uncle now would be the bitterest humiliation of all: to tell Mother of my mishaps would only cause her needless suffering. Patience, patience—stick it out a little longer, and something will turn up, I told myself, though heaven knows I had no grounds for any such optimism. So I worked on as Mr Nishiuchi the moneylender's boy-clerk. My writing-brush I threw away, and never sent a single letter home.

IV.11

Time slips by so fast. More than a hundred days had passed since I left home, though it seemed like only yesterday; already the peach-trees were in bloom. Every time I watched a band of pilgrims climbing up the road outside our gate, their chant of 'Hail to our Glorious Teacher, the Light Eternal' floating on the warm spring wind, I couldn't help but reflect bitterly upon the mischances that had cut short my own journey, and confined me here for three months and more. Tokyo was my goal still; but what chance had I now of reaching it? Mother would assume, unless I wrote otherwise, that I had already arrived in the capital and entered some school there: certainly she would never dream I had fallen so low as this,

I told myself, overcome sometimes by such a stupor of misery that I mixed up the entries in my master's books.

One day when I went down to Uwajima to call at the Police Station with a message from my master, I noticed a westerner, all of six feet tall and with a great red jungle of a beard, though his face looked friendly enough, talking away earnestly—in English, of course—to an inspector and a small group of policemen. The inspector was standing helplessly with a visiting-card in his hand, gaping with the policemen around him at the busily moving lips of the foreigner. Obviously neither understood the other's language, so the conversation didn't stand much chance of getting anywhere. The foreigner seemed to have given up: he shook his head, smiling.

'Awkward, this is. No one around who could interpret, is there?' said the inspector, fingering his moustache.

'How about that doctor who set up a month or two ago?' suggested one of the policemen. Probably the doctor was the only man in Uwajima who had any knowledge at all of foreign languages.

'He left yesterday for Osaka,' said another. That was their last hope gone. Watching them, I had quite forgotten what I had come for, and now, suddenly emboldened by pity for the foreigner in his difficulty, I went up to him and asked him in my halting English, 'What is your business, please?'

Everyone in the room turned to stare at me. The foreigner beamed, like a lost soul stumbling on a Buddha in purgatory, and began chattering down at me like a waterfall. With my meagre English—the teaching at the New School was pretty rough and ready: we had no conversation to speak of, and even in reading we pronounced every word in the Japanese way ('Sir Isaac Newton', for example, we called 'Shiru Eesaku Niyuuton')—more than half of what he said was beyond me. Still, by listening carefully and questioning him repeatedly in Kikuchi English (a fine, forceful, epigrammatic style, with bits of vocabulary fired off like bullets, and never a single conjunction or preposition), I managed to make out the gist of what he was after. Wilkie Brown was his name. He was an American, a Christian missionary, and had come overland from Matsuyama to see a preacher here in Uwajima; but the preacher was out of town, apparently, and he wanted help in fixing up a passage on the boat back to Osaka.

It cost me a deal of sweat to get this much clear, but in the policemen's astonished eyes I was evidently a notable scholar, and the American grasped my hand and thanked me very courteously when he left to go with a policeman to the shipping agent's. I finished my business as quickly as I could—it wasn't pleasant to have everybody staring at me, as if they were all wondering whether this messenger-boy in the shabby, threadbare kimono who could actually talk with the foreigner was some kind of genius in disguise—and ran out of the station.

A man of about forty with a splendid pair of drooping moustaches followed me out.

'A word with you, boy, if you please!'

IV.12

I stopped.

'Where d'you live, if you don't mind my asking?'

When I gave him the moneylender's address, he stared unbelievingly at my well-worn clothes.

'A relative of Mr Nishiuchi, perhaps?'

I told him my name and where I came from, and explained that for the time being I was dependent on Mr Nishiuchi.

'So that's it. I thought you couldn't be from these parts, speaking the way you do. Expect to stay for some time, do you?'

What right has he, I thought, to cross-examine me without telling me who he is himself?

'May I know your name, sir?' I asked.

'Ah, yes—rude of me—.' He took a visiting-card out of his kimono pocket and handed it to me. It read

Ichido Kento
Member of the Prefectural
Assembly

'We can't talk here, though. Come with me, will you?'

I followed the stranger with the moustaches—Mr Kento, I should say—into a little teashop. Must be quite a somebody, this Mr Kento, I thought to myself when I saw how low the old man bowed when he brought our tea. That was a bit of comfort, anyway, though I still didn't know what he wanted of me.

'You can speak English?'

'None at all,' I answered, blushing as I thought of my clumsy efforts at conversing with the American.

'Studied for quite a while, have you?'

'About two years. Not conversation, though.'

'What made you come here in the first place?'

There didn't seem to be any good reason to hide the truth, so I told him briefly the whole story: why I had run away, the troubles that beset me on the journey, and how the moneylender had rescued me in the snowstorm.

'You're not related in any way to Nishiuchi, then?'

'No—he lets me board with him, that's all.'

'Would you consider teaching English?'

I was thunderstruck. Teach English—with barely two years of study behind me? when the furthest I had got was to nibble at the first few chapters of Guizot's *History*, with my head buried most of the time in the dictionary?

'I couldn't possibly *teach*—'

'But it would only be to beginners. The fact of the matter is, we had a Middle School here till last year, with English as one of the subjects; but we had to shut down because of the expense. There are lots of people keep saying they want to learn English if only we can find them a teacher—none of them further on than spelling, I can tell you, and the first Reader or two, maybe. If you agree, I'll speak to Nishiuchi myself.'

By now I was really excited. Nothing teaches like trouble, they say; and absurd though it was to think of myself as a teacher, I fancied I could manage the Readers—especially since it would give me the chance of being something better than a moneylender's errand-boy. Not quite a ticket to Tokyo, perhaps; but a step on the way. Mr Kento had said he would make things right with Mr Nishiuchi. What better luck could I want? Obviously I had to accept.

'If it's just beginners, I'm willing to try, but—'

'Fine. I'll go and see Nishiuchi in a couple of days and fix things up with him. Won't be any trouble there.'

We parted. Treading on air, I hurried back home; but of what had happened down in Uwajima, I told the moneylender nothing.

IV.13

Three days later I was chopping firewood in the afternoon (a job my master had always done himself, on the principle that he would waste less in chips than a servant; but in due course he handed it over to me), the old woman came running up to me. 'Shinta-san!' I used to plead with her to call me Shintaro, instead of cutting it short to Shinta, as if I were an errand-boy born and bred—but without much effect. 'Shinta-san!'

'What?' I asked. I spoke rather brusquely. She had called me 'Shinta' again, and I was having trouble with a knotty bit of wood.

'Leave the chopping, quick! Mr Kento's here, and it's you he wants to see, he says—'

'All right.' I threw my hatchet aside and straightened up.

'You *know* Mr Kento?'

'Of course I know him,' I said complacently, with a did-you-really-think-I-was-good-for-nothing-but-chopping-wood-and-drawing-water look.

'When 'e stood there in the doorway, I never thought but 'e'd some business with the master. But no, 'e said, it was Mr Kikuchi 'e'd come to see—.'

Without waiting for her to finish I hurried off to the front porch, where sure enough my gentleman of the splendid moustaches was waiting—and took him through to the living-room myself, my master being out. As soon as we were seated, he began to speak again of what we had discussed in Uwajima. The students were all delighted, he said, that he had found them a teacher. He wanted me to start next day, if I could manage it, in one of the rooms of the Middle School building, which wasn't being used now anyway—the class to start as soon as possible after supper time, as there'd be some children from the primary school coming; and if I needed a room in Uwajima, I could stay in his house if I liked. The class would be known as The Shikoku English Language Evening Study Group (I was mightily impressed with this title): my salary would be settled later, by mutual agreement. To these conditions I had no objection, so all that remained was to get the moneylender's consent.

Before long my master came home from his round of dunning calls, single-stick in hand and big square satchel slung over his shoulder. Amazement showed openly in his face the moment he saw the visitor (they were acquainted, I heard afterwards, but far from friendly); but when he heard what Mr Kento had come for, he nearly exploded. By now I had become indispensable to the Nishiuchi household. Though I say it who shouldn't, I'm pretty sure my master could have worn out shoes of iron looking in vain for another factotum who would serve him with such ungrudging loyalty. He had come to rely on me both for the daily running of his business and for looking after the house when he was away, and raised objection after objection, not taking at all kindly to the notion of giving me up. Mr Kento pressed him hard all right. Words like 'rights' and 'duty' flew back and forth between them like shuttles on a loom, weaving a fine flowery display of argument. The moneylender held out grimly, stroking his whiskers; Mr Kento striking home again and again, twirling his moustaches faster and faster as his temper rose; Shintaro Kikuchi, who would have liked to be loyal to his master but stood to lose so much if he stayed, sitting silently by; the old housekeeper gaping in astonishment at the three of us; even the dogs, not to be left out, barking away furiously on the veranda—if I had something of Ssû-ma Ch'ien's[10] skill I might have described for you this quaint latter-day Encounter at Hung Meng,[11] but as it is, I shall have to leave it to your imagination to fill in the picture.

The Uesugis of this world may win the first battle, but it is the Takedas[12] who come out on top in the end—and so it was now, as with the heroes of two centuries ago. Unflinching, Mr Kento drove my master before him with such a power of words that soon he was reduced to stammering. What they finally agreed was that since it was only two and a half miles to Uwajima (only, indeed! that's not how *I* would have put it!) and the

10. A Chinese historian of the second century B.C.
11. The celebrated meeting in 207 B.C. of the two rebel leaders who had overthrown the Ch'in dynasty—the peasant-general Liu Pang (who afterwards founded the Han dynasty) and the aristocratic Hsiang Yü. At the meeting, Hsiang attempted, unsuccessfully, to have Liu murdered.
12. Kenshin Uesugi and Shingen Takeda were two famous samurai who fought on opposite sides in the civil wars of the sixteenth century, and were bitter personal rivals. The particular reference here is to a series of encounters between the two leaders and their armies at Kawanakajima.

moneylender would not object (though I would have liked to) to my being away between five and eight or nine o'clock in the evening, I was to stay on with him, and teach every evening in town. A full day's work for Mr Nishiuchi, a two and a half miles' walk into Uwajima, three hours of teaching, the two and a half miles' walk through the night back home. Both my benefactors were satisfied with this settlement—and no wonder, for it did not cost *them* anything. When a little country finds itself caught between two Great Powers, it's bound to be in trouble before long, with the big fellows doing their best to nibble away at it, one from each side. In my case they made a lot of noise about looking after me, protection of minors, etc., but in fact both of them were acting out of pure self-interest—the same self-interest that makes a man suck all the sweetness out of a stick of sugar-cane and then toss it aside casually as soon as he's had his fill. In other words, my position was just like that of our neighbour China,[13] don't you think?

IV.14

The arrangement they had proposed could hardly have been less convenient for me. However, I put the best face I could upon it, and we agreed that I should start the following day. So I made my début as a teacher ...

I still can't forget that day. As it was the first time, Mr Kento took me about dusk to the Middle School building to introduce me to my class. Twenty or more students, all of different ages, were waiting in a lamplit room; they stared at us, abruptly silent, as we entered.

'This is Kikuchi Sensei, your new teacher,' announced Mr Kento, twirling his moustache impressively. Teacher Kikuchi felt the sweat trickling down from his armpits. The students bowed as one man, but I glimpsed a smile here, a sneer there: expressions of doubt that this tiny little fellow could really teach them English. Suddenly I recalled—and with a flood of belated sympathy—that first speech of Komai Sensei's when he took up his post at the New School. Facing silent students, I sat in silence, fingering the pleats of my *hakama* skirt[14] (I could hardly teach just as I was, Mr Kento had said, so he had lent me an old duckcloth *hakama* of his son's to put on over my working clothes).

'How would it be if you used this evening for dividing them up into grades, having a general talk, and so forth, and start the regular teaching tomorrow?' said Mr Kento, looking at me.

This is it, I thought: the moment I had to assert my dignity as their teacher. Straightening up my small body in my chair, squaring my shoulders imposingly, I glanced sternly up and down the rows of faces.

13. i.e. China at the time Tokutomi was writing—1900.
14. See n 2, p. 108.

'Well now. You have all done quite a lot of English, have you?' The voice was mine, I suppose: I didn't recognize it.

'All different stages, aren't you?' put in my sponsor. This started them off, a murmur here, a murmur there, till soon the room was humming. There were some who didn't know A from B, others who had started on the First Reader, others again who had been right through the Second Reader, even. All the time I was anxiously waiting for a real rival to appear, someone who obviously knew more than me. To my relief, however, the most advanced scholar of all had got no further than the beginning of the Third Reader: so I divided them up into three grades, each of which I agreed to teach every evening for an hour at a time.

Next day, then, I started making my daily trips, rain or shine, down to Uwajima and back. After a day's work helping the moneylender with his ledgers and the old woman with the housework, I would pack a few balls of cooked rice-and-barley, clatter down the road to teach school for three hours, and plod back up to my master's house to serve him again, this time as night-watchman. It was a hard grind at first, but I soon got used to it. My embarrassment at my sudden elevation to 'teacher' status didn't last long, either. Students who were big and burly enough to have swallowed me whole were soon accepting their little teacher's authority—as far as our textbook was concerned, at least—without question, nor did they smile any longer at my different dialect, as they had done at first.

A month sped by like a dream. The two yen I received by way of salary seemed like thousands; I was overawed that my rudimentary English could bring in such a fortune—and felt a thrill of long-frustrated hope. A few months of such work, and I should be able to finish the journey I had begun.

IV.15

As the months went by, friendship sprang up between the students and the youthful bird-of-passage they called their teacher. The numbers kept increasing. Mr Kento was delighted with the success of his plan; often I myself quite forgot I was a stranger in the town. Here at least, the little sparrow—a phoenix in his own eyes—was content to rest his wings awhile.

The only snag was that I was still bound so closely to my first benefactor, the moneylender. It wasn't easy, having to switch from odd-job boy to teacher every evening. Most awkward of all was running into my students when I was in town on an errand for my master. This was too much to bear, and I had just decided to appeal to Mr Kento, when Providence smiled on me: a nephew of Mr Nishiuchi's turning up out of the blue, it was decided that he should stay with his uncle—which gave me the chance to escape from my cage. This time, to my surprise, he was quite willing to release me. Partly, maybe, this was because his business had been doing so well lately, one big debtor, in particular, having just paid up in full.

After conferring with Mr Kento, I presented Mr Nishiuchi with a roll of striped cotton cloth, and the old housekeeper with an apron, to show my gratitude.

My removal from the moneylender's having been duly arranged, Mr Kento kindly invited me to stay in his house; but I preferred to take a room in the school. Since its closure, the buildings of the Middle School had remained entirely unoccupied, its chairs and desks unused by any but our English classes. I chose a corner-room upstairs, a big room of about twenty mats, with a huge table in the middle which served as a desk by day and a bed by night. Mr Kento had some bedding sent in. I bought myself two earthenware cooking-pots, a small charcoal stove, a scuttle, a supply of charcoal, matches, and kindling, and started to cook my own meals. My stock of rice I kept in a drawer in the school table; two bottles, one of soy sauce, one of kerosene, stood in lonely state in a corner of the room. When time was short I would eat nothing but rice with a dash of sauce, straight out of the pot; if I wanted a bit of a feast, I bought some bream or *sawara* (both of which were absurdly cheap in the spring—five sen would bring home a good-sized fish uncut, more often than not), dress it after a fashion, and boil it on top of the rice, along with most of the bones and all of the smell. Mr Kento had me to his house for supper sometimes, and now and again a student would bring a dish of boiled fish and vegetables his mother had cooked. I became good friends with the students. If any of them happened to arrive early, they would come running upstairs to my room, smelling a stew, maybe, or hearing me chop onion on my desk, and peep in through the door with a smiling 'Beef today, is it, Sensei—can we help you?'

True it is that 'devil there is none in the wide world.' If a man walks upright through the world, ready to trust and love and serve his fellows, he will snore as comfortably in the enemy camp as anywhere else. Half a year and not a few adventures after leaving home, now for the first time I felt I understood a little of what true human kindness means.

Here was I, abruptly transformed from student into teacher, merely because I happened to be a lesson or two ahead of anybody else—in the country of the blind the one-eyed man is king—but as time went on I must have got a bit of a reputation for serious, helpful teaching, I suppose, for so many new students kept applying to join the classes that I could hardly cope alone. Eventually we set up day classes as well as the evening ones, till they were coming continuously from two o'clock onwards. The students were at every conceivable level. Side by side with some who were just mouthing their first ABC would be others busily translating 'That is a dog', 'An ant has legs'; a Second Reader on one desk, Katzenbach's *Short History of America* on the next, Swinton's *Universal History* here, a *Pocket Grammar* there—and one teacher to help them all. At least I learnt what grown-ups mean when they complain of being 'rushed off their feet'.

As the months went by and little by little the students progressed,

Kikuchi Sensei found himself in difficulty more than once. When a teacher has made a mistake, it doesn't do his authority much good to admit straight out that he was wrong, so I learnt the trick of sticking stubbornly to every point I had made, like Minister Wang An-shih;[15] and then, after a decent interval, remarking casually that what I'd said before was of course *one* way of doing it, but this other way was generally considered the best. Sometimes, in texts like the *Universal History*, I came across words I didn't know in the middle of a lesson. The knack in this case was to glance smartly through the next few lines while a student was reading, leave the room 'on business'—'I shan't keep you waiting a moment'—and return as promised a moment later with dignity unimpaired, having looked up the troublesome words in my dictionary. Three or four times in one evening, if his luck was out, Kikuchi Sensei's lessons might be interrupted by these sudden business calls. It sounds absurd, I know: the truth of the matter is, I had taken on a job that was beyond me, and had to struggle mightily to keep up with it.

The struggle was worth it, though, for the reward it brought each month. For the first month Mr Kento looked after the money side, then I took over; and from then on Kikuchi Sensei acted as director of studies, head teacher, secretary and treasurer all rolled into one. The fee was the same for every class—fifteen sen per student per month. Each pay-day a whole heap of copper and silver coins and old oval pieces of the Tenpo era[16] accumulated in my desk drawer—as much as six or seven yen when the classes were full. Setting aside not more than two yen fifty sen for living expenses and pocket money, I put the rest in Post Office Savings (they went by a different name in those days). Can you imagine how I gloated over my Post Office Book each month, watching the balance creeping up to 10 yen and beyond? Don't misunderstand me: those months as the moneylender's boy hadn't made me a miser. But didn't every entry in that book of mine take me a long step nearer Tokyo, the goal of my ambition?

When I moved to the school I wrote my first letter to my mother. During my stay at the moneylender's I couldn't bring myself to write, however often I tried—what would she think, that proud, strong-willed mother of mine, if she were to hear that her beloved only son was slaving for a moneylender, of all people? Once established in my room at the school, however, my self-respect began to recover, and I wrote at last, shedding not a few tears in the process. First, I apologized for my unfilial conduct in running away the year before without a word to her, and for not having written to her since; then I described in detail all that had happened to me: how I'd been picked up out of the snow in the middle of the night by Mr Nishiuchi, and how Mr Kento had found me a job teaching night classes;

---

15. Wang An-shih (1021–1086), Chief Minister to the Sung Emperor Shen Tsung, and famous for the unwavering self-confidence with which he withstood all attacks on his reforming measures.

16. 1830–1844.

how I was quite well again now, and no longer dependent, even managing to put aside a little every month. Even so, I told her, I hadn't the smallest intention of rusting away here as a country English teacher; before long, as soon as I had saved the money, I would be off to Tokyo. She was to look after herself and not to worry about me, but wait patiently till I finished my studies . . . and so on. Instead of writing separately to the Nodas, I added a postscript asking Mother to give my greetings to Uncle and Aunt Noda and Cousin Suzue.

IV.16

Ten days later came the longed-for reply. The sight of Mother's handwriting moved me so much, as if we were face to face once more, that I wept over her letter as I read:

July 14th

My dear son,

Your letter gave me such joy, and pain too. Reading it was like hearing a message from the dead. Ever since you disappeared last autumn, leaving only that note saying you were going to Tokyo, I have been waiting, waiting every day for the next post to bring news of your safe arrival. But no word came. So I wrote to Mrs Nakajima (Uncle Noda's sister-in-law, with whom my cousin Daiichiro had lived in Tokyo). But she knew nothing either. Then I tried the Matsumuras, whose boy you used to be so friendly with; and when they replied that *they* knew nothing, I even started visiting temple mediums and fortune-tellers—silly, I know, but I was so upset!

Overwhelmed, I dropped my head on my desk. That my mother, with her obstinate courage, her loathing of every kind of folly and weakness, should have—oh, why hadn't I sent her even a postcard before?

Nothing but airy babbling from any of them, though. Give up worrying, Heaven will take care of him, I told myself. But at night I still dreamt of you lying by the roadside, too ill to get up, and every day my heart missed a beat at the sound of footsteps outside, or the postman's voice. So I lived—till in the mercy of Heaven, after seven months, your letter came. How relieved I was! You have had great trials to face since last year, I can see; but I am so thankful to hear that you are working on your own now, and troubling nobody. How kind Mr Nishiuchi and Mr Kento have been. But that's enough of the past! Look after yourself, go carefully, aim high, and do your best. Don't forget the task of restoring our family has fallen to you: be sure you do nothing to bring discredit on the name of Kikuchi. Your success is your Mother's only wish—don't rest till you've made it come true!

These are hard times you have had to come to manhood in. One way and another there will be many disappointments, many tests of your strength and patience. A woman's earnings can't even provide the few yen you'll need for your school fees, however hard she works . . . think what that means to your Mother, if you can. Learn from the men of old who never gave in to hardship and poverty, till at last they raised themselves and their families to greatness. Keep your integrity, Shintaro, if it means you have to go in rags; and never give up!

There is so much more I want to say, but it must wait.

Your affectionate
Mother.

PS. Please take the enclosed letters to Mr Nishiuchi and Mr Kento, and tell them how grateful I am for all their kindness. Never talk of what you do for others, and never forget what others do for you; that is the first rule in making friends.

Your Uncle's family are all well. I thought it best to move not long ago to this place—you'll see where it is, from the address on the back of the envelope (the address she had given was an old samurai house, in the same town but about two miles from Uncle's). I manage by teaching sewing and calligraphy to girls in the neighbourhood. Everyone is kind, and I have everything I need, so give all your mind to what you have to do, without worrying about me.

You must be very short of clothes. I am making a summer kimono, and will send it as soon as it's ready. Do take special care of yourself —

Mother

The other two letters fell out as I came to the end of the scroll—and with them, two one-yen notes . . .

IV.17

Sitting at my desk, my head resting on my hands, I read my mother's letter over and over again. It worried me that she had left Uncle's and was living on her own. Things must have got difficult between her and Uncle after my disappearance: that would be why she had moved. And for this I was responsible, to my shame. Who could tell what she had sacrificed, to be able to send her son this money, when she herself was in such need? Reverently I raised to my forehead the two notes, worth more to me than thousands. How little I deserved the gift!

Two weeks later a parcel arrived, and once more I wept; this time over the fine patterned kimono Mother had sewn for me. Now at long last I wrote to Uncle Noda, apologizing for my past conduct, and begging him to use Mother kindly, whatever he might think of *me*. A reply came by return—in Aunt's handwriting, needless to say—to the effect that Mother was perfectly well, I was not to worry, etc. That was some comfort, though I doubted whether the letter had been written with Uncle's approval. But it did contain one startling piece of news: Cousin Suzue had gone up to Tokyo! There were no details, only the bare announcement that at her own insistence she had left early in March to study in the capital. Aggravating to think I had been overtaken by a *girl*—but I liked her courage. And if even a girl could show such spirit, how long could anyone who called himself a man be content to stagnate in the wilds as a hack teacher of the merest beginnings of English? 'Never tarrying, southward hurries the river'—and time was advancing no less inexorably. If only *my* wings would grow more quickly: they were so slow in coming, I felt like tearing them out in my frustration.

One sweltering day in the height of summer I was sitting half-naked in my room at the school, reading a book, when I heard Mr Kento calling to me from downstairs. Throwing on a kimono, I hurried down. My benefactor had with him a young man of about twenty with bushy eyebrows, his face rather pale but relaxed and serene.

'This is Kikuchi.' Coming straight up to me without any of the usual formal phrases, the young man smiled and gave me a courteous nod of greeting. I had known already that Michitaro Kento, Mr Kento's son, was a student in the department of politics at Waseda College in Tokyo. In this stronghold of the Liberals, his father was the only Progressive of any influence, both in his own estimation and by general consent, and even talked of standing for the Diet. It wasn't surprising, therefore, that he had sent his son to Waseda. A week or two earlier, I had heard them say that Michitaro was coming home for the summer: now here he was, and from the first I took to him. Not that I claim any special ability in face-reading, but more often than not a single glance gives me a pretty fair idea of a person's character. There was nothing showy or wayward in the younger Kento's expression, only a quiet, sturdy manliness. What he thought of me I don't know, but his face kept its gentle smile, and though that first meeting was very brief, no more than ten or fifteen minutes, it proved to be the start of a lasting friendship.

IV.18

With half the students of the evening classes taking a holiday during the hot weather, I felt more than usually lonely in the big school building, and so was especially glad to have this new friend to talk to. He seemed to take to me somehow, and came every day to see me; we quickly dropped any pretence of formal language, and soon were talking like old friends, till one day he complained of not being able to sleep at home, it was so hot and noisy there, and started spending nights with me in my room at the school.

Lying on my massive table for a bed, with the moonlight shining in at the open window, I poured out my story and my dreams, while Michitaro gave me very willingly what I so longed to hear—a detailed account of student life in Tokyo. If I was young for my years, he was old for his, mature already, with nothing of the boyish about him any longer: yet a strange sympathy seemed to have sprung up on both sides, for I kept nothing back, and he trusted me enough to tell me a great deal about his home and family.

Originally a strict Confucian, his father had found it galling to be left behind by all the changes that came after the Restoration and now was doing his best to take the lead in reform. His stepmother treated him (Michitaro) as an intruder, grumbling about him to his father, who was fonder anyway of Masamichi, his son by his second wife, a self-willed, unruly boy of twelve. He himself was engaged to a cousin of his, a girl of sixteen called O-Fuyu. He was supposed to marry her as soon as he finished at College; but in his opinion too early a marriage was a tragedy for any young man; he hoped to get the wedding postponed as long as possible, so that he could travel abroad after graduation. O-Fuyu's parents were both dead; she lived with her grandfather, one of the richest men in Ehime Prefecture, an old miser of seventy-five who stubbornly refused to wear socks even in the middle of winter and would go shuffling round his house retrieving bits of rubbish his servants had thrown away. Even his own father, said Michitaro, was secretly afraid of the old man. So I saw that every house has its troubles. Perhaps the unusually quiet, even subdued air that had so struck me about Michitaro when I first met him was simply the reflection of a trying atmosphere at home. I listened full of sympathy to all he told me.

On one subject, though, I could not sympathize. Michitaro was a Christian. The first night he came to stay with me at the school, he startled me by going into a corner of the room just as we were going to bed, and kneeling, with his face upturned. I peered at him through the dim light.

'What's the matter—headache?' He didn't answer; so still and quiet, he might have been asleep. A couple of minutes later, he stood up, smiling.

'I was praying, Kikuchi.'

'*Praying?* what for?'

'I'm a Christian, you see.'

'A *Christian*?' I shouted.

Michitaro smiled. 'A Christian. Any objection?'

I nearly choked. As a matter of fact I knew next to nothing about religion. Mother hated any kind of superstition, as did Seizan Sensei; at the New School religion was ignored altogether. If the word meant anything at all to me, it suggested an easy way to salvation for the ignorant and foolish. As for Christianity, I had never heard any preaching, nor made any serious attempt to find out what it was about. There was something nauseating about the name Jesus, though: and I recalled how disgusted I had been when years ago in Tsumagome I had seen a man with an inordinately long beard and coarse, vulgar features pointing at a picture of Jesus bleeding on the cross and gabbling something about the shame and pity of it (looking back, I think he must have been a Catholic or an Orthodox priest). Sometimes when walking in Uwajima, even, I heard a wailing of hymns, dreary beyond description, as if all the singers were half-wits, issuing from behind shabby doors over which hung a notice, 'Christian Preaching Hall'. All this had convinced me that Christianity was something no man with any self-respect should have anything to do with. And now here was this friend of mine—whose character I already admired, though I had only known him for so short a time—announcing that *he* was a Christian. I couldn't help feeling disillusioned, as well as astonished.

'Surprised, were you?' said Michitaro, still smiling.

'Is your father a Christian too?'

'No, I'm the only one in the family. I've tried to argue with him, but he won't listen; dislikes me all the more for it, in fact. "What's the good of Christianity," he keeps saying, "to a man who is going in for the new learning, and means to be a politician?"'

For myself I agreed wholeheartedly with Michitaro's father. Michitaro began there and then to expound to me the main points of the Christian religion: the existence of God, the immortality of the soul, human sinfulness, the atonement and divinity of Christ, eternal punishment and eternal life, the meaning of faith, the revelation of God's purpose in the Bible, and so on. Occasionally something he said sounded reasonable, but on the whole it struck me as fantastic nonsense, which nobody with the smallest degree of intelligence could possibly accept. I argued with him furiously (partly, no doubt, out of a feeling that to agree meekly to anything my benefactor's son said would have looked like toadying. The motives of youth are shockingly mixed). I forget exactly what I said—something about Buddhism and Christianity both being nothing but crutches for the lame, myths for the feeble-minded; in Japan, with our Yamato spirit, our Confucian morality, our Bushido, and the 'innate abilities and knowledge' that Mencius spoke of as common to all men, enlightenment and peace can be had without religion. If there was no salvation without religion, how could the innumerable heroes and great men of the past have come by their glorious achievements? Heaven helps those who help themselves, and so, surely, with salvation; what need of a Bible, when we have the Books of the Sages, the Lives of the Wise, the records of famous scholars and men of benevolence to read; what need of Jesus, when we have as many great spirits to look up to as there are stars shining in the sky—all these and other points, as haphazardly as they occurred to me, I bombarded him with. Michitaro listened, smiling as always; he didn't counter-attack that night.

Four or five days later he came to tell me he was going to Matsuyama the next day to see Mr Hachiya (O-Fuyu's grandfather), and asked if I would go with him. As it happened, my classes were officially on holiday just then; and since Matsuyama was no great distance and the journey (according to Michitaro) would cost us nothing, I agreed at once. We set out at dawn next morning, travelling overland.

IV.19

Stopping one night on the way, we kicked off our sandals early the following evening by the veranda of a living-room at the back of a big house in Matsuyama—an oil-merchant's, judging by the great heaps of crushed seeds and husks lying in the courtyard. We went down the passage through the business part of the house, and through a small gate at the end leading to the outer garden and the veranda I spoke of—where we came upon a girl in her teens, dark-skinned, with compact, regular features, sitting with a pile of sewing. She glanced up with a sudden blush as she saw us; bowed, and smilingly pushed her work to one side.

'Guests, Grandfather—from Uwajima!' she called across to the inner garden.

'Oh, it's Michitaro, is it?' came the answer at once, then the old man himself appeared, red-faced with thick white eyebrows, in a sleeveless coat, with a broom in one hand and a dustpan in the other. 'We've been expecting you, Michitaro. Your family alright? Not much wrong with this old fellow, eh? He won't be on his way just yet awhile, I can tell you, ha, ha, ha!' The smile still on his lips, his narrow, sunken eyes turned to stare at me. Michitaro introduced me. 'He's welcome,' nodded the old gentleman. 'No, he won't be in the way—I like young people. Make yourself at home, both of you.'

Washing our feet in a big basinful of water the girl had brought out to the veranda, we stepped up into the house.

Several men and women were employed in the business that was carried on in the front part of the house, but the living quarters at the back were occupied only by old Mr Hachiya, his granddaughter and her younger brother, a sturdy boy of about ten, intelligent and full of mischief, who was presumably the titular head of the family now, a middle-aged woman whom Michitaro called Aunt, and a single maid. After a bath to wash away the heat and dust of the journey, we were shown our room upstairs, and presently sat down to supper. Mr Hachiya was certainly fond of his saké— he emptied three bottles in no time—but neither Michitaro nor I drank, so we started on the meal proper right away, with O-Fuyu to serve us. We talked of many things. When Mr Hachiya had drunk his fill of saké and was swilling his third bowlful of tea, he turned to Michitaro.

'There's something I've been wanting to talk to you about, Michi. It's this girl of mine—,' he jabbed his chin at O-Fuyu.

'Grandfather, you shouldn't—' She tried to restrain him.

'Why not? It's nothing to be ashamed of.' In spite of having finished her elementary schooling, he went on, O-Fuyu wanted more education. He himself didn't think much of this education business—didn't do much good that he could see, only ran away with his money—but she had got the notion that if she didn't go away to a proper secondary school she might be a trouble to Michitaro later on (at which she blushed violently and looked down at the table), and *that* she wanted to avoid, even if it was too much to hope she might be of any help to him. 'So you can see, *you* are involved, and I thought we'd best discuss it with you. There's something else—.' The talk was clearly not for my ears, so I slipped out of the room and went upstairs.

Suzue had left for Tokyo already: now here was another girl following in her footsteps. If these creatures I despised could go so far, how could I hang back so feebly. Gripping the balcony handrail, I spat my anger at the moon, which by now hung bulkily over the laundry platform next door.

IV.20

During the three days we stayed at Matsuyama we visited the castle ruins, and spent half a day bathing at Dogo Spa, besides other trips. The strangest experience of all was when Michitaro took me into a 'prayer-meeting' or 'testimony meeting' or something of the kind, I forget exactly what they called it, at the local Christian church. Aha, I'd better watch out, was my first thought as we entered the building—he's getting even with me for all that I said about religion the other night ...

The hall was quite big, and it was full to overflowing. A bespectacled, kindly-looking man of about thirty, the 'pastor', presumably, was praying. Michitaro knew him, needless to say, but we sat together at the back. Before long the prayer came to an end; and in a gentle, rather reedy voice the pastor began an earnest discourse on some words from the Bible, 'I thank Thee, O Father, Lord of heaven and earth, because Thou has hid these things from the wise and prudent, and hast revealed them unto babes.' I looked around me as I listened. Most of his hearers appeared to be of the lower classes of society; as for intelligence and learning, they looked like fair specimens of the 'babes' of the preacher's text—among them were surely a fishmonger or two (one could tell by the smell) and some dyers (judging by the great stains of indigo on their hands). Several of them got up to pray after the sermon. They used the most preposterous phrases, 'Our Father which art in heaven', 'lay down my life fighting for Lord Christ', and the like, as if it were the most natural thing in the world; but there was a certain strength and dignity about the way each one stood up and spoke—as much as to say that however humble and ignorant they might be, they would bow before none but God—which lent a kind of harmony to all their outpourings.

At one point a huge, rather gloomy-looking man of thirty-five or six got up to give a 'testimony' as he called it. Michitaro whispered that until three years back this man had been a notorious gambler. One winter's night he was on his way to his usual gaming-house, with a bundle of old clothes for a pawnshop under his arm, when he had been caught by some words he happened to hear through a lattice-door—it was this same pastor, preaching in a private house. In that one night he had completely reformed, and was now the respected proprietor of a cake-shop, so Michitaro told me. He was speaking now of the death of a little girl of nine, the daughter of a member of the church. For nearly five years the girl had lain in bed, in constant pain from some terrible disease; yet she had never once grumbled, but remained alert and cheerful to the very end, smiling and singing hymns till the time came for her to fall asleep—such was the big man's 'testimony'. I had heard how the great sage Socrates discoursed on the immortality of the soul while holding in his hand the very cup of poison by which he was to die. But a girl—a little, unschooled nine-year-old—how was it that she could endure such tragedy without a murmur? what power enabled her to smile in the face of death, before which the greatest men have trembled, and act out in her own person the truth of the Greek philosopher's words? A thread of light seemed to flash before me, then fade as abruptly: I was conscious of a strange, deep pain, as if I had been shown for the first time the darkness of my soul.

After the meeting, Michitaro took me to the pastor's house. I found the Reverend Shizu to be a friendly, straightforward person, not at all the superstition-monger I had expected. Great piles of books, Chinese, Japanese and western, but mostly western, filled his study. Somewhere children were laughing. As soon as Michitaro had told him who I was, the pastor asked me a number of questions in a very friendly manner, without the least formality: how long I meant to stay in Uwajima, whether I intended to go on somewhere else for more schooling, and so forth. Of course, I said, my aim was to get to Tokyo; but—and here I faltered. Michitaro helped me out, explaining how I was struggling to save a little money to pay for my future studies by teaching English classes, out of a stubborn refusal to depend on others; otherwise, he said, he himself would have lent a hand. The pastor thought for a moment, then slapped his knee.

'It doesn't have to be Tokyo right away, I suppose? As far as general education is concerned, schools are much the same everywhere. How about Kansei College, in Kobe? That might suit you.' The English there was particularly good, he said, and poor students could earn their fees and keep by gate-duty, bell-ringing, cleaning classrooms and the like. I liked the sound of this. But Kansei College was a Christian school. Did this mean, I asked the pastor, that you were in duty bound to become a preacher when you graduated, as the graduates of Teachers' Colleges were compelled by law to teach? Smiling, he explained that they did train preachers, but in a special theology section, not in the General Studies department, where plenty of the students were non-believers. Kansei College began to seem more and more attractive. Kobe—that would be half-way to Tokyo already; better there than marking time down here in Shikoku. The pastor agreed to write off to the College and find out whether there was a vacancy. We did not discuss religion any more that evening, though before Michitaro and I left, the pastor gave me a Bible and an old copy of the Kansei College prospectus.

Next morning we said goodbye to old Mr Hachiya, to Michitaro's fiancée (she had secured a place in Plum Blossom Women's College in Osaka, we were told, and was to start there in September) and to her lively young brother, and returned to Uwajima by the steamship from Mizu.

IV.21

Thus the trip to Matsuyama gave me the hope of getting my feet back on the road. Michitaro was delighted as I was—a load off his own mind, he kept saying. I didn't tell his father or my students, but wrote to my mother that there was a chance I might be going to Kansei College before long, with a brief account of the kind of school it was and how I hoped to be able to pay my way. Her reply came by return. She was thrilled at the news, and promised to send me clothes and other things I would be sure to need, as soon as it was definite that I had a place. She was obviously worried, though, that I might become a Christian, the school being what it was. Now that I was no longer a boy, she wouldn't interfere, she wrote, but pleaded with me over and over again to stick to my first resolve, and not to allow expediency or the emotion of a moment to tempt me into evil courses.

I wouldn't know whether or not I could get a place till I heard from the Reverend Shizu, nor was he likely to write before the beginning of September (the College term started in mid-September); but I thought it best to make what preparations I could, when I wasn't teaching. According to the College prospectus, the General Studies course lasted five years. I ought to be able to enter the third year, I felt, though my English conversation was weak, and my mathematics more so. Fortunately mathematics was Michitaro's strong point, and he willingly gave me lessons; every day I sweated—how I sweated!—wrestling with Todhunter's 'Algebra' under his direction. We made a rule to speak only English to each other (he wasn't much better than me at conversation), but we hadn't the patience to keep this up: after every other fumbling word we couldn't help slipping back happily into our respective dialects, and soon we gave up the attempt altogether. All my efforts were concentrated now on mathematics. We didn't speak of religion again. The Bible the Reverend Shizu had given me lay shut away in my desk drawer, unread, except for the Sermon on the Mount. Frankly, learning seemed much more vital to me than any talk of religion. A man has no time for salvation when he's trying to get into a College—such was my shallow, worldly, childish way of thinking at that time.

But personality convinces more than preaching, and the spirit hears the message when the ear turns away uncomprehending. Sooner or later the seed that has fallen on the heart's ground is bound to swell and grow. Only a fool gapes at the young plum tree springing up, unplanted, in his garden: the wind has carried the seed, we know, or a bird's beak dropped it, or your boy tossed it in his playing; the earth has covered it where it fell, and there under your foot, where you tread casually, lies the great tree. That gleam of light I had caught in the hall at Matsuyama—it had faded, I thought, in that very instant. Yet it left behind it a strange warmth, that lingered on through the busiest days, as I struggled with my algebra and fought to keep back the yawns through hour after hour of teaching. And to that light Michitaro was a silent witness. His purity, gentleness, sincerity (at first sight there was nothing remarkable about him, only a wholeness of character that grew on you the longer you knew him, compelling love and admiration)—these qualities impressed me more than any number of sermons, and served as a living proof, though I wasn't conscious of this at the time, of the truth of Christianity.

Early in September Michitaro started back for Tokyo. Two nights before he left we talked till dawn in my room at the school, endlessly chewing roasted beans. I told him about Matsumura, from whom I hadn't heard for six months or more, and gave him messages to deliver if they met. On the final morning I went down to the pier to see him off. As the steamer sailed out of the harbour I wept a little, looking wistfully at the 'fading wraith of smoke', as the farewell song describes it. Surely there are other tears besides the poet's 'dew upon the flowers of love'. May not a man weep also for his friend?

IV.22

Soon after Michitaro had left, the letter I was so impatiently waiting for came. I opened it with trembling fingers. While Kansei College could make no definite promise, wrote the Reverend Shizu, they thought they might be able to take me, provided I passed their entrance examination. He advised me to leave at once—the entrance examination would begin on September 10th, and the new session on the 15th—and enclosed two letters of introduction, one to a Mr Ihara, Secretary to the College, and the other to a Professor Shimizu.

So the way lay open, thanks to the Reverend Shizu. But the examination? If I passed, well and good; if not—out of the frying-pan into the fire. No use hesitating now, though. Go I must, and burn my boats, such as they were.

I began at once on the final preparations. My Post Office Savings book showed a credit of just over thirteen yen, which I was loath to use, having laboured so hard to earn it; but out of this little stock of capital would have to come the cost of the journey, and, assuming I passed the exam, the College entrance fee. I decided not to write to Mother till after the examination, to save her from worrying about my fares, and from the shock, if by any chance I were to fail.

Then I had a chance to learn the full extent of Michitaro's kindness. I called on Mr Kento to 'ask his advice', as we say, about my departure (though in reality it was to tell him straight out that I was leaving), fully expecting the news would astound him; instead of which, he merely nodded, as if he knew all about it already, gave me there and then a farewell party (or a farewell meal, anyway: 'party' would be an exaggeration), and finally handed me an envelope wrapped in gift paper and inscribed 'For Your Journey'. Well! Goodwill I was prepared for, but I certainly had not earned a present of money. I was getting ready to refuse in my usual stiff, obstinate way, when I noticed the name 'Michitaro' signed in a corner of the envelope. With all the determination in the world to lean on no one but myself, how could I refuse such generosity on the part of a friend, shown with such tact? I bowed gratefully to Mr Kento.

My students were amazed when they heard I would soon be going. When they came up to me and said dolefully, 'Sensei, we hear you're leaving,' I greeted them with an odd mixture of sadness and excitement, of satisfaction and of regret that I could serve them no further. The day before I sailed, three of them brought me two paper parcels tied with red and white gift-strings. I tried to refuse, but they pressed them on me, and fled. One parcel, it turned out, contained a boxful of bean-jam buns, the other a pair of padded clogs. The clogs being so grand, I couldn't possibly wear them (no such difficulty about the buns!) but it was no good leaving them behind, either, so I rolled them up in my baggage and set out the next day in the Satsuma clogs I had worn nearly flat since coming to Uwajima.

My 'baggage', as I called it, was no more than one cloth wrapper would hold. No, that's not quite true. One well-filled bundle, and the goodwill of several score of my fellow human beings—all this I took with me; and all of it, along with my rescue from the snow and all the blessings, material and immaterial, I had enjoyed ever since, I owed primarily to the moneylender. So to Mr Nishiuchi's I went on my last day to say goodbye, with a bag of crackers to present to him as a token of my gratitude. Blacky, Browny and Mottle charged down upon me with their usual battle-cry the moment I opened the gate; then they recognized me, and I was instantly covered, legs, hands and face with a flurry of affectionate tongues. Up by the house the old housekeeper was drawing water from the well: she turned at the din, peering down towards us.

'Bain't that young Shinta boy?'

I didn't mind the 'Shinta' now, since this would be the last time.

'Shinta-san it is! A long while since we saw you hereabouts.'

'I've been busy. And now I've come to say goodbye—'

'Goodbye, indeed! And where would you be going?'

'To the Kansai—boat to Osaka.'

'The Kansai? What'll you be going there for—the Ise Shrine, or the big temple in Kyoto?'

Poor old woman! Already we were living in different worlds, she and I.

'I'm going to study.'

'Study? Bain't you a teacher then? Why more study, Shinta-san?'

'There's always more to learn.'

A call from the house interrupted us, my old master having recognized my voice. I went inside, to find him occupied as usual with his account-books and abacus. The nephew was nowhere to be seen.

'You've not done badly, to save that much' was his first comment when he heard of my plans. I told him how I hoped to work as a servant at the College to pay my way. He nodded, and started off once more on his lecture on how-to-rise-in-the-world, which I had heard so often before: endurance is the key to success, economy its foundation, never waste a single sen, etc., repeated many times over, until at last he disappeared into an inner room, from which he emerged after several minutes to present me with twenty sen in coins, wrapped in half a sheet of toilet-paper, as 'sandal-money'. This I accepted gratefully, though it didn't seem quite the usual kind of gift. Since they both insisted I should stay for a meal, I was forced to gulp down several platefuls, not without a grimace or two, of the famous fish-salad the old woman was still convinced was my favourite dish; after which the whole household—master, housekeeper, and dogs—saw me off at the gate.

On the evening of September 7th, I said my last goodbyes to Mr Kento and those of my students (many of them still bigger than me!) who had come down to the quay, and boarded the steamer for Osaka. Standing on deck in the evening breeze, as the harbour receded I gazed, entranced, at the lights flickering along the dark line of the Uwajima hills where they rose to meet the Milky Way.

Part V

Four months passed. The cool evening breeze gently rustling the sleeves of my summer kimono on the steamship deck had given way to the piercing autumn winds that sweep down to the Kobe coast from Mount Rokko. Leaning on the window-sill of my three-mat room, I watched a flock of crows chase the setting sun, and recalled my sudden flight from home just a year ago. Below, on gravel paths bisecting the lawn of withered grass, groups of chattering students of all ages from fifteen to twenty-five collected as they left the dining-hall; beyond the lawn, opposite to my window, stood a two-storied rectangular building, many of its long rows of windows open. The scene? The Kansei College dormitories, I don't have to tell you, and here was I, a fully-fledged third-year College student already.

The first sight I had of the College when I arrived from Uwajima nearly knocked me over. (I was still a country bumpkin, don't forget.) The site, to start with: up in the foothills, away from Kobe City proper, with the Rokko mountains behind and over to the right the panorama of Awaji Island and the ships strung out across the Bay of Osaka, like toy boats on a tray—this was overwhelming enough, and on top of it the fine array of buildings: classroom block, dormitories, dining-hall and chapel, all standing on their own—it struck me as much too good for a school. Later, when a fellow-student assured me Doshisha College in Kyoto was more splendid still, and Tokyo University many times grander even than Doshisha, I could only gape. (It didn't take much to set me gaping in those days!) The students who studied in such surroundings must all be paragons, the teachers great scholars, the Principal a genius of learning and wisdom. A hick like myself would never have a chance, I told myself in despair before I set foot on the campus.

But thanks to the Reverend Shizu's letters of introduction, both the Secretary and Professor Shimizu treated me very kindly. The dreaded examinations too, including my special bogey, the sweat-producing algebra, I managed to survive with an average of seventy per cent, which I thought wasn't doing too badly, though I say it who shouldn't. It was English (conversation, not reading) I was most afraid of. Miracles do happen, though. I was sitting waiting in the examination room when the door opened portentously. Enter the foreign examiner.

Ohs and Ahs of astonishment from us both, and we shook hands, the examination (for the moment) forgotten. For my examiner was none other than Mr Wilkie Brown, for whom I had so stumblingly interpreted at Uwajima Police Station. A coincidence worthy of a novel! After we had talked about how I came to be trying for the College, he went on to the examination proper; but meeting him so unexpectedly had given me such courage, I rolled out the most unpronounceable words without a tremor. A poor enough performance it must have been, even so, but he took pity and gave me a generous 7—and capped it with an invitation to come to his home for evening conversation practice twice a week after term began. I was truly grateful for such kindness.

So much for the examination. I paid my registration and first month's tuition and board, and was entered in the third year. The Secretary found me a job as a cleaner in the classroom block, with two rooms to swab out each day, one before school and one after. My 'salary' of four yen would not be due till the end of the month, but I was able to pay my fees and buy the necessary school books, a rickety old table and chair, a lamp and other odds and ends out of Michitaro's gift. Truly I owed everything to others. As soon as term began, I wrote letters, first to my mother, then to Michitaro, his father, the Reverend Shizu, and Mr Nishiuchi, to thank them for all they had done for me.

v.2

Now, after four months, I knew the ropes pretty well. Unlike Seizan Sensei's and the New School, the College had properly organized courses, a full complement of teachers, fine classrooms, and reasonably comfortable dormitories. The 'spirit' of the school was officially Christian, in the same sense that Seizan Sensei's stood for Frugality and Self-help, and the New School for Freedom. Mr Katayama, the Principal, was a samurai from Sendai, who before the Restoration had fought for the Shogunate against the Imperial army in the Shirakawa campaign; afterwards, his unyielding opposition to the new government made him a vehement advocate of freedom in politics, and a heroic worker in the campaign for a Japanese parliament. Then, quite suddenly, he had been converted to the western religion, and ever since had devoted himself to education. Not surprisingly, there was a samurai flavour to his Christianity, which caused a good deal of head-shaking among the foreign teachers but made him very influential with the students. Since it was a Christian school, each morning began with a worship service, and Sunday was of course a rest-day. Most students had Bibles, and if you peeped in at a dormitory window at ten or so in the evening, you were sure to see one or two boys on their knees at a chair, saying their prayers before going to bed. As for the curriculum, apart from the General Course there was Theology Course I, in English, and Theology Course II, in Japanese (referred to by the General Course students, I must confess, as 'the junk-heap'), so that all in all there was plenty of Christianity about.

Wherever a single authority is dominant one always finds both hypocritical timeservers and rebels whose unorthodoxy is merely a pose. So at Kansei College there were not a few, on the one hand, who paid many a secret visit to the gay quarters on weekdays but on Sundays listened with sanctimonious devotion to the most boring sermons and interminable prayers, or who were merely using Christianity as a step in their careers, piously reciting 'for man does not live by bread alone' out of nothing more or less than greed for the largest possible share of bread. With others, sneering at Christianity was a form of showing-off: they would make a point of declaiming passages from the *Kingoro and the Bath Attendant*[1] next to a student reading his Bible, expound the case for atheism, and snigger at the 'Christian weaklings', who were 'so fond of licking the boots of the foreign scum'. As for myself, I wasn't going to accept the school's religion blindly just because I happened to be studying there: I had not lost any part of my resolve to keep my integrity, my sense of independence; nor on the other hand did I see any point in the cheap antics of the mockers. Neutral as far as religion was concerned, I gave myself up wholeheartedly to study.

Though the subjects we studied were relatively few, I was exceedingly busy. In English Conversation and Mathematics in particular, as I hadn't had as good a grounding as the others, I had to work twice as hard as anybody else. About an hour after Lights Out, which was at ten, I would creep out of bed, shut myself up in one of the bedding cupboards with a small lamp, so that no light showed in the dormitory, and grapple with the geometry book. Two evenings a week were given over to conversation practice at Mr Brown's. Then there were my cleaning duties, which took a sizeable slice of time each morning and evening. All this was no strain to me, after the training we had been given at Seizan Sensei's, and the Spartan life I had led at the moneylender's.

But wherever you go you always find pampered young bucks who think it a disgrace to earn one's living, and there was no lack of these gentlemen —fresh from their mother's bosom, a postal order for eight or nine yen dropping into their laps every month without their ever having the bother of asking for it; buying extra woollies for their dear little selves, and bags of their favourite candy, so that they had to send off home for *extra* money by every other post—there was no lack of these gentlemen to sneer and point and turn up their noses when they deigned to notice Cleaner Kikuchi on his way to the classrooms, pail in one hand, broom in the other. No use taking any notice, but sometimes I couldn't help getting angry, like Socrates' wife, and felt like baptizing their jaunty heads into the glories of labour with a few efficacious drops from my swab cloth, or taking a swipe

1. *Kosan Kingoro Kanamajiri Musume Setsuyo*, a romantic novel published in three parts between 1831 and 1834.

with my broom at those soft bellies. However, I gritted my teeth, and managed to endure. Feelings always find some outlet, though: in this case resentment drove me to work still harder, and in the exams at the end of the winter term I ran up to second place in my class of thirty.

v.3

School life doesn't alter much over the generations. Days and months slip by, so long in prospect, so short in recall; you flip over the leaves of your calendar, day by day, week by week and with the speed of a dream the year's end confronts you. How sluggishly we rose on Monday, the first working day; how eagerly looked forward to each Friday evening! Sunday was a rest-day for the soul, Saturday for the body. The evening was the highlight of each day, as Saturday was of the week. Classes over for the day, and supper finished, we strolled about the campus in groups of three or four. The quadrangle between the east and west dormitories, which we had to cross at the start or end of any walk, became our forum: here bigger groups, of ten or twenty students, would gather around the most popular or eloquent of their fellows to discuss anything from religion, politics and literature to the skill or otherwise of the College cooks. Here was perfect freedom of speech, and of sarcasm; admirable miniature parliaments, which any member might join or leave at will, and where College opinion on almost any subject might be tested. On a summer evening when the moon was full, circles of white and patterned summer kimonos would form on the grass, and were still reluctant to break up when the great clock over the classroom building struck eight. After that time, however, we were encouraged to study quietly on our own, so that though you might see lamps burning on desks at window after window, the dormitories could have been empty for all the noise we made. Outside it wasn't always so quiet, though. On cold moonlit evenings in winter, for instance, the big brawny fellows would make the frosty air of the quadrangle resound with flute-like song, lacerating not a few sentimental hearts with the melancholy ballads of Tatsuo Kumoi[2] or Mikisaburo Rai.[3]

But Lights Out at ten was strictly enforced, so that by half-past ten the whole College was silent and unlit, save for the night insects and the moon: and three hundred spirits flitted out to dream their dreams: one to rule his country as First Minister, another to be ruined and spend long years as a humble school janitor; a third and fourth to marry, one a Mitsui or a Mitsubishi[4] heiress, the other a beauty in beggar's rags; a

---

2. A former supporter of the Shogunate who was executed in 1870 for plotting the overthrow of the newly-restored Imperial government.
3. A Confucian scholar and poet, advocate of a return to Imperial rule; executed by the Shogunate in 1859.
4. The two leading *zaibatsu*, or business empires, whose growth was such a prominent feature of Japanese economic development from the 1870s onwards.

fifth to suffer all the torments of purgatory for unpaid debts, pursued by the friends whose pocket-money he had borrowed, disguised as avenging demons; a sixth to fly home to Mother, to suck his fill of candy; a seventh to groan at his performance in the coming exams; an eighth to laugh with delight as the tailor brings the smart western suit he will wear for graduation—to describe them all would blunt the sharpest pen. 'One girl, eight suitors,' we say of the beauty who wrinkles her pretty brow at the difficulty of the choice confronting her: what of the Goddess Success, with three hundred ardent worshippers?

Saturday—a day apart, consecrated to the rites of sleeping-in, day-long snacks, laundry and the weekly bath. Your youthful follower of Tsai Yü[5] stayed snug under his quilt till nine or ten o'clock; woe betide the jokers who tried to whip off his bedclothes *this* morning! Later a crowd of young hopefuls gathered round the well to rub their kimonos, padding and all, in cold suds, with clumsy, unpractised hands, protesting loudly at the destiny that binds such drudgery upon the Han Hsins[6] of this world. Laundry done, in every dormitory room the spinning of the dice, to choose whose money it should be that day—which decided, off would go ambassadors and ministers-plenipotentiary on their several missions, hiking downtown in a flurry of diplomatic foot-traffic, to return before long with ample loads of oranges, crackers, beans, rice-cakes . . . and then the silence! No one at home, you would have said, and no wonder: not a boy but was gagged with food. Chief Products of Kansei College (Saturdays only): orange peel, strips of bamboo wrapping, bean shells—but you're hardly likely to find this in your geography book.

Above all Saturday was for outings. Out of the gate with jaunty flourishing of home-made canes we streamed on a fine Saturday morning in bands of four or five, cool in baggy white cotton trousers, or with red and blue blankets slung over our shoulders on the colder days: at evening, slow of tread and light of purse (whose purse was ever heavy?) the expeditions would return, weary but content, to souse stiff limbs at the well and horrify the cooks with new-found appetites. Truly the spring in Harima and Settsu is a delight, and autumn even more so. The country is glorious, and there are so many places of historical interest: Kusunoki's[7] tombstone at Minatogawa; Ichinotani Shore, scene of Yoshitsune's famous victory[8] over the Taira; the Atsumori Pagoda at Suma,[9] the beaches of Akashi and

5. v. p. 125 above, note 19.   6. See note 5, p. 149.
7. Masashige Kusunoki (1294–1336), one of the greatest exemplars of loyalty in Japanese history. After being defeated in the battle at Minatogawa, he and his brother Masasue committed suicide together at a farmhouse nearby.
8. In 1184.
9. The Pagoda commemorates a moving incident in the Genpei wars towards the close of the twelfth century. Atsumori Taira, a young courtier of sixteen, was riding towards the sea to join his relatives who, pursued by the enemy, had escaped to a ship lying off the shore, when he was challenged by the celebrated warrior Naozane Kumagai. A fierce fight ensued, and Atsumori was soon overcome. Kumagai was about to kill him when he saw for the first time the young and

Maiko and Nunobiki Falls; Ikuta Woods and Shrine—not to mention the glories of Osaka, Kyoto and Nara; and reminders everywhere of Crosspatch High-clogs,[10] Tojiin the Bold,[11] and Naughty Tokichi.[12]

Seeing so many relics and scenes of the most fascinating period of Japanese history, concentrated in one small area a few miles square, and always in surroundings of such beauty, like diamonds heaped in a crystal, I found every step of those spring and autumn walks a thrill. The same breeze that sways the topmost branches of a tree will rustle the grasses at its foot: and the inspiration that made the great Rai[13] sing

> In such a place as this
> One may sense all the vicissitudes of its history:
> Battle upon battle, for a thousand years.
> What need here of written chronicles?

aroused in me, in measure, a new delight in history, a new awareness of its poetry.

v.4

If Saturday stood for expeditions, Friday evening was for speech-making. Writing and speech-making are the two great outlets for student vapourings. At Kansei College we had two student journals—both hand-copied, needless to say—which would make their appearance once a month or so in the reading-room; but compared to the speeches they were featherweights. Every Friday morning the huge wooden notice-board outside the dining-hall would carry (in addition to attacks on the food, 'Books for Sale' notices, an article, perhaps, by a new-found scholar refuting yesterday's lecture on Darwin's Theory of Evolution, a report of the result of the election for the 'Ten Champions', with satirical comments, and every other kind of notice) announcements of meetings of the Lead the Nation Club, or the New Wind Reform Society, with the titles of speeches to be given that evening—'Who Will Come Forward to Pioneer Civilization in The East', for instance, or 'A Plea From The Heart to All Compatriots'—and the names of the speakers. If you had cared to peep in at the time and place appointed, the smallness of the audience for any of these events might

---

beautiful face of his opponent, and wished to spare him. Atsumori, however, begged him to despatch him quickly, being in no mind to accept mercy from an enemy. Accordingly Kumagai cut off his head with his sword, but afterwards was so overwhelmed with remorse that he vowed never to carry arms again, and spent the rest of his life in a monastery.

10. Childhood nickname of Kiyomori, of the great Taira clan (1118–1181).
11. Posthumous name of the Shogun Takauji Ashikaga (1305–1358).
12. Childhood nickname of Fujikichiro Kinoshita, later (and better) known as Hideyoshi Toyotomi, the farmer's son who became Japan's most famous warrior and general (1537–1598).
13. A famous historian and poet of the Tokugawa period, who died in 1832.

have surprised you—fourteen or fifteen, perhaps, sitting around a table with only one small light—but much more the verve and eloquence of the speaker. Every Friday evening the campus echoed with thundered perorations: 'Gentlemen, I beg of you to consider—', and answering shouts (in English) of 'No, No!' or 'Hear, hear!'

Most of my schoolfellows at Seizan Sensei's and the New School were sons of samurai, and came from the same prefecture. The College, on the other hand, claiming as it could and did to be as good as any private school in the west of Japan, drew students from all classes and much further afield. The soft speech of Kyoto mingled with the boorish dialects of Kyushu and Shikoku, the Central Provinces, and even of the Tokyo area, though not many came from the east: sons of peasants, merchants, samurai and artisans, each bringing with him the peculiar ways of his province, his family, and his class, rubbed shoulders in search of a 'Christian' education, like yams being washed in a tub.

There were other divisions besides the classes we were assigned to. Vertically, if you like, the College was divided into two parties: the Worldly (or Vulgar) and the Unworldly (or Believers). Each of these parties was divided again into three: the Stars, the Wits, and the Ordinaries. The Worldly laughed at the Believers as stupid and spineless; the Believers pitied the Worldly for a band of deluded simpletons. From the school's point of view, of course, the Believers were its true sons, and the Worldly an unfortunate accident; but the number of Believers increased the higher up the school you went, so the dividing line between the two camps was more diagonal, as it were, than straight. But with the newcomers too overawed to be vocal, and the seniors fancying themselves as proper adults and no longer so willing to exert themselves, it was classes like mine, in between, that were most active—and that seemed to have more than their share of the personalities.

Akazawa, for instance, chief Star of the Worldly, once a member of the fanatical Genyo Society[14], it was said: a husky, big-chested youth, famous for his swagger, the holes in his shoes, and his politics; reading the newspapers instead of schoolbooks, and forever protesting that the College paid too little attention to current affairs—in which I agreed with him. Or Baba, the leader in my class of the Worldly Wits. Baba never washed with anything but Pears Toilet Soap, kept his hair perfectly parted, dressed himself as smart and shining as a black beetle whenever he went out, and kept Edo romances hidden in his desk drawer; always on the make, he could be affable to anyone if he wanted, but would jeer at the Believers as 'out-of-date' and 'innocent'. Or Endo, our 'philosopher', who would go three days quite happily without speaking, and four weeks or more without a bath, had worn the same crested coat of Maoka cotton every day for five years, and would solve geometry problems by formulas of his own that neither

14. An association of right-wing extremists founded in Kyushu in 1881, and not finally disbanded till 1946.

textbook nor teacher had ever heard of. Endo was our Star Believer; at least he looked the part. Or Kawada, bottom of the class but a smooth talker, sociable, organizer of parties and contact man, our go-between with teachers and other classes; Sato, the tradesman's son, every day dunning some friend for a ten sen debt, invariably disappearing with his own half-sen's worth of baked potato, but leading the rush for anyone else's bag of cakes; Fukami, lisping like the sparrow in 'The Old Man Whose Wife Cut Out the Sparrow's Tongue', smiling Fukami, prince of liars, president of debtors, Mr Never-Pay, Mr Optimist Fukami, dunned by an angry leatherman one day—in the dining-hall!—for the twenty sen he owed for his sandal-linings, and ready as ever next morning to cheat any cakeshop or smallgoods store in town; Kiyoura, the Writer, who decorated his geometry manual in flowery lettering with the legend 'A Noble Brew To Induce Apoplexy' and his *Universal History* with 'Six Thousand Years of Wise Old Men', who would spend an hour working out a simple sum, only to rub it out and glare, defeated, at the blackboard, but answered every question in the history classes, and was always ready with a poem; Kitagawa the Scholar, for ever asking questions, never missing a word in his reading or dropping a mark in translation; Homma the Humbug, who skimmed every book and fumbled every question in class, but earned top marks in nearly every exam; Yamagishi, the Timon of our Athens, son of a wealthy silk-worm breeder, well supplied with cash and candy, and with a touch of sweetness in himself, a combination that attracted a swarm of greedy flies (to his great satisfaction, for he was pleased to see them as tributes to his superior virtue—for did not Confucius say, 'The virtues of the gentleman may be compared to the wind and that of the commoner to the weeds; weeds under the force of wind cannot but bend'?); Sourface Komiyama, the self-proclaimed cynic, sneering at our commonplace minds, but how blind to the surpassing dullness of his own; Sawa, the Trumpet, as we called him, to punish him for his noisy boasting; Mushakoji, who passed exams by faith (so we said) and precious little else besides; Matsumoto the Shaker, a hysterical Christian, who would lie in bed in Sunday service time, happily immersed, with a Bible for a pillow, in Ingersoll's *Christianity Refuted*, and turn up in chapel next day to edify us with tears of repentance and a stentorian prayer: some of these were Believers, some of the Worldly persuasion; some would belong to one party but cross to the other for a while, so it wasn't always easy to say clearly who was what. Down among the Ordinaries of the Worldly party—the Nobodies, I should say—were Shintaro Kikuchi and his friends.

v.5

Great hardships once endured, lesser troubles are easily borne; to him who has nothing, poverty is plenty. Compared to what I had gone through before, I was living now in ease and affluence. True, my cleaning chores cut short the time I had for study, my clothes might be countrified (western clothes were beginning to come in now, even in private schools), my funds couldn't rise to more than one visit to the public bath-house for every three my comrades made (I was particular enough, though, and used to give myself a dowsing every night at the well—the famous 'Kikuchi's Lustration')—but all this was nothing. From the day I entered the College I joined none of the bands of time-wasters: the 'down-with-the-cooks' brigade, the ever-hungry tribe, who would slip out of bed after Lights Out, wrapped in blankets, climb over the school fence and guzzle beef and noodles in downtown eatingshops; the idlers, who read novels in class and looked up startled when questioned by the teacher, to ask him what he had asked; the debtors inveterate, who owed money in so many shops they had to make a back-street detour to reach the bath-house, and hide in a cupboard holding their breath whenever a creditor appeared; the Splendid Ones, who ordered western suits on borrowed money and ate—debts still unpaid—in western restaurants, spurred on by waitresses admiring their dexterous application of knife and fork to lumps of steak, or rode in style in first-class carriages between Osaka and Kobe, sporting cheap gold-plated watch-chains on their chests, determined to be 'gentlemen'. All these I avoided, to be able to concentrate on my studies. I had a rival, for one thing, who set the pace.

Shuzo Yabuki was a classmate of mine, a year older than me. The image of perfection, he seemed—handsome, even-tempered, and unpretentious in his manner, but terrifyingly clever. He spoke but little, appeared devoted to his parents (they were old, we gathered, and far from well-off, with little to look forward to but their son's progress in the world) and though he belonged to the Worldly party, was already the white hope of all his teachers, from the Principal downwards. It annoyed me to see him so effortlessly taking the top place in every test. With my usual pig-headed will-to-win I grimly set about trying to dislodge him. To no purpose. Day by day, term by term, the gap between us remained; we kept our places precisely, like geese flying in formation. While most of us had to struggle to keep up with the class textbooks, Yabuki would calmly borrow—and read—armfuls of western books from the library. In the end I gave up all hope of outshining him.

He didn't have a lot to do with the rest of us. Whether it was that people didn't take to him, or the other way round, I don't know; he was the kind that walks by himself—quite literally, for in the evenings, our great time for exercise, you would always see him walking about the campus alone, apart. In spite of his beating me so easily in schoolwork, though, I liked and admired him, and from the way he looked at me now and again, I felt he made a difference between me and the others; but for some reason, though we met every day in the classroom and dining-hall, we never had a real talk. Never but once, that is. I came across him one evening (towards the end of spring of 1885, I think it must have been) lying on the grass behind the school buildings, with a book in his hand, but not reading it, only staring at the setting sun. Seeing me, he smiled: I smiled back. For a while I stood there, finding nothing to say, but eventually the barrier of silence broke, and for the first time we talked as friends. The book was an anthology of English Poetry: he had been reading Gray's Elegy. I told him how I envied him his easy power of learning, and his prospects for the future. He smiled, a little sadly, and pointed to the sun.

'A man can flog his guts till the day he dies, and what has he got to show for it in the end? Look at that sun: it's setting, but we know it'll rise again; we can count on that. But for a man, when his sun sets, it's the end. Nothing more. It's true: life *is* 'briefer than a winter's day', and what can you do with such a—such a *particle* of time?'

'There's such a thing as "Eternal Life", according to the Christians—.'

'Eternal Life, Eternal Life! It would be nice if that was true. But I'm not a Christian, and I don't believe in their Eternal Life. Man is insignificant, absurd, nothing. Better be a flower for a child to pick' (pointing to the vetch at his feet) 'than any great man in his pride and glory! They talk about purpose: work for a purpose, live with a purpose, they say. I don't understand. Why are men born, to start with? For what purpose? We don't even know the answer to that one. All right, suppose we graduate from here, go on to university, become bureaucrats or professors or something, keep our parents alive until they choose to die. Is that what it's for? If so, isn't it still meaningless? I only have to start thinking, and it's such darkness!'

I was astounded. That Yabuki, the most talented boy in the school, from whom everybody expected so much—maybe too much learning had affected his mind.

But I had another shock coming. We talked no more that evening, and soon afterwards Yabuki went home for the spring holidays. Next term he didn't come back. When after some days the College authorities made enquiries, the startling story came out. Yabuki had shut himself up in an upstairs room directly he got home, it seemed. At first he came down occasionally; but one morning some days later, when his parents went up to see why he had stayed in his room for so long, they found he had hanged himself by his sash from the lintel.

I didn't weep when I heard the news of his bizarre death; I shivered, as if I had suddenly walked under a jet of icy water.

v.6

The famous samurai Kenshin Uesugi dropped his chopsticks in horror, we are told, when the messenger interrupted his meal to tell him of the death of Shingen Takeda, his sworn enemy for so many years: and I was shocked beyond words at the news of my rival's suicide. So Yabuki had died by his own hand, leaving to me his place at the top of the class—and with it his agonized questionings. Often enough when one is standing on a moor in spring, gazing in delight at the smiling mountain ranges on the horizon, a troop of clouds will sail up from nowhere and cut off the sun, depriving the scene of all its charm. So it was now with me. Though I had had my share of troubles and hardship, all my seventeen years I had been happy. In comparison with the great, hardly imaginable delights that seemed to await me in the future, the petty trials of the moment were the lowest of hurdles, to be topped in no time by a boy's nimble feet. Driven by nothing more complicated than joy in learning and in progress for its own sake (and partly too by pride, when they told me I was clever, as a dog runs even faster, panting, when you praise it for its speed), I had studied furiously, though with no very clear goal. Now I was forced to stop and think. Yabuki, dead. That brilliant, perfect boy, the pride of the entire College. All his talents, his promise, his troubles, all buried with a handful of bones.

> Though tomorrow, I know, may bring my own life's end,
> Today, at dusk, I grieve for another's passing.[15]

Truly I mourned for Yabuki. And who could tell when I might be not the mourner but the mourned? For me too the hidden, bottomless chasm would open. Why was I studying so furiously? Where was I going, that I was in such a hurry to get there? If to no goal but extinction, why had I been born in the first place? After death, what then? So long as such questions never come home to him, a man can live untroubled; let him once awake to their urgency, and they will pursue him to the end, sleeping and waking, relentless as his shadow. They bore down upon me now with the force of a Kuroshio Current,[16] the great questions, so old yet eternally new.

Outwardly my life went on exactly as before. Five days of study, two of relaxation, week by week. Gradually 'that clever Yabuki' gave way to 'that clever Kikuchi'. Yet my mind was bowed under a leaden weight wherever I went. As I read history at night by the light of my little lamp, doubts would flit before me like importunate ghosts; after supper, when I was arguing or playing with my friends, abruptly a voice would murmur, 'What is it all for?' Maybe I've been working too hard, I thought; so I eased up on my books, and tried getting out more on weekend expeditions. But it was no good. I found myself trembling at the sight of green leaves tossing in the wind; the evening sunlight fading across Mount Maya warned of the shortness of life. Terrified of being too much alone, I forced myself to spend more time chattering and joking with my schoolfellows; but their

---

15. A poem by Ki no Tsurayaki (?–A.D. 945) on the occasion of the death of his nephew Ki no Tomonori.

16. The Japanese name for the powerful current that flows northward along the east coast of Japan.

shrill, meaningless laughter only mocked me, and I was driven again to solitude. In the quiet, alone, the great questions towered over me, awesome, the Rocky Mountains of the mind. They were inescapable—and insistent. A man must find the answers, or die.

I took out the Bible which the Reverend Shizu had given me, and began to read from Matthew, Chapter 1. So much gibberish. I began to listen to the sermons and prayers in chapel on Sundays, but wasn't impressed: none of the speakers seemed to mean what they said, so that the whole service soundedl ike a string of lies. A strange thing happened in the College just about that time; 'revival', they called it. It really was most extraordinary. How it started, I don't know, but all of a sudden some of the senior boys began behaving like madmen, bursting into tears for no apparent reason, and mouthing prayers incessantly. This curious behaviour spread all over the College, till soon the revival was everywhere: boys weeping and groaning, boys lying flat on their faces in the quadrangle in broad daylight and bawling out prayers, boys staring up at the sky with clasped hands, like animated kites, offering thanks, boys shouting hymns, boys breaking their legs jumping from upstairs windows, boys rushing down to the town to preach and getting warned off by the police—a lunatic asylum, we became, and all classes had to stop for two or three days. More than half of my class had caught the infection. One boy (who was always failing in his tests) grabbed my arm suddenly. 'Repent, believe, and give thanks, Kikuchi!' he commanded, and without waiting for an answer began to pray: 'Our Father in Heaven, look in mercy, we pray Thee, upon this sinful brother —' I began to doubt the sanity of the human race. I have always believed myself to be as susceptible to emotion as anybody; but these revivalists' outpourings were too superficial to be anything but ridiculous, making Christianity seem little better than the Buddhist Hail-to-the-Sutra-of-the-Lotus-of-the-Law mumbo-jumbo we were used to. Religion, I decided, was mental illness under another name. If heaven was a rest-home for lunatics, I would choose hell rather than have anything to do with religion. Having been brought up, as I had, on Ssû-ma Kuang's[17] teaching that one should be prudent in *all* one's actions and do nothing of which one cannot speak in public, the impertinence of this 'sinful brother' claptrap, and the peremptory order to 'repent', merely aroused in me an intense dislike of all the Christians' antics. I shut the door of my heart, and watched them coldly.

The fever lasted about a week, then went out like a straw fire, leaving only sunken eyes and cheeks here and there. In the aftershock of this spiritual earthquake, some ardent converts lost their nerve and tumbled headlong from their pinnacle of faith into the valley of disbelief, to mocking laughter from the Worldly party.

Soon afterwards we had the final examinations of the school year, and the summer holidays began. As soon as they had heard their marks, my friends packed their wicker bags, changed to new summer kimono, and set

17. A famous Confucian scholar and statesman of the eleventh century A.D.

out smiling for home. I had thought I would stay on at the College, till Mr Brown told me he was going to Mount Hiei, near Kyoto, for the summer, to collect plant specimens, and invited me along to help. Anything, I decided, would be preferable to staying behind as fodder for the summer fleas, so towards the end of July I left with Mr Brown to camp on the mountain.

v.7

Westerners are adventurous creatures; it is their custom to take their families to the seaside or up into the mountains in summer, to enjoy for a time a life close to nature. For the foreigners of the Osaka and Kobe district, Mount Hiei is a favourite spot for these holiday expeditions. Somewhere near the eighth station on the mountain path, usually, they choose a piece of ground among the firs and cryptomerias where the slope is less marked than elsewhere, drive in stakes and lay planks between them for beds, then put up tents of thick rubber-coated material that will keep off any rain, no matter how heavy or prolonged. Here they spend the eight weeks or so of the really hot weather. Up to three hundred of them gather here at the height of the season, so that they form a kind of mountain village. They have a special big tent for their worship services; it is a moving experience to peep into the white 'church' tent, set among the trees in their brilliant summer green, and listen to the organ and the voices of the congregation borne towards you on the pure mountain air. One is reminded of the Old Testament and its tabernacles. Faith comes easier here than in the city churches, with their distracting stink of paint.

Mr Brown had brought with him his wife, their daughter, a bouncy little four-year-old, like an animated version of the imported rubber dolls you see in shops, and the Japanese couple who cooked for the family. My 'room' was a little tent which had been intended for Mr Brown's study. Pitched on sloping ground, with one end secured to a rocky ledge and the other to tent-poles, it made a room of three-mat size, and was in fact carpeted in part with two mats we had brought with us. A gangboard connected with the main tent, and except at night, my tent was always left open in front, like a sentry-box. A whitewood table, a lamp, a blanket, and a thin quilt made up my furniture. A little window on the south-west side let in the light; the moon peeped through it at night, and during the day I had only to look up from my table to glimpse through a maze of dark-green branches the smoke from Kyoto chimneys. On wet days, when I shut my door-flap and sat reading a book, listening to the rain dripping down through the branches on to my canvas roof as if determined to dye it green, I felt a veritable Robinson Crusoe.

Though he could be facetious at times, Mr Brown was a kind-hearted, sincere man. He was very good to me, and since he was comparatively free from the besetting sin of most westerners—the constant pushing of oneself and one's own point of view, regardless of the feelings of others—I enjoyed myself immensely. On sunny days we went butterflying, or foraged as far afield as Mount Kurama for rare ferns and all kinds of other plants; reviving parched throats at hidden, moss-lined springs we found under old tree-stumps, guided by the dank smell, and lying flat on beds of hair-moss when hunger called, to devour the 'sandwiches' we carried wrapped in old newspaper sheets. Sometimes we walked so far, it was a shock to glance up suddenly at a bird's cry and catch, through the cryptomerias, the mellowing light of a sun already low, or glimpse the purple mist of evening settling on the ranges across the valley; with every homeward step the valleys would darken, the peaks fade into dusk, as we crossed ridge after ridge with only the faint light of a new moon for guide, till at last—with what relief!—we saw the camplights shining through the gloom. Supper over, I would set to work at once pressing the specimens, and sketching them if I wasn't too sleepy. All in all, my duties were very pleasant. 'Kikuchi, you strong walk' Mr Brown would often say, in Japanese that by now was a good as my English, though that isn't saying very much.

How Michitaro would enjoy camp life, I thought; and wrote him a letter, begging him to visit our camp on his way home from Tokyo. A year had flashed past like a dream. It was when he was home for the summer holidays last year that I had first got to know Michitaro, and already summer had come round again. We had kept up a correspondence ever since he went back to Tokyo, but in writing this particular letter I felt more acutely than usual the swiftness of time's passing.

On my way back from asking the cook of the family in the next tent to post my letter (he was going down to Kyoto for some shopping) I saw a Japanese girl of sixteen or seventeen whom I thought I recognized, coming down the path by my tent with a foreign lady. It may seem almost too much of a coincidence, I daresay, but I was right. The girl was O-Fuyu, Michitaro's fiancée, whom I had met at Matsuyama. A typical girl student she looked now, with her hair done up western-style and cut to a fringe in front. She had come up to the camp the previous day, she told me (Plum Blossom School having broken up for the summer) to catch up on her English, but would be going home early in August, when Michitaro was coming to pick her up. Well! Truth, they say, is stranger than fiction, and Heaven's dispensations, on occasion, are more felicitous than all the contriving of the story-teller.

Michitaro's reply to my letter arrived only a day or so later. I could feel how surprised and delighted he had been to learn where I was spending the summer. 'Must there not be some karma link between us from a previous life? I cannot wait till we meet,' he wrote. I could wait even less. The moment July gave way to August I began to look out for him—so eagerly that very soon I was getting angry with him for not coming, when one day a broad-shouldered young man in a linen summer kimono, cap in one hand and wiping the sweat from his face with the other, came panting but smiling up the mountain path.

Having asked Mr Brown's permission beforehand, I took Michitaro straight to my tent, gave him water to wash in, sugared water to drink, and a change of kimono. We laughed our heads off, said the same things over and over, and behaved altogether like madmen for a while in our delight, then took the good news to O-Fuyu, and the three of us talked the sun down, O-Fuyu's teacher having invited us all to supper. That night Michitaro and I, sharing my single blanket, made up with more long hours of talk for the many months of separation. The moon went down, but still we talked: of the slow decline in the morals of Tokyo students, and of how preoccupied they were becoming nowadays with material security, so that few studied with the old enthusiasm; of Michitaro's hopes of graduating from his school the following year and going on to university, for which he was already preparing in addition to his school work, and of how busy all this made him; he'd been having some heart trouble, apparently, not that it was necessarily the result of overwork, but his breath wouldn't come properly sometimes (I was shocked at this, but Michitaro assured me it was nothing that a few weeks' rest at home wouldn't cure); of how much our meeting the year before had meant to him, and how lonely he'd been since; how he had enquired after Matsumura as soon as he got back to Tokyo, but found he had moved, and left no address; and so on, while I poured a jumble of impressions of the College and dreams for the future that I hadn't been able to write of fully in my letters. That gentleness and modesty of his, that had come through even in his letters, his enthusiasm, so natural and infectious; as we lay side by side after a year apart, his whole character seemed more admirable than ever. Truly a man needs friends, I thought; and of all my friends, I was sure, comparing him with the three hundred students of the College, there was none I liked as much as Michitaro.

Next morning we were still as excited as ever. I insisted Michitaro should stay another day, and after lunch we set out to climb Shimeigatake, the highest point of Mount Hiei. O-Fuyu was too busy preparing for the journey home to come with us. She called Michitaro back when she saw us going off hatless in the full heat of the afternoon sun, and lent him an umbrella and a broad-brimmed straw hat; and off we went, Michitaro with the umbrella and myself in the hat, up behind Enryakuji Temple, threading our way through bamboo grass and under great cryptomerias. We climbed in stages, resting every now and then when Michitaro was getting short of breath, till we reached the spot where the rebels Masakado and Sumitomo are said to have stopped, nine centuries or more ago, to look down at the Emperor's Castle. The whole Kyoto plain lay spread out before us: the City itself, villages, temples half-hidden in the forest, green paddy-fields, the rivers Kamo and Katsura, and southwards, towards Osaka, the towns of Yodo and Yamazaki.

A little higher still we emerged from a forest of fir trees to find Lake Biwa sparkling up at us from the foot of the mountain.

'Superb!' cried Michitaro, panting. Brushing off with my sleeve the sweat that was streaming down my face, I drank deep breaths of the pure mountain air.

We cleared away some rocks under a gnarled old pine, and threw ourselves down on the grass, to wipe off more sweat and gaze in silence at the view. Below us ridge succeeded ridge, like the sheaths of a sprout of bamboo, down to the lake itself, shining brilliantly in the afternoon sun. That ribbon of green lining the shore would be paddy, the tiny knob-like projection on that headland, a clump of pine-trees; those patterns of blue smoke, the towns of Otsu, Yabase, Sakamoto, Katada. The northern half of the lake was hidden behind the mountains, but Hira and Mikami Hill might have been within hailing distance, they stood out so sharply. The Nagahama steamboat had just left Otsu: toylike, it glided across the mirror, trailing a white thread of smoke. Our ears could just catch a tiny sound, like a mosquito's hum—the steamer's siren.

For some time neither of us spoke. Suddenly Michitaro looked at me, smiling.

'Still reading the Bible these days, are you?'

I blushed. Since the famous 'revival', I had had no use for the Bible. The human mind is a devious, slippery creature, and can find any number of excuses to put off facing life's deeper issues. I told him everything. He listened, much moved, to my account of Yabuki's death, and nodded sympathetically when I spoke of my own doubts. When I came to describe my revulsion at the revival, however, he tried earnestly to convince me I was wrong. A revival, he said, was like a tornado: just as tornadoes uprooted trees and sent boulders flying, so revivals led to correspondingly strange phenomena in the spiritual realm. The stirrings of the spirit were not to be judged by the cold, inflexible yardstick of commonsense. Call it inspiration, emotion, call it what you will, did it never happen that one heart could set another on fire?—which was what happened in a revival, only on a bigger scale. 'Horatio, there are more things in heaven and earth than are dreamt of in your philosophy.' The truth of the universe was beyond the reach of man's intellect: only the eye of faith could behold the face of God. With every step in his argument Michitaro grew more eloquent, the fire in his eyes more brilliant. Ever since we met, I had never seen him so deeply, so impressively in earnest.

'Faith is no old wives' tale, Kikuchi. It's what a man is meant for, a worthy calling for true men. Man is a fragment of the universe; he'll never find happiness till he is unified with its great First Principle and Cause. To seek God is the heart's instinct. *You* are seeking Him now—your very doubt, your despair, is a reaching out to your spiritual Father. Why push God on one side? Which is going to make you happier, to shut your eyes and complain of loneliness, or to awake to the truth, that the Supreme

Being is upholding you? Which is better, to die in doubt, or to die in faith? You can't ignore for ever the questions life asks, Kikuchi; time won't stand still.'

Michitaro was silent. Nor did I have any reply. 'Time won't stand still' —the words brushed across my mind like an autumn wind, awaking a boundless melancholy. I don't know for how long it was I sat in silence with bent head, brooding.

Suddenly there was a faint rumbling somewhere in the sky. It grew louder, nearer. All around us the light faded. Over Hira the sky blackened; squads of storm clouds rolled up from the east, then broke into a confused mass, rushing headlong for the zenith. A black shadow streaked across the lake, driving what remained of the light before it.

'A big storm coming!'

'Shelter, quick!'

As we sprang up, shouting, in the same instant lightning tore across the black wall of cloud: five, six purple flashes, flaring over the lake.

'Hurry!'

A damp wind struck in our faces as we ran off, and with it the first drops of rain, as big as grapes. A growl of thunder, directly overhead, cracked open the clouds. Rain cascaded down.

'Get your head under my umbrella!' Michitaro shouted. For a few steps we huddled, chin jostling chin, under his umbrella.

'No good. You follow me!' I broke away, holding my cap with both hands, and ran for all I was worth down the mountainside in the direction of the nearest temple, which was lit up almost continuously by repeated flashes of lightning. By the light of one flash I made out Michitaro, two or three paces behind, drenched—he had furled the umbrella—and breathing jerkily.

'Can you still run?' I yelled.

'Sure!' came back through the darkness. For a split second, in another flash, I saw him smile. Stumbling on against the driving rain, I reached the shelter of some cryptomerias, when an immense sheet of lightning broke over the forest, vividly outlining every tree and hollow through a glistening curtain of rain. An ear-splitting peal of thunder followed instantly, at which the earth itself seemed to shudder on its axis; and I fell to the ground as if struck.

v.8

Of what I went through afterwards, apart from the bare outward record, I can hardly bear to write. When I regained consciousness the storm had dwindled to a shower. Ten or twelve yards away smoke was rising from a blackened cryptomeria—it was split down to the roots. Tense with fear, I looked round hastily for Michitaro. He was lying on his back nearby, his right hand closed round the umbrella. I lifted him up by the shoulders, called his name again and again—but his head fell forward; the blood had drained out of his face and hands. Panic-stricken, I dashed down to the temple for help. A foreign doctor, who by a lucky chance had been sheltering there, ran back with me. It only needed a glance for him to give his verdict—a rupture of the heart: Michitaro was beyond hope.

O-Fuyu, deadly pale, arrived not long afterwards with her teacher, and the doctor, Mr Brown's cook and I carried the body down to the camp. That moment, when the doctor had tried everything he knew, in a hopeless attempt to recall the life that had fled, and shook his head, sighing, for the last time—my pen stops there, the pain of memory is too harsh still.

It was my scarcely less painful task then to hurry down to Kyoto and telegraph to Michitaro's parents and to O-Fuyu's home in Matsuyama. This done, I returned to keep vigil over the body until the relatives should come. Two days later Mr Kento arrived, with a representative from the Matsuyama family. A Christian funeral service was held in the chapel tent (Mr Kento would have refused the missionaries' suggestion for the service, if O-Fuyu had not insisted that it be accepted. O-Fuyu's conduct was admirable all through, in spite of her being so young—entirely worthy of the man she would have married) followed by cremation at Toribe Hill, and a small procession—Mr Kento, O-Fuyu, and I—down to Shichijo Station in Kyoto with the ashes, soon to merge once more with the soil of his native Uwajima. Watching the puffs of smoke of the departing train, I recalled another parting, on Uwajima quay a year before.

A dream—surely it was all a dream. Michitaro's coming was a dream, his death a dream, the long walk down to the station and back, a dream—soon, surely, I could only believe, the moment of waking would come, when I could rub the sweat of so long a sleep out of my eyes and check or quieten my mind's turmoil.

From the day it happened I worked on mechanically at whatever was to be done, dry-eyed, my brain hard and cold like a stone. Noticing me yawning several times, the doctor insisted on taking my pulse, and made up a sedative for me to drink at night. Mr Brown, too, did his best to comfort me, urging the need for faith at such a time. But I wouldn't touch the medicine, still less the faith. I heard Mr Brown in silence, but my heart cried out, 'I won't believe; I would rather die than believe!' I wasn't sick, not in body. I hated God. He had tricked me, played with me, and my tiny spirit burned with revolt. Maybe I would believe, if He could give back Michitaro. But to kill him before my eyes, and *then* demand faith—what could be more ridiculously inconsistent? I *wouldn't* believe, not for a thousand thunderbolts; not out of fear. So I rejected Mr Brown's ministrations, saying little, but thinking what I left unsaid, and feeling more deeply still.

All the thrill of camp life had vanished. I went nowhere, lying alone in my tent, trying to sleep whenever I was free, till on the evening of the fifth day I slipped out and went back for the first time to the hill we had climbed that afternoon. It was a marvellously beautiful evening. The sun had just gone down, leaving hills and forests bathed in the mellow diffused glow that is neither sunshine nor the cold gleam of moonlight. As I climbed the path, memory followed memory, like pictures in a scroll. Here he stopped to rest, there he knelt to prise up a handful of velvet-smooth moss—Michitaro! whose footsteps were those behind me, whose feet advancing through the rustling grasses? I stopped awhile, then climbed higher still, to the old pine-tree under which we had sat and talked. A last ray of sunset still clung to the highest peaks, but the hills and valleys below me were already swathed in mist, with only a faint white sheet to show where the sunlit lake had been. They had just begun to sound the evening bell at Enryakuji. I stood beneath the tree, listening to the great b-o-o-m echoing like a visible presence from hill to hill, from valley to valley. Michitaro! No one in sight, only a voice, trembling on the air, 'Time won't stand still! Time won't stand still!'

Mechanically I started down again. By the time I was nearing the cryptomerias it was already dark, and a melancholy chirring of insects sounded through the dew-laden undergrowth. Suddenly I stopped. Right before me was a burnt trunk, split in two. Unconsciously, like a sleep-walker, I had made straight for the spot where I had fallen, and Michitaro died. I sat down on a tree stump as if at a command, and for long was lost in thought. Something cold touched my forehead—a drop from the stars, a breath of dew, who knows? I looked up. Far above, through the matted darkness of foliage, where the giant cryptomerias pierced the sky, countless stars gleamed like raindrops. Was it only now the sun had set? The hum of insects sounded sad and lonely in the vast night silence of the mountain. If I listened carefully, I could hear my heart beating faint and slow, as if I were asleep.

Out of the dense darkness of the forest abruptly, like a breaking wave, a voice spoke. I listened, suddenly alert. It rustled through the ancient trees of the mountain, and vanished into the infinite sky.

I threw myself to the ground.

v.9

Twice now in my seventeen years I had been moved to the very depths of my being. Once among the graves of my ancestors at Tsumagome, once on the heights of Mount Hiei: once by my mother's words, once by a friend's death. Both of these events marked new eras in my little history. But who was it that made my mother and my friend the agents of the new life that flooded into my foolish, ignorant heart? Let the atheist say what he likes. Let your hedonist, your utilitarian mock if he will—I could not but recognize the Providence of a Supreme Being, so clearly now, as I looked back over my seventeen years, did I see His guiding finger. Could I not see Him through my tears, quietly beckoning—who had borne so patiently my forgetfulness, my wanderings from Him, my cynicism, my childish outbursts? Had I not known His rod and His staff, coaxing, teaching, disciplining, revealing? Even if my lips were still to refuse belief, the spirit within me could not but believe. 'I *will* believe—meekly, like a child—whatever the cost!' I cried inwardly as I lay where my friend had fallen, in the solitude of the mountain-top, under the starlit sky.

Till I die, I shall never forget that night. Till I die, I shall never forget the message my friend's last 'sermon' brought me, sealed with his life. How could I forget this human Christ who bought life for my spirit with his own body's death? For surely Michitaro died for me. Is death then the end of everything? No. Michitaro is alive—of that I am certain: his gentleness, his compelling sincerity—he himself lives on in me, my guide and teacher. In my ideals, in all my struggles, in my sense of thankfulness for life, he lives still.

Every year on August 6th, the anniversary of the day he died, I go apart for a while to meditate. In my study I have his picture (a photograph I got from his father, showing him in a summer kimono about the time he first left home for Tokyo. We kept saying we would take one of the two of us together, but the chance never came). He looks out at me, smiling, from the frame: I have only to glance that way, even now, for my heart to quicken.

A hundred days will rob a flower of all its perfume: but the fragrance of a noble spirit time cannot kill. Always when I think of lives cut off before their time, these two figures of Yabuki and Michitaro rise before my eyes. I grieve for them both—both so outstanding, both taken so soon. But while my sorrow for Yabuki was a tortured cry, the tears I wept for Michitaro were a life-giving rain, reviving a heart parched and weary from life's battles.

Why?

Part VI

My second year at Kansei College began without special incident. To see me rising early as before to wield my bucket and broom, or hurrying about the campus in my shabby country clothes, top of the class in marks and bottom in size, nobody would have noticed anything different from the Kikuchi of the previous year. Outwardly nothing had changed.

But as water may swirl under ice, and a volcano's heart burn beneath the snows, the placid surface of my life concealed a fierce turbulence of the spirit. Of this I spoke to no one, not because I was afraid of the jeers of the Worldly ones, or out of any fastidious unwillingness to inflict my own spiritual perplexities upon others, but rather from a fear of dissipating the blessing of which I was tremblingly aware—the light breaking through the mists, the springs of grace trickling upon my stony soul. As a young girl hides her first love, I kept to myself this vision of new light.

I will not trouble you with the details of my spiritual history. I took up once again the Bible the Reverend Shizu had given me, which I had begun to read six months before, only to throw it aside as soon as I had begun, and read it again and again. On Saturdays and Sundays I went off alone to the hills or woods, to read, pray, and think, now believing, now doubting, now full of remorse and repentance, now thrilling with joy—experiencing in myself, I don't know how many times, the 'revival' that had so disgusted me on a previous occasion. But no more of that. All I will say is that every time I read the Bible, the figure of the Christ, called the Son of Man, towered larger and larger among the shifting obscurity of miracles and strange, hard sayings, till he seemed to reach the heavens, his light more dazzling than the sun; and like the stars before the sun, the heroes I had revered as a boy lost their former brilliance. The more I gazed upward at his glory, the more clearly I realized that this was no refracting prism, but the very source of all light, a revelation of God Himself. I unlocked the gates of my heart—they were unlocked for me—and drank in the light, as a dry sponge soaks up water.

How irresistible—how far beyond the power of words to describe, of thought to conceive—the springs of joy that welled up within me as I let that glorious light nurture my infant spirit; as it caressed my spirit, like a comb smoothing dishevelled hair; as I bathed my whole being in its streams! I would wake up in the night, and find myself weeping for no reason. When I was reading in the daytime, my head would bow of itself in gratitude. In a very torment of joy, I wept that I could not fling away the body, as Elijah cast aside his mantle, and mount like the prophet straight to heaven.

On the first Sunday of the New Year, 1886, I was baptized by Mr Brown. That same day I despatched a letter to my mother, explaining at length how I had come to take this step, and enclosing a pocket New Testament. To the Reverend Shizu also, to whom with Michitaro I owed the gift of faith, I wrote the news, on my card of New Year greetings.

VI.2

One autumn back home in Tsumagome—I must have been about ten, I suppose—I remember how three of us lost our way in the hills when we were out collecting acorns. It wasn't far off sunset; the forest kept getting thicker, and there was not a sound to be heard but the crackle of dry bamboo-grass under our feet. We were staring hopelessly at one another, ready to cry, when suddenly one of my friends pointed to a copse on rising ground not far away. 'Come on. Let's try over there!' We dragged ourselves after him, to the top of a ridge. The view was electrifying. A huge valley stretched out below us; down its centre ran a wavy belt of gold, bordered at intervals by curious purplish blotches, and with here and there blue threads rising into the haze. Marvelling at such beauty, we wondered what valley this could be—till it dawned on us it was our own Tsumagome: the golden belt was our river, the purple clouds our woods and villages, and the threads of blue the smoke of evening fires. What magic had made it all seem so strange? We looked round, half expecting to see some sorcerer with his wand—but there was nothing, only the sun's red orb slipping innocently behind the western hills. I can still feel the awe of that moment of realization.

Sometimes along life's journey you round the brow of a hill, only for strange new hills and streams to spring out upon you, as if from an ambush; you may open your eyes after a nap to find the world you knew has rolled by while you slept and left you rubbing your eyes, wondering where you are and what it might have been, that *other* world to which you had grown so used. 'Let but a new light shine, and the world itself is remade.' Dumb with wonder, I gazed now upon just such a recreated world. It is extraordinary, is it not, how for our tiny minds the operation of light can transform the universe? The lover's rose-coloured world, the glorious landscape of the saints, those new, higher worlds made visible by the flash of contact between another spirit and our own—what do they signify, if not the sudden awakening of the heart's vision after the blinding moment of the flash itself? Nor need an experience come only once. Close observation shows that a man may be born many times after he has left his mother's womb; every day the world can be a new creation; enlightenment may come not once but many times. Truly to grow up, a man must cast off many wrappings of the mind, as a bamboo grows out of its protective sheath. Sometimes there may be only a little to abandon, sometimes a great deal: as with me in the crisis I was now going through.

During the first half of 1886, as I went on quietly with my studies, the light of my new faith flooded through my being with an extraordinary power, changing my ideals, my aims, my whole way of thinking. The things I had always considered the highest goals now appeared no more substantial than drifting clouds; fame, wealth, university degrees, decorations, rank, power, seemed as empty of meaning as the sparks from a child's firecracker. The grandiose dreams that had spurred me on hitherto collapsed: I saw I must rethink the future. Till recently 'society' had been for me the final judge of all conduct, the sole audience before whom I was to act. My goal had been simple: for Shintaro Kikuchi's star to shine more brightly than other men's. Now society was pushed aside: I stood before God Himself.

I pondered much on what God's plan for me might be. The most precious thing in all the world was the light of Heaven—was not the world's noblest work, therefore, the passing on to others of this light? Whenever I could spare the time from my studies, I borrowed all kinds of books on religion from the College library. The lives of famous missionaries such as Xavier, Martin, Henry and Livingstone moved me most deeply. Each time I read of such men, I found myself weeping tears of admiration for their renunciation of the world's attractions, their endurance of the unendurable, the lofty passion which drove them, at the risk of their lives, to carry the light to 'the people which sat in darkness'; and wondered secretly, was I not called to follow where they had led?

VI.3

When Martin Luther was out walking one day, the friend who was with him was struck by lightning, while Luther himself escaped unhurt. The incident was one reason for the conversion of this man, who afterwards became the greatest leader of the Reformation. Luther was a genius, of course; I am not setting my tiny self alongside him. But there was one strong point of similarity, in that my own awakening, like Luther's had been occasioned by a friend's death from lightning. The more I thought of Michitaro's end, the more clearly came a sense of God's guidance, and of Michitaro's unspoken testament. In place of outward honour (which was what really lay behind my dreams of rebuilding the family fortunes) I resolved to put truth first, to throw away all notions of wealth and fame like a pair of worn-out sandals, the better to be able to follow where God and conscience might lead: I felt I was called of God (presumptuous though it sounds) to be an evangelist.

The third night after my baptism, I went out into the pine-woods to meditate; and determined there and then that when I had finished General Studies I would take the College course in Theology, and devote my life to this holy work.

So at last I decided to be a Christian preacher—and began my preaching forthwith. My burden of joy would be unbearable if I did not quickly share it. As the first kiss of the morning sun is for the mountain peaks, so in everything the human heart turns first to where it loves: my mission started with my mother. Directly after my baptism, as I said earlier, I sent her a Bible, explaining my faith and urging her too to believe. When she first read my letter (so she told me afterwards) she tore it in two, threw the Bible from her, and burst into tears. Although I didn't know this at the time, I was astonished at the flinty stubbornness of the disapproval in her reply. Apparently she suspected I must have made a show of believing, in order to get my fees reduced or something of the kind. One fierce, indignant sentence followed another across the page. What good would this cowardly behaviour do our family? Where was my sense of honour—had living with townboys and peasants (I had told her in my letters how many of the students at the College were commoners, not of samurai stock) corrupted me so completely? Surely I hadn't forgotten what she had said at Tsumagome seven years before, by Father's grave? At the very end she wrote that she had been worrying a great deal about my school expenses. For nearly a year now, thinking she might be able to put something together, at any rate to help with the next stage, after I had finished at the College, she had started keeping silkworms, and was managing to find time in the evenings to spin as well. By saving, too, every grain of rice, every scrap of paper she possibly could, for my sake, she had a little money put by already. This she would send me, but I *must* give up this 'dishonourable pretence' of believing in Christianity; 'honour once stained is honour maimed'; now was the most crucial time of my life—and pages more in the same vein.

Appalled at the way she had taken it, I sat up all that night describing at great length how I had come to believe and why, and explaining that with my cleaning wages and my night classes (I forgot to mention before that since late the previous autumn, through a friend's recommendation, I had been making extra by teaching eight hours a week in a school in Hyogo Ward in Kobe) I could easily take care of my school expenses, without the need to borrow a single sen, still less to sell my right to think for myself—and assuring her finally that I was fit and well, and not overworking. Judging from her reply, which came by return, my letter seemed to have calmed her down a bit, though it obviously hadn't satisfied her altogether. 'Don't try to make a Christian out of me,' she wrote, 'and mind you think very, very carefully about what you are doing yourself. Good and bad, young people rush headlong into everything! *Don't* do anything reckless, son. It sounds interfering, but will you *please* tell your mother what you're going to do *before* you do it?' In short, my first attempt at spreading the gospel was a dismal failure. I decided to change my tactics, and to use no other weapons but prayer and patience to bring about a softening of my mother's attitude: but the fact that the 'enemy' in this first campaign *was* my mother made failure all the more discouraging. Mother being so intensely concerned with status and social position, the prospect of the clash when I told her of my decision to spend my life in Christian work worried me a good deal. I wasn't going to change my mind, though. Mother had asked in her letter whether I couldn't manage to come home for a while that summer; but I had decided not to go home for another year. Instead, I went off to Okayama to help in a summer mission.

VI.4

Bible in hand, then, I descended upon the west country, as hare-brained and headstrong a young missionary as you ever saw. Your old Mohammedan went one better, maybe, with the Koran in one hand and a sword in the other, but I was pretty fervent, I can tell you, quite ready to ram the truth down people's throats, and pressure their souls with intimidating sermons. Looking back, I suppose the suddenness of my exposure to the dazzling heavenly light may have turned my head a bit, my brand of evangelism was so vehement. The complaints of the missionaries and Japanese pastors of the difficulties of evangelism in Japan, of the Japanese lack of a religious sense, I put down to faint-heartedness and lack of faith on the preachers' part. If only they all had Xavier's willingness to 'endure ten thousand hardships to save a single soul', all Japan would be Christian in less than ten years . . . even a lay neophyte like me, if he were willing to work till he dropped, even for a brief month, would surely bring home a tale or two of victory. To work, to work! Aflame with zeal, Mr Missionary Kikuchi made his entry into Okayama.

My tasks were two: to confirm and encourage the faithful, and to bring in new believers. I gave myself wholeheartedly to both. The church at Okayama was flourishing already, with three hundred members and a fine building—'citadel of the western provinces' they called it. I went round visiting the members in their homes, as the pastor directed, now quoting to the wealthy ones: 'A rich man shall hardly enter into the Kingdom of heaven', and exhorting them to acts of charity (their contributions to the church's extension work were absurdly small. If I were a man of property, I thought, I'd give it all away, and keep just enough to live on. A have-not's dream, I daresay; once I did have money, maybe I'd be just as bad as these solid citizens I was preaching to. The bigger the purse, the narrower its neck—so it has always been. But in those days I was a real communist); now expounding to a baker in a cake-shop the profound meaning of 'Which of you by taking thought can add a cubit to his stature?' while the worthy man scratched his head, smelling his sponge-cakes burning in the oven. At other times I would burst in upon a group of young men wasting their time in idle talk, and make them promise to attend the prayer meeting next evening—or overawe a girl who was pestering her mother for a kimono of Echigo cloth with a sonorous 'Let women adorn themselves not with gold, or pearls, or costly array, but with good works'. In no time, all three hundred of the congregation had made the acquaintance of Kikuchi the zealot. Some of the young people were so moved by my exhortations that they started coming to me with their complaints about the church, and worked themselves up before long into such a fury of indignation that the deacons were begging me privately not to 'stir up the younger brethren'.

But it wasn't surprising these young people were not happy with the way things were going in their church. There was much that was unsatisfactory about the little community (but what community is ever perfect?). What I found most galling in a church—that by definition should be a society of equals, free of all discrimination, a true republic of the spirit—was the abundance of cliques it had already sprouted, and the jealousy and suspicion and intrigue they gave rise to. (I had forgotten that Christians too are human.) I saw this clearly at a prayer meeting the evening after my arrival. From the Gold-rimmed Spectacles, Curled Whiskers, and Silk Coat tribe in the front row, the gathering presented a progressively dowdier appearance, till you came to the really shabby at the back of the hall. The ones who paid the highest contributions carried their noses, however snub, appropriately high; the prefectural councillor, the official, the lawyer, anyone with a bit of a handle to his name, showed it in the pompous squaring of his shoulders: there were many of these powerful ones, the converts pastors boast about, arranged in rows like the scalps the American Indians used to display as proofs of their valour. Distinctions of wealth, of official rank, of profession—weren't they just as much in evidence here as outside? plus another distinction, between the veteran member, whose rambling testimonies we had to endure, stifling our yawns, and the newly-joined, who as likely as not would find themselves cut short in mid-prayer by a tinkle from the leader's bell.

Worst of all was the handling of a discussion we had after a prayer-meeting one evening to discuss new ways of outreach. A proposal put forward with great sincerity and feeling by a very young man was met with all kinds of objections, and finally rejected altogether; so far, so good, but when a little later a weighty elder got up to make, with a deal of coughing and spluttering, precisely the proposal that had been turned down flat before, it was adopted without a murmur. This particular form of discrimination struck me as so monstrous, I complained about it to the pastor. 'You have to realize age itself is a qualification,' he answered, smiling. 'If words are bullets, trust is the gunpowder you need to fire them. Take your time, and load your gun with powder first.' Many times afterwards, when I had to submit to seeing my opinion rejected as 'immature' (though everyone could see it to be correct) only to be adopted later in some greybeard's name, I couldn't help recalling the pastor's words; they helped me to swallow my anger, or I might have burst out, like the younger Pitt: 'What is there so precious in white hairs? What crime is it to be young?' Even so, I still thought it outrageous that such distinctions should persist in the community of the church. Burning with secret indignation, I waited for an opportunity to launch my own attack—in vain.

VI.5

Kikuchi the Evangelist worked like a fanatic. In the two months or so I spent at Okayama, I never had time to go near its famous Park, I was so busy exhorting the faithful and haranguing the unconverted. Church meetings every night, preaching in the street, praying for the heathen under their very noses, crying 'Lord! forgive them, I beseech Thee' when boys pelted us with stones, smiling charitably at young men who amused themselves by constantly interrupting—waving my arms, shouting, and pointing to heaven, the tears and sweat pouring down, when I was really excited; and feeling no twinge of shame, even, when my hearers swore I was mad. Extending my campaign still further, I ventured alone into the slums and *eta*[1] settlements. Christ's command to 'gather up the fragments that remain, that nothing be lost' surely means also that we are to gather in the outcasts, the souls of those whom society has rejected. I made my way through nauseating smells and filth to rub shoulders with those who had nothing but rags, politely recommending Christian faith to leprous women, shaking the stinking hands of outcast leather-workers and greeting them as 'brothers'. Yesterday when I was hunting through one of my boxes I came across an old diary. The extract I give below was written one night just after I had returned home from one such slum visit during that summer of 1887. Quite deliberately, I have altered nothing—each word is exactly as I wrote it at the time.

'Entered the slum district—stench hit me like a fist. Part of the "town", it's supposed to be, but these huts are nothing but animal pens—four sticks of bamboo or anything else they can find, stuck in the sandy ground, with straw mats thrown over the top. No ceiling, no windows, some of them without a door, even, and no flooring of any kind. After a shower the damp is worse—sodden sand, the smells appalling in the dank air, dirty water drip-dripping like tears through grimy straw roofs. To wear a single rain-clog, with only an old straw sandal for the other foot, is

---

1. The origins of the *eta*, or outcasts, are obscure. One theory is that they were originally tribes defeated in war in ancient times who were subsequently outlawed or forbidden to do any but the most menial work. After 1871 they were no longer officially classified as outcasts, but discrimination continued, and is not wholly dead yet.

luxury for these people—barefoot, most of them. All faces sallow, bloodless. Times are specially bad just now; hardly a wisp of cooking-smoke anywhere.

'Clutching a Bible, opened the door of one of the most miserable huts. Couldn't see anything at first, but made out the roof after a while, black with soot; a floor of sorts, a few roughly-planed planks no more than three inches off the ground; heap of something in a corner, round to the left, it looked out. A white head sticking out of the bundle. It moved, a little. I shook it gently—it detached itself from the pile of rags—turned towards me. An old man of eighty or so, with dull, parched eyes; past weeping, by the look of it.

'Was he sick, I asked. He shut his eyes, pointed to his mouth. Hadn't eaten for three days, he told me, pulling feebly at his rags with one hand. He was hardly breathing. He pointed behind me. A cracked teapot, a blackened earthen cooking-pot, a single rice-bowl, badly chipped, and two or three bamboo chopsticks lay scattered over the floor. No sign of water, or of any means of heating food; everything cold and dry, like the old man's eye. Asked him if he had a saucepan for rice. "They took it away. Took it away—I couldn't pay the tax." "You've no mats for the floor?" "They took them away." I bit my lip. (That summer made me a real revolutionary. Even now I get so angry sometimes, I feel like throwing a bomb at the first lacquered carriage I see.) What with his being so frail, his having no means of earning a living, and the government demanding its money, he couldn't even eat, he said—only lie there and try to sleep as best he could, till the end came, which wouldn't be long anyway. I felt in my sleeve—20 sen. Ran out and bought rice and dried sardines, put them on the floor beside the old man. Crowd had gathered by now. Pitiful faces, staring expectantly at me—but my sleeve was empty. If only I were Shirai —Shirai, one of the richest men in all the district, and a Christian! Suddenly another white head peered up from behind the old man. His wife— she'd been sleeping in the shadow by the wall. Soon, I could see, she would fall asleep in darker shadows.

'Opening my Bible, spoke to them for a few moments, then took the old woman's grimy hand in mine—to murmurs of astonishment that I was willing to touch her—and knelt to pray. All bowed their heads. Came away at last, after urging them all to come to church next Sunday. Has Society no place for these poor folk? The law protects only the rich and powerful; these people know no pleasures, they are born, live, die in an endless cycle of pain and suffering. If they do wrong the sin is not theirs.

Jehovah, Lord of Hosts, have pity upon them!'

They did come to church the following Sunday, a whole crowd of them. At first they hung about shyly by the door, so I took them up to the front and sat them in the best seats, to the alarm of the congregation. Raised eyebrows, indignant stares, superior smiles, stopped noses—every kind of disgust showed itself; evangelism's all very well, but really this is going too far, I could hear some of them murmuring. But the complaints soon subsided: my disciples never came again after that one Sunday. Nor did my mission to the slum-dwellers last much longer. What they needed was not the Way of the Lord but a way to food and clothing. When I preached to them 'Seek ye first the Kingdom of God and His righteousness; and all these things shall be added unto you,' their only reaction was to ask me if Christians got money from the government. I was ashamed. I had been deceiving them, and myself as well. I had given them rice and fish as a reward for listening to my sermon, and sauce to wash down the spiritual meal I was offering: but they only wanted the sauce, not the meal. And the sauce I could provide was so infinitesimal, their need so great. If I had been a Vanderbilt, or at least a Mitsubishi tycoon, I might have done something: the present state of my fortune being what it was, there was precious little chance of my saving a single soul, not if I were to bankrupt myself a hundred thousand times over.

Not wanting to give up altogether, though, I proposed to a church meeting that on the principle of Kuan Tzǔ's[2] 'When one does not have to worry about one's food and clothing, then one may care for courtesy and honour', we ought to try and help the bodies as well as the souls of these unfortunate people; but the idea was dismissed out of hand by the wealthy Mr Shirai. Such expensive souls (the dirty, verminous ones) would be a bad investment for God's money, I gathered—better stick to the cheaper grade, there were plenty of those, *and* they made a better show.

Every time I recall the events of that summer I am filled with shame. How tawdry my unthinking attempt at good works, compared with the benevolence—however superficial—of Minister Tzǔ Ch'an in offering his carriage to help a foot-traveller across the river,[3] or the generosity of the poor man who borrowed vinegar from his neighbour to give to a friend yet poorer than himself! In all my brief exercise in charity, which really was more concerned with my personal satisfaction than with any serious thought of the needs of others, there was no sincerity, only a mixture of curiosity and ultimately selfish desire. Not wholly wrong, perhaps; but childish. Truly I was very young.

VI.6

Yes, I was a boy still. Seventeen years and a few months, with a film of idealism over my eyes that made every mountain seem a valley, a trifling hurdle to be cleared at a single bound. That in reality the way is long and

---

2. A critic (and perhaps a former pupil) of Mencius.
3. The story is told by Mencius—but as an instance of a politician's failure to do his duty. He should have built a bridge.
The source of the incident of the borrowed vinegar is obscure. It may have been invented by the writer here as a rhetorical device to balance the genuine reference to Mencius.

tortuous, that men are bound to travel all their lives in sweat and tears, the goal ever receding even as it seems within their grasp—all this I forgot, in my eager dash forward, and stumbled, panting, on the stony ground.

Those weeks of burning zeal left no more mark than a grain of millet tossed into the sea. What came of all my turgid exhortation of the church members? The older ones merely smiled at such youthful antics. And the mission to those outside? A few lice from the slums dropped in the church, to be swept up minutes after—that was all. Had I failed for lack of faith? The suspicion began to trouble me that I had not been fitted for evangelism in the first place. Maybe my motives were not pure—maybe my faith was not true faith at all. On top of my dissatisfaction with the church and its pastor came something even harder to bear, disgust with myself; I worried more and more, and began to get dreadful headaches, which led in turn to insomnia, something I have scarcely ever suffered from before or since.

Losing the membrane of youthful idealism at the cruel hand of reality is surely more painful than any surgical operation.

> When one is tired of climbing the mountain,
> One has time to enjoy its beauty:
> Do not try to measure the immeasurable!

says the Chinese poet. But who can keep himself from hurrying upward when he sees the mountain gleaming before his eyes? We rush on—but no matter how eagerly we strain to capture it, the ideal recedes like a mirage, till we fall exhausted on the sand, only to raise our eyes a moment later and find it still smiling gently in the distance: the tears we shed then are surely the bitterest, most agonizing of all our lives. 'Give up the struggle!' old men whisper hoarsely in our ears. 'Accept life's limitations. Let the Absolute look after itself.' But what can we do? The beckoning finger of a lying ideal lures us on still; able neither to accept defeat, nor to rise from where we have stumbled, we can only writhe in agony, with self-destruction but a step away. Sleeplessness drove me more than once to the pastor's house in the middle of the night; and as I gazed up at the star-hung sky, my whole body bathed in the gentle stirrings of the night air, I wished very much to die. The vision of Death's embrace held such sweet, mysterious power.

Of all this tumult of my own spirit I said nothing to the pastor. A veteran of the world and its ways, he was not the sort to have taken seriously a boy's outpourings—and even if he had been, after all that had happened I didn't feel like turning my soul inside out for him or anyone. So I suffered in silence. If I hadn't had somebody else's trouble to worry about, I would surely had fallen ill, at the very least. This other trouble was Sone's love-affair.

Sone was a member of the Okayama church, and one year my senior at the College, where he always used to play the clown at our New Year parties. He was strong in science, and often had the pastor in difficulties with his questions. So much I knew already, though I had never spoken to him. It was quite a surprise to learn, after coming to Okayama, that he was seriously in love.

Kinko Ikeda, the girl in question, was a church member too, a beautiful girl of twenty-one, though you wouldn't have guessed she was more than eighteen; very intelligent, and a graduate of one of the few higher schools for girls. (I call her beautiful: I was just at the age when a boy thinks all girls are beautiful, and all beautiful girls are perfect in every other respect. So there may be something more than a little subjective in my description of Kinko. Whether girls go through some similar stage in relation to boys I don't know; if they do, I daresay they lose their illusions quicker—there is a western saying, for example, that Woman soon sees through Man's faults, while Man never ceases dreaming of his ideal Woman and believing she will one day materialize.) She held a certificate enabling her to teach in Middle Schools; was sufficiently fluent in English to have interpreted for Mrs Levitt, a travelling lecturer for the American Temperance Society; played both piano and organ, and sang beautifully—and remained perfectly feminine into the bargain. Once when I was advocating, in a conversation with her, the well-worn notion that women should always be gentle and modest, this delightful blue-stocking burst out with 'Oh, how I do so agree!' but clapped her hand over her mouth and dropped her eyes immediately, as if she had gone altogether far. 'Bingo Province for mats, Okayama for women', they say, but Kinko Ikeda stood out even so. I admired her immensely.

Of the previous history of the love-affair between Sone and this girl I knew nothing. But I noticed to my surprise that Sone began to look very glum when one Kinosuk Kumagae, a government official with a good salary (he was a university graduate who had studied in England, and very elegant—you could smell the perfume ten paces off) came to stay with the pastor, who it seems was an old friend. When Kumagae and Miss Ikeda went for evening walks in the Korakuen Park, Sone, so it was said, insisted on accompanying them. 'A wise bird nests in a safe tree', as the Chinese saying goes: and it is just as natural for a girl to choose a smart, substantial man for a husband. Between an immature boy like Sone and the established, gilt-edged Kumagae there could be no comparison; that goes without saying. Who nowadays would take the trouble to grow timber for his daughter's bridal chests, when they are to be had so easily ready-made, provided only you can pay? Most of the congregation, alas, not just Kinko, had blindly accepted the new philosophy: Why bump along on an ox if you can change it for a horse?

VI.7

One evening Kumagae, Sone, Kinko and myself, together with four or five other young people, met at the pastor's house for a reading and discussion of Longfellow's poems. There was tension in the air, after the rumours about Kumagae and Sone: we sensed a showdown coming, and sure enough, no sooner had we started on 'Hiawatha' than Kumagae and Sone clashed head-on over the interpretation of one particular line. Bristling, Sone insisted he was right.

'You can't persuade the common herd to change their ideas, any more than you can force a horse to drink,' said Kumagae coolly. 'Different brains, different interpretations. Let's leave it at that, shall we?'

'Common herd?' shouted Sone, starting to his feet, but held back by the pastor's restraining hand.

'Oh, come, you don't need to be suspicious,' said Kumagae, smiling. 'I was only speaking of myself, you know.' He and Kinko glanced at each other, only for a fraction of a second. Trembling, Sone threw himself at Kumagae, knocked him over, and stamped on his chest.

Instant uproar, everyone on their feet. Mingled shouts of 'Barbarian!' 'Trample the life out of him!' Thudding noises, like the pounding of rice. A woman's scream (Kinko had been hit in the face, or kicked maybe, I couldn't see by whom, there was such pandemonium).

'Easy, Sone, easy!'

'Get out—quick!'

'I'll kill him, the —'

The house of peace had turned into a battlefield. After five minutes of brawling chaos, I managed with difficulty to drag Sone free and hurried him away home. He lived alone with his old mother in a tiny house on the edge of the samurai quarter—obviously they were far from well off.

I saw then for the first time in my life how painful a dose of love can be, and caught a glimpse too of how parents agonize over their children. I was too inexperienced to have any notion of how to try and comfort Sone; but I couldn't wash my hands of his trouble, either. In the end I sat up with him all night, urging him over and over again to get control of himself. Eventually, just about daybreak, his stubborn silence crumbled in a flood of tears. Producing an armful of letters—Kinko's—from a box in the back of a cupboard, he told me the whole story. Reluctantly, at his request, I glanced through the letters. Some had been written when she was no more than fifteen or sixteen, to judge from the handwriting; some were in a hardly intelligible mixture of Japanese and English; some included poems; some were in the modern colloquial style, which I thought very odd (in such matters I was old-fashioned even then—to me, a letter wasn't a letter unless it was written in the old formal style); some were full of jokes, some sugary with sentiment; some earnestly protesting: 'You tell me I am a flirt, but my love is stronger, I swear, than iron or stone! You think all I want is money and fame—don't you know how much happier I would be to share hardship with a man who was struggling for success than marry one who had already achieved it?'—some dreaming of the glorious future: 'Your Kinko, longing for the day she knows in her heart will come, when your work will open a new era in Japanese science!'—and many more. No signed and sealed contract, maybe, but the understanding they had reached was very plain to see. And now, declared Sone angrily, she had thrown him over for that smooth-tongued Kumagae, as if there had never been anything whatever between them. 'Not that I didn't warn him,' said his mother, weeping. 'These educated girls, they're all the same—so clever at hiding their claws; every young man they meet gets taken in, but all they're thinking of is feathering their own nest. When the moment comes, they drop the mask, and there's no knowing what treachery they won't get up to. I told him this Kinko was no good. But you wouldn't listen, would you? Maybe you can see it now, the tainted look in her eyes, that not all her pretty face can hide? Nothing so hard to bear as poverty, is there, Mr Kikuchi—always someone to humiliate you, whichever way you turn . . .'

The more I thought over what I had heard, the less credible it seemed. That Kinko, of all people—mightn't it all be a terrible misunderstanding on Sone's part? Surely such a lovely, modest girl could not have written such letters! It wasn't any of my business, obviously, but I decided nevertheless to call on her right away to find out for myself.

Kinko wasn't at home. A telegram had come the previous evening, her father told me, recalling her to the school in Osaka where she taught, and she had left earlier that morning. I went on to the pastor's. Kumagae, too, had gone, without staying the night. The rumours were true, then, and Sone's suspicions justified; and that glance Kumagae and Kinko had exchanged needed no more explaining. But that sweet, gentle face—I could hardly believe it even now. Four or five days later, though, when I read the letter that came from Kinko, addressed to Sone's mother, I couldn't help damning her for the she-devil she all too obviously was. The letter was a stringing together of involved and flowery phrases, but the gist of it was that as there had been no definite engagement between Sone and herself, she would not allow any interference with whatever plans she might make in the future . . . My awed respect for Woman took a big blow.

What to do with Sone was a problem. Ignoring his mother, who kept repeating through her tears that she had never stopped telling him the girl was worthless, when he wasn't locked in a morose silence he would break into bursts of harsh, hysterical laughter, or storm against the pastor (whom he had always regarded as the unofficial but willing go-between for his intended marriage with Kinko), or rant wildly about making them pay where it hurt, etc. Eventually it was decided that for the time being, at any rate, he should stay with some relatives at Konpira in Sanuki Province, over in Shikoku. The vacation being nearly over by now, I agreed to see him safely there before going back to school.

So on the tenth of September, in company with Sone, I left this scene of my first attempt at preaching the gospel. With a polite message of appreciation from the church, and tears of gratitude from Sone's mother, light of baggage—an umbrella and one small box—but heavy at heart, a disillusioned zealot escorting a jilted lover, I and my charge sailed glumly out into Kojima Bay. I did not let Sone out of my sight till we reached Konpira —where, after handing him over to his relatives, I said goodbye, entrusting the healing of his wound to time, the Almighty, and the sympathy of his hosts. Duty done, I made my way down to Tadotsu and boarded the steamship for Kobe.

VI.8

Lighters, barges, and bumboats loaded with flatfish, saké, brushwood and every other kind of merchandise hurriedly pulling out of our way, we chugged out of Tadotsu harbour, hooting all the while and churning up a deal of spray. Dumping my baggage in the stuffy third class saloon, I went up on deck. The sun was hot enough, but the ship made its own slight breeze, and the peaceful scene all round us, with an all but waveless sea mirroring the shining, copper-coloured clouds, made the voyage feel like a holiday outing. Most of the passengers had mats laid for them on the deck; some sat cross-legged and half-undressed under the awnings, happily sharing the saké they had brought for the trip with fellow-travellers whose names they hardly knew; some roared out country songs; others talked of this and that: of how fierce, for instance, the competition between the shipping companies had grown, with one firm advertizing a ten per cent reduction in fares and a present of a towel for every passenger, of how you could go all the way up to Yokohama for only one and a half yen; of how, if things went much further, they'd be offering free passages with a cambric umbrella thrown in to tempt you—then would be the time, etc.; and many other such interesting topics. Here was a 'floating world' in miniature, with all its fascination, and pathos, too. Surely there is nothing so moving, so splendid, as a ship! Divided into 'classes' we may be, but this floating world in which we live is indeed one great ship with an unseen captain at the helm, and the famous men of all ages for crew; trailing its white wake of history, now landing its dead, now taking on the newly-born, with its cargo of joys and sorrows, it sails a boundless sea, to a goal as far beyond the vision of the mind as of the eye.

Leaving the crowd, I walked aft, and sat down on the semi-circular grille-deck over the stern, which was quite deserted. Half-listening to the hum of voices from the main deck, the clanking of the engine and the occasional rustling of the flag above my head, I gazed in turn at the long wake we were leaving behind us, like the thread of some great sea-borne spider, the fishing-boats that flowed so swiftly towards and past us over the glassy sea, and the craggy islands, like mountains in a toy landscape, revolving before us as we passed, with wisps of smoke standing over their few poor huts; and I thought of many things: of my disastrous attempt at playing the missionary; of the friend I had just left at Konpira, and his mother; of my own mother—what must be her feelings, when I had ignored her pleas that I should go home this year, fobbing her off with a photograph instead? Seeing Sone's mother had made me realize just how much parents have to go through before their children can stand on their own feet, and what a fearful canker love can be to a young man's life. My thoughts took another turn, to that last time I sailed the Inland Sea, and to the friend who should have crossed these same waters on his way home, when he was struck down so tragically on Mount Hiei. How like a dream is the world, and our human fortunes! Heavy with thoughts too deep for tears, my head began to droop. I was gazing vaguely at the deck in front of me, when over to the left I noticed a long black shadow with a gargantuan head, apparently edging in my direction. I looked up. A huge man in a blue-and-white unlined kimono, tied with a stiff sash, was staring down at me.

'Shingo!' I shouted, jumping up in astonishment. Already, before I opened my mouth, that massive nose was twitching, the narrow eyes twinkling, like threads catching the sun, till the whole great face collapsed in a gale of laughter.

'Ha-ha-ha! So it *is* Shin boy, it *is* my Shin boy after all! Ha-ha-ha-ha!'

VI.9

For a while we just stared at each other, the meeting was so unexpected. How big I'd grown, Shingo exclaimed at last. I could only smile back, wondering at his neat kimono and air of self-possession; a solid, respectable merchant, you would have said. It wasn't surprising he hadn't quite recognized me at first, either. The last time we had met was when I was at Seizan Sensei's—five years before.

'But where are you going now?' I asked, sitting down on the deck again. Shingo sat down beside me.

'Shingo, d'you mean?' (He had a habit of talking of himself in the third person.) 'Shingo's bound for Osaka. And what about you, Shin boy? But you've grown that big!' he said again, looking me up and down for nth time. I explained briefly that I was on my back to Kansei College, after spending the summer vacation at Okayama. 'And you?' I asked in turn; 'I heard you were in Fukuoka or thereabouts. Still selling charcoal?'

'Charcoal it was,' said Shingo, smiling, 'and now it's coal.' A mine-owner in Hizen had taken a liking to him, it seemed; he was now one of the mine's principal travelling agents—hence his journey to Osaka.

'But three days away, and a man must rub his eyes to recognize his friend,' the ancients said, and truly too. Shingo was no packhorse driver now; it was obvious he was well used to having men under him. Always a strong, steady character, whenever I met him he was doing better than before; every time I saw that great jutting nose of his, he reminded me of a great boar, crashing its way imperturbably through a mass of tangled brambles.

'It's a long time, ain't it Shin boy, truly? You're Shin boy still, I can see, though you have shot up so big. Funny, isn't it, I'll be calling you "young master" now, won't I? How 'bout that, eh—young master Shin? Ha-ha-ha-ha!' Jovial old Shingo still—though now that he was 'young-mastering' me, I called him 'Mr Nakamura' instead.

There was so much to talk about, after five years. Shingo had my box brought up to the second class saloon where he himself was travelling, roared out an order to a steward for tea and sweet cakes, spread a rug for me on the floor, produced pears from a suitcase and peeled them carefully for my benefit—all in such style that we soon had all the other passengers staring at us. One question led to another; we finished the cakes, drank all the tea, reduced the pears to a heap of peel and cores, and still talked on.

I told Shingo what had happened to me since I decamped from the New School: my adventures at Uwajima, how I was working my way through the College. He listened carefully, grunting now and then; and when I finished, gave a monumental and decisive nod, as if his great head were stamping a hallmark on the air.

'Perseverance—that's it!' he exclaimed, with such vigour that a passenger who had been sleeping nearby started up as if he had been trodden on, and glared angrily all round the room.

'Shingo's been through it too, I can tell you. He's been through the mill—but the rules helped: the rules the priest wrote—our priest of Ennenji Temple, d'you remember him, Shin boy? "Directions", he called them. Item: never tell a lie. Item: Don't borrow money you can't pay back. Item: keep away from women and gambling, and don't drink too much. Item: What one man has done before, another can do after him. Shingo used to read these rules—read 'em every day, till they really sank in deep. That's how he made it. "This Shingo fellow don't tell lies; Shingo don't steal", it got around a bit in time; "he's no debts; his nose is as good as ever it were",' (guffaw from a passenger on his right)'—and another thing that'll please you, Shin boy, young master: Shingo's learnt a bit since the old days. He can write a pretty letter now, and read the big articles in the Tokyo papers, even—not the poems, mind you, or the chess columns and that stuff, which he can't make head nor tail of—never had much liking for that kind of nonsense anyways. Perseverance—patience and perseverance, that's what does it, Shin boy! The world's a game, to see who sticks it longest—and ain't it fun, Shin boy!'

Shingo's cheerfulness roused me like a bugle-call out of the gloom that had settled over me as a result of the events of the last few weeks. I asked him if he knew how things were at Tsumagome. He'd not been back once since he left, he said, nor had he been in touch with my mother, even, for several years, what with his living so far away now and being so busy: but he'd heard that the other branch of the Kikuchis were in a fine old mess. O-Fuji, the daughter, had left the husband they had found for her (and adopted into the family, incidentally) and run off with a smirking, smooth-faced teacher from the primary school; while Uncle Kengo, the one I used to hate so, had made some worthless woman his mistress. 'Never mind, Shin boy. The net of heaven is wide and full of holes,'[4] don't you worry. The gods side with the honest man; it won't be long before that family ruins itself, and then we'll see! Not much longer your mother needs to hold out. How is she, though, and Mr Noda and all?'

I supposed Mr Noda and his family were well enough, I said, though Mother wasn't living with them any more, so I didn't have any direct news. Just then an old man of sixty or thereabouts sitting nearby, a countryman by the looks of him, leant towards us. I had noticed that he had been half-listening to our conversation—not that he could do anything else, Shingo's voice being what it was.

'Excuse me, sir,' he asked, bowing slightly, 'but would you be a friend of Mr Noda's?'

I was a relative, I told him. He came from a village not far from where Uncle lived, apparently; had handed over the headship of the family to his son, and was just now taking advantage of the drop in steamship fares to visit the Ise Shrine and the great Honganji Temple in Kyoto.

'A great pity that was about Mr Noda,' he added politely.

I didn't know what to say. It was a very long time since I had written to the Noda family, nor had there been any special mention of them in Mother's letters.

'A sad business altogether,' he went on, quite without emotion, as though whatever he was referring to was common knowledge. 'Never could see why he had to bankrupt himself like he did, though, poor man; there must have been other ways out than that.'

Thunderstruck, I asked the old man to explain.

VI.10

This was the story the old man told, wondering that I hadn't heard it already. Uncle Noda's peculiar ways had long been a byword throughout the prefecture, but never so much so, it seemed, as in the last year or two. The culminating example had come earlier this year. To help with the building of a new primary school that was planned for the village (and also for the repair of a local bridge and various other projects) Uncle had asked the prefectural authorities to release—for a nominal payment—a large quantity of timber from government forests. As it happened, the official he applied to was that Mr Kuroki whom Uncle had once punched on the nose, at the Governor's dinner. Not unnaturally, Kuroki took his time over dealing with the application. Whereupon Uncle, furious at the delay,

---

4. Shingo is recalling, somewhat inaccurately, a passage in the Tao Te Ching: 'The net of heaven is cast wide. Though the mesh is not fine, yet nothing ever slips through.' *Tao Te Ching*, tr. D. C. Lau (Penguin Classics, London 1963), p. 135.

ordered the villagers on his own authority to fell the timber themselves, without waiting for official permission. Which, of course, was just what Kuroki was waiting for: he denounced Uncle for stealing government property, and had him arrested immediately. Things looked very serious indeed, till Aunt Noda, 'another lady of the family' (this must have been Mother) and two or three of Uncle's old cronies pleaded so effectively with the Governor on his behalf that it was decided that as his offence had been due merely to an excess of zeal for the public good, he should be released forthwith, on condition payment was made, to the tune of several thousand yen, for the timber the villagers had already felled. But money isn't to be had for the asking. When the village had contributed what it could, and a mortgage raised on the timber, Uncle still had to find two thousand yen himself: so that he had been forced to sell up—land, house, and everything he possessed. So the school got built after all, but at Uncle's expense. He and Aunt had moved to a tiny cottage up in the mountains, ten miles or more away.

'Oh, it's been a sad business, I can tell you, and we're all that sorry for Mr Noda and his lady. But the greed of some can be a frightening thing, Mr Kikuchi, that it can. There's that relative of theirs, what was her name now? Kasa—Kasamatsu, the Widow Kasamatsu: she had lent Mr Noda some small amount a while before, and would you believe it, she bled him for every single sen of it, out of what was left after the house was sold? Mr Noda swore he'd kill her, they say—which must have had his lady worried. The world's grown a plaguy place these days, Mr Kikuchi, when a man can't even do good without watching every step he takes.' The old man sighed deeply as he finished his story.

Shingo looked at me questioningly—he had been listening intently to every word—as if to say 'Here's news'll mean your burden's heavier, Shin boy. Can your shoulders stand it, lad?' And he was right. Uncle had no relatives to turn to for help; and with Suzue, their only remaining child, being a girl, who could they look to but me; and wasn't it my duty to repay the kindness they had shown me by doing all I could to restore the fortunes and dignity of the Noda family, as well as our own? I saw their faces before me, Uncle raging like a wounded lion, Aunt Noda with her hair suddenly grey: I cursed my own laziness in not having kept in touch, so that I should have known of their trouble—and bitterly reproached my mother for never having mentioned it in her letters, though no doubt *her* chief concern had been not to worry me with bad news when I was studying hard, and when in any case there was little I could do.

Harima Channel and Akashi Strait had slipped by without our noticing, so busy had we been with our talk, and already we had entered Kobe harbour, its broad waters a medley of dancing lights. Saying goodbye to Shingo, who was going straight through to Osaka (but promised he would call and see me on his way back) and to the old countryman, I went ashore at once and made my way up once more to the College.

Five days after the beginning of the new term (the first of my third year) Shingo turned up at the dormitory as arranged, gaping at the size and splendour of the buildings. When I had shown him round the campus, he insisted on taking me to the best foreign-style restaurant in Kobe for a meal. Here, in a private room, over our roast beef, we took up where we had left off on the boat. In answer to his questions, I told Shingo I meant to go in for Christian work after graduating. To this he objected vehmently: so, swallowing my half-cooked onions[5] and chewing at the blackened strips[5] of beef, I gave him a speech about the true importance of spiritual labour. Evangelism, I explained at length, ramming home my points at intervals by smartly tapping with my chopsticks the saucepan on the table between us, was a vocation for the man of true public spirit and benevolence—the traditional virtues—and not, as he seemed to think, a mere mumbling of prayers on behalf of the senile. But no, he wouldn't listen for a moment.

'These preachers, or screechers, or whatever you call 'em, may be useful in their way; but Mr Shintaro Kikuchi throw himself away on that stuff—Shingo won't hear of it, no matter who tries to talk him into it. No more will your mother—Will she? These days a man can climb any height he likes if he's got the brains: Prime Minister' (Shingo was well up in the reorganization of the administrative system the government had put through the previous year, now that he had learnt to read the newspapers) 'Army Minister, professor, millionaire—take your pick! Why, even Shingo, who the village clots used to jeer at when they saw him hauling that old horse of his, can dream of getting himself into Parliament! These are the times we live in, so what's the sense in a lad as sharp as you aiming at nothing better than a Jesus-priest? It's throwing your life away, Shin boy. Keep the praying till your hair turns white, not before!'

Shingo's massive body shook so violently from the vigour and earnestness with which he spoke that the yellow glass fly-trap hanging from the ceiling broke loose and crashed into our saucepan; but after a momentary glance down, we went on arguing without so much as a smile for nearly half an hour more. Shingo wouldn't budge, though. Finally I promised to think over what he had said, and we called a truce. He was obviously disappointed he hadn't succeeded in persuading me to abandon Christianity there and then; but he was grateful to me, he said, for giving him a hearing. My getting on in the world, he went on, would give him greater pleasure than any success he managed to achieve for himself. When I needed money for going on to university, or for anything else for that matter, I was to be sure and consult nobody but him; he'd be proud to be my quartermaster, that he would (he kept saying) if so be I would let him.

5. This is no reflection on 'the best foreign-style restaurant in Kobe'—Shintaro would not be so discourteous to his host as to imply any such criticism. He and Shingo are eating 'suki-yaki', in which the customer cooks his own meat and vegetables on a small brazier on the table in front of him; they are too absorbed in their talk to attend to the finer points of cooking.

(If I hadn't shown I was determined to be independent, he'd have offered to pay my College fees from that day on, I don't doubt.) As it was, he handed me a present of five yen, suitably wrapped, 'to help a bit with the books.' When I told him, after a moment's thought, that I would accept it with much pleasure and gratitude, he was hugely delighted, and launched off at once into another round of pleas, as we were getting ready to leave, that I should give up once and for all the idea of becoming a preacher. I presented him with a copy of Benjamin Franklin's *Ways to Wealth*, and we said goodbye.

A few days after Shingo left, I had an answer to the letter I'd written to Mother asking after Uncle Noda. Uncle and Aunt were settled quite happily, she wrote, in their cottage up in the hills; the villagers had shown them great kindness; Uncle, still full of public spirit, had started a maple-planting scheme in the village to increase the local silk-production, and went shooting in his spare time (I couldn't help wondering what birds or animals there could be stupid enough to give Uncle's gun the remotest chance of hitting anything)—in short, I was not to worry.

Together with a letter of apology (for my long silence) and sympathy, however belated, for him and his family in all their trouble, I sent Uncle Noda a tin of beef.

VI.11

My life at the College was as busy as ever. Apart from normal school work, there were my cleaning duties twice a day, eight hours a week of teaching, and the translating of Mr Brown's manuscript *Notes on the Bible*, which latter took up a great deal of time, but which I was glad to do, as much for the practice it gave me in reading his English, as for the modest payment I received. But the more a man is stretched, the better he works; and on top of all these regular activities, I found time for sport, poring over the newspapers, wasting time agreeably with friends, even for extra reading, outside the course, and for bits of scribbling as well. A quaint effusion entitled 'Confessions of a Youthful Evangelist', put together in odd minutes borrowed from other preoccupations, appeared in the College magazine at about this time.

One day we were leaving the classroom after a psychology lecture, when the teacher called me back and asked me to take a meal with him at his house that evening. Mr Kan—that was the teacher's name—was a small, thin man, notorious at the College for the shortness of his temper ('Tea-sticks'[6] was the somewhat riddling nickname we gave him, his inflammability being in inverse ratio to his size.) There can hardly have been a single student who hadn't felt the rough side of his tongue. In religion he was for ever at odds with orthodoxy, so the missionaries didn't much take

---

6. *Edaaumi*, tiny sticks of charcoal, very easily kindled, and used for this reason to heat water in the Japanese tea-ceremony.

to him, either. Academically, though, he was so able and well qualified, particularly in English literature (on which subject, we gathered, he often worsted the foreigners at staff discussions, for all their American degrees) that they had to keep him on in spite of their dislike. Only the Principal, in fact, seemed at all well disposed towards Mr Kan.

As for myself, I knew Kan Sensei had a wife as fat as he was thin, and had heard stories of the violent quarrels they were said to have, but I had never been inside their house, and hardly knew now what to make of this sudden invitation. Try as I could, I couldn't recall having fallen foul of him at all during the last month or so; and why should he invite me to dinner, anyway, if he only wanted to read me a lecture? Summoning up my courage, I presented myself that evening at Kan Sensei's house.

I was shown straight through to his study, a four-and-a-half mat room with a desk and such a confusion of books sprawling over the floor that there was hardly room to sit. Here we talked, Kan Sensei puffing at his pipe, I nibbling at rice crackers. 'A devil at a hundred paces, a fellow human being at fifty; a stranger at fifty paces, a brother at ten,' the saying goes; and so it was with this martinet of a professor, who turned out to be surprisingly gentle when you once got close to him. Presently we were summoned to dinner—bowls of rice with sliced burdock roots, terribly salty: the fat wife's home cooking, I suppose. (Kan Sensei can't have been very well off in the first place, and he obviously spent most of his salary on books. Hence, no doubt, the domestic strife.) Then back to his study. This time we relaxed, both of us sitting cross-legged. Then he began again. What was I going to do after graduation next year? I told him I was thinking of taking the Theology Course, with a view to going in for Christian work. (I was still quite sure that this was what I wanted to do.) He'd heard something of the kind, he said, and had realized how strong my convictions were from reading my article in the College magazine. 'How about writing as a career?' he went on. 'Ever thought of that, have you? Not that I'm against preaching; but you don't have to be a preacher to do the Will of God. A carpenter can't build a house all alone; a regiment of gunners doesn't make an army. God gives us the lily alongside the rose—don't you think it must be His Will that every plant should bear its own flower? A man's first duty is to find out where his talents want to take him, his second, to give them all the rein they'll take. Ideals shine so very brightly when you're young, they can dazzle you into mistaking altogether what you are really fitted for. Listen to me, Kikuchi. I'm not pushing you, mind: take me for an old woman if you will. But if I'm seeing straight, and I think I am, there's a vocation clearly marked out for you. It struck me again when I read your 'Confessions' the other day. Evangelism, teaching, politics—I've nothing against any of them, but your work, I can't help thinking, lies elsewhere. There are other ways of spreading the gospel than praying in a pulpit, mixing the communion wine and preaching sermons on Sundays; and if teaching means lording it over a bunch of boys in a classroom, it's a pretty tedious way of going about it, don't you think? But put a pen in your hand, and you can turn out sermons enough for a hundred years of Sundays: take all Japan for your classroom, if you will! To my mind, there's nothing so pitiful as a man who doesn't know for certain where he belongs. A Prime Minister who's not sure of himself, or a primary school teacher who is—which do you think is the happier? Which is doing God's Will, which conforming to His plan for the world? There *are* evangelists, I daresay, full-time professional preachers, who manage to write, and write well, at the same time. But one stout stick serves your traveller better than two fancy canes. Genius will out, of course: like a compass needle, a man's real gift is bound to make itself known sooner or later, whatever the pressures. Burns sang with his hand on the plough; Lamb wrote his *Essays of Elia* because he *had* to, from his desk in the East India Company Office. If he's given the chance, though, a man wants to choose the path that suits him best—Eh, Kikuchi? You're near the crossroads now, getting ready to make that choice; and that's why I'm telling you all this.'

VI.12

One rainy Saturday night early in the term, all my classmates had crowded into my room for a party. When eventually we had tired of fooling and consumed the evening's stock of buns and beans, someone suggested a bout of communal fortune-telling, for each member of the class in turn. Off we went, in order of the English alphabet; somebody proposing a career for so-and-so, others coming up with 'amendments', till the final choice was made by majority vote, and recorded by one of our (self-styled) Masters of the Brush. Akazawa—to be chief of Tokyo Metropolitan Police ... Baba—to inherit a restaurant, by marrying the owner's daughter ... and so on. We had among us in embryo, it seemed, a university professor, a district governor, a speculator in rice, a Christian pastor, a bailiff, a minister-plenipotentiary. Groans or shouts of delight from each victim at the announcement of his destiny. Soon it came to my turn. 'Novelist!' yelled a voice. 'Hear, hear!' shouted somebody else in English. 'Never! Moody, Whitfield, that's Kikuchi's line—isn't he always telling us? Put down "preacher"!' 'Wrong again! Kikuchi for College President!' etc. etc., amendment after amendment. But 'novelist' won out in the end, for all my frantic protests. It must have been a malicious reference, I suppose, to a remark I had made about the famous novel *Kajin no Kigu*[7] (the first part had come out not long before: everybody was talking of Yuran and Koren, and the College had sprouted its own crop of would-be novelists).

7. *A Strange Encounter of Elegant Ladies*, a fanciful romance of love, patriotism and revolution, which was a best-seller for several years after its publication in 1885. Yuran (Mysterious Orchid) and Koren (Crimson Lotus) are the Ladies of the title—Yuran being Irish and Koren Spanish.

'Admire a trashy book like that, do you? I'd do better myself, if I ever took up writing,' I had boasted, half-jokingly, to the classmate who had now saddled me with this fate. A novelist, indeed! I was furious. A petty scribbler: as if a gentleman, a man of any honour at all, could stoop so low! This was carrying a joke too far.

'Wasn't Disraeli a novelist, though?' someone tried to placate me. 'And didn't Hugo answer, "Make them read my novels!" when Itagaki asked him for advice on how to preach liberty and equality to the Japanese? There's nothing to be ashamed of in writing novels. It's what a man makes of it, no more, no less. Stop the sulking, Kikuchi; it's not like you. Accept the verdict, man!' So, in the end, they brought me round.

My feelings were pretty confused, too—different though the circumstances were—when I listened to Kan Sensei deliver his bolt from the blue. To have Kan Sensei, of all people, the irascible, unpopular, odd-man-out Kan Sensei, talking to me thus kindly—this was a pleasant experience, certainly; and there was something too in what he said. Yet the question was such a big one, I couldn't answer him either way then. I'd think it over, I said, and asked him finally what field of literature he thought I ought to go in for. Nodding repeatedly, he told me to keep up the study of English literature, and inevitably, in time, the question would settle itself. Before I left, he lent me some of his own books: a commentary on *Hamlet*, Carlyle's *Heroes and Hero-Worship*, and a *History of English Literature*.

The little fortress I was building had already to face a savage attack, before its walls were dry or its arrow-holes prepared. Most alarming of all, I discovered a traitor lurking within. I had been so sure of myself, so sure of standing on the solidest of ground; now, to my terror, it was beginning to slip away from beneath my feet. This was no rock where I had started to build, but a floating island. After less than a year, my resolve to give my life to preaching the gospel was wavering.

A bout of the blackest depression followed. If I could give up as easily as that, what chance was there I would ever achieve anything at all? A man's duty, if he called himself a man, I told myself grimly, was to stick to what he had once decided, no matter where it led him. But had my decision really been God-given? Or was it no more than a passing emotion: in which case to hold to it would make no more sense than for a samurai to immolate himself on the death of his lord's usurper; and more than that, the blame for neglecting my true vocation might all be on my own head. No! such doubts only showed a cooling off of faith, a reborn worldliness. I had tired of the lonely struggle, the thorny road to Heaven, and longed only to strut down the broad avenues of this floating world, a slave to fame and fortune. Wait, though: fame and fortune, blindly served, could destroy me, yes; use them rightly, and what a weapon they might be! What's the good of preaching sacrifice and the 'peace that surpasses all worldly achievement', when the preacher himself has achieved nothing and never possessed anything worth giving up? Maybe there was truth after all in the popular idea that praying and white hairs belonged together, as Shingo had said? The half-baked piety of a boy of seventeen, solemnly telling his beads—assuming he isn't just a spiritless half-wit—can only be an illusion. If I didn't know my own mind now, what would it be like when I was older? And wasn't it inevitable anyway, the urge in a young man's blood to be up and doing in the world? There's nothing meaner than staying neutral because you're afraid of losing, or more pitifully absurd than to take up preaching because you haven't the guts to succeed in the world: better far to go out first into the arena and try one's skill, not to show off, but for one's own inner satisfaction—win fame and fortune by serving others, not oneself, learn the limits of one's strength—and *then* toss all achievement willingly aside, ready at last for a purer, more spiritual life! Not to start by fawning, empty-handed, at the steps below God's throne, endlessly mumbling Amen, Amen; but to use the hands, the feet He gave you, try your bow (if you have one) upon the moors, bring home your prize—some shedding of blood there must be—to burn it upon His altar: *this* is surely His Will.

Don't deceive yourself! The devil was ever a plausible advocate, dragging men and women to the pit with his smooth words. Only prayer could help me now, I knew. I knelt. 'Open Thou the eyes of my spirit, O Lord, and show me the right—' But how happy Mother would be if I gave up the idea! 'What do you mean, interrupting when I'm in the middle of praying?' I rounded on my rebellious thoughts. But then again, why such anger and argument? 'Let water flow, and it will dig its own channel'—wasn't this the best rule of all for a good life? Instead of sticking stubbornly to one's own petty claims, instead of brandishing one's own minute talents, why not let life flow as nature wills, let feeling be the guide for speech and action? In the end this might be the true obedience to the Will of Heaven, I told myself comfortingly. But I could discover no clear answer to my questionings.

Every day, though, I found my resolve weakening, till I was keeping to it out of little more than a sense of guilt. By now I was thoroughly disgusted with myself, which made me so irritable that people began to ask whether I was ill. No, I wasn't ill, not physically anyway; my sickness was of the spirit.

But one there was who *was* ill, and seriously ill at that—Uncle Noda, in his cottage three hundred miles away. On December 24th, 1886, a letter came from Mother with the news that Uncle had had a stroke, and might not survive the winter.

VI.13

I decided to go home at once. Fortunately the winter vacation began the following day; so after collecting the money due to me for the translation of Mr Brown's Notes on the Bible, I caught the boat from Kobe that same day. Two days later, early in the morning, we reached Hakata, from where I took a rickshaw. Watching families everywhere busy with house-cleaning, *mochi*-making, and other preparations for the New Year, I was reminded that it was just three years since I had slipped out of the New School that night, to start my long journey to the capital. Three years, four years— they flit by as lightly as the flap of a bird's wings, as it sails from its perch in a tree. And life stays still no longer than the turning wheels of a rickshaw. So Uncle Noda, that massive, robust, energetic man, as I had known him, was dying. If only I were not too late . . . Mother couldn't have expected me so soon, though, surely. Anxiety ran ahead, making the wheels below me sound cruelly sluggish. The ferry across the Chikugo River, buffeted by the cold down-river winds, a night at the post-inn at the village of Fukushima, an early start next morning: it was nearly nightfall again when I reached the castle-town that had once been my home.

Mother had told me that she was living in a cottage in the old samurai quarter on the edge of the town. Most of the houses on either side of the narrow lanes looked alike, each with its strip of hedge and tall lattice doors. I was riding up one lane and down another, looking at the names on the doorposts, when a boy of ten or so—supper just finished, no doubt—came running out from a house just ahead of me with a dog. I stopped him, and asked if he knew where a Mrs Kikuchi lived.

'Kikuchi? The lady Big Sister goes to for sewing? Up there behind the bamboo.' He pointed to a house a little way up the lane, the second or third from where he was standing. I jumped down from the rickshaw. The boy was right. In the half-light I could just make out the name, inked on the wooden nameplate in Mother's writing, 'Shintaro Kikuchi'.

I knocked, trying to curb my excitement. A servant-woman of about thirty appeared with a lamp.

'Who is it, sir, if you please?'

'Is Mother here?'

'Well I—if it isn't the young gentleman! Of course it is, and welcome, sir, too, I'm —'

'Where's Mother?' I repeated, peering past her.

'Come in, sir, please—Mrs Kikuchi left yesterday for Mr Noda's —'

'Of course—how is Mr Noda now?'

'None too good, sir, none too good,' the woman answered, hurriedly preparing a brazier for me. 'It might be two or three days before she was back, Madam said, depending on how she found him.'

'Did she? I'll go right away, then.' I got up.

'But you'll be worn out, sir—let me get you a bite of supper first!'

She went to the kitchen. Sipping tea, I looked round the six-mat room. The alcove was decorated with an arrangement of young daffodils still in bud and a familiar scroll painting—a branch of a plum tree under a pale moon, with perched among the blossoms a grotesque bird I had scribbled over it when I was six or thereabouts. I had spent half a day locked up in the shed for drawing that bird; the scroll had been in the family for generations, and was one of the few things we kept when Father went bankrupt. A small desk in one corner; a big sewing board in another; a much-patched sliding partition, half-open, and beyond it, in a smaller room, a silk-loom, with a dust-cloth thrown over work just begun, and my letters in a home-made rack hanging from one of its posts: everything in perfect order, not a speck of dust on the threadbare floormats.

I gulped down a bowl of hot rice, while the woman gave me news of Mother, and then, wrapped outlandishly in an ancient red blanket the woman insisted on giving me to keep out the cold, I set off for Uncle Noda's. Yamashita Village was ten miles from the town, up in the hills; I knew it from having been that way once or twice on our rabbit-hunting expeditions from Seizan Sensei's. No need for a rickshaw tonight: under the frosty white light of a seventeen-day old moon, with only my shadow for company, I hurried on, my clogs click-clacking on the frozen road.

It was a lonely walk through fields, for the most part, with two or three miles between each hamlet, and no travellers at this hour of the night. After about seven miles the road led up to the bank of a river, beyond which, in the distance, a range of hills showed black and hump-backed under the moon. I took a narrow track, following the river upstream. Gradually the hills drew closer, the river curving to meet them, till the track crossed a bridge and began to climb more steeply. On the bridge I passed a countryman with a packhorse making the most of the night—he was taking a load of whitebean branches down to the town to sell them early next morning as New Year decorations. Did he know Mr Noda's, I asked. 'Mr Noda—aye, sir,' he said, with evident respect for Uncle's name. 'The thatched cottage is where 'e lives, on the rise across the river.' I pushed on up the stony track to the top of a small hill, to find myself looking down on Yamashita Village, and the moon shining up at me from a stream that neatly cut the village into two, with some sixty houses on the far side, and fifty more immediately below me. The nearside, under the brow of the hill, was pitch-dark; but beyond the stream I could distinguish every house, tree and stone, scupltured under the cold, over-arching light. By now it must have been past midnight. There was not a single light to be seen, not a voice to be heard, save for a dog barking in some distant garden. Now and then came a slow, grinding *gi—i—i* from some invisible rice-mortar nearby, and in the intervals only the murmur of the stream—like a breeze among pines—as it darted along its stony bed, shattering the moon into dancing points of light. I stood gazing down, as if in a trance.

Coming to myself abruptly, I hurried down the hill, crossed the stream by some stepping-stones, and climbed up the other side, as the countryman had directed, looking out all the time for any thatched roofs; but I could hear nothing, nor see any cottage that matched his description. If only I could find someone still awake; or maybe I should knock somebody up and ask? I turned right into a still narrower lane, and was just passing a night-soil tank when I noticed a thread of light, too yellow for a moonbeam, lying across the track. It came from a house on the higher ground to my left, filtered through a mulberry hedge. Here at last was somewhere I could ask the way.

I crawled under the hedge into a tiny back garden. Voices sounded from behind the shutters, blurred by the tiny drum-beats of water dripping from a bamboo pipe. Tiptoeing up to the shuttered veranda, I listened.

'It must have been a shock for him when he heard.'

My heart nearly missed a beat—and the next instant was racing furiously.

'No doubt of that. I dreamt last night he'd come—'

'Mother!'

The voices stopped—I could hear the sudden catching of breath. I knocked on the shutters.

'Who's there?'

'It's me—Shintaro, Mother!'

'. . . .'

The shutters slid back instantly, so that I was standing in the full glare of the light.

'My boy!'

'Shin-chan!'

Clutching at my hands, Mother and Aunt Noda pulled me up over the high veranda.

VI.14

Half-climbing, half-dragged up into the little six-mat room where Mother and Aunt had been keeping vigil and wondering how I had taken the news of Uncle's illness, I sat down with them over the charcoal brazier. For a while none of us could find words.

'It's a miracle you were able to come home so soon,' said Mother at last, turning up the wick of the lamp and fixing on me those clear, cool eyes of hers I remembered so well. But her face—I could hardly bear to see how she had aged in the three years I had been away.

'Your mother and I were only now talking of you,' said Aunt. She stirred up the charcoal embers. 'It was good of you to come, though. And how you've grown!'

'How is Uncle?' I managed to ask at last. He seemed to be asleep: I could hear the rise and fall of his breathing from the other side of the sliding partition, which had been left open a few inches.

'A little better today,' replied Aunt, glancing through into the other room. 'He'll be so happy to see you when he wakes up. But weren't you frozen, Shin-san, travelling so late at night?'

'You must have left directly you saw my letter?'

'Yes, Mother. I got home this evening, and came on here right away.'

'So quickly? It *was* kind of you, Shin-san,'—Aunt looked at me intently—'and you are truly welcome. Why, only the other day Suzue was saying—Suzue! Where are you?'

'Here, Mother.' A girl with her hair done up in the western style appeared in the doorway, tying the braids of her *haori* coat. So this was Suzue. She was changed astonishingly in three years: taller, more confident, looking every inch the high-school girl. Three months after I ran away she had gone to Tokyo to study, and this was her first visit home since then— she had travelled alone, I was told, her aunt, with whom she was lodging, and who should have brought her down, having been prevented from coming by trouble with her feet. The four of us sat round the brazier, sipping hot tea, and talking now and then, but as softly as we could, for fear of waking Uncle. Since they had moved to the village in the spring of that year, Aunt said, Uncle had been surprisingly cheerful and active, hunting, climbing, preaching the advantages of silkworm-rearing to the farmers, persuading a doctor to move in, and urging everyone in the village to stop relying for their health on 'praying and potions'. The locals had soon come to look up to him; they often brought him new potatoes, and had sent lots of freshly-made wheatcakes for the Lantern Festival. But just when it seemed Uncle had been given a new lease of life, and they were wondering in pleasant surprise whether his bankruptcy hadn't been a blessing in disguise, it happened. Uncle had collapsed halfway through a meeting to mark the purchase by the Young Men's Association of a new fire-pump, and had not got up since. He could speak, but had difficulty in understanding; the doctor they had called in from the town had feared Uncle would have a struggle to get through the cold weeks ahead.

Soon we fell silent, but sat on as before, staring at the quietly-burning charcoal.

A moan from behind the partition, then a cough. I followed Aunt Noda into Uncle's room. It was a six-mat room, like the one where we had been sitting. Uncle lay on his back, his head propped on a raised pillow. Suddenly, in the light from Aunt Noda's lamp, he saw me.

'..... Daiichiro ... Daiichiro! Why have you come?'

I was too taken aback to say anything. Mother turned away; Aunt Noda bent her head.

'It's Cousin Shintaro, Father!' Bewilderment spread over Uncle's face as Suzue spoke.

'Shintaro ... Shintaro ...? Why, it's Shin boy! Where have you been all this while—come closer now!'

The hand he tried to give me fell limp. I took it, kneeling beside him.

'Uncle!' The fine phrases I had planned on the journey vanished; I could only stare in silence at the wasted cheeks, the glazed, lifeless eyes and childish smile.

Uncle lived on till the last day of the year, his mind flickering like candle-light. He would call me Shin-boy one moment, Daiichiro the next, and talk of all manner of things. 'Must get more silkworm eggs sent down from Kozuke for the village,' he would mutter sometimes, or (imagining he was back in the old house), 'We'll knock down the pigpen and keep bees instead,' or again he would launch out on a rambling account of the battles of Fushimi and Toba,[8] only to interrupt himself with an indignant 'Hasn't that fellow Saigo[9] come to his senses yet?'—but always with the same gentle smile, except for moments of petulance when he wanted his food and it didn't come in time. Aunt Noda and Mother cooked special delicacies, and Suzue fed him, as he couldn't manage chopsticks any more. (He'd been thrilled with the tin of beef I had sent, they told me: alas, I had left Kobe in too much of a hurry to think of bringing anything with me this time.)

I stayed at Uncle's bedside night and day, turning him over when he wanted it, massaging his arms and legs, and generally helping with the nursing, which certainly made things easier for *me* to bear, whether he knew me or not. Looking down at the deathlike stillness of his sleeping face as I massaged his great limbs, I wondered sometimes whether I should speak a little, when he woke, of the blessed peace that awaited him: but invariably, when he did wake, the sight of that strange childlike smile checked any such thought, and I could only pray to God to ease the passing of this generous, unfortunate soul.

On the afternoon of the 31st, Uncle seemed particularly cheerful. Asking for the sliding windows to be opened (the winter sun shone bright and warm that day), he watched with delight the villagers trying out their New Year kites. But when evening came he sank into a deep coma. We sent a messenger after the doctor, who on seeing his patient apparently so comfortable had returned to the town in the afternoon; but before he could get back, just on ten o'clock, Uncle suddenly opened his eyes wide, forced himself up on his elbows, and cried out: 'The Diet they promised—has it met yet?' Alarmed, I jumped to his side—in time to catch his body, as it fell back like a great tree. Uncle Noda's spirit was no longer of this world.

VI.15

On a journey, ill,
and over fields all withered, dreams
go wandering still.[10]

So the poet Basho not long before he died; and so must Uncle's spirit, after his death in that remote mountain village, have looked back wistfully at the world in which he had planned so much and achieved so little. His life reminds me of those prickly water-lilies that abound, I am told, in the

---

8. Fought between Imperial forces and the Shogunate army in 1868.
9. See note 2, p. 75.
10. The translation is by Henderson, in *An Introduction to Haiku* (New York, 1958), p. 30.

River Amazon, with no flower worth the name to match their enormous leaves; or of a great eagle lying wounded and squirming on the ground, no strength in his broken wings to obey his still imperious spirit, so that even the common kites dare openly to mock his fall—till in a last mad burst of fury at his fate, he tears out his own entrails. Truly it was sad to see Uncle die thus—sadder still to watch him in those final days, bankrupt and dying, his mind no longer clear, yet concerned to the very last moment for his beloved country and its welfare, like the old warhorse of the Emperor Wu's poem—

'A hundred miles a day' is still his dream
As now he lies, all strengthless, on the stable floor.

I couldn't keep back the tears as I looked down at the dead face, and said goodbye.

So he was gone—Uncle Noda, who for four years had loved me like a son: gone beyond hope of return, before I could begin to pay the debt I owed him, when there had hardly been time even to repair the breach between us. But at least I had arrived before the end. In this thought, and in the knowledge that though there would be no guard of honour to escort Uncle to his grave, he had died peacefully, in the loving care of his wife and daughter and surrounded by the unfeigned sympathy of the villagers, I sought consolation.

On January 3rd, while the New Year holiday was still in full swing, Uncle was laid to rest alongside his son Daiichiro in the shadow of a big oak tree in the grounds of Seisenji Temple, across the river. Daiichiro's grave had been moved here when they sold the big house. 'Bury me next to Daiichiro. No priests, mind you, and no showing off with a big gravestone!' Uncle had insisted. The funeral was exceedingly simple. Uncle's eccentricities had made him so many enemies and the village he had retired to was so remote, that the only mourners besides ourselves were two or three relatives (the widow Kasamatsu and her son Sanjiro being among the absentees), one representative of Uncle's old friends (Seizan Sensei was away at the time), three or four former neighbours, and the people of the village. The latter were wonderfully kind, turning up in almost embarrassing numbers to shoulder the coffin, dig the grave, and help in the kitchen afterwards. Their memories went back to the days when Uncle's grandfather had served as local Commissioner for the Shogunate. During his period of office he had done so much for the community—planting cryptomerias systematically to help conserve water, setting up temple-schools for the teaching of writing and arithmetic, raising moral standards by organizing easy-to-understand public lectures on ethics, not to mention a host of other admirable projects—that the Noda family had been held in special regard ever since.

The two or three days following the funeral were as desolate as the aftermath of a typhoon. I doubt whether Aunt and Cousin Suzue could have stood it if Mother and I hadn't been with them. The evenings were especially lonely. Sitting round the brazier in the six-mat room at the back of the house, we talked of the dead, who till a few days ago had been lying in this very room, and whose spirit now gazed down upon us through the incense-smoke from the memorial-tablet on the family shrine. Anecdotes galore had always gathered around Uncle; but in the three years since I ran away there seemed to have been a specially rich crop. How he once stopped an itinerant fishmonger in the street, bought up his entire stock of sea-slugs and distributed it gratis among the passers-by—loaded three horses with *warabi*, the bracken-stalks you make starch from, and sent them to a friend as a present—called on all his friends and relations, riding on a white horse and with a subscription book hanging from his belt, to collect money (like Hikozaemon Okubo[11]) for his own tombstone ('Can't see the point of waiting till a man's dead to give his family "condolence offerings" or whatever they call them; I'll take mine now, if you please!')—left his horse at a little restaurant as security when he found he'd forgotten his money and couldn't pay for his bowl of eels and rice—borrowed his rickshawman's last hard-earned farthing to tip the waitress in a teahouse—lectured a burglar he caught in the house, then treated him to saké and sent him home—there was no end to such stories. He had been very upset, apparently, at having to leave the old house: the day before the purchaser was due to move in, he dropped everything and spent the last few hours wandering about the house and grounds, stroking the fruit-trees and urging them to 'go on doing their best', as if he were saying goodbye to a crowd of promising children. To all these stories I listened intently.

Now that Uncle was dead, it was decided, after due discussion, that Cousin Suzue should return to her school in Tokyo, while Aunt would go to live with Mother in the castle-town as soon as Uncle's affairs were cleared up and she could dispose of the cottage. The villagers seemed to know at once what was in the air. They came to plead with Aunt not to leave them: they themselves, they told her over and over, would see to it that she should never want for anything. Aunt's tears flowed once more.

On the eighteenth day after Uncle's death, the first period of mourning over, Mother and I left Yamashita Village together.

VI.16

We walked back to the town, Mother in her velvet-thonged clogs, with an umbrella for a stick, I with the faded red blanket wrapped round my neck, my broad Satsuma clogs clop-clopping noisily on the stony path. There had been so much to be done after the funeral, and so many callers, that for the last ten days we had hardly slept, let alone sat down quietly together; now at last, as we walked the ten miles home, we could ask and answer at leisure. I learnt then what joys a lonely, frost-bound country track can offer.

11. See note 10, p. 87.

I described to Mother the adventures I had kept out of my letters. She told me of Uncle's fury at my running away, which had finally decided her to leave his house and live on her own; of Aunt's frantic efforts on Uncle's behalf—unknown to Uncle—when he went bankrupt; of how she herself was managing to make a very modest but adequate living—it had been easier, strangely enough, after she had started living alone—by rearing silkworms in the spring and summer, weaving all through the autumn and winter, and teaching sewing and penmanship in her spare time to the daughters of respectable families in the neighbourhood—little by little she was putting cloth by, too, for my future needs; of how she had been asked recently by a group of local people to act as superintendent of a small school for girls which they were about to start, mainly for instruction in English, but was thinking now of getting Aunt to do it instead. I spoke of my meeting with Shingo, and heard from her how after years of silence old Katsusuke, O-Ju's father, had called on her one day (he had come to town to give thanks at the shrine of Kiyomasa[12] for favours received) with news of Tsumagome. Our priest of Ennenji had gone to his rest at last; Uncle Kengo, after losing most of his money speculating in coal mines, had contracted cancer of the stomach, apparently, and was in terrible pain; O-Yoshi, his younger daughter, burdened with a sick father and a mother who was too weak-willed to be of any help, was struggling single-handed to preserve such of the family property as Uncle hadn't thrown away on his mistress—she was too ashamed to write, but had begged Katsusuke to bring us her greetings.

Then we turned to my future. I told Mother I would probably stay on at school for another year or two after graduating, though I had nothing definite in mind. She was less concerned about my plans than I had imagined from her letters. She would not interfere in any way, she said. I must not sell myself too cheaply, that was the chief thing, nor worry in the least about her, for she could wait years if need be: only let me keep aiming for the highest with the same steadiness of purpose and refusal to depend on others with which I had made my way till now. This, rather than coming home every year or sending her presents or rushing to get myself some comfortable salaried job, was the way of true filial duty.

Absorbed in such talk, we reached the 'Tiger Stone', about halfway back to the castle-town. A rock as big as a small house crouched beside the track like a sleeping tiger; over it a huge nettle-tree spread its branches, leafless now but festooned with *shimenawa*.[13] A tiny teahouse nestled in the rock's shadow with a slender stock of straw sandals, horseshoes, cheap cakes, sweets and shrivelled oranges, and behind the counter, in a patch of sunlight, an old woman of seventy or so, busily spinning. Here we rested a

---

12. Kiyomasa Kato, a celebrated general of the sixteenth century. There are two shrines dedicated to his memory in the city of Kumamoto.
13. A kind of rope used in Shinto to mark off sacred ground, or to distinguish natural objects held in particular reverence.

while, quenching our thirst with the bitter tea the old woman ladled us out of an iron pot. She commiserated with us on hearing of Uncle's death (she had recognized Mother when she saw us coming)—'such a strong, upstanding figure of a man'—then came out with the inevitable anecdote. (Stories of Uncle were scattered everywhere between his village and the town, like stones on the track.) One night early last year, just about the time of the spring harvest, she had been terrified by a knock on the door so violent that she had thought the little house would collapse about her. As if that wasn't bad enough, the sight of the giant looming above her in the darkness outside nearly knocked her out; all she could do was to grab what little money she had and offer it there and then, cashbox and all, to the huge bandit, begging him on her knees to spare her life. But the 'bandit' only roared with laughter: he didn't want her money, only a bite to eat, as he was dying of hunger. After downing seven or eight bowls of boiled rice-and-barley, he complained of the cold, borrowed an old coat of hers to throw over his shoulders, and stalked out, booming at her from the doorway that he'd no money just then, but would send her something later. Overwhelmed with relief that she'd escaped with her life, she told everyone she met in the next few days about the ferocious night robber. Then one morning she was summoned outside by an imperious 'Hey!' from a horseman, who did not trouble to dismount. There was her giant 'robber', alias Uncle Noda, smiling pleasantly down at her. 'Apologies for the other night—'fraid I'd left my money at home—pay with this—' and he tossed her a tobacco-pouch fitted with a beautiful metal clasp, one of the few valuables he had been able to hold on to when they sold up.

As we listened with mingled laughter and tears to the old woman's story, the clack-clack of approaching clogs sounded from the stony track outside. An elderly man in a sealskin cap, a crested coat of black silk, and clogs with thongs of unusual thickness, both hands tucked inside his kimono for warmth, looked in at us as he passed. A boy servant carrying a light green bundle walked at his side.

'Seima's father!' I jumped up, astonished.

The old gentleman stopped, but looked puzzled. 'And who might you be, young sir?'

'I'm Kikuchi, Mr Matsumura; Seima's friend. Have you forgotten?'

'Ah, Shinzaburo, is it?' (he'd remembered my name wrongly). 'Here's a strange meeting!'

A strange meeting indeed, in a most unlikely place. Six years had passed since that spring when Seima took me home with him to spend the holidays with his family.

VI.17

Mr Matsumura stepped inside. Mother bowed politely, and invited him to join us.

'Shinzaburo's mother, no doubt?'

'Yes, sir, Shintaro is my son. I am honoured—' Mother had never met Mr Matsumura before, despite the fact that Seima and I had been such close friends for so long; he had called briefly on Uncle Noda once, but for some reason she had missed him.

'You are still living in the town?' asked Mr Matsumura, turning to me.

Mother was, I explained, while I had come home from Kansei College to be with the family because of Uncle's illness. I enquired after Seima.

'How sad about Mr Noda—forgive me for not having spoken of it earlier. A great blow for you all, indeed ... Seima is well; he is up in Hokkaido now.'

'In Hokkaido?'

'At the Agricultural College in Sapporo. I'm thinking of making a farmer of him.'

So Seima was in Sapporo. It was three years since I had last heard from him.

When had Mr Matsumura come up from his home on the coast, Mother asked.

'Of course, you wouldn't know. My son (the older boy, that is, not Seima) thought the castle-town would be better for business. And besides, we felt we'd all go silly, young and old together, if we stayed on for ever down there in the country; so we moved, last October, it was. I called at Mr Noda's about a month ago—I had met him once before, of course, and he had been kind enough to get me some excellent poultry, and chrysanthemums for my garden. But the name on the gate had changed, and I was told Mr Noda had moved out into the country. Ever since, I've been meaning to call—until yesterday, quite by chance, I heard of his death, and a great shock it was. I'm on way now to pay my respects to his grave.'

'How good of you to make a special journey! My sister will be so grateful. Might I ask where in town you are living?'

'Sakamachi. And you? Enoki Lane? Why, we are almost neighbours: I had no idea. Shinzaburo, you and your mother must come and see us. But you'll be going back to Kobe soon, no doubt?'

I would certainly be leaving within a few days, I said, as school had already started.

'Well then.' Mr Matsumura stood up briskly. 'Goodbye, Mrs Kikuchi —forgive me, but I can't bear the formal greetings and farewells people seem to think are so necessary. No, I know the way,' (he must have overheard me whispering to Mother that I would go back with him in case he got lost) 'Goodbye!' Calling to the boy, he walked off at once, but turned back at the entrance.

'Have you forgotten something, sir?' said the old woman.

'To pay for my tea!' Mr Matsumura threw five or six big *tenpo* coppers on the matted floor, and went on his way.

So we had one more topic, Mother and I, to discuss as we walked the rest of the way back. Knowing Mrs Matsumura as I did, I was delighted, though I kept my feelings to myself, that Mother would be able to have her for a friend.

Soon after we got home, Aunt decided Cousin Suzue ought not to stay away from school any longer, and brought her to town, leaving friends in the village to take care of those of Uncle's affairs that still remained to be cleared up. They lodged with us, our two households uniting once more; with both Suzue and myself preparing to go back to school, the tiny house seemed tinier than ever, and everything in it inadequate—there were no proper rice-bowls, we were short of chop-sticks, extra bedding had to be borrowed. 'Mother, where have my vests gone? Have you seen my needles, Aunt? Cousin Shintaro, you don't know what's happened to my case, do you?' Suzue would be asking all day long, till Mother laughingly declared that no doubt she couldn't help losing everything because 'the house was too big', and produce the missing articles in triumph from the shelves where she had carefully stowed them away. Fortunately Aunt seemed to find some relief in all the bustle and confusion.

I was kept so busy with the duties that fall to the man of the bereaved family on these occasions—paying courtesy calls on everybody who had come to the funeral, and suchlike formalities—that I had no time either to visit the Matsumuras in their new home, or to speak to Mother and Aunt of Christianity (once indeed I did quote a Bible passage in an attempt to comfort Aunt in her grief—she was grateful for my sympathy, but ignored the quotation), or even to visit my old school friends. One place in particular, though, I did go to see, or tried to—the New School. It wasn't far out of my way when I had to call at the Municipal Office to register Aunt Noda as a temporary resident.

Every bit of the country for half a mile round the school was so familiar to me still, I seemed to know each blade of grass. Here were the wheat-fields where we used to hold mud-fights in winter, 'training for the revolution' we called it; the hump-backed bridge where Takahashi had stumbled one night, and fallen into the stream below; the raised path between paddy-fields where the farmer had caught us making a bonfire out of his hay; and waiting to greet me at every turn of the road, it seemed to me, a mischievous fourteen-year-old, the Shintaro Kikuchi of days gone by. Smiling with excited anticipation, I hurried towards the bamboo grove that had so far hidden the school from view.

The tall bamboo behind me, I looked up, expectant. There was nothing. Nothing—nothing but a great sweep of fields.

I stopped, astounded.

VI.18

Was it just possible I had mistaken the place after all? But there was the great gingko-tree we used to see from every window, still jutting into the chilly sky above Yawata Village; there too the cemetery with its crowded grey tombstones, and the two cryptomeria trees we pinned our namecards to in the night as proof of courage; there the farmer's dung-heap that served as cover for many an ambush in our mud-fights, a solitary crow still perched upon its weather-covering of straw. What could have happened to the famous New School?

I walked through the wheatfields, my clogs heavy with mud after the morning thaw, to the place where I was certain the school buildings had stood. Only the fields surrounded me on every side, patterns of green woven over the brown earth and lit up faintly by the wintry sunlight. 'Where could it all have gone?' I murmured to myself. In a sudden sharp gust of wind the long ranks of corn shook their heads from end to end, as if pleading ignorance of the mystery. 'But where —?' I asked the shadow at my feet. The solitary crow rose with a harsh cawing from his perch on the dung-heap and flew off towards the village. What did they mean, these fields, and my memories of the New School, of Komai Sensei? Was I another Urashima[14], that so much had changed?

At last, with a sigh, I began to retrace my steps. An old farmer with a few dried radishes in a bamboo basket slung over his shoulder was trudging towards me.

'Can you tell me what's become of the school there used to be hereabouts, grandpa?'

'What's that? A school, eh? Aye, there was a school there all right, and a fine mess they made of our fields too, playing at fighting or summat, I dunno. Closed it, they did, more 'n a year since.'

'And it doesn't exist any more—it hasn't moved or anything?'

'Closed, it were. The buildings were sold up, they say, and the timber took away. Come here wanting to go to school, did you?'

'No, nothing of that sort—but thanks all the same.'

I wondered afresh at the mad pace of change in the world. (The year after I ran away—so I heard later—the school had gone to pieces for want of a good principal: the buildings had been sold, the students went home, till nothing was left of its glory but old Mr Myope teaching a handful of boys in a private house in some obscure corner of the town.) Thinking much of Komai Sensei and of my schoolfriends of former days, I walked slowly back to the house in Enoki Lane.

Cousin Suzue was stitching away, with a very unpractised hand, at a long under-kimono.

'We're going to have good company on the journey, Shintaro.'

'Who?'

'Mrs Matsumura is taking her daughter to Tokyo. She's just been here to tell us.'

'Seima's sister?' Of course—O-Toshi, the smiling little girl I had met

---

14. The Japanese Rip Van Winkle.

when I went to stay with the Matsumuras; she must have been about eight then.'

'That's right. She's thirteen, and a sweet little thing. I'm going to look after her.'

The notion of Suzue looking after anybody was too much. I nearly told her she'd better start by looking after that tear in her own sleeve, but managed to stop myself in time.

'Fine; the more bluestockings the better,' I said, half to myself.

'What's a bluestocking?'

'A clever, bookish girl—like you.'

'Stop teasing! Why shouldn't girls study, anyway, just like boys? Look at Mrs Fawcett[15] —'

'Of course; I'm all in favour of it myself: Japanese girls all getting degrees, the men fussing in the kitchen —'

'There you are, laughing at me again, when I was trying to be serious! You've lost your manners since you went away!'

But her sally missed its mark. Smilingly declining further combat, I went off to find Mother. Aunt Noda had called at the Matsumuras' a few days before (so Mother told me) to thank Mr Matsumura for his visit of condolence. When she had mentioned that Suzue would soon be going back to the capital, with me accompanying her as far as Kobe, O-Toshi, who had been pleading for some time to be allowed to go to Tokyo, was at once eager to join us. The Matsumuras loved their daughter too much to say no: till then they had thought it would be better to wait until she had finished at the Middle School, but now that she had such good friends for the journey—Mrs Matsumura was to go with us too, to help O-Toshi settle in, and to see something of the sights of the great city. The two of them had called earlier to make the arrangements. Mother and Aunt Noda were delighted, for their part, that we were to have such company.

So the days slipped by till January 15th, the date fixed for our departure.

This time we were to go by sea all the way—by sampan down the river, then across to Nagasaki, and on from there by the Yokohama steamer. Mother and Aunt came down to the quay to say goodbye. The Matsumuras were waiting for us outside the shipping agents', the mother and daughter all ready for the journey, the old gentleman to see them off. I greeted Seima's mother formally, for it was so long since I had seen her; and there behind her, in a coat of fine black silk over a yellow kimono with the edge of a purple under-kimono showing delicately at her throat, a gay floral ornament setting off her gingko-leaf hairstyle above a complexion of the purest white, stood the slender, smiling figure of O-Toshi. That summer I had stayed at their home, she had been humping dolls around on her back, pretending they were babies, a small girl with hair parted

---

15. Mrs Millicent Fawcett (1847–1929), wife of the blind politician Henry Fawcett, and a prominent figure in the English suffragette movement.

childishly down the middle—could she have grown precocious enough already to talk of leaving home to study?

Parting is a sad business, whatever the circumstances. After Aunt Noda had straightened the neck of Suzue's coat for the nth time and given her all kinds of messages for her aunt in Tokyo, and Mrs Matsumura had urged their servant over and over again to take good care of his master till she came home, all of us were feeling pretty down when the time came to board the boat.

'The best of company, the best of weather—it even makes *me* feel I'd like to go away to study.' From where she stood on the jetty steps, Mother broke the melancholy silence.

'Aye, it's such a relief they can all go together,' said the old gentleman gratefully.

'Goodbye, Mrs Matsumura! Look after Suzue, won't you, Shin-san?'

'Take care of yourself, Shintaro! Suzu-san, my greetings to your aunt!'

'Goodbye, Father. Sorry we're leaving you all alone!' O-Toshi spoke for the first time, her voice like a silver bell.

'Don't worry, don't worry, I'll take care,' answered Mr Matsumura. Even he was tearful now.

Slowly, to the splashing of oars, the sampan moved out from the jetty.

VI.19

At Nagasaki we transferred at once to the Yokohama boat. As we steamed past the Five Islands and up into the Genkai Channel, the sea roughened quickly, with cold winds sweeping down from the ice-fields to the north, till we were pitching so violently that Mrs Matsumura and O-Toshi could hardly get up from their bunks, and even I, though no stranger to sea travel, felt pretty shaky—only my stalwart cousin, placid as ever, managed every meal as usual. Calm weather returned, however, when we entered the Inland Sea, and with it the passengers' spirits: the prostrate ones rousing themselves and exchanging greetings for the first time with the occupants of neighbouring bunks. Mrs Matsumura, overcoming at last her disgust at the smell of paint and the rumbling of the engines, struck up a lively conversation with her neighbour; Cousin Suzue sat knitting (one of the latest 'modern' fads) and supplying O-Toshi with a quantity of historical and geographical information, full of the most grotesque mistakes (according to her, Miyajima[16] was somewhere quite different from Itsukushima[16]; Hakata[17], which we had passed the evening before, was the celebrated

16. Two alternative names for a large island off the coast of western Japan, famous for the Itsukushima Shinto Shrine.

17. A port (now included in the city of Fukuoka) in Kyushu, the scene of the Mongol invasions of 1274 and 1281. The great military leader Hideyoshi was not born till 1537.

place where Hideyoshi (sic) had massacred the Mongols', etc.)—to all of which O-Toshi dutifully listened, silent but plainly incredulous, while I read with disgust in a borrowed newspaper of the latest goings-on at the Rokumeikan[18]—a 'dance' one night, a 'fancy-dress ball' the next, a play given in English by students the next—looking up now and again to make an appropriately sarcastic comment on Cousin Suzue's monologue. In the sunny intervals we all went up on deck, to marvel at the long chain of tiny rocky islands, like miniatures on a tray, an endlessly turning kaleidoscope of beauty as we passed. Suzue would have preferred to stay down in the saloon most of the time, eating buns and biscuits, had not O-Toshi, who was still, no doubt, excited with the novelty of it all, kept urging her on deck.

O-Toshi was a strange girl. Just when I was beginning to suspect from the way she was invariably smiling that she must after all be rather stupid, she spotted a tear in my kimono sleeve that neither Suzue nor Mrs Matsumura had noticed, and whispered to her mother to mend it. She hardly spoke as a rule, but listened intently, as if quietly making up her youthful mind on every subject we discussed. Sir Kikuchi spent much thought on the care of the three ladies entrusted to his charge, but with the best will in the world a mere man is far from adequate in such cases: when Mrs Matsumura (for whom this was the first long journey she had ever made) started feeling lonely and anxious about how things were going at home, and even Suzue, normally so cheerful, showed her feminine side by succumbing to bouts of homesickness and tearful memories of her dead father, till they were quite beyond any ministrations of mine, it was O-Toshi who quietly comforted them both. Not that she *said* much to them; what she did, she did with a subtle skill, undetectable by eye or ear, the delicacy of feeling that flows of itself from a fresh, innocent heart—an example, I suppose, of the power to influence others by apparent inaction of which Lao Tzu[19] speaks.

Suzue was highly delighted to act the elder sister, and was incessantly 'looking after' her, as she had promised—did her hair up in the western style, in spite of Mrs Matsumura's misgivings (English conversation and a western hairdo were two great musts for young women at that time), insisted she must enter the Seiyo Girls High School, where Suzue herself was studying (I know nothing about this institution, but if Suzue was anything to go by, the education they offered was eccentric in the extreme), and reminded her to 'take particular care with the steps, they're so dangerous', without ever noticing how her own kimono sleeve was saved from disaster only by a deft movement of O-Toshi's, lifting the sleeve quickly to one side as she followed behind her sisterly protector up a companion-way.

Good company shortens any journey, and no sooner had we passed the

18. i.e. 'The Mansion of the Baying Stag', the name of a building in Tokyo which became from 1883 onwards a centre of social intercourse and entertainment for Japanese notables, from the Prime Minister downwards, and foreign residents.

19. 'Hence the sage says, I take no action and the people are transformed of themselves.' *Tao Te Ching*, trans. D. C. Lau.

Sanjuroku Channel than the port of Kobe lay before us, ships' sirens echoing through the evening sunlight over Settsu Bay. I had told the ladies that if time allowed I would take them to see the famous beaches of Suma and Akashi; but, the ship's stay in Kobe having been cut short in order to make up for time lost in the rough weather we had encountered in the Genkai Channel, the plan had to be abandoned. Entrusting my charges to the care of a merchant and his wife we had got to know during the voyage, I prepared to leave.

'Thank you, Mr Kikuchi, for all your kindness. I shall write at once and tell Mr Matsumura how good you have been. We shall be so lonely now,' said Mrs Matsumura as she helped me on with my cloak.

'Goodbye, cousin!' from Suzue. O-Toshi bowed without speaking.

'Goodbye!' I called back as I jumped down into the lighter with my little wicker travelling-box. The lighterman pushed off; I took off my cap and bowed to the three ladies, who were watching me still from the upper deck.

'Goodbye! Mind you come to Tokyo soon!' shouted Suzue. O-Toshi was still staring after me, her hands on the rail.

I bowed once more and sat down—to jump up again in astonishment at the sight of another three-oared lighter hurrying towards us from the shore, with two passengers.

'Kan Sensei!' For Kan Sensei it was, and his ample wife with him.

'Kikuchi, for a wonder!'

'Where are you going, sir?'

'Tokyo.'

Before I could find out why he was going, or ask him to look after Cousin Suzue and the Matsumuras for the rest of their voyage, his lighter had passed out of earshot.

VI.20

The news of Kan Sensei's resignation and departure for Tokyo was the first thing I heard when I got back to the College. As to why he should have left at such an odd time—just after the New Year holiday—he was the victim, so I was told, of a united campaign by the missionaries to drive him away. What with his religious views, which as I've already said clashed at many points with orthodoxy, his fiery, uncompromising character, and the contemptuous displays of his own superior learning with which he would show up the shallowness of the missionaries, there had long been latent hostility between Kan Sensei and the foreign teachers.

The immediate cause of the breach was a lecture Kan Sensei had given to the whole school on the first day of the new term. Under the title 'Superstition and Faith', he had argued that Abraham's readiness to sacrifice his son Isaac owed much to a certain barbaric superstition then current among the Chaldeans, and was certainly not to be taken as a model of faith.

Superstition could take root easily in any age, and to be so preoccupied with mere rites, such as baptism or the communion service, as to forget the true spirit of faith—this in itself was nothing more or less than superstition, and a crime against religion . . . The lecture had been met with bitter criticism from the missionaries. The most senior of them, who already had a grudge against Kan Sensei for his having worsted them in a controversy on teaching methods, campaigned openly for his expulsion, maintaining that to give expression to such heresy, and with the whole College for audience, was an insult to the missionary staff, and that Kansei College, claiming as it did to offer a 'Christian' education, could not possibly continue to employ such a teacher. His final stroke had been to threaten that if Kan Sensei were not dismissed all the missionaries would resign in a body. Was the College prepared, he had asked, to accept the withdrawal of all foreign support that such a step on their part would entail? The Principal had tried to avoid a final break, and Mr Brown in particular had done his best to mediate, even to the point of alienating many of his fellow-missionaries; but by now the fire was beyond quenching. The upshot was that Kan Sensei had resigned, not wanting to embarrass the Principal, and left at once for Tokyo. Clearly there was reason enough for the angry flush, unusually pronounced even for him, that I had noticed in his face as he passed me in the lighter.

I myself was filled with anger at what I had heard. Who were these missionaries, to lord it over our College? And what sort of students were we, content to watch Kan Sensei being hounded out before our very eyes without so much as a single cry of sympathy or protest? I went to bed, but couldn't sleep. At eleven o'clock I got up again, took out my brush, that was still wet with the ink of a note I'd written to my mother to tell her of my safe arrival, and committed to paper, under the tiny dormitory nightlight, my burden of solitary indignation. The books Kan Sensei had lent me lay on my desk. I saw again his tense, clouded face staring at me from the lighter. My hand flew over the paper.

I wrote and wrote and wrote with hardly a single pause for thought—fifty pages, till at last, as dawn filled the window, I tossed the brush aside: 'Who are the false Christians?' was my title.

'I am a believer,' I wrote. 'I am under no obligation to Professor Kan; neither do I bear him any ill-will. But in the face of what has happened I must not, I cannot, remain silent! Fellow-students, my three hundred comrades—I beg you, in the name of Christianity, in the name of this College of ours, in the name of freedom of conscience and of speech, to hear what anger has driven me to reveal!'

After this beginning, I reminded them of Kan Sensei's great learning, of his fearless, forthright character, and deplored the inability of a great school like Kansei College to find room for a scholar and teacher of such independent spirit.

'Who are the false Christians? Who are they who monopolize Truth—God's gift to all the peoples of the world, not to them alone? who pour scorn upon the Pharisees, yet clutch to themselves the keys of the Kingdom? who call themselves the Children of the Reformation, yet act like princes of the Papal church? Who, I say, are the false Christians?'

Sentence by sentence I pressed home my attack, castigating those who went by the name of Christian but were so pitifully lacking in tolerance and charity, who built barriers even as they preached love, who smeared the noble banner of Christianity with the filth of their own narrow prejudice.

'Emperor Yao had the unworthy Tan Chu for a son; the mediocre Hsiang was younger brother to the Emperor Shun: not all the descendants of Washington and Franklin inherit the greatness of their ancestors. Those whose learning is so superficial that they must envy the ability of others; whose aim it is to impose on a foreign people their home-grown bigotry, forgetful of their own adage "when in Rome, etc."—these are the false Christians! Those who are so arrogantly conscious of their own charity, whose self-importance renders them incapable of respecting a people with customs different to their own—these are the despoilers of Christianity! "Foxes have holes, and the birds of the air have nests; but the Son of Man hath not where to lay his head"; but these—who covet their high salaries, build themselves fine houses, hire cooks for their pleasure, seek refuge in "resorts" from the cold of our winter and the heat of our summer—and still dare to preach "the Way"! What is this "Way" of theirs? Truly, they are not missionaries of any Way, but mercenaries, feeding on the Christianity they claim to preach. I do not argue, as did many in the past, for the expulsion of the foreigner from our shores: I repudiate all who would discriminate between men because some are yellow and some are white, because some write down the page and some across it; for all are equally the children of one Father. But in face of this breach of Christian charity, this slur on the good name of all independent Colleges, I *cannot* be silent. Who are the false Christians? Who will shed a tear for him they have wronged—Professor Kan?'

Finally I called on the whole College to unite in pressing for the reinstatement of Kan Sensei. At last I finished. Binding the manuscript as carefully as I could, as soon as day dawned I took my manifesto down to the reading-room, then pinned on the notice-board outside the dining-hall a summary, in thick black headlines, of its contents.

VI.21

By breakfast-time a dense crowd had gathered in front of the noticeboard. Watching from my window the subsequent procession in and out of the reading-room, I was secretly delighted that the shot I had fired so boldly had not missed its mark.

What with Kan Sensei not being overly popular in the first place, and the missionaries having been so vehement against him in the second, feeling among the students had not run very high while the dispute was still going on; but now, with Kan Sensei's expulsion a reality, the effect of my protest was dramatic. Everywhere I went people talked of nothing else, till I was driven to stay in my room to avoid being stared at; and then I had a constant stream of callers. Some complimented me on having the courage to write as I had; some were worried that I might have to suffer for being so outspoken; some again mocked the would-be evangelist for the bitterness of his attack on the missionaries; some came to ask what would be the next move in the campaign; some supported me with an embarrassing fervour, declaring themselves ready to 'tear out those obscene red whiskers and pound their big noses out of shape'. Akazawa, champion of the Worldly Party (and by unanimous vote future chief of the Tokyo Metropolitan Police) and two or three leaders of the Believers told me they were ashamed it had been left to me, who had been away all through the dispute, to strike the first blow; now, at least, they would join me in working out what to do next. Altogether, apart from the naturally meek and submissive, and a few who asked me with a cynical smile what I could hope to gain at this time of day, when the damage was already done, there was hardly a student who did not catch in some degree the fever of indignation that swept through the College. Astonished, as well as encouraged, to see the fire I had lit spread so fast and fiercely, I published a second instalment on 'The Next Step'. Feeling rose quickly throughout the College. The following Saturday morning representatives from every class and each of the two 'parties' met in the wood behind the College to plan further action. After a long discussion, we decided to petition the Principal for the reinstatement of Kan Sensei; and voted to withdraw from the College, if this proved necessary in order to secure our demands.

I was chosen to head the committee that was to draw up our petition. Very much aware of the responsibility on my shoulders, I shut myself up in a deserted classroom and sat down to write a draft:

1. The enforced resignation of Professor Kan being inconsistent with the spirit of Christian tolerance and forgiveness, and causing moreover grave harm to the College and its reputation, we request his immediate reinstatement.

2. We regard the part taken by certain of the missionary staff in the events leading up to Professor Kan's resignation as mean, dishonourable, and unbecoming to those who call themselves Christians. We therefore demand that after Professor Kan has been reinstated they shall offer a public —

The door opened as I was still writing. 'Here he is,' came the janitor's voice as he opened the classroom door. To my surprise, Mr Brown and Professor Shimizu were behind him.

'Kikuchi—you doing terrible thing!' said Mr Brown in his not quite perfect Japanese. He sounded very concerned, almost tearful.

'Haven't you been a bit hasty, Kikuchi?' asked Professor Shimizu. 'And only six months before you're due to graduate, too!'

According to them, the missionaries (Mr Brown himself was a missionary teacher, of course, but had always shown himself sympathetic towards us Japanese, and frequently acted as a kind of bridge between us and the main body of missionary staff) had been so incensed when they learnt of the inflammatory effect of my appeal that they were demanding the severest punishment for all concerned, and in particular for myself as the instigator—their hatred of me being the more intense because of my known intention to take up Christian work, and the hopes they had consequently placed in me. The Principal had sent Mr Brown and Professor Shimizu to try and persuade me to take a more moderate line, while he himself attempted to mollify the senior missionaries, with whom he was at that moment in conference. For more than an hour my two visitors urged me to withdraw my 'manifesto': it was such a pity, they told me, that one from whom both staff and students expected so much should have acted so rashly when Kan Sensei himself had shown his understanding of the difficulty the Principal was facing by resigning of his own free will. If only I would give up all thought of further 'agitation', the Principal would do his best, as would they themselves, to pacify the angry missionaries, etc., etc.

Swallowing with difficulty the counter-arguments that rose so readily to my lips, I told them I would think over very carefully what they had said; and as soon as they had left went off to the classroom-block with the draft of my petition sticking out of my breast-pocket. Just then Akazawa and several others of the group known to less excitable spirits as the 'Soda-Water Brotherhood' (because they were always effervescing over something or other) were coming out of the chapel in little groups, some obviously deep in thought, some looking tearful even. I guessed at once what had happened. A tear or two from the Principal, and the student blaze had been extinguished there and then.

Once again we called a meeting in the wood. Speech followed speech, till finally it was agreed that though we were disgusted by the missionaries' campaign to remove one of our teachers, Kan Sensei had in fact left at his own request, with his honour unscathed, so that to reinstate him now would certainly harm the reputation of the College, while for us to agitate for his return would be to ignore both the sincerity of our beloved Principal in the dispute and our own finer feelings. The Principal had said he took full responsibility for what had happened, and expressed his regret. Wasn't that enough? Our demonstration had given the missionaries a fright; even in war, according to Sun Wu,[20] one should not press the enemy too hard when he is in difficulties, for if you do he will only fight the more stub-

20. Traditional author of the Chinese military classic *Sun Tzŭ* (The Art of War).

bornly. The general feeling was, in short, that it was time to let the matter drop. Two or three still maintained that this would be too much of a climb-down altogether, but by now the straw fire had burnt itself out, leaving only flatness and despondency in place of passion. But for me, who had started the fire, things were not so simple. When they asked me, 'Any objection, Kikuchi?' my muttered answer, 'Me—oh, I'll have to think it over some more', only served to hide the unutterable shame of a cause betrayed: betrayed by myself, by my fellow-students, by the Principal—by everyone and everything in my world.

That evening, and again the following Sunday morning, Principal Katayama himself sent for me and advised me, very courteously, to go no further with my protest. He spoke of his own earlier years. 'Experience has taught me one thing, Kikuchi: impulsiveness never achieves anything. The world and its affairs are infinitely complex; and if you let your feelings take charge, you'll collide with somebody or something at every step, and for you of all people, with so much before you, there could be nothing more tragic than to waste all your energy on pointless quarrels!' Could I not bring myself to accept defeat this once—call off the protest, and admit publicly that my manifesto had been too extreme? (Try as he might to persuade the missionaries to moderate *their* attitude, they still insisted on nothing short of a public apology; leniency, in their view, could go no further.) He himself realized only too well the generous feelings that had driven me to act as I had done. He asked me, nevertheless, to understand his predicament, placed as he was in charge of so many young students and having at the same time to hold the balance between the native staff and the foreigners; and earnestly pleaded with me to emulate the great Han Hsin[21] in courageous acceptance, on this one occasion, of a personal sacrifice.

VI.22

I thanked the Principal for his kindness, and promised to give my final answer next day. As soon as I got back to school Mr Brown invited me to dinner, to ply me yet again with advice. Afterwards, I don't know how many hundred times I walked through the pine-wood and back that night in the cold night wind. Every single one of my allies had surrendered: I was entirely alone. (So is it always with the commander of a defeated army.) Should I surrender too—'understanding the difficult position' of the principal, and following the good Mr Brown's advice? Perhaps that was the brave way, after all. Yet I could see no reason to withdraw a single letter of my manifesto. If my language had been headstrong, everything I had said was true. If I were in the wrong, I would go on my knees to a beggar and ask his pardon; but if not, how could I grovel meaninglessly before these

21. See note 5, p. 149.

missionaries, when I prided myself on bowing my head before none but the Almighty and my beloved mother? No, I would not apologize—never! What dignity would remain to a general who saved himself from the enemy by 'apologizing' for his untoward presence? And how, having once surrendered, could I bear to earn my fees with broom and swab, in servile dependence on College charity? How endure every Sunday, with simulated piety, the sermons of the foreign preachers I had attacked so bitterly? No, I could not apologize. Yet I could not ignore the sympathy Mr Katayama had shown me. How could I respond to his kindness, while preserving my self-respect? Finally, after long cogitation, I decided that the only way out was for me to leave the College of my own free will. When graduation was only six months away? But why should you be so greedy for a graduation certificate, came the reproach: for a mere piece of paper . . .

Climbing over the fence (the gate had long been locked) I came back at last to the little three-mat room of which, fortunately, I was the only occupant. As noiselessly as possible I stuffed my wicker trunk with books and clothes, and roped it securely; swept and tidied the room, arranged on my desk the books I had borrowed from friends, leaving a marker in each with the owner's name; and finally wrote six letters—one to the Principal, one each to Mr Brown and Professor Shimizu, one to my classmates, one to Philosopher Endo, who had been a special friend (this last to ask thim to sell the bedding I was leaving behind and use the proceeds to forward my trunk to me in Tokyo—for this, needless to say, was my destination—as soon as I sent him word that I had arrived. This time, at least, I was determined to take my leave by day, instead of absconding at midnight; but fearing that if the signs of my coming departure were too conspicuous, attempts would be made to keep me from going, I hid the trunk away, and left the rest of my possessions—desk, lamp, rickety old chair, and a few other odds and ends—to be taken over in due course by fellow-students as poorly-off as I had been. Fortunately there was still a clear six yen left in my purse out of what my mother had given me, so the journey to Tokyo would be no problem. Debts I had none; and my fees for that term were already paid) and one to the friend who had got me the evening teaching job in Kobe. I couldn't help recalling as I wrote that other fateful night, four years before, at the New School. Running away then, running away now—was it just that I hadn't the courage to stick it out? Was I heading now for a repeat of all the troubles, the wasted months, that had followed my last escapade? I took out my Bible and opened it at random, praying for guidance—to read: '. . . the elders of the people took counsel against Jesus to put him to death: and when they had bound him, they led him away, and delivered him to Pilate the governor.' Puzzled, I shut my eyes again and tried a second time: 'And in the same house remain, eating and drinking such things as they give . . .', the words stared up at me. 'Go not from house to house . . .' Doubts redoubled. The way seemed less clear than ever—when there flashed upon my growing uncertainty the closing words of Ch'u Yuan's poem 'On Divination', which I had studied at Seizan Sensei's:

> Times there are when the mind is beset with doubt,
> And the gods themselves do not know all.
> At such times act as your own heart and will bid you:
> For neither divining-sticks nor tortoise-shells will then avail.

Here was the answer, surely! I nodded eagerly, and hurriedly finishing my letters, crawled under my iron-cold quilt.

At dawn I got up as usual, washed, and went down to the dining-hall, taking secret inward leave of every friend I met. After breakfast, when the bell rang out for morning prayers and the whole school began to converge upon the chapel, I slipped out of the dormitory, bundle in hand and my letter to the Principal in my kimono pocket. Just as I was going out of the gate, Professor Shimizu came running down the road, late for chapel. Hurriedly I dropped my bundle out of sight behind the gate and tried to look my usual self.

'Hallo, Kikuchi. Aren't you going to prayers?'

I mumbled some sort of reply, my heart thumping. Was I found out already? But the Professor was in too much of a hurry to suspect anything.

'What about this manifesto of yours? Have you decided yet? The missionaries were on at the Principal again last night, I hear. The longer we leave it the worse it'll be —'

'I'll be seeing the Principal this morning.'

'Will you now. That's fine, fine. See you later, then.' He ran off again towards the chapel.

Retrieving my bundle, I looked back at the College. Across the campus came the rise and fall of massed voices singing the morning hymn, like distant waves. I bowed, and strode out of the gate.

Down at the Kobe waterfront they told me there was no boat leaving for Yokohama that day or the next. I decided, therefore, to take a boat from Yokkaichi instead; and set out on my last and most difficult duty—to pay my respects to Principal Katayama at his house. Although I had said not a word of farewell to my friends or to any of the other teachers, Mr Katayama had taught me so much over the last two years, not to mention his understanding attitude in my present trouble, that I felt bound to thank him in person for his kindness, and take my leave openly, with proper courtesy. A thousand oxen could not have dragged me back to the College now, but I was eager this time to have no shadow surrounding my departure.

Twenty past nine, said a clock in a shop-window. Mr Katayama should certainly be back from chapel by now. Bundle in hand and heart pounding, I stood in the porch of the Principal's house and struck the bell. A maid opened the door.

'Is the Principal back yet?'

'Yes, he came back a few minutes ago' (the pounding grew fiercer still) 'but left again immediately; a message from the College —' I gave a great sigh of relief and regret, as a duellist might when told on his way to the fight that his opponent has dropped dead. After a moment's thought I took from my pocket the draft petition and my letter of withdrawal from the College, and handed them to the maid.

'Tell the Principal I'm sorry to have missed him. I came to say goodbye.'

I hurried off to Sannomiya Station.

Taking the train to Kyoto, I walked from there to spend the night at Ishibe, pushing on through the snow next day (the fires of indignation burning so strong in me still, I hardly felt the cold) to cross the Suzuka Pass and come down into Yokkaichi in time to catch the night boat. After a continuous buffeting from heavy seas and driving sleet all along the Totomi coast, by the time we reached Yokohama I was as limp as a jellyfish, inside and out. With difficulty I clambered aboard a train; and at long last, at four o'clock in the afternoon of January 27, 1887, at the end of a journey huddled among a dense-packed mass of human beings, every one of them with the face of a pickpocket, my teeth chattering audibly with the cold as I stared through half-clouded windows at the grim metropolitan world outside, I arrived—four years after leaving home—at the goal long since familiar in dreams: Shinbashi Station, Tokyo!

Threading my way somehow through the muddy, jostling mass of men and rickshaws, I climbed to the top of the stone steps, clutching my bundle. As I stood there in the incessant sleet (*mizore-buru* in Japanese: it sounds so like the English 'miserable' that every time I come across the foreign word I remember that day), gazing at the vista of drab sodden streets, I could only wonder, 'Can *this* be Tokyo—this *filthy* place?'

Part VII

Anyone who happened to be walking down the western Ginza at nine o'clock on the morning of January 28, 1887 must have noticed (not that they are likely to remember!) a solitary youth standing stiffly under the willow-tree in front of the offices of the *Nippo Daily*, bundle in hand, umbrella-less in the intermittent rain; a black broad-brimmed cap, now grey with age, perched on the back of his head like a Buddha's halo, a strained, derisive smile disguising the mingled curiosity and fear of the countryman new to the capital. There I was, who now write that young man's story, on my way to Hongo after staying the night at a Shiba inn. Even now, whenever I pass that way—childish though it may seem—I want to shake my fist in anger at that inn where I spent my first night in Tokyo, though the owner has changed long since and the building itself been replaced. Imagine the feelings of a poor student at the end of his solitary journey, knocking at door after door with his little bundle, to be rejected everywhere for the all-too-obvious shallowness of his purse—no tip likely there!—till at last he is more shoved than shown to a filthy three-mat 'room', and forced to drink the pallid, lukewarm apology for tea, that silent witness to the city-dweller's cold, insipid heart. He claps his hands in vain when the tiny fire dies in his brazier. And the 'supper' they bring him after a wait of two hours or more!—rice all but cold and with a plentiful mixture of grit, *miso*-soup as clear as water, with hardly a hint of vegetable, a fragment of boiled fish of as doubtful provenance as the maid who sits impudently watching, lacquered tray on her knees, when she has set the table. Together with a few slices of pickled radish, a sample of this city-world's true taste of bitterness to set against the sweetness of its talk, and hard almost beyond crunching, I forced down two bowls of rice, and curled up on the miserable quilts (so thin and small and hard and stinking that if only he had been born in our modern century the King of Wu[1] himself might have preferred them for his bed) I had got them, only after tearful pleas of utter physical exhaustion, to lay. 'I knew that Tokyo's a cold place,' I thought to myself bitterly before I dozed off, 'but not that city folk had frozen hearts!' If ever I succeeded in this world, I would build an inn of my own, ten times bigger than this, in the very centre of the city; and when the high officials and rich merchants, splendid

---

1. Famous for having slept for years on a bed of firewood as a constant reminder of his duty to avenge his father's murder.

in their crested kimonos, came crowding in their carriages to my door, 'I'd have a smart young maid turn them disdainfully away, 'No gentlemen, I am sorry, this inn is not for you . . .' But the young travellers in simple soiled clothes and tattered caps, with the mark of the future bright upon their foreheads—these I would run out to greet myself and give them all a princely welcome . . . Deep in these and other vain imaginings, eventually I fell asleep.

Breakfast over in the morning, I paid the bill and hurried out. I had thought of emptying my purse to tip the proprietor, so that I could give myself the pleasure of castigating him for his contemptuous attitude of the previous night, and force him to apologize; but knowing too well I could ill afford such vanity in my present state, when every sen was worth a hundred silver yen, I shut my eyes and ears and ran out of the building like an escaping criminal.

Shaking off the dust of my feet on the place, I crossed Shinbashi Bridge and made for the famous Ginza Avenue. Though less spendid than I had expected, it surely deserved its reputation as the noblest street of Japan's noblest city, with its rows of busy shops and vast moving crowds that filled it from early morning. I found myself continually sidestepping to avoid colliding with the citizens of the capital, as my eyes wandered this way and that in naïve astonishment at every new spectacle. Outside the Nippo building I stopped for a while, to marvel at its size and look up wonderingly at the first-floor offices where (I supposed) the celebrated journalist and novelist Fukuchi wielded his eloquent pen. What did the passers-by think, I wonder—if any noticed him at all—of the shivering student beneath the willow-tree? *His* mind was busy with its monologue: 'Tokyo, Tokyo! so intent upon your struggle to survive, you have no time, have you, to notice Kikuchi's arrival? You passers-by, you glance my way, but you see nothing, though our sleeves touch, you feel nothing, as you push your own way through the crowds. But wait; you shall hear the name of Kikuchi yet—read in the paper you scan so eagerly' (a little knot of readers had gathered in front of the board displaying that day's issue of the *Nippo Daily*) 'of this boy standing at your backs; one day, I promise you, you will stand aside for Kikuchi, stand on tiptoe, maybe, to see him pass—eh, old willow-tree?' I stroked the smooth trunk beside me. It was midwinter now: the tree was stripped bare, its trunk blackened with the cold—no hint of spring there. But spring would come; not two months more, and that dead tree would breathe again the green life of spring. When would *my* spring return, *my* life put forth its shoot of green? Not till I had fought and won the battles of a far longer winter, my season of toil and sweat and blood . . . five, ten, twenty years?

VII.2

I put up at the Matsuya lodging-house in the Yushima Tenjin section of Hongo Ward. My old friend Matsumura had once stayed there, for one thing; and it was convenient for the final goal of my journeyings—Tokyo Imperial University, whose threshold I was already crossing in imagination with the first step I took outside the gate of Kansei College. Strictly speaking, if the truth be known, my dreams had led me even earlier through the great Red Gate.[2] Even without Shingo's attacks and Kan Sensei's advice, my resolve to become an evangelist had already declined from its first high summer into autumn. Only the slenderest restraining thread still bound me to the College, to the possibility of a theological training and a life of Christian work: the higher my ambition flew, the brighter shone that other world of learning—as new landscapes unveil themselves to the soaring balloonist—and the weaker grew the thread that held me, till it was ready to snap at the first puff of wind or touch of a knife.

Such a knife was the affair of Kan Sensei. A magic mirror thrust across my deepest feelings might have shown, behind all the anger and disillusionment of those days, a smile of secret joy. But of this I knew nothing consciously, or maybe did not want to know; as far as I was concerned, I was leaving the College less of out of sympathy for Kan Sensei than as a scapegoat, a victim of the missionaries' narrow-mindedness and bigotry, a willing martyr in the cause of true Christianity. Certainly I was not leaving of my own accord: the College had driven me out. Events had forced me to abandon the resolve I would otherwise have kept: every step (so I told myself)—my sudden exit from the College, the giving up of my cherished ideal of a Christian career, and now this final journey to Tokyo, and, perhaps, to the University—had been forced upon me.

I had picked up a few scraps of information about Tokyo University while at the College, but as soon as I had settled into my lodgings I went to check up on the details of the entrance examination: the date, the fee, how many references were needed, and so forth. The next examination would be held early in September, it seemed. The list of subjects didn't look too terrifying, except perhaps for science and mathematics; and even in those I ought not to fail if I studied hard for the next six months. The only problem was how to keep myself alive till September. All I had left was two yen and a few odd sen, less than a month's room-rent. As for asking Mother for money—after I had got into the University, perhaps; but to appeal to her now, 'I've run away from the College, come to Tokyo —cash please!' No, I couldn't do it. Shingo would help me at once if I asked him, but I didn't like the idea of that: as spiritless a way out as the other. Of all the million citizens of the capital, I knew, in effect, no one. There was Kan Sensei, of course; and no doubt Endo at the College (the friend I had asked to send on my trunk) could tell me where he was lodging; yet it wouldn't be honourable to approach him, either, not for money. Cousin Suzue and the other women (they would surely never dream I had followed them so speedily) were out of the question. If only Seima Matsumura were here instead of in Hokkaido, or my dead friend

2. i.e. the main entrance of Tokyo University.

Michitaro—but why waste time complaining? I sent for the landlord (an honest-looking fellow in his fifties, Shinshichi by name; he spoke with a strong northern accent), told him exactly how matters stood, and asked him if he knew of any way of earning a modest living, preferably at night, so as to leave the day free for study.

After listening carefully to my story, he assured me that he well understood my position. He himself, carrying on the kind of business he did, had had a great deal to do with 'young student gentlemen'; indeed, some who had long since established themselves in the world still condescended to speak kindly to him when they met—an honour indeed! What students needed most was staying power, endurance. It wasn't easy nowadays: all round Hongo and Kanda there were more night-class teachers looking for work than pupils wanting to learn, and precious little night-work of any kind suitable for a respectable student, unless it was helping on a printing-press, or a milk-round, perhaps, or pulling a rickshaw, if that wasn't too hard . . . But delivering newspapers—that was pretty light work once you got used to it; and wait a moment, he'd thought of something. With that he left me, but knocked on my door again that same evening to tell me he had heard from 'a friend of a friend' of his, who was in charge of the general affairs section of the *People's Daily*, that the paper had one vacancy for a delivery boy at twenty-five sen a day. Would I try it?

Though I had hoped for something better, I was in no position to refuse even a doorkeeper's job. Rickshaw-pulling might bring in more, but would be beyond me physically, and if it had to be a delivery-round I'd rather it was brain-fodder I was delivering than milk. To see what sort of brain-fodder, I bought a copy of the *People's Daily*: it proved to be a better-produced, maturer version of the earlier *Torch of Freedom*, over which we had fought so eagerly at the New School, with an eloquent editorial evidently written by someone well-versed in French history and culture. Distributing such sentiments as his, I should be walking the streets to some purpose, I decided. Before long, therefore, through the good offices of Mr Something-or-Other Akagi, the aforesaid friend of a friend of my landlord, I was appointed to the post of delivery boy for the *People's Daily*.

VII.3

On January 30th I presented myself for the first time at the Yakenbori office of the *People's Daily*, and after two nights of following the boy I was to replace up and down the streets of Koji-machi (the 'pitch' to which I had been assigned), on February 1st I started on my own.

What would Mother have thought if she could have seen me walking the Tokyo streets, a wide-mouthed canvas sack stuffed with newspapers slung over my right shoulder, more papers in a bundle under my left arm, one hand clutching the delivery list, a *People's Daily* lantern swinging from the other? Or my comrades at the College? In those early weeks I came to know Tokyo best late at night—when everyone slept but prowling thieves and night-police, and rickshawmen hunting for late fares, and wayside cooks hawking their stew and macaroni and bean-filled ricecakes.

It wasn't so bad on spring nights, with a pale moon shining and the rows of willow-trees lining the broader avenues half-veiled in mist; or in summer, with the silver galaxies gleaming bright above the 'eight hundred and eight streets' of the ancient city; or in autumn, when the moonlight fell chill, like frost, on the innumerable tiled roofs. But those first nocturnal skirmishes with Generals January and February daunted even my youthful spirits. The snow blowing in your face no matter how low you pulled your wide-brimmed wicker hat, your lantern, without which you were helpless, going out every fifty yards, on clear nights the jagged frozen bumps on the roads standing out in the moonlight like the pinnacles of the Sword-Mountain,[3] the wind whistling so cold and fierce that even the soft flute-call of the blind itinerant masseurs sounded like a scream of agony . . . the alleys made into seas of mud after three days of rain, nights when the skies poured hail or driving threads of sleet as sharp as drills, till your oiled-paper cape was as wet inside as out, and your body shivered from top to toe—at last every limb went numb, and then you fell flat in the mud, and saw your precious, precious papers slithering in the filth . . . Indeed these times of trial were bitter enough to have made me cry my heart out, had I been a few years younger. I still remember the old man, near seventy he must have been, at whose tiny stall at the bottom of Kudan Hill I would stop for a couple of his farthing rice-cakes and a moment's conversation. 'You're a brave one, to start so young!' he would say approvingly. I couldn't help recalling Charles Kingsley's 'Men must work and women must weep'; and if that old fellow could stand out there by the roadside, exposed to the cold winds every night, to earn his meagre living, what right had I to complain? Courage renewed, I would plod off up the hill once more.

If only the City Assemblymen could each be given a newspaper round for ten days or so, we should get a bit of progress in road-making, not to mention other civic improvements. 'Our great metropolis,' they say, 'our capital, first city in the land'—the appalling roads, the crazy patchwork of streets, the unintelligible system of numbering! Trying to find houses in Koji-machi was like wandering through a maze without a single clue. Night after miserable night, till I learnt my way about, I wandered helplessly down one alley after another, or found at dawn I had been walking round and round the selfsame block, to be greeted at last, at the customer's door, by a pert young maid, 'Early, aren't you? But we don't want *old* news, thank you!' Complaints were coming in from my round, they told me at the office; I must be loafing on the job . . . Clearly this was a battle you couldn't fight without first knowing the ground: so for a while I set all other work aside and spent the days as well as the nights walking the length

3. A mountain in the Japanese Buddhist hell, planted with inverted swords.

and breadth of Koji-machi, till the supports of my clogs were all but worn flat. Even now I could easily draw you an exact map of the whole area.

Not that my expeditions were confined to Koji-machi. One of my delights for some time after my arrival in the capital was to wander among the Yamanote residential districts. I didn't feel drawn to the downtown bustle of Ueno, Asakusa and Mukojima; for me it was a keener pleasure to seek out, on the Yamanote gateposts, the names of the great ones long familiar to me from newspapers and journals—best of all, to catch a glimpse of my heroes in person. Sometimes, indeed, I would linger on and on outside the gate of one I held in particular awe, daring myself to enter, till even the dogs inside would bark furiously and patrolling policemen turn suspicious eyes my way. Seeing Mount Fuji with your own eyes for the first time is a disappointment: it is so much less imposing than you had heard. As with mountains, so with the famous. They look truly awesome in the misty distance, but go a little closer, and there is a deal of ugly volcanic ash about, and not much else.

But all this I didn't yet know. Your youthful genius will see through the high and mighty of this world and learn to look dispassionately at men and affairs before he is seventeen; yet here was I, I am ashamed to say, at nearly twenty an innocent enthusiast still, in such awe of the famous that like Su Che[4] I dreamt of the inspiration a meeting with any one of them would supposedly bring. More than once, if I am to confess, I presented myself in my innocence at a great man's door. At one house a notice 'No interviews without an introduction' sent me packing, at another the dismissal was less abrupt, with a bland 'We regret we do not deal with itinerant gentlemen' from a bowing maid; at three more the great ones were 'not at home' (though two assuredly were); two sent word they were too busy to see me (I could hear the click of chessmen); one enquired if I had 'called on business'. At the very last house I tried, however, the master was in, and would see me—to my amazement: he must have been more than usually bored, I supposed. Ushered into the presence, I found his Excellency decked in gold-rimmed spectacles and a coat of Oshima silk.

'Well, what is it?' he asked, twirling his moustache.

'I've heard so much about Your Honour —'

'Ha, ha. After a job, eh? That's it, isn't it?'

'A word or two of advice, I thought, perhaps, for young men like myself —'

'Advice be hanged! Money is might, might is right, and mind your stomach—that's the real wisdom!'

Reeling from such an icy blast, I took myself off in a hurry. The mania for calling on the famous lost its grip on me after that experience. Youth takes both love and hate to extremes. The great often have faults in plenty to match their greatness; and if you fall blindly in love with one side regardless of the other, the shock of disillusionment is so great, you want

---

4. A Chinese poet, statesman, and scholar (1039–1112).

to murder where you loved. The few choice words of wisdom tendered by my gentleman of the gold-rimmed spectacles proved, I must admit, an effective antidote to my feverish adulation of the great.

VII.4

I stayed on in the Yushima boarding-house. The three-mat room I had chosen for its cheapness (it faced west, and was next to the toilet) turned out to be a torture-chamber, suffocating in summer and ice-cold in winter. Between the three-foot strip of veranda and the charcoal-merchant's warehouse opposite, a garden 'as big as a cat's forehead' served as a permanent receptacle for a mass of orange-peel, paper handkerchiefs and bamboo wrappers tossed out of the upstairs windows. A dark, noisy, stinking place it was, but my landlord, the good Shinshichi beforementioned, was so honest a fellow, and his wife—Taki her name was, or Kaki, I forget which—such a cheerful, sensible woman that it was heaven indeed compared with the Shiba doss-house where I had spent my first night in the capital. Taki's (or Kaki's) one eccentricity was the speed with which she changed the maids, thirteen times in my first month alone; some said it was all a subtle scheme devised by Taki for hiring servants without ever paying them. But it was a steady, respectable house for all that, and my fellow-lodgers a company of 'very *sound* young gentlemen', as landlord Shinshichi delighted to call them. True, it was a little trying to hear them rock my ceiling with bouts of wrestling or judo, or bawling out at the top of their voices 'The battle lost, in Edo now I languish!'[5] of a Sunday morning, when I was resting after a long night's tramping on my round; but better that kind of din than twangings on the Chinese guitar and drooling songs and loud-mouthed obscenity.

Apart from these four stalwarts overhead, there was a medical student, as quiet as a cat, a picture of his girl back home stuck proudly in his pocket; another would-be Pen Ch'iao,[6] likewise up from the country to take his qualifying exam—always complaining of his weak stomach, he was, yet a great hand with dried cuttlefish and saké, reaching for his pills in a panic after every feast—and four or five others besides. About one, landlord Shinshichi gave me due warning. 'Not a *bad* young gentleman, Mr Kimura: but don't you lend him anything, Mr Kikuchi!' Kimura was from Nagasaki. He was still in the process of failing his Higher Middle School

---

5. A poem written in prison by Mikisaburo Rai (third son of the historian and poet Sanyo Rai [see note 13, p. 186], who was arrested by the Shogunate in 1858 for his support of the *sonno joi* ('exalt the emperor and expel the foreigners') movement. The poem laments the failure of Rai's personal efforts to rally opposition to the Shogunate in Kyoto (the seat of the imperial court), and his consequent arrest and imprisonment in Edo (Tokyo).

6. A celebrated Chinese physician in the period of the Warring States (4th–3rd cent. B.C.).

exams, I gathered, but had learnt how to play the Tokyoite, all charm and wit. The day after I moved in he had looked in at my room with a breezy "Scuse my butting in, old fellow—we'll be friends in no time, eh?' and before the week was out he was back, asking for a loan of one yen 'for a day or so'—he had a money-order on the way, of course. 'Not a sou to spare,' said I. 'Could you lend me a coat or an old kimono then' he tried again, a little put out, 'just for a few hours, don't you know?' 'What, are you so cold?' I countered—a masterstroke, this: It would hardly do to tell me in so many words he wanted it to pawn, and so, with an unconvincing smile, he withdrew.

Once, though, I had reason to be grateful to this same Kimura. When the *People's Daily* was banned (papers that came out at all strongly against the government—no others—were constantly being banned) it was through him I found some copying work at half a sen a sheet of 200 words. I learnt afterwards, I may say, that the real rate (Kimura paid me, on behalf of the author of the manuscript) was one and a half sen per sheet; two thirds of my wages disappeared in transit, you might say. I didn't complain, though. Who offers his services nowadays without expecting a commission? Not that it's very relevant, but once when I was given the job of transcribing a college teacher's lecture notes for publication, he suddenly sent me word, *after* I had finished the first twenty sheets, if you please, that he didn't need me after all; ostensibly because of mistakes in the copying, but in fact, I am sure, out of pique at the corrections I had made—heaven knows why I bothered!—to his appalling style.

Coming home to a late breakfast of stone-cold soup and rice after finishing my round and checking out at the paper's offices, I would take a nap, and then, armed with a box of pickled plums and rice-balls, start off for Ueno Library. Here I could study in peace for the entrance examination, saving the cost of books and avoiding the din of the crowded streets near my lodging. Turning night into day meant loss of sleep, inevitably, till I got used to it. At any moment in the Library, my head would sag feebly over the pages of a Euclid or a Todhunter's *Algebra*; once I caught myself snoring—and woke up blushing to face the amused or angry looks of my fellow-students, young and old, who filled the reading-room. After that I took to slipping out at the first signs of drowsiness, to sit on a bench in the garden among the birdsong and the fresh sweet scent of early plum-blossom; half-an-hour's doze in the balmy sun and breeze of spring would send me back to my books refreshed. When the Library closed I would stroll down through Ueno woods to Shinobazu Pond, while the last gleam of sunset was lighting up its placid waters. I love those woods still: trees, like truly great men, delight and inspire by mere proximity.

Back at my lodgings by lamplighting time, after supper I would either sleep for two or three hours, if I were particularly tired, or else go out again (to save lamp-oil—how Nishiuchi would approve, I often thought; if ever he wanted to adopt a son, there's no doubt who'd be well qualified!)

to the *People's Daily* building. While my fellow-roundsmen lay around on straw mats and snored or dreamt of better days, or wallowed in each other's dirty jokes, I would sit on the long bench by the brazier in the middle of the earthen floor, reading by the dim light such papers as I could borrow from the general office. As mere roundsmen, we knew next to nothing of what went on in the editorial department upstairs; but many a time, as I listened to the carefree laughter from the floor above us, I bit my lip to check the tears.

VII.5

One evening late last autumn I leant against a seat on Atago Hill and gazed down over the darkening city. I was quite alone. As the evening bell tolled from the great Zojoji Temple and one by one the streetlamps winked up at me through the twilight haze, I listened. All sounds, all voices seemed to merge into a single sad melody, like a weary giant's sigh. I stood as in a dream, till slowly before my eyes the city lightened to a vast grey sea . . . and in a fearful vortex at its heart, innumerable as autumn leaves, bobbed black motes of seething, squirming humanity, their groans borne to me on the wind like the roar of distant waves. I looked outward, to the horizon. From every quarter, new hordes flowed towards the fatal centre: some, I saw, were sucked instantly into the maelstrom, as if plucked by an infernal hand; others floated lifeless on the surface; others, not yet dead, spun round helplessly upon the current; only rarely did one here, one there, struggle free to smoother water. But as fast as the victims disappeared, others, blind to every danger, swam up eagerly to take their place. Again and again, tense with horror, I longed to scream a warning . . . The shadows deepened about me on Atago Hill. Tokyo spread itself below, a broad sea lit with fishing fires; I caught the hoarse, sad music of its waves.

I wiped the sweat from my forehead, and breathed deeply of the night air. Of the million men and women in the capital, jostling to raise themselves above their fellows, how many count themselves happy? All their lives they only scurry, panting, back and forth. What makes them cling so avidly to their city? Is not the world wide open to them still—Formosa, for instance, or the Kuriles? Is not country air purer, country water sweeter? Why must they breathe such poisonous air? Why should they be for ever so intent upon squeezing empty glory from a city as hard as stone, when 'at home the fields neglected lie'[7]? Yet men must live, and fight to live; seek fame, earn money. So great is the gulf between the city and the country that once a man has tasted city rice, he'll never again feel at home in his village; so, worn thin with hunger, tubercular maybe, his eyes as narrow and greedy as a pickpocket's, dying on his feet, he slaves away in the city

---

7. From the well-known poem *Kuei-ch'ü-lai tz'ŭ* (Returning Home) by T'ao Ch'ien (?372–427) who gave up public appointments to live a simple rural life

still. And every year new waves of bright-eyed youth pour in—as I myself had done—to fatten the monster's cavernous belly.

But two months or so after my arrival in the capital, when the bare Ginza willow-tree in whose hidden promise of life I had seen my own hopes imaged was hung with threads of green, and plum-blossom carpeted the streets and alleys of my round, even I had grown a little used to Tokyo, and my new life took on a steadier rhythm. Mother had approved of my second flight from school, more enthusiastically than I had expected; my visit home had been a comfort, no doubt, and I daresay she was particularly pleased that I was aiming at a proper university rather than grind on indefinitely at Kansei College. When he sent off my trunk, Endo wrote to say how much staff and students had missed me, but otherwise I heard nothing from the College, for Endo was the only one I had told of my address, and that only under promise of secrecy. I was on my own entirely.

A carefree life—and a very lonely one. Early one Sunday morning, as I was on my way home as usual from my round, two glossy heads of hair done up in the western way, one neck hidden in a yellow shawl, the other in a brown, turned out of a side-alley ahead of me. Cousin Suzue and O-Toshi! Pulling my hat down, I ran up another turning. They had no idea I was in Tokyo—I had made Mother promise to tell no one of my move, not even Aunt, at least until after the entrance examination. Truly, for creeping through life unnoticed there is no place like Tokyo, where it matters nothing if you know a man's face but not his name, or know his name but pass him by without so much as a nod of greeting .

Faithful to my mother's admonition not to make myself ill with study, I spent my Sundays (except when there was a special edition to deliver) sleeping, going to church, or exploring the city. The theatre billboards gave me a taste of Kabuki drama; exotic smells wafted from the fashionable Seiyoken or Yaozen restaurants, my fill of metropolitan food and cooking; I hurried past the big bookshops with eyes closed to their displays. A certain extravagance I did allow myself on this one day: three sen's worth of roasted sweet potatoes, or a bowl of whale soup from a cheap tavern, when I could pluck up the courage to enter such a place. On rainy Sundays I stayed quietly at home, amusing myself by writing pieces for the *People's Daily*. This brought me a reward of another kind from the wages I earned for delivering the paper. The *People's Daily* encouraged anonymous articles and letters from the public, and published a great many, some of them absurdly trivial and obviously only put in to catch the vulgar eye. Eager to try my hand again, I scribbled something myself, modelled on a piece I had read in the Miscellany column, and dropped it (taking care no one was looking) in the box displayed for the purpose outside the office. I could hardly wait till the next evening's printing. When we were given our bundles I peeped inside the first paper, pretending it was easier to fold that way—and there it was, in print.' I had 'published' articles at Kansei College, but this—in a Tokyo newspaper, with four or five thousand readers!

I couldn't keep back a smile. Whether any of the paper's readers read that article I don't know; its author did, though, scores of times, by lamplight on his round ... And pushed every copy of the paper into its waiting letter-box that night with very special, if wholly selfish, care. The taste thus acquired, I wrote similar pieces whenever I could spare the time, and eight or nine times out of ten they were accepted. Bravo, I thought, I'm a journalist already. Not that any of it brought me in a single sen, of course; nor had I any inkling of the editor's opinion of my writing. To appear in the paper—that alone was reward enough.

Along with the editorial and the Miscellany column, my favourite reading in the *People's Daily* was the 'Letter from Paris', over the signature 'Tetsurei'. Tetsurei[8] was the pen-name, I was told, of a Mr Sato, who had gone to live in Europe three or four years before, but would be coming home soon, so it was said, to take over the editorship. As well as the beauty of his style, the thoroughness of his reporting, and the force of his arguments, there was something else about his writing, something quite indefinable, that excited me strangely, like a bugle-call that stirs the heart at once with its own haunting beauty and with the memories it revives of martial music heard long since.

VII.6

In due course Mr Sato returned from France and took over the editor's chair, as rumour had prophesied. I heard reports of the welcoming dinner and of his speech of thanks and greeting, but could find no chance to get a sight of the man himself. One evening, however, about cherry-blossom time, I was sitting in the roundsmen's room reading a borrowed magazine by the light of an oil-lamp, when an unusually well-dressed figure I did not recognize (he was in western clothes) came clattering down the steps from upstairs. This must be Sato, I thought, for I knew all the other editorial staff by sight. He bowed slightly in my direction as he passed on his way out. For a moment the light caught his profile—and I sprang to my feet ... Not noticing, he walked on towards the door. I dashed after him.

'Sensei! Komai Sensei!'

He looked round in surprise, one foot already on the waiting rickshaw.

'Who called?' That voice—after four years! I could hardly speak for delight.

8. Literally 'Iron Mountain.' The name is made up of the first character (*tetsu* = iron) of Sato's given-name Tetsutaro (see p. 261) + *rei* = mountain peak. Apart from the obvious implication of 'iron', 'mountain' has for the Chinese and Japanese an ancient association with the ideal of ethical goodness and quiet steadfastness of character. Cf. Confucius, *Analects*, VI, 21: 'The Master said, The wise man delights in water, the Good man delights in mountains. For the wise move; but the Good stay still. The wise are happy; but the Good, secure.' (tr. Arthur Waley).

'Sensei, have you forgotten—Shintaro Kikuchi—you taught me, at the New School —'

At the words 'New School' Komai Sensei took the rickshawman's lantern and shone it in my face. Smiling, he seized my hand at once, to shake it several times in the French manner.

'So it *is* Kikuchi—grown so big I didn't recognize you! But come inside: we can't talk here.'

Sensei hurried back towards the stairs. Past the wondering stares of my comrades, my heart racing and my whole being trembling in an inexpressible tension of shyness and delight, I followed him. Halfway up the stairs I suddenly realized I still had on my mud-caked sandals. My fingers catching in the thongs, I tore them off, kicked them aside and ran on up the stairs to where Sensei was standing smiling under the gas-light in the reception room.

'It's been a long time, Kikuchi. I'm surprised you still remembered me.' He sat down, pointing to a chair for me.

Even if it had been ten times longer, how could I ever have forgotten him, I longed to say; but was speechless, only laughing like an idiot for joy.

We had only a few minutes for talk then. I told Komai Sensei very briefly what I was doing in Tokyo, he gave me a visiting-card with the address of the Nihonbashi inn where he had been staying since his return from abroad, and we agreed to meet there next day. More thrilled than ever, I could hardly answer without breaking into tears the astonished questions that assailed me downstairs. Truly the strangest of meetings! It seemed incredible that the Mr Sato I had heard of should be my Komai Sensei. Sato was his real name, I gathered; he had been adopted into the Komai family some years back, but only temporarily, so as to avoid military service.

Next morning I called on Sensei directly I had finished my round—before he was up, in fact. With a fluency born of excitement I told the whole story of my flight from the New School, my setting out for Tosa with the aim of finding him at his home, the mishaps and adventures that befell me at Uwajima, the years at Kansei College, Uncle's death, the reasons for my sudden flight to Tokyo, my present life and hopes for the future. Sensei listened intently. When at last I had finished, he thought for a moment, then asked if I had a specimen of my writing I could show him. As it happened, the paper had printed one of my little pieces that day, so I showed him this, thinking all the while I'd have done much better if I had known *he* was going to see it. After reading it through, he picked up out of a heap of books in the alcove the English magazine *Contemporary Review*, and told me to bring him a translation of one of the articles, an essay on 'Problems in the Far East'. I started work on the translation as soon as I got home, finished it the following morning, and took it straight to him at his office. He must have read it at once, for he sent for me again that evening; the translation was pretty creditable, he said, and if I would do this kind of work for the paper, not only would it help with my studies but he would see—though they couldn't afford to be generous—that I was paid enough to cover my keep and school expenses. Which meant, of course, that I could give up the delivery round.

But there was a greater thrill to come. He was expecting soon to move into a house of his own, Sensei went on to say: he'd be needing some help with his work—there'd be no women in the house—would I come and lodge with him, sharing his life, as we had done in the old days at the New School?

Was I dreaming? If I was, the dream came true. At the end of the month I left my lodgings and moved into Komai Sensei's—Sato Sensei's— house.

VII.7

Tetsurei Sensei, campaigner of the pen, took up his new headquarters in a little house in Kami-negishi surrounded by a wall of oak-trees. Sensei himself, Shintaro Kikuchi, two other students, and an old woman who came in to cook made up the household. While the old woman looked after supplies and my two comrades acted as janitors and cleaners, my own duties, such as they were, were mostly secretarial—in fact I was treated more like a friend and guest than a secretary, even. My days I spent at the Library as before; in the evenings I would translate articles from foreign newspapers and magazines, or help the other two with their English, or sometimes when Sensei was free I would pester him with questions about life in Europe. The change from my previous state was so sudden I couldn't believe it. The listlessness induced by long cold nights spent tramping the streets, the pale, haggard look (I couldn't help noticing my reflection in shop windows) began to disappear, the sunken cheeks to fill out, and I began to feel human once more—all this thanks to Komai Sensei (if I may continue to call him this, for I could *not* get used to 'Sato Sensei').

The story of Sensei's own career after leaving us at the New School did not take long to tell. After his father's death he had gone straight back to Tokyo, to be sent to Europe before long as supervisor to a group of students, the sons of leading families of his own clan of Tosa, a post which had still left him time to attend lectures on politics at the University of Paris and to study at first hand the workings of European parliaments and political parties; and in Paris he stayed till his return three years later to take up the editorship of the paper. In appearance, he was no longer the austere, somewhat awe-inspiring figure I remembered from New School days, but a smart, up-to-date and easy-mannered gentleman, as befitted one who had trod the streets of Paris. But the transformation was only in externals. In spirit he was still the old Komai Sensei, as keen a student as the youngest of us; behind the polished façade there was the same fiery idealism, the same iron will we had tried and failed to break. Before half the week was out I was under the spell once more.

Sensei's tastes and habits were simple in the extreme, as if the noble fire within him had burned up every other passion. Or if he had a passion, it was love of students. 'Others go abroad to study systems,' he said once. 'I studied men. It's men our country is short of, not money. If ever any power came my way, there's only one thing I should ever want to use it for —education, the freedom to teach in my own way. If they made me Prime Minister, I'd keep a school at home to teach each day before I went to Cabinet!' Whenever he could spare the time he would send for us students and talk to us endlessly over a bowl of baked potatoes, of the danger of empty heads in politics, of the need for public spirit among the scholars of the land. And always he would urge us to read. Sometimes he would throw me a book with an 'Out you go, and read this!'

I had no cause to complain my practical education was neglected, either. I had the right of entry now to the editorial offices I had contemplated so long and enviously from my bench in the roundsmen's room. Sometimes when I handed in a translated article or review I would be given some small job to do—how eagerly I listened then to the easy, confident talk among the staff from Sensei downwards, talk of men and their virtues and failings, of the paper and its problems, of home and foreign affairs, of teacup village scandals; great issues rolled back and forth on witty tongues like so many candy-balls, by masters of the art of extracting sense from laughter and hiding humour in solemnity. In short, I witnessed time and time again the process of a newspaper being brought to birth; and these short hours I spent at the editorial offices taught me more of the world than I had learnt elsewhere in all my nineteen years till then.

VII.8

1887 was a lively year in Meiji political history. The negotiations for the revision of the unequal treaties with foreign powers, in particular, led to bitter attacks on the 'government of the western clans', and popular opposition flared up again to something like the pitch it had reached in 1870 and 1871. The leakage of Foreign Minister Okuma's proposals for treaty revision and of a paper in similar terms by a foreign adviser in the service of the government added fuel to the flames: the newspapers organized big protest rallies; opposition leaders rushed from meeting to meeting; political gangs mushroomed; inflammatory manifestos, secretly printed, penetrated to every corner of the land. Indignant country patriots poured into Tokyo, threatening crowds surrounded Ministers' houses—passions rising higher and higher with the sticky summer heat of the city, till the anti-government forces had acquired a dangerous strength. Komai Sensei, needless to say, had thrown himself and his paper into the thick of the struggle. When the great demonstration of popular feeling had its effect, as before long it did, and it was officially announced that the negotiations for treaty revision were suspended, and the Foreign Minister had resigned, Sensei clapped his hands in jubilation: 'One more heave, and they're out, Kikuchi!'

With all the comings and goings I got to know most of the opposition leaders by sight, and often heard them in discussion the other side of my partition wall. (I was prejudiced, maybe, but for me, there wasn't one of them to touch Komai Sensei, though he was younger than most.) As one of Sensei's assistants in a small way I couldn't help rejoicing whenever an opposition salvo landed squarely in the enemy camp. If I didn't quite succumb to the general political fever and stopped short of joining the crowds at the Foreign Minister's gate, it was because I had another battle to fight—a battle that I had burned my boats to face, abandoning theology and Kansei College for a newsboy's round. For the honour of the College that had taught me, if for no other reason, I was determined to succeed in the University entrance examinations. As the great teacher Fukuzawa lectured on unperturbed with the roar of the guns in his ears during the pre-Restoration fighting—if one may compare the great with the small—so I continued at my books, tucked away in the headquarters of an anti-government army, in preparation for my private ordeal.

Endo wrote from the College to tell me of his graduation and hopes of coming to Tokyo in the autumn. Everyone in the class had missed me, he said, but I was too preoccupied to feel much moved. Everything—the honour of the Kikuchi and my own self-respect, Mother's happiness, the prospect of reward for the years of endurance—depended on success in the examination; and I could think of nothing else. Early in September I made my final preparations. Two friends of Komai Sensei agreed to act as my guarantors and sponsors to the University if I should pass. I sent my application to the Dean of the College of Literature, paid the five-yen examination fee, and sat back to wait for the day. My head was heavy, unfortunately, with a cold I had felt coming on at the beginning of the month; and when Sensei sent out for a chicken to put me in condition again (I had taken practically nothing but tea for three days) I could hardly eat a mouthful, grateful though I was for his kindness. Ashamed of myself for such feebleness, I tried to get my energy back by stripping every few hours and dousing myself at the well in the garden. But the pain in my head only grew worse.

The day of the examination arrived at last. Feeling as shaky as ever, I determined to shock myself out of it—leapt out of bed, ignored the way my feet shook as I washed, and took my place as usual at table. But not a grain of rice could I eat. Komai Sensei looked at me suddenly.

'You're very red, Kikuchi—surely it's fever of some sort?' He took my hand. 'You're burning—better see the doctor at once!'

Managing a smile, I refused; struggled with trembling fingers to slip on a borrowed *hakama* over my best kimono, opened the door to leave—and nearly fell on my face. The rest of our 'family' came running out, Sensei among them.

'It's no good forcing yourself, Kikuchi. You'll have another chance to take the exam. Or if you must go, see a doctor first!' He called to one of the other boys to fetch a doctor. Frantically I begged him to send for a rickshaw instead. (A doctor, I knew, would never let me go.) Realizing I was not to be persuaded, he brought me some fever-medicine in a glass of water. I raised it gratefully to my forehead, and forced myself to drink.

'Goodbye!' I got the word out somehow, my teeth clenched against another fit of trembling, and after a final bow to Sensei was turning to step into the waiting rickshaw, when the ground slipped from under me and everything went black.

VII.9

Often, though huntsmen crowd round his mountain lair and hide their best marksman in the bushes by the track he is bound to take, their prey will still escape. Man may work his will nine tenths of the way, but always one obstinate tenth remains, where Heaven alone disposes. So I found myself entering not the College of Literature but the University Hospital, suffering from a severe bout of typhoid fever, the more virulent for my having held out against it for so long. For a long while after they carried me away from Sensei's house on a stretcher, infuriated but inert, I lay in a coma, with a temperature so high that the doctors were amazed, so they told me afterwards, that I managed to survive. Much of the time, apparently, I was babbling examination answers for hours together; but I myself remembered only a continuous torture by burning, as if I were being roasted in the fires of hell—the slender thread of life barely kept from breaking by the ice they plied me with a hundred times a day, ice pillows, ice poultices, crushed ice in my mouth. I too wondered that I did not die.

But happily my journey's end was not yet. After two weeks the fever began to abate, my body's elements slowly took shape out of the vapour into which they had dissolved, and Kikuchi floated back to earth. Two blank walls, I made out, a door this side, a window that—an isolation cubicle, three yards by three of frustration; and the body on the bed, myself. The fever had left me little more than a burnt-out shell: my tongue was black, my lips parched and cracked, my throat too exhausted to cough, even, my mind incapable of thought. I was alive, that was all. When Sensei came to visit me, as he somehow found time to do, I wanted to tell him to keep away, the illness being contagious; but the effort of a murmured 'thank you' left me no strength to say another word. I was more helpless than a baby in his cradle. But youth has its own resilience: little by little, as the fever left me and I could take nourishment, my wasted body picked up, till I entered at last on the infinitely tedious period of convalescence.

As health returned, however, so did my gloom increase. Komai Sensei having written to Mother that I was out of danger, I was free of anxiety in that direction, but the collapse of my plans I could not get over. A year's delay in getting into University—not much to make a fuss about, perhaps. Yet it was to do just this—enter the University this year—that I had turned my back on Kansei College a mere six months before graduation (I might claim the missionaries had expelled me, but the truth was otherwise) and struggled on for so many months alone. To have failed the examination would have been disastrous enough; but for the soldier to drop down on his knees without ever having struck a blow was too ignominious, too absurd. I had failed them all—Mother and Komai Sensei and my friends, students and teachers alike, at the College. As I stared at the ceiling through long sleepless nights, it began to seem as if a malevolent Heaven had broken off deliberately my new bud of hope, and instead of thanking the Supreme Being for my deliverance I was more inclined, in my blindness, to charge Him with vicious injustice.

By the time I was able to talk, visitors came pretty often to help me while away the long autumn days—Komai Sensei, or when he was too busy, one or other of the boys, my fellow-lodgers in his house; and on Sundays, Cousin Suzue. She hadn't known of my illness, of course, or even that I was in Tokyo, until Aunt Noda wrote to say I was in hospital, which had brought her hurrying to see me. Along with her sympathy she gave me a good scolding.

'What d'you mean by coming to Tokyo all that time ago and never even sending a postcard?'

When I told her (as I invariably did) not to stay unless she wanted to get the fever herself, she was more indignant still—planted herself in a chair at my bedside with her knitting and started to talk: of how her Aunt here in Tokyo was still having trouble with her feet, how Mother (my Aunt Noda, that is) had helped to start a new school back home, how Matsumura's sister O-Toshi was studying at a Girls' Higher School near Hitotsubashi Bridge; how one day last summer O-Toshi had sworn she had seen me at Ueno, walking in the opposite direction, and Suzue had insisted it was impossible. '*Very* naughty of you!' she wagged her finger at me, with such feeling that her sleeve knocked over a big bottle of medicine.

VII.10

From lying all day like a baby, unable even to turn over without help, to sitting up against a pile of pillows—from the first two or three steps, clutching the bed-rail, while the nurse smiled encouragement at her clever toddler, to the great undertaking of a walk right round the bed unaided (wondering, as I fell back afterwards among the pillows exhausted and caught my reflection in a medicine bottle, from what graveyard such a ghost could have strayed): so six weeks went by, till one day when Sensei sent a sprig of chrysanthemum, in my weakness I nearly cried. Could it be chrysanthemum time already? Bored by now almost to the point of accusing the doctors of holding up my recovery, I lived only for meals and visitors and the hope of release.

Now and again I had some special visitors apart from those I spoke of earlier. One of the most unexpected was old Shinshichi, from the lodging-house in Yushima. How he had heard where I was I don't know, but more than once his shining bald pate lightened my gloomy sickroom. Scratching his head, he would pull back to the door the chair the nurse had put by my bedside, resisting all my pleas to come nearer where we could talk. I marvelled at his shyness, till it struck me suddenly it wasn't that at all; he was only protecting himself. There's sense in that kind of shyness, I thought, smiling at my mistake. I can't tell, though, how grateful I was to him for coming: for who, in the ordinary course of things, would take the trouble to visit anybody so insignificant as a penniless sick student?

Another surprise was a visit from Professor Kan, who was teaching at a private college in Tokyo now. He had known nothing of my flight from Kansei College till Principal Katayama, up in Tokyo on business in the summer, had told him the whole story (adding that he would have liked to help me in some way with my future studies, if only he could find out where I was living; as it was, he knew only that I was somewhere in Tokyo. Evidently Endo had kept my secret well). Since then he had been on the lookout; till one day a friend at the University had told him he'd seen my name in a list of applicants, whereupon he had gone at once to Komai Sensei, and thence to the hospital. 'Why didn't you call on me, Kikuchi?' he scolded me. 'Modesty is a fine thing, but you don't need to push it *quite* so far!' But the memories of the College Kan Sensei's visit revived served only to mock my present state, shut out as I was now from both College and University, so that I cannot honestly say I was wholly glad to see him.

At last the word came through for my discharge. Wrapped in a padded robe (which the boys had brought me in place of the light summer kimono I had been wearing when I entered hospital) I rode home to Komai Sensei's through streets decked with flags in honour of the Emperor's birthday, wondering at the holiday crowds, like a spectre condemned to wander in the land of the living. When we reached the house my legs shook, from sheer relief at leaving hospital, I suppose, and I fell, though only for a moment, where I had fainted eight weeks before, in Sensei's porch.

That evening Sensei called me to his study. 'I envy you your mother, Kikuchi. There aren't many like her,' he said, after congratulating me on coming home, and cutting short my attempt to thank him (which I couldn't find words for anyway) for his kindness. When he had sent her a telegram saying simply that I was ill, Mother had telegraphed back asking him to hide nothing, but tell her exactly what the doctors said; and on his replying that though the attack was severe, I would probably recover, had sent him fifty yen with the request that he would see that everything possible was done for me, 'as there seemed to be no immediate need for her to disturb us by coming to Tokyo herself.' Komai Sensei showed me another letter he had just had from her, written when she heard I was to leave hospital. After thanking him profusely for all his wise teaching and guidance in the past and his fatherly care during my illness, to which I assuredly owed my life, she wrote, 'you will know my son well enough by now to realize how keenly, too keenly, he will feel what may appear to him for the moment as a failure—something for which he himself is to blame. I beg you therefore now above all to guide him in everything, that he may not be restored to bodily health only to succumb to a weakness of the mind and spirit, and so fail in appreciation of all that you have done for him so far. Tell him also that not a hair of his Mother's head has yet turned white; and that she will wait for him as long as need be; her patience will not weaken with the years.' Komai Sensei glanced at me as I rolled up the letter-scroll, my head still bent. 'We've both to watch our step, eh, Kikuchi, if your Mother's not to laugh at us for a pair of good-for-nothings!'

On the doctor's advice, and positive orders from Komai Sensei, three days later I went to convalesce by the sea on the Boso Peninsula.

VII.11

I spent almost as many weeks in an inn at Hojo as I had in the hospital. The habit of sea-bathing had just recently caught on, and in the summer, I was told, the fishing villages were crowded with students and other visitors from the capital. But now, in November, there was not a city face to be seen in Hojo, Tateyama or anywhere else, nor any whisper of Tokyo except for such letters and newspapers as the little mailboat brought, chug-chugging across the bay; only the chanting of the fishermen as they hauled their boats up the beach, occasional shouts of excitement over a big catch of tunny, and the raucous gaiety of a credit club that met in a big empty house nearly opposite the inn, disturbed the stillness of the autumn days.

Thus cradled in peaceful Nature, my body took its ease. A first walk of a hundred yards along the sand tired me out; I lay flat to rest, which set a fisherwoman screaming that the 'gentleman visitor from Edo' was dying on the beach. But each day fresh air and fresh fish gave me back more strength and flesh, till by the time the fishermen all knew me and were bowing in recognition every time we met, I could walk the three miles to Nago-Funagata and back. Books, too, I began to open again; soon I was able to write at some length to both Mother and Komai Sensei. In the bath, particularly, my arms and legs still looked thin and brittle enough, but my face, 'as white as gourd-shavings' when I arrived, according to my landlady, had acquired a colour in the good salt wind, and by degrees the joy of life rose within me.

'A man's thoughts are like arrows shot from a bow; they can only fly where his mind takes aim.' For the last year my mind had been so engrossed with the struggle for mere existence, there had been no time for quiet reflection. Now that illness had thrust leisure upon me, I lay awake through many long nights pondering the future, hearing in the sighing of the wind in the pinetrees above the eaves, in the roar of the waves, in the beating of rain on my window, the voice of Heaven rousing me from forgetfulness and sleep.

One evening I sat in a wood by the mouth of a little nameless stream between Hojo and Tateyama. The sun had just dropped behind Izu; Mirror Bay slowly paled from molten gold to white, and the distant outline of Mount Fuji, rising purple on a golden ground between two tiny offshore islands, darkened to indigo. As the evening bell boomed through the wood from the temple of Nago Kannon, a blue haze slid quietly across the bay and seeped, tree by tree, to where I sat, knees clasped in hands, against an ancient pine. Decoy lights gleamed here and there from fishing-boats far out at sea. There was not a soul left now on the whole length of the beach, no voice to be heard through the mist but that of the waves, and the roll of the temple bell once more, sweeping over the bay with its long, slow echo. As I listened, I seemed to hear again the bell I heard on Mount Hiei two years before, after Michitaro's tragic death, and glimpse for a fleeting instant my friend's face smiling among the shadows. Covering my face, I wept.

And what tears were these? Tears of submission, if they must be given a name; of a sad awakening to truth. How foolish I had been! For a year I had plunged madly ahead, blindly confident of my own strength: ambition had crowded out faith and the impulse to wait calmly till I knew the Will of Heaven; I had seldom opened the Scriptures; if I had prayed, it was not in humility and truth. My attack on the missionaries—hadn't ambition been the hidden motive even there, in spite of the heroic pose? If the hardships of the last eleven months had been a necessary medicine, had not ambition, like a lingering impurity in the blood, undone their work? To such questions I could not answer no. Truly I had run where I should have walked, and they who run too rashly must stumble.

But my heart, as hard as any rock, ignored the rounding action of the breakers that beat upon its stubborn edges. More bitterly than ever I rebelled at Heaven's injustice, with no gratitude for my narrow escape, only anger at the narrowness of my failure.

Yet in the end that evening on the shores of Mirror Bay did soften my recalcitrant spirit. What is man's little life, confronted with infinity—or the stubborn human will, confronted with the vast purposes of Heaven? To what goal had I been racing, when I could run for a million years and never leave the hand of the Buddha-Lord, on which all creatures have their being eternally? The seasons march, tides rise and fall, with unhurried, stately motion. Yet I—I had been out of my mind, disdaining to walk mere earth.

My illness was an alarm, then, sounded to wake me out of too deep a sleep. How could I accuse Heaven of injustice, when it had twice given me warning, first by ordaining that I should witness my best friend's death, and now by bringing me to the very edge of death myself? Once more hot tears rolled down my cheek.

Almost completely recovered after more than fifty days on the Peninsula, far longer than I had expected, on December 25th I boarded the boat back to Tokyo, where I landed at Reiganjima Quay. It was dark when I reached Komai Sensei's house. As I stepped down from my rickshaw there was a sudden grating of shoes from a sidepath. Two or three dark figures stepped out of the shadows. A lantern shone in my face. I peered past the light. A sergeant, apparently, with two policemen.

'You wouldn't be Tetsutaro Sato, would you, mister?' said the sergeant, looking puzzled.

'No—Shintaro Kikuchi is my name.'

'Got business with Sato, have you?'

'No, I live here. Do you want to see Mr Sato?'

As I was speaking, lights appeared at the end of the street, followed by the clatter of wheels. Seconds later, three rickshaws, the first carrying Komai Sensei, drew up where we were standing.

'Welcome home, Kikuchi!'

Before I could answer, the sergeant confronted him.

'Mr Sato?'

'Yes. What can I do for you?'

The sergeant took a paper from his pocket and handed it to him. Sensei glanced at it, dumbfounded.

'A banning order—forbidden to live within eight miles—what, I'm to leave Tokyo?'

'That's correct. You've three days to obey the order, Mr Sato!'

VII.12

I had read in newspapers and letters from Komai Sensei how the government was preparing stronger measures to defend itself against the increasingly bitter attacks that followed on the success of the opposition's campaign for the suspension of negotiations on the unequal treaties; but that they would take such drastic punitive action just at the tail-end of the year had never occurred to me—nor, I suspect, to Sensei himself.

'The brutes—shall we deal with them?' growled one of my fellow-lodgers, all of whom (there were three besides me now) had tumbled out of their rickshaws behind Sensei's. Rebuking them, Sensei apologized to the sergeant for having kept him waiting, took us inside for a moment to give us a few hurried instructions, and was just getting ready to leave when there was a shout of 'Sato, are you there, old fellow!' from the front door. Kyoshi Aoyama, the former editor of the *People's Daily*, and something like an uncle to Komai Sensei, was swaying in the porch, reeking of saké.

'They've done it, Sato. Never thought they would, but they've done it at last. Proper *coup d'état*! How long for you? Two years? That makes two of us, ha-ha! I called on Mr Brandy just now—notable foreigner—celebrate impending exile. They'll give us a police escort now fit for Ministers —*Ministers*, no less, how's that now!' The words spurted out on a saké-laden tide of anger, hysterical laughter and tears.

The excitement and confusion of that night and the next day were indescribable. More than five hundred and sixty people, including many whom I knew, were served with notices under the Security Ordinance banning them from the capital for two or three years; householders were ordered to leave within three days, others within twenty-four hours. The slightest attempt at resistance was met by instant arrest.

After two days of dashing around in a two-man rickshaw to settle his most pressing affairs, Komai Sensei left for Yokohama, where I joined him as soon as we had finished (the other boys and myself) shutting up the house. Most of the victims of the Ordinance headed for Yokohama (hence the verse that got about, based on a popular song of the time, 'You go today/And drown your sorrow:/The others will come/By train tomorrow') so that the city was soon crowded with 'refugees' of all kinds. Some were on their way home to the provinces to build up a stronger base there, some hoped to start country newspapers, some planned to stay in Yokohama but continue the fight from there; others merely fumed ineffectively, unable to decide what to do; others again wanted to return to their homes in the country but could not till they had begged the fare from their friends or colleagues. But Komai Sensei, I gathered, had made up his mind from the start. He would be going abroad again, he told me, as soon as his passport came through. (The *People's Daily* had been banned, along with the expulsion from Tokyo of its editor. Plans were being discussed to publish it in Osaka under a different name; but Komai Sensei had already resigned the editorship. A wealthy friend of his, a business man named Nakagawa, had undertaken to pay for his trip.) There was little he could do in Japan, he felt, so rather than stay in such a restrictive atmosphere he had decided to spend another two or three years abroad to continue his own education, and also in a small way try and dispel some of the suspicions foreigners felt about Japan, as his personal contribution to the honourable modification of the unequal treaties.

For some days I travelled up and down the Tokyo-Yokohama line on business for Sensei, till at last his passport was ready. A few hours before he was due to embark he found time to walk with me for a while on Noge Hill, overlooking the harbour. Of the many wise things he said then, I remember the following few sentences so vividly, I can quote them still:

'We shouldn't worry too much about the way the leaders of the western clans cling to power in the government. They can't last for ever—nature will take care of that. No, what should trouble us is our own people. These 'men of public spirit', as they call themselves, grieving so unselfishly over the future of their country—you've seen them, Kikuchi. How many of them are capable of rational speech, let alone thought? Either ignorant, or stupid, or corrupt, most of them. And these are the people we expect to take over the government of our country! It's a depressing thought. I tell you, Japan won't be able to get by for long on the platitudes they've fed us with till now. The race will go to the swift, not the empty-headed! The real testing-time in politics will come after the Diet gets going in 1890—and in everything, not only politics: the further Japan advances on to the world stage, the more opportunities for the really able. Now's the time for true patriots to prepare themselves, Kikuchi, without counting the cost: and by "true patriots" I mean every single loyal citizen in every walk of life who has a mind to serve his country!'

So Sensei urged me too never to lose the larger patriotic spirit as I hurried on toward my own immediate goal. To these parting words, spoken with such earnestness and depth of feeling, I listened as to a deathbed testament, shedding womanish tears in spite of myself—as I did again next day, January 3, 1888, when with many other of his friends I walked down the gangway of the liner *Oceanic* that was to carry my beloved teacher to America. 'Two hands so tightly clasped,/And torn so soon asunder!'[9] might have been written of Komai Sensei and myself.

'The crowded capital is empty now', wrote Po Chu-i on his friend's departure from Ch'ang-an; but to me as I gazed numbly after the receding liner, all Japan seemed empty. My spirit, too, had sailed with the ship, leaving only a lifeless corpse standing on the Yokohama quay.

9. From a poem by Kao Ch'i (1336–1374).

Part VIII

Having seen my beloved teacher Komai Sensei off on his foreign travels on that last day of January, in September of the same year I at last entered Tokyo University, and started courses as a first-year student in the department of English Literature. After Sensei's departure I went back at once to old Shinshichi's lodging-house and resumed the narrower life I had lived before. Among all his final preoccupations, Komai Sensei had not forgotten his young disciple: with the help of an introduction he had given me to a Mr Ando, the editor of the *Meiji Review*, a reputable journal that had somehow slipped through the Security Ordinance net, I was very soon self-supporting again, and if the money I earned by translations and the like was hardly enough to pay for fancy meals and a private rickshaw, at least I could keep up with the rent and get my underwear washed occasionally without having to go back on a newspaper round.

Apart from infrequent visits to Professor Kan, one to Cousin Suzue's aunt to thank her for the fruit she had sent to the hospital, and one or two calls a month at the office of the *Meiji Review*, I went nowhere and saw no one during those months, but shut myself up in my room as quiet as a cat, the better to study. Having lost a year already, for a while I had hopes of getting so much work done now that I would be able to go straight into the second year after the examination; but the strain proved too great, my health not recovering completely for a whole year after the illness, so I settled for a cow's pace, slow but steady. As the examination drew near I was almost indifferent—far less tense, certainly, than before.

I passed safely, though, with the highest marks obtained for several years by a candidate who hadn't been through one of the great State High Schools, so I was told afterwards. Welcome though it was, the news didn't thrill me as it would have done a year earlier, and I reported only the bare fact to Mother, to Komai Sensei in America, and to my two sponsors—Mr Nakagawa (the business-man who was paying Komai Sensei's expenses) and Professor Kan. Some comfort, at least, it must have brought to Mother, who seven hundred and fifty miles to the west would turn her face towards Tokyo each night and morning and pray for my success. For all her stubborn courage she was still a mother: every line of her reply to my letter shone with relief and joy. A few days later she sent a new lined kimono and a *hakama* shirt, the latter much longer than any she had made for me before; now I had entered the University, I suppose she felt I had truly grown up all of a sudden.

So, two years after leaving Kansei College, I started regular school and dormitory life once more. Tokyo University, which my still childish imagination had viewed from outside with such awe, as the highest seat of learning in the land, proved on entry to be not so formidable after all. Distinguished doctors and professors there were—and others very noticeably commonplace. (It was a shock to find Kumagae, my friend Sone's rival in his tragic love-affair at Okayama, already an Assistant Professor, and very conscious of his dignity. Not long ago I would have been ready enough with a sneer when we met; but now—well, even I had grown up, I suppose. I nodded, no more, and never spoke of our former meeting. He asked me to his house several times, but I always refused, and so never had a chance to see what kind of wife Sone's Miss Kinko had made.) Of my classmates, some were brilliant, some very definitely not. I kept very much to myself so that I could concentrate on my work ('Kikuchi the Silent' and 'Hermit Kikuchi' were my two English nicknames) and did so well in the tests at the end of the year that I was given a scholarship for the second year.

VIII.2

What with the formation of the great coalition of opposition groups, the ceremonial promulgation of the Constitution, and the breakdown of the attempt at treaty revision, the three years preceding the opening of the Diet in 1890 were a spectacular period. In literary history, too, they made their mark: public interest in the arts revived, scores of talented young writers appeared, and printing and publishing flourished as never before. Yet I shall hurry past this period with hardly a glance, for I have so little of interest to record in my own story. I was busy, of course, but only mentally, that's to say; not with much that's worth spoiling paper for.

Every one of my schools so far had been a privately-run institution with its own special aims and atmosphere. It wasn't long before I discovered how wide a gap separated someone like myself with this kind of background from the majority of students at the University, who had come up through the state schools; and time only strengthened this impression. Just as an erupting volcano spews out the biggest rocks first, so in the history of a school, or of a nation, for that matter, the most heroic spirits are brought to birth in the tonic air of its time of founding or reconstruction: young gentlemen brought up in comfort catch cold too easily. The University was past its first youth, when students throve on pickled radishes and mad dormitory meetings, and swore to turn the country upside down by the sheer power of learning; it had come by now to years of discretion, no longer brisk but merely cosy, an incubator for bureaucrats, money-makers and docile scholars—so it seemed to me. A fount of learning, yes: but the waters were far from invigorating. Most of my fellow-students looked on study only as a short cut to worldly success, currying favour with professors, and busily making 'contacts' among the wealthy and powerful, while running up debts with all manner of extravagant pastimes. With such undergraduates, and a deal of unsavory intrigue among the professors, the place was more like a 'factory for the mass-production of time-serving bureaucrats', as one brave journalist had angrily called it, than a school for true patriots and public men. How disappointed I was! The day of the truly great teacher, whose influence moulds a whole generation, may be past, but I could find neither friend nor teacher of any kind worth the name. So long as I stayed a member of the University, I decided, I would swallow the mental food it offered, but refuse to breathe its atmosphere; if I was too insignificant to influence others, at least I could make sure I wasn't influenced myself.

So, like Po Yi,[10] 'not looking on an evil face, not listening to an evil sound,' never touching saké, never calling on the professors in their homes except on business (Kan Sensei I did visit sometimes, for the stimulus of hearing him discourse on history); on Sundays going quietly to church, Bible in hand, or walking in Ueno wood, or further afield; never throwing away the smallest pencil-stub, using salvaged waste-paper for my notes (and toilet-paper, even. Not wanting to sponge on Mother, I had accepted the scholarship of four yen a month—repayable—which the University had offered me. With this, plus what I earned by translating for the *Meiji Review*, and small research jobs Kan Sensei found for me, I could just get by); taking refuge in the library in vacation time whenever my fellow-lodgers grew too boisterous or their chatter too offensive; strolling down to Shinobazu Pond occasionally to lie under the maple-trees and think—so month by month I kept stubbornly to my straight and narrow way, till to my classmates I was 'Snob', 'Boor' and 'Miser' as well as Kikuchi the Silent and Kikuchi the Hermit.

VIII.3

I didn't pay much attention, though, to my classmates' opinions. Solitude implies loneliness, but also freedom; there are times when friends are a nuisance and unpopularity a blessing. To dislike others is deadly poison for the heart, but to be disliked hurts no more (if one's conscience is clear) than a scratch on the skin. 'A travelling companion makes the journey bearable'—true, but if no companion presents himself there's nothing for it but to walk alone.

Fortunately I kept my health: if anything I was even stronger than before, as if the end result of my illness had been complete physical renewal. A dullard like me would have to live long if he was ever going to achieve anything (what a waste when your genius falls before his time, the

10. See note 10, p. 117.

prize within his reach!) so I took great pains to keep fit. Hermit Kikuchi surprised his friends by his diligence at every kind of outdoor sport—baseball, boat-racing and the rest; at every University athletics meet he won the six hundred yards (sixth nickname—Longshanks Kikuchi), and in the swimming championships in the summer of 1890, with the skill he had learnt at Seizan Sensei's and kept up ever since, swam zig-zag thirteen times across the River Sumida (seventh nickname—Merman Kikuchi). With health and hope, no coach to ride in but books in plenty to read, the ancients for my friends (pompous though it sounds), and the freedom to wander among the inexhaustible treasures of literature, beside which all the wealth of India is as nothing, I was truly happy.

And busy too. For besides my regular school classes, reading sessions in the library, the translating and occasional reviewing (under a pen-name) I did for the *Meiji Review*, and the collecting of material to send to Komai Sensei, who was using his time in America to write a History of Japan in English, I had started work on an interest of my own—the study of Japanese feudalism under the Tokugawa Shogunate. Since coming to Tokyo I could never look up at the walls of the Shogunal, now the Imperial, castle, or walk in the grounds of Kaneiji Temple among trees that still showed bullet-wounds from the fighting of 1868, or feel under my hand, as I passed, the great stones of the Shogunate's watchtowers; or see, still left in the very centre of the city, the mansions of the feudal princes; or read in the papers of the death of some 'Japanese Robin Hood' or other greybeard survival from Edo days; or stumble, while strolling on the University campus, over a broken tile engraved with a plum-blossom crest[11]—without visualizing the whole spectrum of our feudal past.

All such sights and sounds fascinated me, merging with half-remembered bedtime stories Mother and Father had told me long since, and with tales from the old-fashioned picture-books that were my first reading. On my way home from Komai Sensei's one autumn evening, I had just passed some workmen busily demolishing a row of old samurai houses—vivid reminders of our history!—near the top of Kudan Hill, when through the gently settling haze a sunset bugle rang out from the barracks of the Imperial Guards Division in the Castle grounds. I stood by the obelisk commemorating those who died in the pre-Restoration battles. Three crows swept croaking past me, their shadows darkening for a fraction of a second the still waters of Ushigafuchi moat, in the direction of the distant Nicolai Cathedral. Simultaneously there flashed through my mind the lines

> Watching the last light fade
> Beyond the hushed, smokeless plain
> I ponder our country's ancient past

11. Emblem of the Maeda family. In pre-Meiji times Lord Maeda of Kaga was the richest daiayo (feudal lord) in Japan. Tokyo University occupies the site of the former Maeda estate in Tokyo, the only surviving relic of which is the 'Red Gate' (v. note 12, p. 251).

—and in that instant I decided. Truly the phases of history are as fleeting as the shadow of a bird's wing. A mere twenty years since the Restoration, and already the Shogunate was shrouded in the mists of time. How little of that era would my children know, and their children's children after them? Now, when memories were still fresh and old men still alive who knew the period at first hand; when records and monuments still abounded; when we stood just far enough removed to discern the objective truth: surely this was the time to trace its outline firm and clear on the historian's canvas? I would attempt the task myself, not as history proper, but in the form of a novel (I was reading Scott's historical novels just then), a living picture of feudal Japan. Let others list the facts, elucidate dates and places, and classify minute particulars: my concern would be to reveal what lies behind such history—the true face, the true spirit of our feudal period; my book, a successor to the great Rai's[12] *Chronicles*. True, at the age when I first conceived this upstart dream, Rai had already finished the first draft of his immortal work. He was a genius, I a plodder. Yet, perhaps, if I took my time—lived to a hundred or thereabouts . . .

Such were my fancies as one by one the lamps gleamed out above me on Kudan Hill that evening.

VIII.4

Not forgetting, in the midst of all these preoccupations, to seek spiritual refreshment in the Scriptures, each Sunday I either attended church or went out into the country to walk and meditate. Most of my comrades laughed at me. It was preposterous nowadays, they said, particularly for a student at the country's leading university, to indulge in anything so out-of-date as religion. But for my part, it was not merely that I had found in Christianity a rock upon which I myself could take a stand. How *could* one neglect religion, I came increasingly to feel, when everywhere beneath the surface of the vast expanse of the literature and philosophy of England one could see the never-resting current of religious thought, that had inspired so many of her grandest achievements? 'Knowledge without faith leads a man only into pride or despair.' If the truth of religious intuition may sometimes appear commonplace—

> So clear is the water of the lake
> Surely, doubts the mind,
> It must be shallow?

—the profundities of the scholar, as often as not, may only mystify. For myself, I was determined to keep this one thread in my hand as I wandered in the labyrinths of thought.

12. See note 13, p. 186.

In which resolve I found an unexpected ally—Mother. So often do things obstinately refuse to happen when we strive to bring them about, only to happen of themselves when we have forgotten or given up hope. Time is an easy-going workman, but at least his memory never fails. Coming now, when ever since the failure of my first attempt at proselytizing I had not spoken to her of religion, Mother's letter announcing her acceptance of Christianity was a surprise indeed. For some time now she had had trouble with her eyes, no doubt because she often stayed up late sewing, and had grown so bored with not being able to read for herself that she started asking anybody who called to read to her—books, papers, magazines, anything. I sent her several of the latest novels, but she soon tired of them. Anything new, it seemed, was welcome.

As it happened, she had a visit just then from O-Fuyu, who was to have married my friend Michitaro. (Aunt Noda had written me earlier that summer that she was looking for a woman teacher of English for her little school. Cousin Suzue had just finished the general course at her High School, but wanted to stay on for another two years of advanced English and then go abroad; a country teacher's job was far beneath her now, for all her mother tried to persuade her. When by chance I noticed O-Fuyu's name in the list of mission-school graduates in the *Christian Weekly*, I wrote at once to the Reverend Shizu in Matsuyama to ask him to put her in touch with Aunt Noda; and sure enough, at the end of August O-Fuyu took up her duties as English teacher in Aunt Noda's school. It was my recollection of the wonderful courage and good sense she had shown at the time of the tragedy on Mount Hiei that had led me to recommend her to Aunt, who soon wrote to thank me for having found her such an exceptionally good teacher.)

O-Fuyu offered to read to her, and suggested the Bible, since she seemed to have heard everything else in the house. So the little Bible I had sent her when I was baptized was produced from the closet where it had long been shut away, and Mother heard for the first time the strange, compelling language of the gospel. How moved she may have been on that first day I don't know, but from then on she had the Bible read to her every day, till by the time she had finished the New Testament her heart was softened; her eyes too improved miraculously, as if to match her new spiritual insight. She was ashamed, she wrote—apologizing openly to her own son—to remember how lightly she had rejected all that I had so earnestly pleaded in favour of the new religion, when her years should have taught her more humility. More zealous a convert now than her son, she soon prevailed on Aunt Noda to accept the gospel; and towards the end of that year both of them were baptized. From then on she would speak in every letter of the comfort it brought her to think that however far away *she* might be, there was One who would care for me always; and pleaded with me again and again not to let my faith grow dim from too much study.

VIII.5

Closely tangled though the threads of joy and sorrow invariably are in the pattern of our mortal lives, I was shocked almost beyond belief by the report that reached me, only two days after the good news of Mother's baptism, of the sudden death in England of my beloved teacher, Komai Sensei.

Since I saw him last at Yokohama in January of the previous year, Komai Sensei had spent six months on the west coast of America and more than a year in the eastern states, studying, lecturing, and compiling his English-language *History of Japan*. With the date for the opening of the first Diet approaching, however, he had decided to come home, and planned to return to Japan via Europe in time for the general election in July. It was only two months since he had left New York for England. From his letters, the articles and reports he sent to the *Meiji Review*, and references to him in the American papers, he seemed to be in perfect health, and constantly deepening his knowledge of the West. With a man like this for my teacher and friend, I couldn't help thinking, I would have to look about me if I weren't still to be laughed at for a provincial know-nothing after three years of university. What stories he would bring home from his travels, for our delight and instruction! How his character, his knowledge, his eloquence would dazzle the first parliament in our country's history! I was so impatient for his return. And now—had the poisonous fog and smoke and cold of London killed him? Barely past thirty, such a single-minded, passionate idealist, and with so much still to achieve, focus of the hopes of so many friends and younger men; snuffed out at the other end of the world.

I was stunned, beyond weeping. The very next day, by the diabolic irony of fate, a postcard arrived from London—from Sensei. (Such was the shock of seeing his handwriting, I thought for a moment he must have written to correct the report of his death.) It was dated mid-November. The English winter looked like being severe, he wrote, so as soon as he had finished what he had to do in London, he would be leaving for the Continent, probably early in December. He was well, and would I give his greetings to Ando (the editor of the *Meiji Review*). That was all. He must have fallen ill before he could leave England. The pity of it, that he should die while this card was circling the world, till at long last it delivered, as if nothing had happened, these few lifeless words!

About six weeks after the fateful telegram a box containing Sensei's hair reached Mr Ando from the secretary of our Legation in London, together with a letter giving details of Sensei's illness—acute pneumonia—and death. Japanese friends had taken turns to watch at his bedside. Even in delirium he had spoken often of the Diet: made speeches, even, to imagined crowds; at other times he would call the name of his elder brother far away at home in Susaki, in Tosa Province. When the end was obviously near, he had raised himself suddenly on the pillows and cried out, 'Diet—Keep faith!' before sinking into a last coma. The English doctor had been astonished at his courage: the English friends he had made during his short stay in the country had without exception praised him as a 'charming, cultured gentleman.' So much we learned from the secretary's letter.

A few days later, with Sensei's brother, who had come up from Tosa (a typical countryman, nothing whatever like Sensei) and a number of other friends, we laid the hair to rest in Yanaka Cemetery. How moving it was to see so many exiles, victims like Sensei of the Security Ordinance, risk going back to Tokyo specially for the funeral! On my way home that day I called on Asai (do you remember, from among my comrades of the New School, clever Asai, the small youth with the large voice? He had entered the University's College of Law this year, after coming up through the First National High School. We had renewed our friendship after a chance meeting one day in a dormitory. Quite a sophisticated young Tokyoite he was by now, having come to the capital a good while before me; but give this veneer the slightest scratch, and there was the old Asai still, impish as ever) and I talked with him of our New School days under Sensei's reign. Back in my lodgings, I lay for many hours unable to sleep, till I could bear it no longer and went out to walk in the little garden. The night was frosty; I shivered in the chill wind.

VIII.6

A wild goose broke the stillness with a harsh cry as it skimmed over the rooftops. I looked up. It was an awe-inspiring sky. From every corner innumerable stars, massed as if in readiness to fall, poured down their fierce cold light: such a sky as I had watched through the cryptomerias on Mount Hiei four years before. But no, this sky was even loftier, brighter; each star in the whole vast canopy shone with an incredible intensity, more piercing to me than needles of ice. For a long while I stood staring upwards, with feelings too deep for tears.

> There is
> One great Society alone on earth:
> The noble Living and the Dead.

says a western poet, and truly so. The souls of great men do not die, but live on through the ages to inspire all who obey their silent call to reject the commonplace, the mediocre. How insignificant are the distances of time and space! And what are differences of race or creed but lines drawn on an ocean, where they can leave no trace? Were they stars, those glittering lights, or the spirits of all those, past numbering, who since the beginning of the world had lived nobly in the flesh and entered by death's gate into infinite life, looking down from heaven upon our nether world? Komai Sensei, my beloved teacher, Michitaro my friend, were surely not dead, as the world claimed, but alive, brilliantly alive, in that shining, heavenly world! Which lights were theirs? Men are born, men die: Man marches onward unceasingly. Whither? To what end? My two guides dead, I must walk alone at last. Alone? *Alone?* Never! Hidden though they were, I could hear the tread of multitudes all about me, my companions on the way. Forward then, to the limit of my strength, not for myself only, but for their sake too who had fallen after setting my feet on the way; no time to waste in girlish tears. Forward, however bitter the road! That last appeal of Komai Sensei's, to 'keep faith': might it not—must it not—have been intended for me, as well as for others more exalted?

All these feelings I poured into an article, 'Komai Sensei, the Beloved Teacher', written by lamplight the moment I got back to my room that night. The piece appeared in the next issue of the *Meiji Review*, and was later included in Kyoshi Aoyama's *Life of Tetsurei Sato* under the title 'Tetsurei as Educator'. I look forward to compiling a more detailed *Life* myself some day, to repay a tiny fraction of the debt I owe Sensei.

No more tears, I had promised myself; but this was another promise I wasn't able to keep. When I called on Mr Ando on business some weeks after the funeral he handed me a little western book, bound in white sheepskin, with gilt lettering; it had come with Sensei's effects from London a few days before, he said, and was marked with my name. It was a copy of Milton's Poems. My lip quivered in spite of myself when I opened the book and saw, inscribed with a western pen on the flyleaf, the simple words

> For Kikuchi
> A small gift
> from
> Tetsu

in the hand I knew so well! He must have meant it for a Christmas present, and been taken ill before he could post it. With tears and inexpressible gratitude I received my dead teacher's gift. I have it still—its pages are well thumbed now from years of reading, and their gilt edges faded, but three layers of wrapping have kept the sheepskin cover as white as snow. The *Poems of Milton* and Michitaro's photograph are the two most precious objects in my study. More than anyone else in my life, except my mother, Komai Sensei and Michitaro have been my inspiration—he through whose inner calm and strength of character the light of Christianity shone, and he whose life was the perfect image of passionate yet uncorrupted patriotism. Whenever I find myself despairing at the corruption of the world, at the impossibility of ever attaining ideals that recede with every step we advance, the faces of my teacher and my friend rise before me to revive and encourage me. Even if there were no other evidence, such moments as these convince me that men's spirits cannot die.

VIII.7

Gradually the bitter north wind that had blown our hair about our heads at Komai Sensei's funeral grew less harsh. As the smiling plum-blossom gave way to the drowsy green of the willows and pale pink buds formed on the cherry-trees of Kaneiji and Sumida, great crowds of country folk gathered in the capital to see the Exhibition of New Industry.

When Professor Kan left in January to take up an appointment as professor at the Second National High School in Sendai I had to find someone to replace him as my second guarantor. I turned to Mr Nakajima—Uncle Noda's brother-in-law, and Cousin Suzue's uncle. The present head of the family (Mr Nakajima senior had retired and given up all family responsibilities) was a lieutenant-commander in the navy, and away at sea most of the time; his wife Kaneko was a pleasant, easy-going person, as was his father, who spent all his time chanting Noh texts—with the result that Mrs Nakajima senior was the real power in the household. Mrs Senko Nakajima was fifty-six. When her feet were giving her more trouble than usual she would bark at her husband, who had a Court decoration and a fine dignified set of whiskers, as if he were an impudent seven-year old; and good-natured old man though he was, if he ever scribbled in his diary a list of 'Things Truly to be Feared'[13], it must have run like this:

1. Globe-fish.[14]
2. Faces of bill-collectors on the last day of the year.
3. Wives.

(though in his case *taikun*[15] would have been a more appropriate description of the good lady than *saikun*[16], for as befitted a sister of Uncle Noda she was a massive, foursquare woman, with a presence quite as commanding as any Tokugawa Shogun). At the first sign of one of her moods he would shut himself up in his room and wait (you could hear him almost panting with fright) till all was clear. As for his mild daughter-in-law, a chameleon was nothing to her: she was turning red and white all day long, like a fire under a blacksmith's bellows. The only one who took no notice of the elder Mrs Nakajima's outbursts was Cousin Suzue, relaxed and cheerful as ever, and little Fujio, the small grandson of the family.

But it was not without reason that Uncle Noda used to speak of 'that

---

13. In the manner, perhaps, of Sei Shonagon, the tenth century poetess and diarist, who included in her *Pillow-Book* similar lists under such titles as Awkward Things, Things That Make One's Heart Beat Faster, Things That Give One a Hot Feeling.
14. Poisonous unless cooked in a special way.
15. i.e. 'ruler', 'prince' (cf. English 'tycoon'). 16. 'wife'.

marvellous sister of mine'. Among her qualities were courage and a sheer solidity of character rare in a woman, together with the charity of a Lu Lien and the dependability of a Chi Pu.[17] Such was her love for students, she would pawn her husband's best clothes to help a boy in difficulties, and empty her purse (or her daughter-in-law's, if she herself had nothing) to give any student caller a meal. Quite a character, in fact. Among the younger generation she was especially popular, and I myself often enjoyed her hospitality.

One day at the Nakajimas' house Suzue told me she had heard from O-Toshi that her father would be coming up to Tokyo soon to see the Exhibition. Mother had never been to Tokyo; here was a chance to show her the city at an exciting time, and what better travelling companion for her than old Mr Matsumura. I wrote at once urging her to come. Her reply came by return. She longed to come, she wrote, and had the money for the trip put away; but there was work that had to be finished before the silkworm breeding season, and anyway she didn't feel she could come without Suzue's mother, who was too busy with her school to be able to get away just now. So it would have to be later, unfortunately. She added, though, that she thought I would be having an 'unexpected visitor' soon, from whom I would hear all her news.

An unexpected visitor—who could he be? Five or six days later, still not having solved the mystery, I was putting on my cap after breakfast with the idea of going to Ueno—it was the first Sunday of the Exhibition—when the maid came to say there was someone to see me. Downstairs in the little reception-room a huge man in a black morning coat stood beaming. It was Shingo.

'Shingo! What a surprise!'

He looked me up and down with his tiny eyes as thin as threads, his huge nostrils twitching incessantly (the infallible sign in Shingo—in case the reader has forgotten—of the most intense delight).

'That's right. Got here only yesterday, Shingo did—made sure you'd be surprised, ha-ha-ha! There ain't nothing could please Shingo more 'n meeting you like this —', and he choked with laughter. I couldn't help laughing too.

'So you're the "unexpected visitor" Mother wrote me about!'

'Ah, your Mother now—I seed her again this year, after eight years... It were the year of the Dog you showed me round Kobe, weren't it, young Shin—young gentleman. That makes it four years since *we* met. This year's a lucky one, ain't it? So you took Shingo's advice and got to University. Your Mother'd cry for joy, if she'd a chance to see the grand young man her son's growed up into!'

---

17. Two Chinese worthies of the third century B.C., famous for the qualities mentioned. Lu was always willing to help others without thought of reward, while Chi Pu's faithfulness is remembered in the proverb, 'Better Chi Pu's word than a hundred pounds of gold.'

We both fell silent for a while in the sheer excitement of meeting after so long.

'And you're here on business, like the last time?'

'That's right. But this'll make you happy, Shin-boy: Shingo's no mine-owner's agent any more. Got a little bit of a mine all his own now, he has!'

A couple of years before, at the time of the unrest over conditions in the Kyushu mines, Shingo had been dismissed for having 'sympathized' with the miners. With his very modest savings he had bought up for next to nothing a little mine in Fukuoka Prefecture that had been closed as a bad investment, and started to work it with some of the 'refugee' miners from the Takashima collieries. Results were better than he had expected. The wholesalers he had dealt with before trusted him, he was lucky enough to be able to acquire two other nearby mines working the same seams; till by now—well, it wasn't much so far, he told me, but in north Kyushu anyway you'd find they knew who you meant when you talked of Shingo Nakamura. 'Shingo's only started; no more. He's got one stone laid, good and proper, Shin, young master, that's why he goes back to Tsumagome after all these years to see your Mother, and then steps up this way to get a sight of Shin-boy, as well as do a bit o' business and look around the big city and the Exhibition and all.'

'Have you seen it yet, the Exhibition?'

'What are you talking of, Shin-boy? Wouldn't I come to see you first, young master?'

'Why don't we go now then—together?'

We left my lodgings to walk to Tatsuoka-cho, Shingo turning every now and then to stare at me and murmur, 'A fine young man he's growed into!'

'It's you that's the fine one! Western clothes suit you, Shingo.'

His shoulders squirming uncomfortably. Shingo wiped the sweat off his forehead with a handkerchief the size of a sheet of newspaper, and tried to loosen his collar.

'Suit me, do they? That's what the wife said —'

'The wife?'

'And I never told you—ha-ha-ha! What a blunderer Shingo is, ain't he? Shingo's fixed up with a wife at last. Used to think a man had to be single to make money, he did, and now he's got wife and money both, ha-ha!' She was an orphan, a samurai's daughter of some education who had suffered much since her parents' death. As to her looks, 'like marries like', according to Shingo, but 'ah, her character!' he went on, 'North Kyushu wives are cold and cunning, they say, but mine's from down south. She's a warm one, she is' (He himself, of course, was from the north.) She spoke and wrote beautifully, was skilled with the abacus, and could manage everything on her own, from keeping Shingo's accounts to dealing with the wholesalers. This being Shingo's first visit to the capital, she had insisted he must wear western clothes. He had hurriedly ordered an outfit from Fukuoka, and set out for Tokyo the moment it was ready. Thus instructed as to their history, I looked again at Shingo's clothes. With a red line showing where his huge boar's neck bulged above the chafing collar, and the two bottom buttons of his waistcoat tugging at their threads, his breath came in jerks with each step, as if his lungs hadn't room to expand. Oddest of all were his feet—in two-toed Japanese socks and wooden clogs.

'What's happened to your shoes?'

'Ah, them shoes now!' He had bought an outsize pair at the best shoe-shop in Fukuoka. Even so, they weren't quite big enough, being ready-made, but he'd get used to them in time, his wife had said, and 'anyway, in the west it showed you belonged to the upper classes if you walked with your heels sticking out above your shoes.' Thus encouraged, Shingo had worn the shoes on the journey in spite of the pain they gave him. By the time he got to Tokyo, though, the skin was peeling off his heels; he couldn't even take a bath. So he'd doctored them with some sticking-plaster at the inn the previous night, and come out today in the strange mixture he was wearing now, occidental above, oriental below. A fearsome character his wife must be, I thought, if this was her doing, but Shingo wouldn't hear a word against her. 'A good wife is what a man needs most, Shin, young master, wait a while now, Shingo'll find *you* one too!'

VIII.8

Shingo's vast bulk, his odd get-up, and most of all his voice booming out the details of his domestic felicity, attracted stares all the way, to my embarrassment, though not to his. At the end of Ikenohata Street we joined the crowd filing into Ueno Park like a procession of ants.

Ueno in early April: the cherry-blossoms in all their glory. For this first Sunday of the Exhibition night-showers had washed the sky to a clear pale blue; the sun was warm already, the shade of cryptomerias inviting. Caught in a mass of thousands upon thousands of spring revellers, all pushing their way towards the Park, the women with perfumed kimonos and gay ornaments stuck in their hair, we drifted forward in a haze of dust and sweaty breath and jostling faces, themselves as red as any cherry-blossom. I shouted encouragement to Shingo—even he was beginning to look over-awed by the crowds—and together we struggled slowly up the steps of the Park entrance.

'Ah, but it's a big place right enough!' Shingo stopped at the top of Cherry Hill to look back at the city below, but not for long. I had to show him everything, with explanations: the monument to the last Shogun's loyal retainers, who would not accept their lord's surrender and held out in Kaneiji Temple till 1869; the cherry-tree about which little Aki wrote her famous poem,[18] with its blossoms reflected magically in the dark green well-water, and the rest—but Shingo was breathing so heavily and mopping his forehead in such obvious discomfort that I gave up playing the guide and took him to Mortar Hill, away from the crowds. What joy when the cool air of the woods struck our melting faces! Inhaling the scent of the trees with a positive snort of delight, Shingo strolled under the great firs and cryptomerias, stopping now and then to measure the width of a trunk, or tap it lovingly, as one strokes a favourite child.

'Fine trees, young master—must be government timber, eh?'

But it was time to visit the Exhibition. We made our way down, and had nearly reached the open ground around Shinobazu Pond when suddenly through the trees I noticed a sealskin cap and a pale-blue parasol, coming down by another path only a few yards away. That cap, surely, I knew . . . A couple of seconds later I was standing in front of Seima's father.

'Mr Matsumura!' I took off my school cap and bowed. He looked puzzled, but only for a moment, and slowly took off the sealskin cap I had recognized.

'Well—Mr Shinzaburo! A long time since we met, indeed,' he said—or rather that was all I heard, in my wonder at the vision revealed by the quiet folding of the blue parasol—a vision of smiling eyes . . .

I doubted my sight. *Could* this vision be O-Toshi—or was it not rather the spirit of the cherry-blossom? Four years we had lived in the same city and never once met (though once I had seen her, you may remember, on my newspaper round soon after I came to Tokyo). Blessings on you, years, months and days, who had made O-Toshi so beautiful! When I first saw her, she was a winsome little miss of eight, the second time, a charming girl of fourteen; and now, at nearly eighteen—how can I find words to describe her? Cherry-blossoms, of Ueno, can you still boast of your beauty?

My legs shook, my body trembled, my head spun; my eyes stared in front of me, but saw nothing. The battle was already lost. In the language of the Spring and Autumn Annals: in the spring of the twenty-third year of the Emperor Meiji's reign, in the King's fourth month, O-Toshi Matsumura slew Shintaro Kikuchi.

VIII.9

When at last I recovered from the shock, Shingo, tired of waiting for an introduction, was talking on his own to Mr Matsumura. Hurriedly I got

18. The poem, one of the most famous of countless *haiku* on the cherry-blossom, is as follows:

    Cherry-blossoms
    By the well-side
    Danger—a drunk!

(lit. 'The cherry by the well is in danger—there is drunkenness approaching'). A monument in Ueno Park marks the spot where Aki, the daughter of an Edo confectioner, composed this *haiku* at the age of 12.

out some incoherent sentence about this being my friend Shingo Nakamura from home.

'And when did you arrive in Tokyo, sir?' The voice—it was mine, apparently—shook most oddly.

'Three nights now I've slept here in the capital. We should have called on you before now; I've been too busy resting, I'm afraid! Mrs Matsumura and I see a lot of your mother at home. What's that—what's that?' (O-Toshi was whispering into his ear. How I envied that ear!)—of course, how forgetful of me: I should have thanked you for looking after Mrs Matsumura and this girl of ours on the boat. Most kind of you. You've grown so big, though, these last three or four years, I hardly recognize you.' Once again he looked me up and down. Behind him, two bright eyes shone like black stars . . . I looked away, blushing. If only I had known (I shouted inwardly), I'd have washed that morning six times over, put on a clean collar and cuffs, polished my shoes, even—but look at me now!

Had they seen the Exhibition, asked Shingo, still beaming with pleasure at this unexpected meeting with my friends.

'Not yet. We tried a while ago, but the crowds were so thick, we came up here for a rest first. You haven't been in yet either? What a pleasure to have company then—and perhaps Shinzaburo will show us round?'

How could I refuse, when I had just been praying I might be allowed to be her guide, and not to the Exhibition only, but to the future and all the joys of Paradise! Elbowing a way through the still dense crowds, I led our little party to the Exhibition building. We passed under the entrance, which was gaily hung with crossed purple banners inscribed with the names of the prefectures in white, and joined the stream of sightseers in its slow progress between the stands built up on both sides of the long hall like river banks—staring like everyone else at the mass of exhibits. But none of them could interest me, I was so furious at the way all the younger ones in the crowd, both men and women, turned to stare at O-Toshi. I watched their faces, wishing in an agony of jealousy I had a magic cloak and hat to throw over her so that she should be invisible to everyone but me, or an ointment to blind all eyes but ours.

At the Okinawa stand, Shingo had the attendant fix a 'Sold' tag to two rolls of patterned Ryukyu cloth (one for my mother, I gathered, and the other, no doubt, for the 'lady from the south' he was so proud of). Mr Matsumura bought a lunch basket woven from *akebi* vines, a product of Aomori Prefecture, 'to use on picnics at home.' O-Toshi, naturally enough, was attracted by the marvellous fabrics on the Kyoto stand (though she didn't spend much time on the gay Yuzen silks), most of all by a length of black velvet curtaining embroidered in silk with a moon, white-crested waves, and here and there a plover among reeds. With one hand clutching the purse in my pocket (contents: one yen and a few odd sen) I gazed wistfully at the price-tag—over 1,000 yen. It was some small comfort when we came to the Niigata Prefecture stand and Mr Matsumura bought his daughter some fine Echigo grass cloth (she insisted he buy two more rolls, for her mother and sister-in-law). I loved (and envied as much as I loved) the old man for loving his daughter as he did.

By the time we reached the Art Gallery, Mr Matsumura had had enough, and Shingo was yawning continually; but O-Toshi was stopping to look at every painting, so the 'guide' was forced to stay with her, leaving the others to walk on ahead. My heart was pounding.

'Do you—like oil-paintings?' I said hoarsely—I had to say something —half my voice getting no further than the back of my throat.

'They're interesting—but I don't think I really understand them.'

The cool, flowing purity of her voice!

VIII.10

O-Toshi stopped to admire a picture of a girl playing a Japanese harp. But to me she herself was a thousand times more beautiful than any painting ... so I would have told her if I had been as relaxed then as I am now—if I had not been so callow, and had had a bit of courage inside me instead of an inexplicable whirl of agitation, which smothered the gallant phrases before they could find a way out. As it was, I stepped back a pace or two, the better to admire the admirer of the painting. What gracefulness in her figure, as she leaned forward a little on her parasol, gay in striped kimono and straw-coloured sash (I was too dazed to notice details) to examine the picture more closely; how charming the glossy black coils of her hair, only needing to be unwound to turn into a mirror ready-made; the delightful flush of excitement in her cheeks, the cool depth of her eyes, the sweet little chin, the delicate neck set off so perfectly by the pale blue collar-band with its pattern of cherry-blossoms—pretty before, she was perfection now. How could less than four years have made her so beautiful, I wondered with a secret sigh.

'Kikuchi! Kikuchi!'

I jerked round, thunderstruck. Saito, a fellow-student with a venomous tongue, was standing just behind me, smiling.

'Nearly knocked you over, did I?' he sneered.

'I'm still standing. Alone, are you?'

'I brought a bunch along, but we got separated in the crowd. Oil-painting's a long way to go yet, don't you think, when people swarm round such trashy stuff as this? What about you, though—you seem to be as fascinated as anybody?'

'What d'you mean?'

'Don't blame you though; she's a beauty all right,' he said with a wink in the direction of O-Toshi, was was standing four or five yards away, looking at another picture.

'Hey—young master!' Shingo's voice boomed out, careless of the crowds—my chance to escape.

'Coming with us?' I asked, implying that he'd better not.

'I would—but not now you've got such company,' said Saito, smiling nastily.

Not finding a ready retort, I threw him a curt goodbye and went over to join the others in front of a painting of Heita[19] fighting the snake. He was still grinning at us, I noticed, but when we moved on a moment later to the 'Dragon-headed Goddess Kannon', to my intense relief there was no sign of him any more. I turned to contemplate the Kannon painting. Not with any aesthetic emotion, I'm afraid. I was thinking how much more sublime the effect would be if the picture was of O-Toshi instead of the Goddess. . . .

We hurried through the rest of the Exhibition, missing a great deal, but even so it was well past midday when we came out. The crowds were bigger than ever; merry-makers yawned under blossoms that had lost their freshness and hung limp in the afternoon sun. I too was strangely lightheaded, though not with wine. At Shingo's suggestion all four of us went to the Matsubara Restaurant to celebrate our unexpected meeting with a meal. I could hardly manage a single one of the exotic dishes set before us. Tokyo cooking? fair but short on salt, pronounced Shingo, happily clearing bowl after bowl of unsalted Tokyo delicacies. Mr Matsumura declared himself disappointed with the rice, O-Toshi had smiles for us all, and I drank endless cups of tea.

Years later I laughed over Dickens' description of how David Copperfield, when he was in love, 'lived principally on Dora and coffee.' But did not I myself, on that day, dine at the Matsubara on no more than 'O-Toshi and tea'? True it is that love 'weighs heavily upon the stomach' . . .[20]

VIII.11

We parted outside the Matsubara, Shingo to return to his inn, the Matsumuras to take a rickshaw to their relatives' house in Kanda, and I to walk home to my lodging with O-Toshi's 'Thank you' lingering in my ears, and my head working on a new formula, Shintaro minus O-Toshi = 0. Two days later I showed Mr Matsumura and Shingo over the University, and the following week invited the Matsumuras, their relatives, the Ishikawas (whose only son, I was greatly relieved to hear, was still a very small boy; the father, by the way, was an army doctor) Cousin Suzue and the Nakajimas (the old gentleman couldn't tear himself away from his Noh chanting, but his wife came all right—Suzue's aunt: you can guess how the talk

19. Hero of two *joruri* (puppet dramas), and also of a Kabuki play.
20. The reference is to a well-known passage in the fourteenth-century book *Tsurezuregusa* (see note 4, p. 328) where the same phrase is used with less literal implication: 'I have let my pen run on aimlessly, because it weighs heavily on a man's stomach if he does not say the things he feels.' (*Tsurezuregusa*, 19.)

flowed when I introduced her for the first time to Shingo and the Matsumuras) and, of course, Shingo, to the regatta on the River Sumida. Alas, a wretched cold that was going around just then chose stupidly to attack O-Toshi instead of me. Collapse of all my joy—but Mr Matsumura and Shingo were thrilled with the races, and the prospect of describing them back home.

Shingo stayed in Tokyo ten days altogether. Luckily his visit coincided with the spring vacation, so I was free to show him the city. I took him to meet my guarantor, Mr Nakagawa (a formidable character who had raised himself from messenger-boy to millionaire. I hadn't had a great deal to do with him—the pride of poverty!—but Shingo asked to see him, so I took him along. As one might expect with a man of Mr Nakagawa's experience of the world, he saw Shingo's qualities at once, and was not too busy to talk to an ungainly countryman who brought nothing with him but an introductory note from an insignificant student, and give him useful advice, apparently, on the running of his business. For all of which, said Shingo, absurdly, he had *me* to thank) and a couple of well-known politicians, friends of the editor of the *Meiji Review*. For some reason, though, the politicians didn't make anything like such an impression on him as Nakagawa. 'Names—names is nothing!' he muttered, with evident disgust. Probably they had been cold with him on account of his huge uncouth figure and country accent. Not that one can blame them altogether, when even Confucius once had to confess he had misjudged a virtuous man merely because he didn't look the part.[21]

Shingo wished he could have stayed the year out and seen the opening of the Diet. He counted out my age on his fingers. 'A long time yet till you'll be thirty, young master,' he said with a sigh. 'But Shingo'll be so rich by then, he'll not let you spend a penny of your own when you stand for Parliament!' The day before he was due to leave for home, we talked for hours at his inn in Bakuro Street. He described all manner of trials he had been through: the struggle it had been to get started, his difficulties as an employer; but most startling of all was the news he had heard, on his visit to Tsumagome, of the fate of my Uncle Kengo. Truly 'the flowering of evil is but for a season.' All that wealth of Uncle Kengo's—after Father's death he was said to have been the richest man in the valley—had shrunk to nearly nothing. His perverse infatuation for his mistress, in defiance of his family and everybody else, was the start of it all: the risky deals he specialized in began to go wrong, one loss bred another so fast that the villagers were muttering 'the devil himself must be striking him down, for all his brains and cunning'; he was robbed by his mistress, who had tied up with some crook from Osaka or Tokyo; and just when the crash was round the corner, his elder daughter (who loathed the husband they had found for her and adopted as the family heir) disappeared with a schoolteacher

21. See note 7, p. 114.

and nearly all the money there was left, leaving behind her six-month-old baby. Her mother was sick with anxiety by now, and before long Uncle himself fell seriously ill.

For nearly three months his screamings and groanings terrified the neighbours, till the disease had worn him out, but even then the attacks would come on suddenly just as he was dozing off, so that he got no proper rest. He kept waving a skinny hand above the bedclothes, as if to ward off a blow. 'Kentaro —' (my father) 'Kentaro's holding me down—I can't breathe!' he gasped, cold sweat pouring off his forehead, when they asked him what the matter was. Sometimes they would hear him confessing his crimes, frantically pleading for forgiveness—to an empty room. Eventually his spirit broke altogether. Terrified to be left alone, he wouldn't let Yoshi out of the room; and so, with her hand in his (more truly, it was she who held *his* hand), in agony to the last, he died. On the day of the funeral it rained so fiercely that the grave was completely flooded, filling up as quickly as they emptied it: not one of the few mourners but had paled at the sight of the coffin floating restlessly on the muddied water.

'Who'd 've known they were father and daughter, those two?' went on Shingo. Poor Yoshi! Still barely twenty, and now the sole prop of a tottering house, the strain she must have been under, all those months of nursing a dying father and comforting a mother half-frantic, and herself mothering her sister's baby: struggling to keep alive a slender thread of hope for the future of their branch of the Kikuchi. After her father's death they had shut up most of the house. Yoshi was wearing herself to a shadow with work and worry; but even so her mother, a semi-invalid now, never gave her a kind word, whimpering incessantly of how she missed her other daughter, the one who'd disappeared, even threatening to go in search of her herself, till Yoshi, nearly beside herself, was praying daily to all the Buddhas and Shinto gods and pleading with everyone she met, Shingo included, to help in finding the runaway.

The fear the villagers had once felt of Uncle's family, as of some vengeful god, had given way in time to hatred, and the hatred, at last, to utter contempt, but Yoshi was different. Gradually, in spite of themselves they started calling on her with some little gift of vegetables from their fields, to show their sympathy. Even Shingo, who had listened unmoved, except for satisfaction that retribution had come so soon, to the story as they told it to him, had found himself so near to tears when he saw Yoshi washing clothes at a well in their little yard, her sister's baby on her back, that he had gone in to talk with her, though he had never intended to do anything of the kind. She knew we would have done what we could, she told him, if things had been as they should between the two branches of the family, but as it was, her aunt and Shintaro (she had wept as she spoke of us) must look on all their side as devils, past all saving.

'She's a fine girl, young master; though how a man like him can have a daughter like her, there's a mystery for you. Now if only she had the learning of that Matsumura girl, not to say the looks too, she'd make as fine a wife as any man could wish!' Shingo sighed.

VIII.12

Four weeks after Shingo left for home, green leaves had replaced the cherry-blossoms, and with the departure of the crowds a strange air of desolation settled over Ueno Park, like the aftermath of a typhoon.

And over my heart. Why? I killed myself, very painfully—that's why. If that's not quite clear—well, I gouged my heart out, the better to scrape off a certain image engraved thereon.

I determined never to think of the Matsumuras, of O-Toshi, again. Never.

But why? On whose objection? Because O-Toshi had found out, and would have nothing to do with me? But no one knew, least of all O-Toshi; or so I thought. No, it was my own decision, and no one else's—to kill myself.

Ever since that day at the Exhibition, Shintaro Kikuchi had ceased to exist in this world. His spirit guarded in its prison by a cruel and much-loved gaoler named O-Toshi; only his dead flesh walked in the land of the living. Kikuchi the free, the independent, the self-reliant—quietly murdered by a gleam from O-Toshi's bright eyes, and his body made her slave.

I concentrated all my love upon my one and only Mother. Who was O-Toshi anyway, to descend on me so abruptly in Ueno Park and steal that great love?

O-Toshi's smiling face appeared on every page of the text-book on aesthetics I was studying. When I was translating foreign articles, my wandering brush would scribble 'Matsumura', 'O-Toshi', in the margin: the characters of her name flashed like lightning between the newspaper and my reading eyes. On Sundays I would walk the streets near her relatives' house (where she often visited) or gaze at the school that was her home in term-time; when her father left Tokyo I missed a whole morning's lectures to see him off at Shinbashi Station, ostensibly to ask him to take a present to Mother. I paid a special visit to the Nakajimas' in the hope of at least *hearing* something of O-Toshi, but lost the courage even to get her name out in front of Cousin Suzue, who couldn't make out what had come over me, and said so. I wrote a hundred O-Toshi poems in a single night, drew execrable portraits of her in pencil, caught my breath at every yellow sash on the other side of the street, shivered at the sight of any hairdo remotely resembling hers, stood petrified whenever a blue parasol showed on the horizon, shaved off the beard I hadn't grown, scrubbed my face till the skin was near to peeling—in short, turned utterly insane. Who drove me mad? Miss Matsumura's was the crime: none to be punished but she.

I had read of love in novels, seen love-scenes on the stage—and had laughed at my own friends' antics when they were smitten. Now 'the rice-bowl passed to me'. Little Kikuchi, all five feet three of him, lay languishing in love's prison. If O-Toshi had but beckoned, I would have jumped the pit of hell to go to her. Fortunately, however, or unfortunately, neither she nor I had much time to spare from our studies; and even when we were both free there were very few opportunities to meet. I was far too shy and timid anyway (this was my first love, don't forget) to tell her openly I loved her. When very occasionally we did happen to meet, I was tongue-tied, or managed at the most an incoherent greeting, but parting was worse: I would walk home in despair, cursing myself for a coward and a weakling and a fool, for how could she ever respond if I never told her? And so home to my lodgings, with a dousing of well-water for Kikuchi's feverish head, and a pen to jab his trembling knees and startle him out of his dreams and folly.

VIII.13

While I was in this state a strange thing happened. I had to go to Ishikawa-jima Prison one day (to see the editor of the *Meiji Review*, who had been gaoled for 'insulting a government official') and there, to my astonishment, I met Sone—*Warder* Sone! I couldn't believe it: he looked away, confused. It was four years, no less, since I had witnessed—so unexpectedly, that summer at Okayama, when I was trying my youthful hand at evangelism—the painful end of Sone's love-affair, and from the day I waved goodbye at Tadotsu in Sanuki Province after taking him to stay with his relatives, I had heard nothing of him. True, every time I came across Assistant Professor Kumagae I couldn't help recalling his old rival and wondering how he was faring: yet all the time he was here in Tokyo—'distant as a thousand *li*, close as a single foot,' as the saying goes—and doing *this*!

It was all we could do just then to exchange a brief word or two of greeting, both of us were so taken aback by the suddenness of the meeting; but later, when I called on him at his lodging in Tsukiji, he told me his story, and a pitiful one it was.

Not long after the break with Kinko his mother had died, leaving him an orphan. The double shock, grief on the one hand, and disappointment and frustration on the other, turned him against his native place, where both blows had fallen; selling what little property they had possessed, he drifted to the capital. Originally he had aimed high—science degree, graduate school, study abroad, a life devoted to 'probing the secrets in Creation's store'—but the loneliness, the hurt and lack of hope, broke him: soon he hadn't a farthing left. No mitigating circumstances can sway the verdict of the Supreme Judge: as a man sows, so *must* he reap. For months Sone tramped the city streets . . . and so at last to this.

Yet with his education, his English, the science that came so easily to him—surely there was something better than that he could do, I asked him. He shook his head. In a world overrun with bragging, shameless upstarts he wanted only to hide. Reputation, career, meant nothing to him any more. He had come here with the idea of spending the rest of his life caring for the unfortunates whom the world called 'criminals', but he had found the same world inside the walls as out: the power of money not a fraction less, the pride of rank as arrogant, the selfish and sordid as universal. At first he had had extravagant notions of reform, dreams of one day becoming Chief Warder or even Governor, and managing the place *his* way: those too had long since soured, and now he kept his eyes and ears shut, content, if he could keep the job, to live life out as a common gaoler. He spoke too of Kinko, though I had avoided mentioning her. One of his reasons for coming to Tokyo, it seemed, had been the idea of revenging himself somehow on her husband. Once he had stood for a while outside their door. Once on the Ginza she had passed him in a rickshaw with her baby boy; as he stared at her, still as a stone, she had glanced down at him, smiling, bowed, and passed out of sight. (Sone bit his lip to stop the tears.) For a time he brooded over a plan to kill them both, and then himself. But the longing for revenge had cooled, and the whole affair seemed now to have faded to a dream.

'I'm beaten, Kikuchi. A man who's been crushed as I have doesn't have the strength to resist, even when he's trampled on. I've no hope any more. Just keeping alive till life goes out—that's enough,' he said with a tired sigh, like a sick man in the last stage of a fatal illness.

Indeed, if Sone was left to himself he wouldn't last long, that was certain. Wasn't there somewhere he could go, something he could do that would bring him back to life? I thought and thought—and suddenly remembered: hadn't Shingo said he was looking for a man to do his paperwork for him and lend the engineer a hand when he needed help? That would be better than the prison, surely. There would be Shingo's laugh, for one thing, like a bugle-call sounding the charge—that would rouse him out of his gloom, if nothing else would.

I wrote to Shingo at once. By the end of September I had talked Sone into making the move, and sent him off to Kyushu.

VIII.14

The Sone affair moved me deeply. When I saw him off at Shinbashi Station he looked so listless and shadow-thin, it was obvious the wound of four years still had not healed. Inwardly I cursed love for a vicious maniac.

My eyes opened wide. The maniac had *me* in his grip, too. Truly, one cannot be too careful in this world. While I was dreaming idly of making Miss O-Toshi my own, she had quietly taken me captive, all the five feet and more of my manly dignity; and without intending it, either. Now that

I came to think of it, my behaviour of late hadn't been very impressive. What had happened to that 'manly independence' I had been so proud of? I was bound hand and foot, with O-Toshi holding the rope's end, though doubtless she didn't know it. My school work had been falling off too: I was reading little, looking up less, behind in everything. Frugal Kikuchi, who till not long back had grudged every penny of unnecessary expense, and saved every farthing he could possibly spare, found to his disgust when he looked through his diary that he was spending far more than he earned—on soap, toothpaste, haircuts, collars, cuffs, new shoes, handkerchiefs, and a quantity of other such vanities.

Since he met us at the Exhibition, Saito must have been broadcasting the story, no doubt with additions of his own, for even my glazed eyes couldn't help noticing the amusement in every look my fellow-students gave me. One day when I was quietly reading a voice just behind me burst out with 'Who knows the short way to make a man a gentleman?' 'Find a Venus for a sweetheart!' came the prompt answer from Saito, to an explosion of laughter. That didn't worry me much, but other taunts struck closer home. 'How come Kikuchi's so smart and smooth these days? Pretty powerful baptism *he* must have gone through!' In a word, when I should have been devoting every minute of these most precious months to study, I was living in a dream. In a world that will trip a man up though he keep his eyes open as wide as saucers, here was I charging ahead with eyes shut tight—perhaps with the loss of all my hopes only a step away. And all for the sake of the slender figure of a girl. Was she worth it?

Perhaps—so my heart said; or perhaps not. Who can tell with a woman? And what guide less sure than a boy's infatuated eyes? Kinko had been an angel in heaven to Sone—till she betrayed him. Even I, an outsider, had been deceived. How much greater the risk now, when I myself was involved? 'Love is folly, and marriage a lottery!' Suppose this pronouncement of Dr Johnson was merely the angry outbrust of a man saddled with a wife he couldn't stand: Sone's example was warning enough of how pitifully a man can sacrifice himself to a girl who is utterly undeserving of his love. Truly Woman is a mystery, and love a great danger. With so long a journey still before me over moor and mountain, and life as quick to fade as the autumn sun, were the flowers of the plain to hold me back, however beautiful?

Never! I must forget O-Toshi, I decided. The bitter pain of giving up even a one-sided love: the desolation, the emptiness, the chill in the heart, as of a hearth with a dead fire! Yet love, the vicious fellow, is not to be killed so easily, trample on him how you will. Slowly the dead ashes flickered into new life, recalling from the dark a smiling face . . . For antidote, I summoned up another image, of Cousin Yoshi, as Shingo had described her. Poor Cousin! If the story of Uncle Kengo's miserable end made one shudder, who would not weep for Yoshi in her tragedy? While worthless stones are found in plenty among the gems of the city, so expensively wrought and polished, precious jewels abound among the pebbles of our country uplands. Ten full years it was, though it seemed only yesterday, since Yoshi had said good-bye to Mother and me at the little teahouse that morning when we left Tsumagome, and given me as her farewell present—struggling with her tears—the little box painted with vines. Ten years, and I had never once written. How she had suffered, and how admirably she had borne her trouble! It was girls like her that made the best wives, even if they hadn't much claim to beauty or education.

So I heaped praises on my cousin—like a conscientious second wife listing the virtues of her predecessor's daughter.

VIII.15

With Sone gone, and O-Toshi given up (?) I plunged back with frantic energy into my studies. Give it the smallest chance, and my undisciplined heart would be liable at once to attacks of loneliness and memories, so I set my brain to work and work and work, with hardly a second to relax. When what should confront me one morning but a letter—a letter, after long, long silence, from Seima Matsumura in Sapporo. He had written, he said, three years ago, when he had heard from his sister (sister! I shouted; the word had me so dizzy with joy, I had to read the next sentence five times before it made sense) that I was at Kansei College, but the letter had been returned marked 'Gone away'. Eventually news had reached him of my entering Tokyo University, and he'd been meaning to write, if he hadn't been so busy, etc., etc. Then just recently his father had written from Tokyo about how we had met in the capital and how kind I had been. He himself was hoping to graduate this June, and would probably be coming down to Tokyo soon after.

Why this new temptation, I couldn't help thinking, just when I was struggling to forget the name Matsumura. Still, whatever awkwardness I might feel where his sister was concerned shouldn't make me shy with *him*, I told myself, and replied straightaway. Then came the end-of-year exams, which nearly drove all thought of the family out of my mind. Not long after they were out of the way, however, a visiting card was brought to my room. I ran out, to find a young man in a summer kimono and old undersash, standing in the doorway smiling.

'Kikuchi! Sorry we've been out of touch for so long —' How mature the voice sounded, so different from former days! He was taller and broader too, and wore a thin moustache under his nose. There was a fresh tint to his cheeks, borrowed, no doubt, from the apple-orchards of Sapporo. But in the simple warmth of those smiling lips and eyes (a touch of the Hokkaido bear about them, too!) I saw unchanged the friend I had said goodbye to eight years before at Uncle Noda's gate. One glance at a friend's face after a long separation usually gives a pretty accurate indication of how life has treated him in the interval, and of whether you are likely to stay friends or drift apart; and if I wasn't mistaken, I recognized in Mr Matsumura, Bachelor of Agriculture, my old Kyushu comrade Seima. His years of study up in the plains of Hokkaido, close to nature and in a college where Professor Clark's[22] influence still lingered, had given him a freshness of complexion and straightforwardness of manner one rarely meets with in Tokyo students.

'My fault as much as yours, Seima. On your way home, are you?'

'Yes—came down on the train last night. Term's over here, I suppose?'

'The exams have just finished. Are you going to stay in Tokyo for a while?'

'Me? I'm hoping to start graduate work here in Tokyo in September. I'll be going home before then, but not just yet; our relatives here, the Ishikawas, are going down the coast for a few days, for the sea-bathing —'

'Sea-bathing? Very stylish! Where are they going?'

'Somewhere near Enoshima.'

'Come to think of it, *my* relatives were saying something about spending a few days at Oiso.' I remembered hearing Aunt Nakajima speak of taking Suzue and her little grandson to the seaside for a holiday.

'The Nakajimas, you mean? So I heard; but the bathing's nothing special at Oiso, and it's too crowded and noisy—according to the Ishikawas, anyway. The last I heard was that we'd probably all be going together, your people and mine, to this village near Enoshima; I've forgotten the name, though. You'll be coming too, won't you, or are you going home?'

'I'm not going home, no.'

'Then come and join us! Nothing to keep you in Tokyo, is there?'

'No; but —' Suppose she was going too—my beloved enemy, my good-and-evil angel? Seima pressed the invitation: we'd hardly begun to talk, and he was leaving Tokyo next day, but down at Enoshima—we should all be friends, there'd be no need of constraint (oh yes there would!); I *must* come, he insisted again as he left.

Certainly I longed to have more time with Seima; but for fear of one who would be with him (for I took it she was going too, though I hadn't the courage to ask), and also because I was busy helping with the preparation of the *Meiji Review*'s Summer Supplement, I sent only non-committal replies to the reminders Seima began to shoot off at me like arrows from Kugenuma, the seaside village where the party were staying. One day, however, Aunt Nakajima herself wrote, practically ordering me to come.

22. William Smith Clark (1826–1886), an American of forceful personality and evangelical Christian faith, who taught chemistry for some years at Sapporo Agricultural College. Many of his students became prominent in Japanese life, the best known being Dr Inazo Nitobe, who was Under-secretary of the League of Nations from 1919 to 1926.

The scenery was magnificent, the fish cheap and marvellously fresh, there were no noisy crowds; I was to join them at once for a rest—besides which, there was a matter she particularly wanted to discuss with me.

A 'matter to discuss'—this sounded rather alarming, but I couldn't possibly refuse this time, so as soon as they no longer needed me on the *Meiji Review* Supplement, I threw a couple of summer kimonos, a towel, and a book or two into my ancient suitcase and caught a southbound train.

Part IX

It was five o'clock in the afternoon when I reached Fujisawa Station. Stepping down off the train among a sweaty crowd of pilgrims bound for Enoshima Shrine, I saw instantly, with an uprush of excitement, three straw sunhats beyond the station fence, framing three expectant faces ... they had recognized me; six eyes smiled a welcome. It was Seima and his sister and Cousin Suzue.

Seima grabbed my case as I came through the barrier.

'An obstinate old solitary you are, not deigning to come till we'd asked you twenty times over!'

The girls took off their hats and bowed.

So there she was—after all the time I had spent wondering whether she'd be with them or not, and vainly telling myself I didn't care either way—lying in wait for me: my arch-enemy, the presiding spectre and bogey of my life. But where else in the world could you find such a charming spectre? With her face, of a purer white than snow at other times, burnt to a delicate olive by the sun and sea-wind, a hint of roses in her cheeks, a smile playing about sweet lips and cool, restful eyes, one hand deftly tucking away a few unruly strands of hair; as slender as any Spanish beauty as she stood there, hat in hand, in patterned white *yukata*[1] and crimson sash—to me this spectre was more sublimely beautiful, more awe-inspiring, than an angel direct from paradise. My firm resolve—to greet her, if we *did* meet, with a fierce, sour stare, the kind you use to silence a yammering child, and speak, if I had to, in words as hard as bullets—began to crumble. Hopelessly, I felt a smile spreading.

'Admit it—you've kept us waiting too long altogether.' Seima still wouldn't let me off.

'Sorry; I've been so busy.'

'You won, though, O-Toshi!' laughed Suzue.

I turned to ask her what she meant, when Seima saved me the trouble.

'You've let us down so many times, even when we got your postcard yesterday I was sure you wouldn't keep your promise—so sure, I said I wouldn't go to the station; but my sister would have it you were really coming this time. We were betting on it in the end, she for, I against.'

'Really?' I said with attempted coldness; but my heart was dancing. Once again a disobedient smile showed itself.

1. See n. 18, p.122.

To Seima's 'Well, now he's come—a dose of energy to start us walking!' we set off, he and I in front and the two girls following, laughingly holding up their *yukata* sleeves to protect themselves from the dust we raised. A little way past the level crossing Suzue suddenly remembered she had left her shopping at the teahouse near the station, and went back with O-Toshi to fetch it. Seima and I strolled on, talking, up the sandy track through fields of soya bean and mulberry and sweet potatoes.

'Must be hot in Tokyo.'

'I'll say. Different from here.'

'It's pleasant here all right, with the sea so close, and the fish, and the quiet—but lonely, too, with no one but the girls around.'

'Mrs Nakajima said in her letter how she enjoyed having you come over now and again.'

'She's a character, certainly. I spend a good deal of time with her. Not many women have as much sense.'

'It's no wonder, seeing she had my Uncle Noda for a brother.'

'Ah, Mr Noda—sad about him, wasn't it? Father was always singing his praises.'

'Poor Uncle—fate went against him.'

'Miss Suzue's not much like her father, is she?'

'Not in looks, but she has his temperament—warm-hearted, placid kind of a girl; never gets worked up over trifles, like most women.'

'She's so straightforward and pleasant. Doesn't waste her time on clothes, either. Nothing the least bit gaudy or affected about her, my sister says.'

'My sister'—I pricked up my ears at the word, and waited eagerly for more; but Seima was warming to *his* subject.

'Then she's so level-headed always. I was really impressed the other day, I can tell you —' The owner of the house where Mrs Nakajima and Suzue were staying had got into a quarrel with some young men in the village, Seima told me; there had been a scuffle, with dire threats on both sides, and the good man had come running home for his life. Suzue promptly hid him (Aunt Nakajima was out at the time), went out alone on the veranda to face the youths, who were on the point of breaking in, read them a lecture and sent them packing. Cool she certainly was, as befitted the daughter of a man who had snored contentedly in the middle of the enemy camp.

We had come about half a mile, and were resting in the shade of a mulberry tree, out of the evening sun, when Cousin Suzue and O-Toshi, each with a bundle of shopping, caught up with us. I grabbed the bundles and walked on unsteadily, one dangling from each hand, feeling as stiff and awkward as a puppet.

The sun had set when we entered the village, though the cicadas were chirruping busily still. After five or six hundred yards, at a stone memorial tower, the track divided into two.

'It's a bit out of your way, but won't you come and see the house where we're staying? We've the best water in Kugenuma!' At Seima's invitation we took the right-hand fork, and a couple of hundred yards from the tower turned through a gap in the tall hedge of bamboo, honeysuckle and camellia, to find ourselves in a farmyard. The farmhouse was a big one; they even kept silkworms in the loft, judging by the window in the roof. The farmer's eye for beauty showed in the little flowerbed in the corner of the yard, brilliant with orchids, bellflowers, lilies and touch-me-nots. Near a shed to the left of the house a few hens pecked at scattered grains of barley; to the right, the branches of a zelkova tree were draped with bathing costumes and towels hung out to dry. While I was greeting Mrs Ishikawa at the door, O-Toshi slipped inside to fetch us some of the 'best water in Kugenuma', flavoured with lemon-oil and sweetened with white sugar.

That water! Even now the very thought of it makes me shiver with delight. O-Toshi's drink distilled such fragrance, I was intoxicated. It's a question with me still whether I swallowed that glorious nectar or the nectar swallowed me.

IX.2

Mrs Nakajima, with Suzue, her grandson Fujio, a little boy of five, and O-Kichi, their housemaid, was staying at a pretty little farmhouse less than a quarter of a mile to the east of the Matsumuras' lodging. They gave me a six-mat room, facing east, all to myself, and I was glad to get to sleep that night. Next morning, after a night of dreams washed by the sound of waves and the gentle sighing of the pines along the seashore, I woke early, and went round to the back to wash—under a trellis draped with morning-glory and white-flowering kidney-bean—in the purest well-water imaginable, in whose depths the stars of dawn still bathed. A few minutes later I was gazing entranced at the Katase Hills as they slowly defined themselves against the morning sky, when a shout of 'Kikuchi—aren't you up yet?' sent me running round to the front. Seima was standing in the yard barefoot, *yukata* tucked up and a towel stuck in his sash.

'Aren't you coming for a swim?'

'Bit early, isn't it?'

'Early morning's the best time. Come on—no, leave your clogs! It's so fresh and cool at this time of day.'

Stopping only to give way to farmers out to make an early start in their fields, we ran down through the pinewoods to the beach, kicking aside the dewy tangle of convolvulus and reeds, and drenched before ever we touched the sea in the blue mist—a blue so delicate and ethereal, such must surely be the colour of dreams—that floated from branch to branch among the trees. The view from the beach took on an extraordinary beauty in the pure dawn air. The sun had not yet risen, and Enoshima Island lay sleeping at the edge of a pale grey expanse of sea; above the tops of the pine-trees lining the long sweep of the bay to our right, we could just make out, still hazy as if in a lingering dream, the outlines of Mount Fuji and the Hakone and Ashigara Hills.

Braving the cold, we plunged in for a swim. Soon the sun rose; we thrashed about like ducks playing on a golden sea. And then to rub the cold out of your shivering skin, and sit back at last with a contented sigh—*yukata* shaken free of sand and tossed over your shoulders, the salt water brushed like a shower of gold from your tousled, smarting head—to watch the passing sails: what pleasure can equal this?

'It's a pity, but it looks as if I'll have to go home right away,' said Seima suddenly as he wrung out his towel.

Abruptly the splendour faded from Mount Fuji and Enoshima and the sparkling sea. (Till then I had imagined the sun as the presiding spirit of that glorious morning, but now I knew: what was 'the sun' but another name for O-Toshi?)

'Why on earth? What's happened?'

'I got a letter from home last night, after you'd left. Not that there's anything special they need me for. They wrote several times last month, though, telling me to come; and I've put it off for so long, they're a bit upset now. I'm to leave on receipt of this letter, they say. I can't really see why, seeing they know I'm bound to go home anyway before the summer's out. Still, that's the way parents' minds work, I suppose.'

'They haven't seen S. Matsumura, B.A. yet—that'll make all the difference. But you can't leave *now*—not immediately I come!'

'Can't be helped, I'm afraid. Your punishment for keeping us waiting so long.'

'Not today, anyway. They can spare you for another week, surely. I'll write to them myself. No, you just *can't* disappear the moment you've got me down here.'

'I don't want to, I can tell you. My sister likes the place so much, too.'

'Then stay on another week. We'll see each other again in September, won't we?'

Making a seat for ourselves with a thwart from a boat that was lying beached close by, we settled down to talk. Seima planned to enter the new Agricultural College in Tokyo and take some of Dr Jansen's courses, he explained, in order to learn more of veterinary science before starting his own stock-farm; since he was the younger son and his parents not by any means old, the pressure on him wasn't so great, so that for a while at any rate he could decide things for himself. I told him something of my own hopes.

'You're the idealist, I'm the practical one. Not that I'm that good even at the practical side.' Seima sighed. 'I've no imagination, no taste, nothing of that sort—unlike my sister.' He was always so open, so sincere. I loved him for such candour—especially, of course, when he spoke admiringly of his sister.

By now the sun had climbed quite high, and reluctantly we got up to go. On the other side of the pinewood we met Suzue and O-Toshi, who had been looking for us. O-Toshi, in a crepe *yukata* of pale lilac with a red sash, and hempsoled sandals, carried a bunch of wild pinks, still glistening with the dew. A few stray curls of hair escaped from beneath her wide straw hat, which was tilted back a little on her forehead, to lie enchantingly about her shoulders. The instant she saw me she let down the skirt of her *yukata*, which she had hitched up for easier walking, and smilingly took off her hat. A single white ribbon kept her hair in check—how beautiful, how maddening, that hair!

'Thanks—for your hospitality last night' was the limit of my eloquence, however. I was ready to cry at the thought of their going home so soon.

Together we walked back, now in the shade of pine-trees, where dew still tinted the path, now in brilliant sunlight, till we came to the fork.

'You'll try to manage it the way I said, won't you, Seima?'

'I'll talk about it with O-Toshi. Goodbye for a while. He and his sister turned into the right-hand track.

'What did you mean "manage it the way I said"?' asked Suzue from behind me.

'They've got to go home.'

'What!' Suzue was flabbergasted. 'Just when you've got here? What's happened?'

I told her of the letter Seima had had from his father. 'I think I've persuaded him to stay on just a few days more anyway. You do your best with O-Toshi, will you?'

'I'll try. But I don't think she'll need much persuading.'

'Why not?' My heart, anticipating too eagerly the 'Because you came, of course!' that my ears longed to hear; but Suzue only murmured something vague.

Aunt Nakajima wasn't too surprised when we told her. 'It's only natural—they want to see their boy,' she said. She looked thoughtful, though. After breakfast she had Suzue go back to the Matsumuras for a while, as 'Minister Plenipotentiary' to plead for a five days' postponement of their departure, and sent Fujio out with the maid to play. Having thus cleared the house, she called me into her room.

IX.3

Aunt looked unusually serious and formal. I felt pretty nervous as I sat opposite her—as if I were about to lift the lid of some Pandora's box of fortune's secrets.

'It's about Suzue.'

'I see.' I swallowed. How solemn her expression was, and how exactly like her brother's, that day when he was so furious with me for refusing to marry Suzue and become his heir! I was a bit frightened, I must confess.

'She's of an age to marry now, as my sister keeps reminding me. I've been thinking about it a good deal, naturally.'

Whatever was she going to say? I waited, silent and tense—when the current swung round, as you might say: 'How would it be,' Aunt went on, 'if young Mr Seima married Suzue, and Aunt Noda adopted him, so that he would take Uncle's name and be the new head of the family?' He was a younger son, she had heard, which made it easier; she had seen for herself how steady and pleasant a young man he was; her sister, she knew, would be delighted at the idea. Would I find out from Seima—if I had no objection—what his reaction was? She asked in quiet, confidential tones, so different from her usual exuberant manner.

'If I had no objection'? Of course I was in favour, passionately so; if anyone was so wrong-headed as to object, we'd turn ourselves into an army—with Aunt Nakajima as the General and S. Kikuchi for her spearhead brigade—and crush him as easily as you crack an egg for cooking. As a matter of fact, I had been thinking quite a bit about Suzue, just as Aunt had. How could I help it, when she was the only daughter of a man to whom I owed so much, and we had been brought up together as brother and sister in Uncle's household, and still felt we were no less? I was absolutely sure that our relationship could never go beyond that of brother and sister. It happens often enough that a boy and a girl who have grown up together from childhood and know each's temperament inside out never fall in love, however marked out for marriage they seem to others to be; and so it was with Miss *Oyomei*[2] (for the uninitiated, I had better explain that you can write the great philosopher's name with the characters for 'easy-going niece', hence this code-name—of my mother's devising: she went in now and then for such faintly malicious witticisms—for Cousin Suzue) and Shintaro Kikuchi. For Miss Oyomei, or rather Cousin S, treated me as an elder brother, with whom she could talk without the least constraint; while I for my part could like her and laugh at her at one and the same time. But never anything more.

Another factor was that I was the sole support of the house of Kikuchi, and Suzue was expected, as the only surviving child of *her* family, to marry someone who would be willing to take the name of Noda; so that on that account too marriage between us was out of the question. Mother and Aunt Noda were as well aware of all this as we ourselves—as was everyone who was the least bit acquainted with the circumstances. But if marriage between us was out of the question, that didn't mean I wasn't concerned about Cousin Suzue's marriage. Having once refused to marry her myself,

2. The Japanese name for Wang Yang-ming (1472–1529), a Chinese philosopher whose teachings had a wide following in Tokugawa Japan. The Wang Yang-ming (or Oyomei) school emphasized the primacy of practical morality rather than the study of the ancient Confucian texts, and appealed especially to those who were impatient with the pedantry of the more traditional philosophies.

I felt I had a real duty (to my dead Uncle, to his widow, and to my dear 'younger sister' herself—though she punctured my vanity on occasion by playing the *older* sister: in fact she was born four months before me) to help in finding a suitable husband for her and a son-in-law and heir for Aunt Noda. No wonder I had been conscious of a queer awkwardness that morning, as if I myself were directly involved. So now I raised three (inward) cheers for Aunt Nakajima's initiative.

Judging by what he had said about her the previous day, Seima could hardly be averse to the idea, while her liking for him was obvious even to my half-blinded eyes; so it would very probably work out. And if it did, what good fortune for the Nodas! Seima's plan of stock-farming fitted in perfectly; if my dead Uncle could come back to life, I could see him making more of Seima than of his own daughter. A husband for Suzue, the perfect wife for Seima, peace of mind for Aunt and Uncle Nakajima, and who knows what satisfaction for Uncle Noda, asleep in his long grave beneath the oak in faraway Yamashita Village? Mother and I, too, could feel a small part, at least, of our debt to the Nodas repaid. And if they did marry, perhaps—no, I mustn't, I daren't say it!

Of course I approved, I told Aunt Nakajima, prophesying too that it wouldn't take long to arrange. I promised I would let Mother know at once if Seima's response was favourable, so that the two of us could help in any way possible. Aunt Nakajima's gravity dissolved in smiles.

Just as we finished, Suzue came back, her mission successful: they had agreed to stay another five days. So far, so good—Aunt Nakajima and I smiled at each other. Suzue had also brought me an invitation from Seima to go over and lunch with them that morning.

'Suzu-san! Am I to be left out?' laughed Aunt.

'You are, Aunt—but not to worry, there'll be another chance for you later, I gather. Today it's for Shintaro and me alone. They're hard at work already. Seima's gone to buy some fish and O-Toshi's busy peeling potatoes. You won't mind if I go and help her, Aunt?'

'Of course not. But I warn you, Shin-san, take along some flavouring and a box of stomach powder if you're going to eat Suzue's cooking!'

'Aunt, how can you! It's only boiled fish—even I can manage that.'

'Charred fish, you mean!' Thus Shintaro.

'Don't you enjoy yourselves, you two? All right, Shin-san, charred fish it shall be!' Laughing, Suzue set off again to the Matsumuras'.

IX.4

Seima himself called soon after, and I went back with him. Their eight-mat living-room had been swept spotless, and a table and a desk put together in the middle, with a graceful arrangement of pinks and bell-flowers in a glass as centre-piece, standing out vividly against the white table-cloth—O-Toshi's delicate taste, needless to say. Here we sat down, with Cousin Suzue and myself for guests, Mrs Ishikawa, with the Matsumuras, as hostess, and the maid to wait on us, though as she also had to mind Tsu-chan, Mrs Ishikawa's baby girl, Mrs Ishikawa and O-Toshi often left the table to serve in her place. The menu: sea-bream soup, sliced raw bonito, tinned salmon, and mashed cucumber, with a 'dessert', after the new fashion, of steamed new potatoes and Japanese pears in iced water. No sign, happily, of the charred fish Suzue had threatened me with. My only complaint was, I wished they had stuck a label on each dish to show which ones we owed to O-Toshi's sweet fingers. I couldn't ask, of course, so I had to sample everything, and praised everything I tasted. (True, I detected Suzue's hand in the sweet potatoes, they had such solid hearts; but this didn't prevent Seima, fresh from the wilds of Hokkaido and unused to such delicacies, from downing a bowlful.)

'It's a long time since we shared a meal, you and I.' Seima seemed ecstatically happy. And so was I. With such food and such a cook, I made up that day for my miserable performance at the Matsubara in Ueno Park, and ate and ate as if I were all stomach. How could I not, with O-Toshi to persuade me so charmingly?

Busier and busier our tongues grew with food and talk. Mrs Ishikawa, as you would expect of a lady Tokyo-born and bred, kept us laughing with a stream of stories—of the countryman who blundered into an eel-house, for instance, and demanded beefsteak. 'No beef, only eels here,' apologized the waitress. 'Then bring me eelsteak, and make sure it's off the best cow in town!' Or there was the Tokyoite who stopped at a country inn one evening in early summer and asked the maid for a *biwa* (loquat) after lunch. After a while the landlord put his head through the door and mumbled apologetically that 'they had no *biwa* (lute), but if one of them old Chinese guitars would do . . ?'[3] Mrs Ishikawa could have beaten our professional story-tellers at their own game. What explosions of laughter amongst us as she rambled on, till the last barriers of stiffness and formality were toppled!

3. More is involved here than the simple pun on the two meanings of the word *biwa*, or the inability of the country innkeeper to provide the dessert ordered by the sophisticated city-dweller. There is an implicit reference to the famous story of Ota and the *yamabuki*-girl. Ota (1432–1486), a distinguished soldier, engineer and poet, was out hunting in the country when a sudden storm led him to seek shelter in a peasant's cottage. The rain showing no sign of stopping, Ota asked the peasant's daughter if she could lend him a straw coat. Instead of replying, the girl went outside, broke off a sprig from the *yamabuki* (Kerria japonica) in front of the cottage, and handed it to Ota, explaining herself with an extemporized poem:

Nanae yae	Flowers abound
Hana wa sakedomo	On the *yamabuki* bush:
Yamabuki no	How melancholy the lot
Mino hitotsu dani	Of one too poor to own
Naki zo kanashiki	A single coat!

Ota was filled with shame that while the girl could respond to the beauty around her in such a poetic way in spite of her extreme poverty, he himself, the man of culture from the town, had been concerned merely to keep himself dry.

When the talk turns to food, it's a sure sign (among us Japanese) that the party is warming up. We ranged pretty wide over the subject, from Lien P'o's mammoth meal of rice and meat[4] to Bismarck's *omelette à 50 oeufs*, till I put forward the theory that a healthy, powerful mind in a healthy body is the exception rather than the rule. 'Patriotic indignation' wasn't the only product of an empty belly, or a sick one: many of the masterworks of literature, both ancient and modern, could be traced to some such origin—Carlyle's prose, for example, or the poetry of Tu Fu—and if a man could write well on a healthy stomach, like Macaulay and Po Chü-i, the inferiority of these two to Carlyle and Tu Fu only proved my point. Clearly therefore (I concluded manfully) the prime requisite for progress in literature was over-eating. (Usually in O-Toshi's presence I was as dumb as if my tongue were stuck with a lump of sour persimmon—what loosened it now I can't imagine, unless it was the salmon.)

At once Seima trotted out his favourite theme, the importance of meat-eating. According to him, the example of Europe and America showed that the great nations were the ones that ate most meat. The power and scale of Chinese literature, such as it was, was to be explained in the same way—and what a contrast with our own classics of the Heian period, the work of a people who fed on little else but rice-gruel and sardines! No, the vitality of a people depended on the vitality of its individual citizens, *their* vitality depended on their physical condition, and whether their physical condition was good or bad depended on how much meat they ate: so that in the end of the great Meiji campaign for 'a rich nation and a powerful army', for the spreading of enlightenment and modern civilization, meant simply 'eat more meat'—the inevitable conclusion being (conveniently for Seima!) that stock-farming was far more important than education, or religion, or working for a Diet and a party Cabinet. The only true patriots, the country's only hope, were the cattle-breeders. 'Just wait a while, and I'll be producing cattle and sheep and goats as good as any in America or Australia, and so many of them it won't be long till we get every family in the land eating three pounds of meat a day and thinking no more of it than they do of eating bean-curd now!'

Suzue listened admiringly, I noticed, to this effusion.

'Now you're going a bit too far. Meat's not that almighty!' I put in. 'The Scots "cultivate literature with oatmeal", they say; and there are any number of vegetarians in the West: from Tolstoy, to begin with —'

'Nonsense, that's only because they want a change from eating so much meat; like a drunk pouring himself a glass of water. And for the Japanese, who practically live on fish anyway, to preach vegetarianism—no, it's too much. My sister is keen on it, though.'

O-Toshi was peeling pears for us, her fingers moving with quick deft grace. She smiled, blushing a little.

'I'm a vegetarian!' I announced.

4. See note 21, p. 131.

'What! Who was it said 'meat' when Aunt asked you last night what you liked best? I don't think much of sudden conversions!' Suzue was paying me out for the charred fish. We all laughed—myself ruefully, O-Toshi out of uncomplicated happiness, I suppose, Seima and Mrs Ishikawa in hearty enjoyment of the joke. Even the hens beyond the veranda set up a sympathetic cackling. The meal ending thus happily, the girls went off to the kitchen. 'Come and see where I take my siesta!' Seima took me round to the back of the farmhouse.

IX.5

Outside, the fierce noonday sun shrunk our shadows to our feet, its heat reflected all around us from the burning sand. A fine white dust covered the fields of soy and sweet potato. Our eyes smarted from the brilliant light, and before we had walked a hundred paces we were bathed in sweat. But beyond the sandy fields, over the dunes that bordered them, a breeze blew cool among the green rustling shade of a pinewood. From the shadiest spot halfway up a little hill within the wood, Mount Fuji and the peaks of Hakone peeped through the trees, and below, white sails festooned Sagami Bay; we could see the caps of the sea-bathers, but hear none of their shouting. The wind combed gently through the branches, weaving restless patterns of light and deep green shade, and pouring such fragrance into the air around us that sleep in such a spot would surely have brought pine-scented dreams. Here even the chirruping of the cicadas sounded cool.

Seima slung the hammock he had brought with him between two sturdy trees.

'Take a seat! I come here every day after lunch and sleep for a while. Crabs wake me up with a bite on my toe sometimes, if I leave a foot dangling. Why don't we just sit and talk; I'm not sleepy today, are you?'

So we sat on the low-slung hammock and talked, while our toes traced letters in the sand among the shifting patterns of shade. Even students have plenty to talk about when they haven't seen each other for nearly eight years. Memories of Seizan Sensei's school, Seima's life in Tokyo and then in Sapporo, the long story of my own ups and downs, my admiration for Komai Sensei and Michitaro, and sorrow that Seima had never had a chance to meet them—so it went on, the shadows lengthening without our ever noticing, till we came to speak of Seima's family.

'You'll be starting a separate branch of the family, I suppose, rather than live with your parents?' I asked.

'Probably, though I haven't thought a lot about it yet. I'm not much interested in family honour and status and all that, as you know. So long as I can do the work I want, that's all that matters to me. My brother's dependable and hard-working, so Mother and Father have no worries, and I propose to go on studying for a while yet.'

'How would you feel about carrying on the Noda family?'

'How d'you mean?' Seima looked mystified.

'Have them adopt you as the head of the house.'

'You're joking!'

'Not a bit. Seriously, wouldn't you consider marrying Suzue and succeeding Uncle Noda, as it were?'

Seima stared at me. 'Why do you ask so suddenly?' he said after a while.

'I may have put the question suddenly, but a lot of thought went into it beforehand. I'm not joking, I promise you.'

Seima was silent again. 'No, I couldn't possibly. It would be presumptuous—'

'Don't be absurd, the presumption would be on our side! You know as well as I do all the Nodas have been through. There's only the mother and daughter now, and they've literally nothing in the way of property: only the name, that's all. Frankly, I feel we ought to apologize to you for asking. But won't you think it over, now you know how much we want you?'

Another silence. 'I'm only a student still, and shall be for some time.'

'No one's asking you to marry and raise a family all at once, only to say what you think of it as a plan for the future, something to look forward to. Of course, if you're not that fond of Suzue the question doesn't arise.'

Seima blushed. 'The whole thing's so sudden, I can't think.'

'You didn't get much warning—agreed; and now it looks as if I'm trying to squeeze an answer out of you here and now. But we wanted to have some idea of your reaction before you go home. As far as I'm concerned, it's hardly surprising I want to see you and Suzue married, is it, when you and I are such good friends already? Look out though, there's someone coming–' A white kimono flickered among the shadows further down the slope. It proved to be Mrs Ishikawa's maid, sent to tell us tea was waiting. She went straight back; we followed a moment later.

'I don't know what to say . . . give me a couple of days to think. I'll talk it over with my sister, too. My parents will have the last word, naturally.'

Back at the farmhouse, O-Toshi and Suzue were sitting on the veranda weaving baskets of straw, with brown-faced Fujio and the paler Tsu-chan looking on over their shoulders. Even in their weaving my biased eyes could pick out the difference in the two girls' characters: O-Toshi's basket was close-woven and taut, Suzue's big and loose, and with gaps here and there wide enough to let a loquat through. Seima would have a different interpretation, no doubt. When Suzue turned her comfortable face and smiled a welcome, he turned as pink as the plums laid out on the veranda to dry; and even while we drank tea and nibbled *katase*[5] buns (the local speciality)

---

5. Named from Katase, a village (now part of Fujisawa City) on the coast opposite Enoshima Island. It is well known in history as the place where the envoys sent by Kublai Khan in 1275 with a demand for tribute were beheaded and where Priest Nichiren (1222–1282), founder of the Nichiren sect of Buddhism, was miraculously saved from execution by the breaking of the headsman's sword.

he seemed to have lost the power of speech and turned all stiff and hard, as if he'd been starched from head to foot, or hidden whalebones in his socks and sleeves.

IX.6

Around dawn next day a storm blew up, and it was still pouring after lunch. I started out for the Matsumuras' (their maid had come to ask if they could borrow my copy of the *Meiji Review*) but thought better of it and turned back: it wouldn't do to disturb them if they were talking over my proposition, as they very probably would be. The afternoon dragged on. Aunt lay snoring; Fujio too had fallen asleep at last, clutching at her shrunken breast, after whining all the morning. So I felt wretchedly lonely. For want of any other way to pass the time I fished out a textbook on aesthetics I had brought with me. It was no use, though. For all the learned theorizing of Schopenhauer and Hartmann, a beautiful object delights, and whatever has once delighted him a man longs to see again. It's as simple as that. A hundred volumes of aesthetics are nothing to a single work of art. I tried some short stories in a couple of magazine supplements I'd packed right at the bottom of my case. But I couldn't get on with them either. Finally I threw them away and sat yawning under the thatched eaves, staring gloomily at the filaments of rain. In the next room Suzue (Aunt had stopped her going to the Matsumuras') was trying to play 'A song of ennui, not of beauty or of skill' on the concertina. The drowsy melody of the part beginning 'When I remember', tapped out time and time again by Suzue's unsure fingers, merged with the monotonous thud-thud from the shed, where the farmer's aged father was pounding straw, into a single limp, depressing rhythm. I yawned once more.

Why so bored and sad? Of course—I hadn't once seen her today, not once! Suddenly I remembered the promise I had made myself a month back, never to *think* of her again. Where's your pride, your shame, I began to tell myself—but there was more at stake than hurt pride: hadn't I *vowed* to give her up, solemnly and deliberately? What if I had, though? My heart couldn't help loving her still. Even if marriage did mean goodbye to dreams of the prestige of a career in officialdom, riding through life in the comfort and dignity of a lacquered rickshaw—what would that matter? If I *were* ever to marry, it had to be her.

Just as I was yawning again the musical torture from next door stopped, and Suzue slid open the door.

'Why haven't any of them been over today, d'you know?' she asked.

'They're angry with us. I quarrelled with Seima, so we're both sulking.'

'Liar.'

I hadn't the energy to tease her any more. Suzue stood by the door, twirling a fan.

'O-Toshi's grown into a charming young miss, hasn't she?'

My heart jumped. Danger—fire round the corner!

'She's doing very well at school, I gather. Painting, especially. She's bright, you know.'

'Really.'

'Don't you think so?'

'Do *you* think so?'

'You slippery eel! I'm asking you seriously, what do you think of her?'

'H'm—that she's a student, the sister of one Seima Matsumura—'

'Oh, stop it!' Suzue paused. 'Myself, I like her a lot.'

'Better marry her then.'

'If I were a man I certainly would.' She laughed.

Aunt turned over. 'Don't make such a noise .You'll wake Fujio!'

'How different a brother and sister can be,' went on Suzue, lowering her voice abruptly (it was a trick of her father's, the way she could switch in midstream from megaphone to whisper). 'Look at O-Toshi and Seima now—'

I changed the subject hastily. 'Suzue, you'll be graduating next April, won't you?'

'I hope so.'

'What will you do then? Study abroad?'

'Maybe.'

'Are you still thinking of staying single all your life, and founding a women's college, like you said once?'

This time she didn't answer.

'A woman unmarried is a woman incomplete, Suzue. The Bible says it's wrong for men and women to live alone, you know. Of course, if he or she has some great work to do in the world, it's different. One has to stay single then. But they're the exceptions: there isn't one such in ten thousand. "Good wives and wise mothers" are still what the world needs most. Good marriages, good families are the bricks we need to build a great country. A woman who has no time for her family is a disgrace. I've no use for the kind of feminism that lets a child go in rags and feeds a husband on burnt rice—'

'What am I supposed to do then?'

'Find the right man, run a home and raise a family—and then take on something outside, if you've still got the energy.'

'Running a home's so dull—'

'Don't be absurd; it's a woman's duty. Or if you really can't stand it, live in lodgings with your husband.'

'In lodgings—how awful!'

'All right, have a home of your own after all. Try it and see. You'll find it much more absorbing than you expect; it can be so enjoyable—'

'All right, grandfather!' Suzue laughed.

'Now supposing—just for argument's sake, mind you—that Seima—' (she reddened perceptibly)'—or any other young man for that matter, educated and with a good character and a bright career ahead of him—suppose someone like this comes along and says he'd like nothing better than to make a home with you, what'd you do then? Tell him to apply elsewhere, because you've no taste for housework?' Suzue blushed redder still. 'Turning down a man like that would be a disgrace you'd never live down. No, you'd *have* to take him, whether you wanted to or not.'

'Who ever heard of such a cruel go-between?' she said, laughing.

'It may seem a bit cruel, but a girl can miss the best chance of her life by imagining she can afford to wait till Prince Charming comes to carry her off one day in a rickshaw made of solid gold. She puts them off and puts them off, till one day she has to throw herself away, like the greengrocer in the *haiku*—remember? "Autumn already/Water-melons galore/A penny each!" Do you want to be dumped like overripe fruit? If I had my way I'd pass a law compelling women to marry by such and such an age: better still, I'd go round and lecture the choosy spinsters one by one—'

'Now you're turning grand*mother* as well!'

'I'm not joking, though; it's true.'

'Then a woman has no right to choose for herself?'

'How sure can you be that a young girl will choose sensibly, or a young man for that matter?' (Except, of course, in *my* case, I told myself.) 'Allowing young people nowadays to choose for themselves would be like asking someone who was colour-blind to buy a length of Yuzen silk.'

'But to give a girl no say at all in who she's to marry—no, it's too unfair.'

'That's where education comes in. I don't mean only school education, but "social" education as well. Young people don't choose right because they're not used to each other: boys haven't had enough experience of girls, or girls of boys, either. It'd be much better not to keep the sexes so separate. Bring in co-education up to Middle School, say, and give them lots of opportunities to mix at home, with their friends and relatives.' (Then there'd never be any time for housekeeping, she might have come back at me—which only went to show, would have been my answer, how great was the need to modernize our Japanese houses and way of living. But luckily she didn't notice the inconsistency.) 'Don't you agree?'

'With that much, yes. So off you go and get to know O-Toshi better!'

That stopped me dead. I wasn't expecting such a subtle stroke—not from Cousin Suzue!

Suddenly the room went dark. There was a roar of thunder, and another burst of rain: the signal for a truce in our small cousinly war.

As if to spite the rain we had had since dawn, this new storm called up reigiments of thunder and lightning for a desperate, pounding onslaught on the thatched roof; but at four o'clock precisely, as if by command, the sky lightened, and the great white ropes of rain shrank to silver threads. Too impatient to wait for it to stop altogether, I ran out barefoot. The last drops struck cool on my face; rainwater trickled under my feet, to be swallowed instantly in the soft sand. Beyond a dripping clump of bamboo, hens clucked happily.

I walked on without thinking, till I noticed suddenly I was nearly at the Matsumuras'. After a moment's thought I turned back, and took a roundabout way down to the beach. The rain had stopped by now. Inky thunderclouds still hung massed over Oshima Island to the south, but round towards Mount Fuji the sun was peering timidly through a slowly thinning fleece of cloud. The sea lay tired and still, grey under the clearing sky. Though Fuji itself was still hidden, the hills behind Oiso and Kozu and Odawara stood out sharply, as if new-rubbed with indigo. Enoshima Island seemed ready to detach itself and float away, the water stood so high around its wooded rim. A fisherman, stripped to his loincloth, was baling water out of his boat close to the water's edge; from the bow of a larger boat, drawn up nearer to where I was standing, rainwater dripped delicately, like tea from a bamboo whisk,[6] piercing tiny holes in the sand. I turned to face the rain-cooled breeze, and strolled on, round the big fishing-boat—to run straight into O-Toshi, carrying Tsu-chan pickaback.

'O-Toshi-san!' As usual, my heart began thudding away, O-Toshi being the accelerator. 'Isn't your brother with you?'

'He's resting.'

'Nothing the matter with him, is there?'

'No, nothing. It's just that last night we were up rather late talking—' She blushed.

Neither of us spoke for a moment. Tsu-chan, gay in white bonnet and pink smock, began bouncing up and down on O-Toshi's back.

'She's too heavy, surely. Let me take her! Come on, Tsu-chan—' I held out my arms, but she hid her face, laughing, on O-Toshi's neck.

'What are you afraid of, Tsu-chan?' O-Toshi smiled over her shoulder. I smiled too, fatuously, in a kind of trance. Suddenly it occurred to me I hadn't thanked her for the meal the evening before.

'A wonderful meal that was last night!' I said, scratching my head like a fool.

O-Toshi bowed. A shaft of silver broke aslant through the clouds, to set Enoshima and the sea around it smiling.

'Beautiful, isn't it?'

6. Such as is used to help dissolve powdered tea in the tea-ceremony.

'Wonderful!' Half-blinded by the sudden brilliance, O-Toshi gazed with me across the bay, her hair dancing in the gusty wind over her adorable forehead and cheeks.

'Your brother told you, I expect—?' I asked in a burst of determination; and as far as I was capable of judging in my state of exaltation, she said yes, he had.

'Is he angry?'

'Not at all' she smiled.

'What do *you* think of the idea?' I marvelled at my boldness.

'I could hardly—it's not for me to—' she faltered; but her delight showed through.

'Does your brother ag—'

'Mummy, Mummy!' Tsu-chan twisted round suddenly. Mrs Ishikawa was coming towards us in a big straw hat, smiling, with her hands outstretched. I liked Mrs Ishikawa: she was a pleasant, friendly woman, as well as being a relative of O-Toshi's; but at that particular moment, I must admit, she struck me as a singularly unnecessary phenomenon.

Next morning the Matsumuras, Mrs Ishikawa and Suzue and I went to Enoshima. One the way home, Seima glanced back at O-Toshi and Suzue, who had fallen some way behind. 'If my parents have no objection,' he half-whispered, red-faced, 'neither have I.'

It hadn't taken him long to decide.

IX.8

As soon as we got back I told Aunt Nakajima, who called Suzue at once to give her the message. No longer mystified by my hints of the day before, Suzue began to raise all sorts of objections, imagining it wasn't dignified, I suppose, to accept all at once, but Aunt silenced her with an abrupt 'Leave it to me, and don't talk such rubbish!' Which wasn't as harsh as it sounds, for anyone could see what Suzue's real feelings were. Anyway, on the principle of striking while the iron is hot, Aunt wrote off immediately to Mrs Noda, and I to Mother; and after supper I hurried out to post the letters in the box at Fujisawa Station.

It was dark when I left the station—too early yet for the dew, but I felt the breeze cooler on my cheek, and evening insects were humming busily among the roadside grasses and in the fields of soy and mulberry beyond. The moon would be up before long, to judge by the faint yellow glimmer on the hilltops beyond Katase. Drums and flutes sounded from a village ahead of me—the local Bon Dance,[7] perhaps, as today was July 15th by the old lunar calendar, which a few communities in this district still hold

---

7. Part of the Bon Festival, or Feast of Lanterns, when people visit their ancestors' tombs and invite their spirits to their homes.

to for their annual festivals, though most have gone over to the new. A mood of mingled gladness and vague melancholy enfolded me. The gladness was for Seima and Suzue, obviously, but the gloom I couldn't define, except as an emptiness, a chafing frustration: like having to view the cherry-blossom through a paper screen. I was in love—no doubt about that. Was my love returned, though? I went over every word she had spoken, every tiny gesture. Maybe it was only conceit on my part, but it did seem as though she didn't dislike me. But how could I be satisfied with seeming? Two more days, and she and her brother would be gone. Chance might not bring us together again for months, perhaps never ... if so, then all my joy till now was only a fading dream. I longed to act, somehow, but what *could* I do? Ask her openly if she liked me? Impossible, when already even to speak to her made me shiver with fright. Ask someone else to act as emissary? More terrifying still. If only there were two of me, I thought peevishly; a second self, detached and brazen ... But grumbling would serve no purpose. I gave my stick an angry swish, silencing for a second the chattering insects.

The stick gleamed as it fell. I turned. The full moon had risen: orange-tinted, it hung low over the hills like a paper-lantern. Slowly it climbed, whitening steadily till silver beams flowed everywhere among the soy and mulberry leaves, and the insects sang louder and louder, as though drunk with the light that bathed the rain-washed, dew-fresh air. I began reciting Shelley's poem to the moon, 'Art thou pale—' but it sounded so flat I cut it short in the middle with another furious whirl of my stick. What good was poetry or moonlight when my O-Toshi was leaving me the day after tomorrow—perhaps for ever? The sky might vaunt its clear calm air, the moon its rounded wholeness; but without O-Toshi my spirit could be neither calm nor whole.

So down the grassy country path I went, with a weary tap-tapping of my stick, to the cottages of Kugenuma Village, dark among its many trees. No one was at home, I found, not even Aunt Nakajima; the old grandpa, who was sipping saké and airing himself on the veranda in nothing but a smock (he had been left to look after the house, I gathered, while the farmer and his family enjoyed themselves at the Bon Dance) told me they had all gone to Mrs Ishikawa's. To the Matsumuras', in other words. I went off again to join them.

The moon had risen quite high by now, but all through the village only a pale gleam, no brighter than the glow of fireflies, filtered through the trees to the sandy ground. When I came to the Matsumuras' farmhouse, I found the papered sliding doors all round the house shut, and I couldn't hear a sound from inside, though a light shone through.

'Seima! Are you there, Seima?'

I heard someone getting up, and then a small cough ... a coil of hair, magnified in silhouette, but infinitely charming still, took shape against the paper panels. The door slid back at once, and there was O-Toshi, looking

(I thought, though I couldn't see very clearly, as she had the light at her back) rather over-wrought, as if she had been crying, even. More flustered than ever, I asked if Seima were in.

'He's gone out with the others—'

'For a walk, I suppose. But you—you don't look well!'

'It was nothing, only a little headache.' She straightened her hair.

'You were lying down, weren't you? Was it very bad?'

'No, I feel much better now. But do sit down—' O-Toshi offered me a rush cushion.

'Perhaps it was the heat?' I said stupidly, still standing on the veranda.

'Won't you sit down?'

'Thank you. Have they gone to the beach—your brother and the others?'

'I think so, but they'll be back any minute. Do sit down, though—', which at long last I did, very hesitantly. O-Toshi gave me a fan.

'But you should be lying down.'

'No, it's quite gone. I'll be glad if you'll stay and talk—' with a smile —'the farmer and his family have all gone to the Bon Dance, so I'm all alone.'

The ground was opening under me . . .

'You've been to Fujisawa?' O-Toshi broke the silence.

'Yes—to post—we wrote to tell them at home—'

'We must thank you', bowing her pretty head.

'On the contrary, it's we that should be grateful. Seima agreed so quickly. Aunt is quite thrilled, and so am I. But what do you suppose your parents' reaction will be?'

'They'll be very happy, I'm sure.'

'Will you help to persuade them? Seima was saying they'll agree at once if only *you* approve.'

She smiled, her head inclining demurely to one side, as if to disclaim any such influence.

Till then the moon had been peering through gaps in the tall hedge round the yard, no more than a collection of glow-worm-points of light. Abruptly, it seemed, it rose now above the bamboo and shone full-face among the zelkova branches; at the same time, a cool breath of wind rustled the leaves overhanging the veranda—and blew out the lamp behind O-Toshi. Moonlight streamed into the room.

IX.9

O-Toshi gave a little gasp of surprise, but quickly struck a match and tried two or three times to light the lamp; but the breeze had grown too strong. Finally she took it into the next room, drawing one of the partitions across as a shield. We sat down again, myself on the veranda, and O-Toshi four or five feet away in the eight-mat living-room, turned slightly away from me, gently waving her fan; while the moon, with no lamp now to challenge its liquid light, poured in to scatter the gloom. Shadows of the bamboo and zelkova in the yard bestrode the veranda and the room itself, till even our *yukata* were dyed with patterns of light and leaves. With the cold gleam on the *tatami* mats fading and brightening as the moon shone clear or obstructed, and the quivering of the trees' chiaroscuro on the veranda, I recalled the ancient poem 'Shifting shadows in a moon-filled night . . .'. The ethereal sweetness of O-Toshi's smiling face in the play of shadow and moonlight, the charm of her tiny lap beneath the moving fan, of her breast and hanging sleeves, of the leaf-shadows fading and reforming across her white *yukata*—was not such beauty too elusive, too fleeting-perfect, not to dissolve at the touch of outstretched arms?

I heard again the insects, chirping in the grass at the bottom of the hedge, and the sound of distant flutes and singing.

'How beautiful the moon is!'

'Isn't it wonderful!' O-Toshi sighed.

'I still can't quite believe it—being here like this with you and your brother, and feeling so at home. I stayed in your home once years ago—I don't suppose you remember, you were still quite small. I was fourteen then. Seima and I used to frighten you terribly sometimes when we played spooks. I'm afraid we were always up to tricks of one kind or another, though.'

'I remember very well. I've still got the pictures you painted for me.'

'Have you?' My heart was ready to burst. 'Hasn't the time gone quickly!'

'It has indeed. It must be four years already since you looked after Mother and Suzue-san and me on the boat to Kobe.'

'You'll be graduating next year, won't you?'

'I'm sure I shan't pass the exams.'

'Nonsense—Suzue says you're good at all school work—'

'Not true!'

'You paint too, she says.'

'Not true again.'

'And write poetry—'

'No, I'm very ignorant. I wish my brother would help. I tell him so sometimes, but he never has the patience.'

'I envy you both, having each other,' I said, and then, with an abruptness that surprised even myself, blurted out, 'You and Seima must come and see me!'—without a word as to time or place; but the invitation was stupid as well as vague, since I was living in the University dormitory now, and O-Toshi, as she very well knew, couldn't possibly visit me there. But she smiled faintly through the moonlight, as if such stupidity were not unwelcome. I sank deeper into dreams . . .

'You'll be going home with Seima in a day or so?'

O-Toshi didn't answer. I thought I heard a tiny sigh; but maybe it was only the zelkova leaves.

'I'll be so lost without Seima, I—I think I'll go straight back to Tokyo when you leave.'

'Seima wanted desperately to stay,' murmured O-Toshi with bent head.

If only I had been born a Westerner, a European! I would have gone down on my knees before her, taken her pretty hand and told her in so many words: 'My darling, my heart, could you ever dream, even, of sharing your life—of marrying such a vulgar pitiful object as Shintaro Kikuchi?' But as it was I might have been bound hand and foot: I could not advance an inch, still less retreat—only sigh . . .

O-Toshi sat staring at her fan. The zelkova branches swayed gently in the wind, their leaves transformed by the moonlight to a shower of glancing jewels.

IX.10

As a rule I don't have to search for words, but none would come that evening—or rather I was saturated, body and soul, with a power no clumsy human words could convey. A perfect opportunity to tell her of my love; but I could neither speak nor act . . . and at any moment the others would be back. *Now* was the moment—this very instant! Heart racing, but tongue adamant, I could have torn myself in two.

'Haven't I made you tired with talking?' I found myself saying, to my disgust—more nonsense.

'No.' O-Toshi didn't look up.

Silence again. The breeze was freshening, yet the air between us seemed so congealed and oppressive, I could hardly breathe. Surely my heart would crack if I did not speak!

A minute passed, or a hundred years. The wind caught something in O-Toshi's shadow: I saw white pages flapping.

'What book is that?'

'It's the magazine you lent us yesterday.'

'The *Meiji Review*? I'm afraid you must have found it terribly dull.'

'Oh, no—I've enjoyed it very much.'

'Did you read the story translated from the Russian?'

'Yes, it was fascinating.'

'How these Westerners can write! We've a long way to go before we can catch up with them. That same writer has written a whole collection of brilliant short stories.'

'What are they about mostly?'

'There are so many of them—'

'Tell me one, then.'

So I started.—A young Russian girl of eighteen, a nobleman's daughter, is living in a villa in the country. She is beautiful, clever and gentle—altogether charming ('exactly like you'; the words rose to my lips, but got no further!). Two men fall in love with her. One is a handsome middle-aged gentleman of rank and fortune, who brings her a present of costly flowers, worth I don't know how many score of roubles, on every visit. If she will but marry him, he promises her a lifelong honeymoon: he will take her to America, to Japan; escort her, decked with diamonds, to the great balls at the Winter Palace—bring her, everything, in short, that the world calls happiness. The other suitor is a mere student (exactly like me, though I could no more say it of myself than of her) and a commoner into the bargain, with neither money nor title, nor even looks, and no one to depend on for his future but himself. Only in his love for the nobleman's daughter is he strong, ready to challenge the whole world if need be; to go smiling through fire and water, or to die, even, if she but say the word. Yet he is so diffident and shy, he can find no way to tell her, and so remains ever silent, though he is dying of love—

I stopped suddenly—what was I saying!—then, after a pause, started again. But my story had tied itself in knots; I was past knowing whether I was talking of Shintaro Kikuchi or the penniless Russian of the tale. I stopped again, and this time couldn't go on.

Several seconds passed, till a faint sound of weeping broke the silence. O-Toshi's head was bent forward over the *tatami*. I couldn't see her face.

'What is it, O-Toshi-san?'

She looked up. Tears like pearls were streaming down her cheeks. Her lips moved, but I couldn't catch the words. She hid her face again.

By this time I was nearly demented. 'O-Toshi-san—O-Toshi-san!'

'I . . . I . . .' Tears smothered her voice.

'O-Toshi-san! Forgive me if I upset you—' No longer knowing what I was doing, I caressed her shoulder—when suddenly burning fingers caught at my hand: in an instant it was wet with tears. 'Forgive me—forgive me!' I repeated again and again like a madman.

'. . . . . . .'

'It was my fault—forgive me—'

'I'm sorry, Shintaro . . . I—I'm so—happy . . .'

The world faded as we stood alone on the bridge that links men to eternity—the Bridge of Dreams. The moon shone down, the wind blew, the insects made their summer music, but we neither saw nor heard.

How many seconds or hours or ages went by I can't tell, but when laughing voices the other side of the hedge—Seima and Mrs Ishikawa returning—woke me out of my trance, our hands were still tightly clasped, O-Toshi's and mine!

Part X

In the main my optimistic prophecy in the farmer's living-room at Kugenuma was justified. Seima Matsumura was adopted into my late Uncle's family, Cousin Suzue became Mrs Seima Noda—though the realization of Aunt Nakajima's project took a great deal more time and trouble than we had anticipated. '"A go-between wears out a thousand pairs of sandals" they say, but I never knew an engagement so difficult to arrange as this,' my mother said afterwards; it was she who did all the negotiating, and truly she had her work cut out to bring it to a successful end.

As soon as the Matsumuras had left Kugenuma for home, I came back to the dust and scorching heat of Tokyo. A laconic postcard from Seima announced their safe arrival in Kyushu, but I heard nothing whatever from him about his family's reaction to our proposal till he walked into my room some weeks later, explaining rather shamefacedly that he had been back in Tokyo four or five days already, and would have called earlier if he hadn't been so busy getting himself registered for his courses at the University. But from Mother's letters to me and Aunt Nakajima's reports of what *she* was hearing from Mrs Noda, I got a pretty clear picture. Mr Matsumura senior had been delighted from the start: 'for one so worthless as his son Seima to inherit the distinguished name of Noda was the greatest good fortune for the boy himself and an honour for his parents' etc., etc. Suzue's open, straightforward temperament ('so unaffected—no smell of facepowder about her—there's a great man's daughter for you! Too good for Seima altogether') appealed to him particularly. But Seima's brother Kinji (who had been adopted into the family, and had been its titular head since the old gentleman's retirement) began to raise objections. For his brother to change his name would 'lower' the family, and that it was his duty not to permit; and more than that, he could not, he insisted, allow Seima's share of the property to be made over to a family that was both penniless and landless, however distinguished the name of Noda might be.

That wasn't unreasonable, perhaps, but there were other obstacles. Mrs Matsumura had ideas of her own for Seima when he finished at graduate school in Tokyo. The bride she had in mind was O-Fuyu, apparently ('a clever, alert girl, though it's true her skin's a bit dark'). But O-Fuyu had kept very much to herself since Michitaro's death, and in any case there was talk of her having to go home to Matsuyama to look after the house there, as her grandfather had begun to fail and her brother, the present head of the family, was too young to be left in charge. So *that* came to nothing. But still the good lady couldn't bear the thought of the Nodas 'walking off' with her splendid son, or of such an easy-going girl as Suzue for his wife: on the pretext that it was too soon for him to marry anyway, she held out as stubbornly as a besieged garrison. That her defences were finally overcome, and even Kinji's solid fortress breached (after a campaign at whose inexpressible rigours the letters we received could only hint) was due to Mother, who threw herself into the struggle with single-minded loyalty (and, though this wasn't generally known, to my O-Toshi, whose slender arms helped not a little to crumble the enemy's fortifications).

So it was that the maple-trees I passed on my morning and evening walks round the University campus were already turning a yellowish-brown when the engagement broached at Kugenuma in high summer at last found acceptance. In view of Aunt Noda's plea that the happy event should take place before the fourth anniversary of Uncle's death, and as everyone, I think, after all the complications over the engagement, wanted things settled before any further hitches could develop, it was agreed that the wedding should not be delayed. Aunt Nakajima dragged her swollen feet around Tokyo doing the necessary shopping; back home Mother sewed her fingers into a mass of callouses making new kimonos and altering old ones. Finally, almost at the end of the year, Aunt Nakajima left Tokyo with Cousin Suzue, Seima following three days later; and on December 28th, in the midst of the usual year-end frenzy of bill-collecting, the pair were solemnly united.

Unfortunately I couldn't attend the wedding (nor, I heard, was O-Toshi there). I sent them a telegram, though, timing it as carefully as I could. It arrived, I gather later, exactly as the company were sitting down to the wedding feast. When Kinji had read it out in his halting, stilted manner, Aunt Nakajima moved out to the front to bow to Mother and thank her for her trouble in arranging the marriage, assuring her in full voice that she 'looked forward to showing her gratitude by finding a wonderful wife for young Mr Shintaro'. Aunt, too, wrote in her letter of thanks to me that now Mother and I had been instrumental in making her so happy, her only remaining wish was to see *me* settled . . . etc.

X.2

The little school that Aunt Noda had charge of was expanding so fast, and Aunt herself was so well trusted by the girls' parents, that for the time being at least she felt she must stay down in Kyushu. But early in January the bride and bridegroom came back to Tokyo with Aunt Nakajima (Seima was in the middle of his course in veterinary science, and Suzue still had four months schooling ahead of her till graduation) and hung the nameplate 'Seima Noda' on the gatepost of a neat little thatched house in Shibuya.

I had heard, of course, that marriage marks an altogether new period in people's lives, but even so I was astonished by my first sight of the new couple. Seima's infant moustache suddenly seemed a mark of dignity, and there was a distinction, a new seriousness in his bearing. Suzue too looked more attractive, more womanly than before. Even to the casual observer a happy couple make a pleasant sight, as instruments perfectly harmonized are a delight to hear; and I was glad for Seima and Suzue to see the wind set fair in their new home, particularly as I myself could claim a share of the credit for the marriage. It was an odd sort of home, certainly—more like a school dormitory, with bridegroom off each morning to the University, and the bride, shawl thrown over her shoulders and lunch-box in hand, to her Koji-machi school. Aunt Nakajima lent them her maid O-Gin to look after the house while they were out. Most days, until four or five o'clock anyway, O-Gin must have had a pretty lonely time of it. She was marvellously impressed, though, by Seima's thoughtfulness for his wife. According to O-Gin he cared for her like a child, fetching her shawl and putting it on for her before she left each morning, and telling her to take a rickshaw if the weather looked the least bit threatening, and be sure not to catch cold: about the only thing he left to the maid was putting her clogs out ready.[1] The moment he came back in the evening, too (he was the first home) Seima's foot was hardly over the threshold before he would be calling to O-Gin 'Have the tea ready now—the mistress will be home any minute—and hurry with the charcoal for the footwarmer!'—with an almost embarrassingly tender concern for his wife, which made O-Gin tell Suzue she wished she could have her time over again, if only a man would treat *her* as kindly.

Suzue was no less considerate. Often she would buy a bag of bean-cakes on her way home, and toss it on to her husband's lap with a smiling 'Good for the brain, they say!' I longed to see Seima's satisfied face as he sat munching the cakes, weightily twirling what there was of his moustache.

The thrifty man dresses perfectly but saves on food; to feed well at the cost of appearing shabby is no true economy, so one of our pundits has said. By this standard, a wife like Suzue could hardly be called thrifty. Whether her husband's meat-eating theories had influenced her I don't know, but it was certainly *her* philosophy that since nothing was possible without good health, and good health meant good food, one *had* to eat well, whereas simple cotton kimonos were all anybody needed for clothes, provided you didn't actually wear anything dirty: so meals accounted for most of the Noda budget. Meals apart, it would happen pretty often that 'there were some marvellous apples in that shop I pass on the way home, I

---

1. To touch anything that comes into direct contact with someone else's feet was, and often still is, considered unhygienic, so that Seima would have had to wash his hands if he had put out Suzue's clogs for her in the porch.

just *had* to buy them', or that 'it was so miserable having to stay in all day because of the rain, I sent O-Gin out for some cakes,', while the instant a guest arrived O-Gin would be out again, this time to the fishmonger or the noodle-shop—so that all in all their budget was 'out' just about as often as O-Gin, or so I gathered from the faithful O-Gin herself, who (it was not surprising to learn) complained secretly about their extravagance to Mrs Nakajima.

If husband and wife lived in perfect harmony, the house itself was scarcely a model of good order. Such a marvellous variety of objects was packed into their four rooms—two six-mat, one three-mat and one two-mat—that there was hardly space to sit. Her shawl and his overcoat were kept stuffed in the bedding cupboard; in the alcove, instead of the usual scroll or flower-arrangement, agriculture textbooks jostled with the latest numbers of the *Women Students Journal*; pins and half-burnt matches lay strewn over Seima's desk; Suzue's sewing box could hardly be opened for the surrounding jumble of cake-plates and packets of cigarettes. The Eighth Noteworthy Sight of Shibuya, O-Gin called the perpetual confusion of the house: how chaos could take charge again so instantaneously whenever she had got everything tidy, she could not imagine. O-Toshi arranged the rooms to perfection when she went over on Sundays, but even so, by Monday they were invariably back to normal.

Adding to the confusion was the stream of guests. Not that there was anything odd in O-Toshi, myself, the Nakajimas and Ishikawas calling fairly frequently, but there was something almost laughable in the alacrity with which Suzue's girl friends and a host of new acquaintances of Seima's flocked to their house. The girls liked Seima's courtesy and gentleness; Suzue's wifely welcome and hospitality, that called to mind Kung Jung[2] with his 'never-dwindling throng of guests and never-empty cask of wine', delighted the men.

So popular was their home that whenever I looked in on a Sunday the place was jammed with close-cropped heads and raven hair done up in smart western coils, and voices buzzing to match: Suzue stuffing them all with cooked meat and cakes hurriedly got in on credit, Seima at her side, beaming with pleasure at the popularity of his Empress Josephine, and disposed around them their friends: Mr A with his peering near-sighted eyes, Mr B with the jutting chin, Mr C the born comedian, Mr D with a face as puddingy as the American pumpkins they were growing at the University, Mr E the exquisite; Miss F, the Beauty of the Teeth (they lit up the darkest, plainest face you ever saw), Miss G, as pale as a white melon, Miss H, all beef and bulge (she might just as well have given up school and joined a troupe of female wrestlers), Miss I, so vain she could have sat all day murmuring 'You and I, the twin beauties of the world' into a mirror . . . There was such a din of chattering and laughter, I had no chance to talk to

2. A Chinese statesman of the second century A.D., said to have been a direct descendant of Confucius. His hospitality became proverbial.

my friend and cousin. When I tried to suggest that they might scale down their hospitality a little, Seima only smiled and pulled at his moustache, while Suzue neatly quoted against me the sermon I had preached her at Kugenuma on the social mixing of the sexes. A wry smile was all I could manage this time—not finding it convenient to admit that at Kugenuma I had been more concerned with one particular girl and one particular boy than 'the sexes', for all my theorizing.

Worse still, I couldn't even get a moment with O-Toshi when we met at the Nodas'. It was irritating too, the way Suzue acted the elder sister with her 'Just do this for me, will you?', 'Run round and fetch it for me, there's a dear!'—but it was agonizing having to watch the crowd of lively, smart young men, none of whom knew anything about O-Toshi and me, darting their glances at her from all directions, like huntsmen aiming at a deer. I dreamt of setting up a notice 'Private Property of S. Kikuchi. No Shooting Allowed x yards east & x yards west of this board'—and suffered in silence. O-Toshi must have felt the same. She looked so disgusted whenever Miss Melon-face or the Lady of the Teeth smiled in my direction; while if I so much as gave a civil answer to any of the girls she turned crimson to the ears, and though she said nothing, her eyes flashed at me like lightning.

x.3

Ever since that moonlit evening at Kugenuma my relationship with O-Toshi had changed completely. Without either written pledge or spoken avowal, let alone formal acknowledgement by our families, that single ecstatic joining of hands had united us for ever. Of this I was certain, and knew that O-Toshi shared my certainty. Yet each memory of that evening was a curious mixture of joy and shame—shame at having been so carried away as to reveal a love that should still have been kept secret. Call it mean or reckless or what you will, when the girl was so young, and my best friend's sister, I had to admit it wasn't much better than if I had deceived a sister of my own; and repented bitterly of such foolishness. What marvellous good fortune, on the other hand, to find ourselves in such perfect sympathy already, to have achieved such understanding without the need of words or pen! Though if things hadn't happened the way they did, sooner or later we should both have fallen ill, or just collapsed, I shouldn't wonder, out of sheer frustration. After leaving the Matsumuras that night I walked for hours up and down the moonlit beach. No poor words of mine can describe the joy I knew then: where it had been empty, my heart was filled to overflowing: I was no longer alone in the vast universe, no longer incomplete, for the lost half of my soul had leapt from heaven to heal my divided being. My love was returned. The gentle, the clever O-Toshi, beautiful as a flower, but with an inward fragrance of spirit yet more pure and perfect—she loved me! Surely, I told myself, it was either miracle or dream.

Now at last I knew her deepest feelings. Whatever the world said, she was my wife. My wife-to-be: for from the beginning I hadn't forgotten, needless to say, the weeks of comings and goings and formalities that the world demanded before it would acknowledge her to be mine. The boat lying before me on the sand would have told me as much. The soul of a boat must long to put out to sea, and the sea to receive her lover; but for fulfilment both must await the tide, and the strength and skill of fishermen who will come in due time for the launching. Now that we understood each other so perfectly, everything could really have been left to settle itself, but inevitably we should have to call on others to help, and put ourselves in the hands of those who wished us well. Good manners and the rites must be observed, though the pains of love cut like a knife. To be patient in love and faithful in waiting: for us there was no other way. If I had a regret, it was that on that one occasion, because of my impatience, love had broken bounds, and spoilt a little what should have been a more gradual growth.

So there was nothing but a sheepish silence between us when we met again at Kugenuma the following morning. Even when we said goodbye at Fujisawa Station we merely bowed politely to each other, though it tore my heart to see the tears forming in her bright eyes. I even left out 'regards to your sister' in the letters I wrote to her brother, and after they came back to the capital avoided the Ishikawas like the plague, though it was ten to one I would find her there if I called on a Sunday. If we did chance to meet, I gave her only the most perfunctory greeting, and changed the subject whenever Suzue spoke of her. Shallow eyes would have deduced a quarrel; but O-Toshi and I knew that however far apart we seemed to be drifting, we were bound to meet again—like travellers around the world in opposite directions. It wasn't only for Suzue's and Seima's sake that we rejoiced in their marriage, for it seemed such a wonderful prelude to our own. Reading Mother's report of the wedding was like hearing a neighbour's plum-tree has blossomed, when your own is still in bud. Why waste time lamenting your garden's backwardness, if spring has already arrived next door?

A woman still, for all her lack of niggling feminine ways, Cousin Suzue was well aware of my feelings for O-Toshi, and of hers for me. Seima too, judging by the peculiar delight he took in talking of his sister whenever I was present, may have known more than he cared to admit; nor would Aunt Nakajima have promised Mother at the wedding to find me a partner if she hadn't had *some*one in mind. The special smile Mrs Ishikawa always had for me suggested that she would be yet another ally to be called on in time of need. And what of Mother, most important of all? She need only see O-Toshi to love her: Mother's sharp eyes couldn't mistake her gentle, considerate nature, her quick intelligence and depth of feeling, not marred by the smallest hint of affectation or conceit. The Matsumuras too would hardly reject as a son-in-law one who was both O-Toshi's and Seima's choice, and who could at least lay claim to 'prospects', though now he hadn't a quarter-acre to his name.

So I proved to myself that victory was certain—before ever battle had been joined.

X.4

With O-Toshi's love no longer in doubt, and our prospects as favourable as they seemed, what need had I of impatience or sickly pining? Why hurry when a steady walk would bring me to my goal? No lovelorn melancholy for me, or silly smirking if a friend should accuse me of being in love, however well such play-acting might suit the pale-faced nerve-ridden heroes of fiction. In the world of learning, the aspirant *must* go forward till his name is made; so in love, the lover's road is charted for him, till at last he take his partner in marriage. Such thoughts filled me with courage.

Fortunately I had been fitter than ever since my illness three years before; scarcely ever catching a cold even, sleeping well (though for a while, before going to Kugenuma, I hardly slept at all) and with plenty of energy to dispose of my little problems before they could start disposing of me. For a student, the days and months flit by so quickly. It seemed only the other day I had entered the University, and here was graduation looming up already, this very summer. Kikuchi was quite a senior by now. Now and again, in some small corners of society outside the University (if you will forgive the admission) you might hear a mention of 'Kikuchi of the College of Literature', prefaced with a 'promising' or an 'up-and-coming' or some such commendatory phrase; the literary articles I contributed to the *Meiji Review* not only brought in enough to cover all my school expenses, but attracted some little notice from the readers of the *Review*, or so I was told, despite their *naïveté* (not so surprising, perhaps, when our whole literary world was so naïve and underdeveloped): in particular, some essays I wrote while convalescing—to pass the time more than anything else—earned a far more generous reward than they deserved.

Gradually, as in my leisure hours I wandered at will among its corridors, the treasure-house of Oriental and Western literatures revealed its inexhaustible riches, at once evoking a wistful admiration for its glories, so far beyond my own reach, and fanning a mad ambition to emulate them —as of an ant resolving in his tiny pride to sway the towering tree. I saw how stupid had been my earlier impression, that past generations of scholars had left us no more fields to plough; even in my own little study of the Tokugawa period, which I had started simply as a hobby at school, the horizons kept expanding, with points to be studied more deeply and new subjects to write about cropping up everywhere like stars in the sky, till I longed for a hundred lives at least to do them all justice.

Poor I was, one of the poorest of all the students in Tokyo Imperial University. Yet I had a mother; I had O-Toshi; I had health, and hope, and dreams, and the will to make my way alone whatever it might cost. I envied neither X his wealthy family who would be sending him abroad after graduation, nor Y his aristocratic friends, whose brandy, on such occasions as they chose to invite him to their homes, turned him a bright brick-red, till he had to be sent home to our dormitory, triumphant, in the care of a liveried rickshawman. I envied no one, and was in every way content. If I had one single worry, it was the idleness and pranks of my dead friend Michitaro's young stepbrother. Mr Kento had finally got himself elected to the House of Representatives as one of the members for Ehime Prefecture, and on coming up to Tokyo last autumn to take his seat had brought this boy of sixteen with him and asked me to keep an eye on him. Masamichi,[3] they called him, but straight he certainly was not, and I could do nothing with him. It was inevitable: a spoilt child grown up is a trouble to everybody.

A stream begins to race when it's nearing a waterfall; and with the milestone of graduation less than six months away more and more of my comrades, as well as working frantically, began to wear themselves thin with rushing around trying to fix themselves up with the promise of a comfortable post. Like the rest, I had to think about the future. But in fact I had settled on my course long since. I was not going into politics, still less the army or business; the sea of officialdom and bureaucracy was not for me to swim in, nor the stock exchange a stage on which I cared to act. The pulpit had lost its former attraction. No, my battlefield was to be a book-lined study, my weapon the pen; though even a writer must live, and of private longings I had plenty: to travel abroad, for one thing; to collect a library-full of books, to start a school, to train a thousand poor youngsters like myself . . . The rich were welcome to their safes, their splendid mansions and carriages and country retreats; for I wanted for my own mother the best of everything Japan could offer, and for O-Toshi's engagement present, at the very least a necklace of diamonds each as big as my thumb. Oh yes, I had my share of dreams, to last me till the sap was dry and the fires burnt out at last.

But the road from a student's dormitory to such glories was long indeed. True, there was no lack of short cuts, if what one heard was true. But I would do no kind of thieving, nor bow and scrape my way to prosperity (I'm almost ashamed to recall it, but once when I was still delivering newspapers and had all but lost hope of ever doing any better, I threw away the princely sum of ten yen on a Ginza fortune-teller, a physiognomist. 'You've a hard time coming, lad,' he murmured after a long look into my face—I can hear him still—'for you'll not bend your knee to any man!) Maybe when the time came and fortune smiled I too might ride in a gilded rickshaw; but to raise oneself by lowering one's dignity, by a mix-

3. Lit. 'straight road', a common given-name.

ture of unctuous smiles to superiors in public and whining and intrigue behind their backs—this I could not and would not do. Let them laugh at me for a stubborn fool, or abuse me for a narrow-minded rustic if they would; I didn't care, I was made that way, that's all. The smallest degree of restriction or constraint affects me like a physical paralysis, so that I can hardly move, let alone write. Hence my simple rule: if wealth and rank came of themselves, I would accept them gratefully as Heaven's gift, or go out to seek them even, if they were to be had justly; but if the price were 'sell yourself', I'd shake my head till they struck it off. When the abler of my comrades, preparing to flaunt their genius in the ranks of officialdom, taunted me with the Chinese tag: 'The fool will do nothing but draw water all his days' I retorted with another: 'Though he lack both rank and fortune, who but the humble man of letters has true power?'

For the time being, at any rate, my only course was to eat simply, drink water, and wield my pen to the best of my ability. Of all my needs and longings, the most immediate were a niche in society where, apart from professional restraints, I could be truly free; a modest income, enough to keep me alive; time to spare, and peace of mind: and teaching in an elementary school would supply me with all these. A long wait, perhaps, till I could send for Mother to join me, and O-Toshi; but happily Mother still had perfect health and was single-minded and stubborn enough herself to look sympathetically on my purpose, and as for O-Toshi—one day, I knew, she would be my wife, to cook my rice with her own fair hands in time of need.

x.5

Early in March a message came from my guarantor, Mr Nakagawa, inviting me to a family plum-blossom party he was giving the following Sunday, 'only for the family, quite informal', at his villa in Koume, near the Sumida River.

As I've said before, I had all the pride of the poor plus the samurai contempt for money, that made it seem a dishonour even to go near a rich man's house. Unlike some rich men, Mr Nakagawa had made all his money by honest work and thrift. He had offered of his own free will to pay for Komai Sensei's trip abroad, and was as polite and courteous to a struggling student as to the highest in the land—a gentleman-merchant, in fact, of the English type, with none of the stink of brass about him. All this I knew. Still, he was rich; and I had never called on him except when strictly necessary. His villa in Koume I had never even seen, though I had heard him speak of it; so that this invitation out of the blue puzzled me not a little. It would be discourteous, though, to refuse, so when Sunday came round I gave up my usual visit to the Nodas', carefully brushed my student's uniform and cap, and set off—in state, for they sent a rickshaw specially to pick me up.

Over the Sumida by the Azuma Bridge, three or four hundred yards down a lane to the right, past a black fence overhung with long branches of oak, their leaves still touched with yellow from the frost, and I clattered under Mr Nakagawa's gate, to be greeted almost at once in the porch by the old gentleman himself. He was sixty-two this year (so I had been told) and of small but compact build, as if he had been beaten into shape with a hammer; with a steady gaze and straight, firm lips went the smooth address and manners you would expect from one who had raised himself from nothing to a place in the list of Japan's half-dozen wealthiest men.

'Glad you could come—I've been meaning to ask you for a long time. Plenty of time to talk today. Only one or two others will be coming, otherwise it's just the family. I'll get my daughter to play her harp for us—not that *we* can lay much claim to the arts and graces—but I've one boast, and that's my garden: you'll be expected to admire it, I can tell you.'

He had a right to his pride in the garden, which was a masterpiece of clever landscaping by his old Edo gardener. A small lake, the centrepiece, was supplied by a channel drawn from the River Koume; a decorative bridge of brushwood spanned its banks at one end, where the lake narrowed to rejoin the river. One could picture at once the beauty of the scene when lotus and iris were in bloom. In a secluded corner, where birds chattered and acorns carpeted the ground, a shrine to Inari the Fox-god nestled among shadowy camellias; elsewhere a bank of rose-bushes and beds of peonies and chrysanthemums, of the 'seven herbs of spring' and the 'seven flowers of autumn', brought to mind the brilliant display each season would provide. There were pine and cherry trees such as the Priest of the Three Hills[4] wished for in his garden, a maple you could hardly reach round, a clump of Tung-p'o bamboo. In the exact siting as well as the rarity of every tree, each carefully chosen piece of rock, one could gauge the old man's lavish expenditure, which alone could create such harmonious beauty. I walked under plum-blossoms of a dozen different shades of pink and red, set off here and there by pines and bamboo; some overhanging the lake, others cunningly placed where their flowers would fall like coloured snowflakes upon a bank of soft green moss. A nightingale sang sweetly among the shadows. And who had hung from those branches the strips of coloured paper inscribed with poems in a woman's hand, that danced in the cool east wind?

No, I didn't grudge my host, as he led me through his garden, the admiration he had asked for. Tucked away among the plum-trees was a simple little summerhouse, with three or four porcelain stools. Here my

---

4. Priest Kenko (1283–1350) is said to have been living on one of the Three Hills on the edge of Kyoto when he wrote his famous *Tsurezuregusa* or 'Idle Jottings', in which the following passage occurs: 'Trees that it is desirable to have about the house are the pine and the cherry. Of pines the *goyo* [pinus parvifolia] is good. Single [cherry] blossoms are best ... the double cherry is exaggerated and specious. It is an oddity. It is better not to plant it ...' (*Tsurezuregusa*, 139, tr. G. B. Sansom in *Transactions of the Asiatic Society of Japan*, Vol. 39, 1911).

host and I sat and talked—of Komai Sensei, of Shingo (I've described already how I introduced Shingo to Mr Nakagawa. The old man couldn't praise my good friend enough. Not long afterwards I heard in a letter from Shingo that my guarantor had lent him more than a hundred thousand yen at very low interest, as capital for his business—which impressed me tremendously. That's how they did it, I thought, the men who make the millions: never lend a farthing of your money when you can't be sure of the borrower, and shovel it out in thousands when you can), of my plans after graduation—till we were interrupted by a girl of eighteen or nineteen, her hair done up in the *Takashimada* style, and blushing as pink as the blossoms above her head, with the announcement that 'refreshments were prepared'.

The only other guests were a man of about forty in a Japanese *haori* coat with a Triple Triangle crest,[5] another merchant by the look of him; a pock-marked gentleman in a western suit, rather younger; and two or three others. Mr Nakagawa's family made up the rest of the party—one man in Japanese dress, one in western clothes, two uniformed schoolboys, a *komarumage*[6] and an *omarumage*, the *shimada* already mentioned, a *momoware* and a *chigomage*; a regular crowd, and all of them well used to saké— unlike myself, for the third cup defeated me altogether. Fortunately Mr Nakagawa came to my rescue at once: 'Apologies—not many abstemious young men about nowadays. Bring Mr Kikuchi some vermouth instead!', and I could breathe again. Sipping vermouth and pecking at some *sashimi*[7] to hide my confusion, I wondered what O-Toshi was doing.

After saké came the entertainment. First a tune on her harp from the daughter who had come to fetch us from the summer-house, then it was the old man's turn to treat us to his party piece, a recitative from the Noh play Hachinoki, which I had to endure in the proper respectful posture (he was my host after all, as well as my guarantor), sitting stiffly upright and struggling to forget the pins and needles in my feet. In such a highly respectable household we were of course spared the commoner favourites, such as geisha ballads and the like. But even Mr Nakagawa unbent rapidly, now that the more formal half of his party was over. 'The sun is setting already!' he cried, 'look at the flowers in the fading light—how exquisite! A dish for your eyes to feed on while I serve you tea.' Escorting us to another room, he prepared ceremonial tea for us 'with the tranquil mind of greatness', according to the strict rules of the Senke school. The bowl of thick tea, offered to us one by one after the master himself had taken a sip and delicately wiped the rim with a cloth of purple silk, brought a headache

---

5. A design of three triangles arranged in the shape of a pyramid, the badge or heraldic sign of the ancient family of Hojo.
6. Shintaro classifies the female members of the family by their hairdos. *komarumage* = younger married lady; *omarumage* = older married lady; *shimada* (or *takashimada*) = girl of marriageable age; *momoware* = girl of sixteen or seventeen; *chigomage* = little girl.
7. Raw fish, eaten with soy sauce and Japanese horse-radish.

when it came round to ignorant Kikuchi: how *did* one drink it? I hated to copy the others, and didn't want to offend my host by any lack of manners. All right: 'the true philosopher follows no school but founds his own': so now for the founding of the Kikuchi School of Tea Ceremony, I decided. Grabbing the bowl, I drained it instantly, and gobbled the proffered beancake, to such obvious titters from the *shimada* and *momoware* sitting demurely at the bottom of the room that I couldn't stop myself blushing, and even Mr Nakagawa smiled.

Truly I have never known such a trying party. Once outside the gate, when at last the entertainment, or affliction, as I'm almost tempted to call it, had come to an end, I sighed aloud with relief.

But why had the old gentleman invited me? The question refused to fade like the vision of the blossoms and the harp music and the sonorous phrases of the Noh. Five days later the mystery solved itself, and I faced a startling dilemma.

x.6

I was certainly unprepared for the proposal the gentleman of the Triangles had to make when he wrote asking me to call at his house for a talk on the evening of the fifth day after the party. After asking about my plans and whether I had any dependents, he grew more formal. Taking into consideration, among other factors, the link that had existed between us since the death of Mr Sato (Komai Sensei), announced the Triangular gentleman, Mr Nakagawa desired to be of assistance to me in the future: should for example I wish to travel abroad, he would be very willing to discuss the detailed arrangements with me when the time came; and would further be glad if I would state openly, ill-mannered though such a request on his part might be, any ways in which he could be of service, etc., etc. In this connection he (Mr Triangle) ventured to enquire whether, now that I had seen Miss Nakagawa at the recent flower-viewing party (O-Ito was her first name; now just eighteen, she was in fact the daughter of a relative, but had been adopted by the Nakagawas. She would be graduating this summer from the Peeresses' School. Though not perhaps of exceptional outward beauty, as I had no doubt remarked, she was of a naturally pleasant, gentle disposition, and had had, he was sure, an excellent upbringing—so said Mr Triangle, in the habitual language of the go-between) would I do them the honour of accepting her, in due course, as my wife? If I would allow Mr Nakagawa to adopt me as his heir, he would be doubly grateful, but such a further step was no doubt impracticable, since, as he had been informed, the fortunes of the house of Kikuchi rested entirely on my shoulders.

Though I might find it hard to believe, in view of the suddenness of this present approach, Mr Nakagawa had long had his eye on me, if the expression might be allowed, as a young man of quite exceptional qualities, of whom his daughter was certainly unworthy; nevertheless, he had permitted himself to entertain the hope, etc., and would consider himself fortunate indeed if I were able to give my consent. Needless to say, Mr Nakagawa should have spoken to me himself, but to avoid any possible embarrassment to myself, he (Mr Triangle) had been entrusted with the mission, etc., etc.

Such was this gilded bolt from the blue. I was astounded. I left that night with a promise to think over the proposal, but it was clear already what my answer would be. I was no genius like Hakuseki,[8] with a mind above worldly things; if a certain name hadn't been written across my heart already, I can't say but that I might (might, not would) have been attracted, for all my Yüan Hsien[9]-like contentment with virtuous poverty, —at least to the extent of needing a fortnight or so to make up my mind. I knew the taste of hardship and the power of money; and could picture to myself as vividly as anyone the countless advantages (all of which the single word 'no' would throw away) of having one of the richest men in Japan for a father-in-law. If I had a sweetheart already, there was no formal engagement between us, only an unspoken understanding. To dismiss the moonlit interlude at Kugenuma as an empty dream, accept Mr Nakagawa's offer, and snap my fingers at the world as his heir, would be nothing out of the way in present-day Japan. Yet thanks to O-Toshi the temptation came too late. If a Princess of England, famous for her beauty, could reject a suitor who vowed he would bring her the Bank of England in his pocket and all India in a carrying-case, twenty or thirty thousand yen stood little chance with me: riches without O-Toshi would be like a golden frame without a picture. I sat down to write my reply as soon as I got back:

I am greatly moved by the honour Mr Nakagawa has shown a poor student in making his proposal, which I ought no doubt, to accept at once with the gratitude it merits. Unfortunately, however, I have to decline. May I explain myself fully, in return for his extraordinary kindess?

I would not, I am sure, be a suitable son-in-law for Mr Nakagawa. Apart from my lack of ability, of which he is already aware, I live rather in the world of ideas than in that of practical reality, and the profession I have chosen has little to do with worldly success or advancement; it looks for no quick recognition, or early harvest from its labours. If I were to accept, out of gratitude for the kindness Mr Nakagawa has shown me, I should certainly be unable to repay the smallest part of the obligation I should owe him and his family. For myself, in all frankness, such a connection would seem inappropriate, while the house of Nakagawa could

---

8. Hakuseki Arai (1656–1726), a celebrated Confucian scholar and adviser to the Shogun.

9. A disciple of Confucius, remembered for his modesty and happiness in spite of great poverty.

only lose by acquiring a son-in-law with so little to offer. Young men of talent and character are as plentiful in the University as trees in a forest. Many have not only great ability, but are planning careers more suited to such an alliance than that which I intend for myself—among my own close friends there are those I could warmly recommend. (I was thinking of Arai.) To have been chosen in preference to others far more suitable is an honour I do not deserve. I cannot however believe that it is in the interest of the house of Nakagawa, and am therefore bound to reply, after careful thought and with the deepest gratitude and respect, that I am unable to accept.

So there it was. Let a prince inherit the kingdom, not Kikuchi! Even now, though, I can hardly tell whether it was I myself or O-Toshi within me, as it were, that wrote this letter.
An answer came by return from Mr Triangle.

I have lost no time in informing Mr Nakagawa of the contents of your letter. He is greatly impressed by your frankness and modesty, and earnestly hopes that you will see your way to accepting his proposal. There being no need for haste, he begs that you will consider the matter further at your leisure.

This did put me in a quandary. If I said simply that I was already engaged, that would be an end of it; but I wasn't free to say that much yet. Fortunately I was particularly busy just then, with the end of the spring term not far away, and could take advantage of the request to 'consider the matter at my leisure' to put it out of my mind altogether for a while; but in the meantime the message had got through to Kyushu, it seems, for a letter came to remind me, in Shingo's enormous scrawl, each character a solid square inch or more. Young Sone was doing well enough, he wrote, even if he couldn't be said to be cheerful. One surprising piece of news was that my cousin Yoshi had got married to a steady young army lieutenant; her mother and all the rest of the family had moved to Fukuoka to be near the couple. Which brought Shingo to the point: 'he'd heard talk of a certain proposition' . . . as for Shingo himself, he'd once thought of Yoshi in the same connection—and then there was the Matsumura girl, with her looks and education and personality, 'made to measure for Shintaro, you might say'—in fact, he'd said as much to my mother not long before (my pulse leapt as I read this!). But this piece of luck, why, it was marvellous, he went on, and the god Hachiman be his witness, he wasn't after any feathers for his own nest, but 'if a man didn't accept what Heaven bestowed, he'd be refusing what couldn't hardly be said to be refusable altogether'. (This I didn't perfectly follow. Shingo had his passages of near-nonsense at times, which might take a bit of deciphering; but to me they were charming reminders of how entirely Shingo owed his success to his own efforts and character, and not at all to any schooling.) So he hoped very much I would say yes.

If that were all it wouldn't have been so bad, but Shingo, the rascal, must have passed on to Mother what he had learnt, for a letter from *her* followed immediately on his. Having heard something of the approach that had been made to me, she had been waiting every day for a word from me, or a visit, even, and was disturbed by my silence. No doubt I had reasons; but what sort of girl *was* this—I was to write and tell her everything at once. Choosing a wife was the most important decision in a grown man's life: this, if nothing else, he *must* discuss with his mother, etc., etc.

I couldn't keep silent after that, and took precious time off to write her a letter yards long, explaining everything and listing thirteen good reasons for not marrying into a wealthy family. I did have *some* ideas, I added, about the sort of woman I wanted to marry, and might have written to her earlier on the subject; if I hadn't, it was because after all I was only a student still, and in no hurry to marry. But after what had happened I had to tell her what was in my mind, to prevent any misunderstanding. My ideal wife would be educated, healthy and strong, kind to her husband and gentle with her mother-in-law, refined, and willing to make do with very little—for example, somebody something like Seima's sister, O-Toshi-san (furious blush as I wrote her name); but of course when the time came I would be guided by Mother's opinion and advice . . .

With all these distractions, two or three weeks went by without my making my usual Sunday call on the Nodas at their home in Shibuya. The evening I posted my letter to Mother, a postcard arrived from Seima, enquiring if I was ill, it was so long since they had seen me. His mother ('not the new, the old') had arrived from home the night before, partly to see him and Suzue in their new home and partly to fetch his sister home—she would be graduating in three days' time. She had brought a message for me, and there was something he himself wanted to see me about; so would I call on them the coming Sunday?

X.7

The spring term having just ended, I went over to Shibuya a day early, on the Saturday afternoon. Suzue was sitting alone, with the sliding doors open to the veranda on the south side of the house—sewing, for a wonder. Seima, she told me, had gone out with his mother and sister to call on the Ishikawas and the Nakajimas. I hadn't had much hope of finding them in, but was disappointed nevertheless.

O-Gin brought me tea. Why was the house so silent, without one of the usual crowd of visitors, I asked. 'They've not shown themselves since the master's mother arrived,' said O-Gin with a smile before she disappeared into the kitchen. Mrs Matsumura—a strange scarecrow indeed!

'What shall it be, Shintaro-san—noodles, or rice and fritters?' asked Suzue, with her customary enthusiasm to provide everyone in sight with a meal; but I managed, with difficulty, to restrain her, and we sat talking of 'graduation year', as indeed it was, with herself and O-Toshi finishing school as well as me. Before long I got up to go, saying I'd back back next day if Seima and the others were going to be late; but Suzue wouldn't let me.

'Why should you go, when there's so much to talk about?'

'What, for example?'

'Something that'll surprise you—'

'What?'

'Guess!'

'Stop playing, Suzue! What is it?'

'You mustn't be upset, then. It's about O-Toshi; there's somebody wants to marry her.'

'Don't be silly!'

'It's true.'

'Now you're a housewife yourself, you've taken up gossiping.'

'It's true, I tell you.'

I realized with a shock she wasn't smiling.

'What's happened then?' I asked, or shouted, rather; more like a madman, I'm afraid, than sober Kikuchi.

'Didn't I say you weren't to get excited? All right, I'll tell you.'

The wretch who was proposing to rob me of O-Toshi was one Tokuro Kabaya, a Dietman of the National Party, who had been elected recently from the Matsumuras' home constituency, a gentleman of thirty-three with an imposing beard, educated and with substantial expectations, but a widower, who had lost his first wife before the last election. O-Toshi had taken his fancy when he called on the Matsumuras during a round of courtesy visits to thank constituents who had helped him in the election (Seima's step-brother had been one of his supporters, apparently). O-Toshi and Seima being at home just then for the vacation; and he had approached her parents soon after she left again for Tokyo. The Matsumuras had refused then, as O-Toshi was still at school, but now, having heard she was very soon to graduate, he was trying again.

'And he's found himself the most extraordinary go-between. You remember the boy you had that fight with back home—ages ago, by the well—Kasamatsu—'

'Not Sanjiro!'

'No, not Sanjiro; his mother, that dreadful widow.'

'No!' In that instant, I must confess, I committed mental murder. The widow Kasamatsu, of all people! If she had been there I'd have given my life for the privilege of taking hers. 'And what have they said this time?'

'With Mrs Matsumura coming to Tokyo anyway, they promised to get in touch with him again after she had seen O-Toshi and Seima and me, and heard what we have to say.'

'I see—and what does Mrs Matsumura think of him?'

'She wishes he were a bit younger, she says, and that this wasn't the second time; but since he hasn't any children, and there's a lot to be said for him in other ways, she's willing to leave it to O-Toshi to decide. Seima's brother Kinji is all in favour—it might come in very useful to have a Dietman for a brother-in-law, he says. Mrs Matsumura has to be careful how she treads in *that* direction, with his being only a stepson, and not really hers, so—'—If only I could kill him along with the widow!—

'What about her father—Mr Matsumura?'

'I gather he's not very keen to part with her yet.'

'And Seima?'

'Seima says there's no special hurry—she's still very young.'

Was that all? I boiled over. 'So Matsumura—Seima—wants her to marry the Dietman, you mean?'

'Nothing of the kind. That's why he wanted your—'

'Congratulations to all concerned! The wedding won't be till after O-Toshi's gone home with her mother, I suppose.'

'*No*! O-Toshi—'

'What about her?'

'—wants to stay on in Tokyo for a while, to improve her English.'

'Nonsense, with the Girls Higher School behind her, she'll make a perfect wife for a Dietman already. She'd better stop the dithering—make up her mind and get married right away!'

'There's no need to get so angry.'

'I'm not angry! What is there to be angry about, anyway? Congratulations, I said; and now I'd better be go—'

'Wait, Shintaro-san! You're not listening to a word I say.'

'What difference would it make if I did? A wedding's a wedding, isn't it—stupid? Stop the nonsense and let me go.'

'Wait! haven't even *I* a right to—'

'I know, you're on that Dietman's side like the rest of them.'

'No!'

'I tell you you are, the lot of you!'

'Why must you get so worked up? Calm down a bit. Haven't you forgotten Seima and I have a say in all this? You'll be safe with us, Shintaro-san.' Safe with them? Surely, as safe as Old Badger in his boat of mud,[10] I nearly said, but didn't, though I was seething inside.

What a month of misfortunes! First for me, and now for O-Toshi—and how much better if I had had the courage to tell Seima last summer, instead of cursing them for being so little help now, when it was too late!

10. In the old folk-tale of *Kachi-kachi Yama* or The Badger Who Got What He Deserved, a badger kills an old peasant's wife. A white rabbit persuades the wicked badger to take a sea-trip with him, and builds two boats for the purpose, one for himself, of wood, and one for the badger—of mud. The badger discovers too late the trick that has been played upon him.

x.8

Suzue tried her best to soothe me with wine and slices of Korean cake, but by now the flame of bitterness had turned to ashes; I was only listless and indifferent. What could I do?

'You haven't the least need to worry. Nothing has been decided yet. Why don't you go and ask for her yourself?' She wasn't joking, apparently.

'I'm not a Dietman!'

'Now you're off again! All you have to do it to ask—what's wrong with that?'

'I'm not a beggar, either.'

'Shintaro-san, what are you saying? I know what O-Toshi feels about it, anyway. No, don't sneer, it's true—as far as she's concerned, she'll be Mrs Kikuchi, or stay as she is.'

'More nonsense. Let her marry your Dietman and have done with it!'

'Can't you stop harping on the Dietman? O-Toshi wouldn't thank you for it—she'd be in tears if she could hear you.'

'She can cry her heart out if she wants, it's no concern of mine.'

'Listen, Shintaro-san! *We* don't want to give O-Toshi away to somebody none of us know, any more than we want you to marry a wife who's a complete stranger. I've known about you and O-Toshi all along; Seima and I talk about nothing else. That's why we asked you over, so that we could talk it over with you first, and then tell Mother (Seima's mother, I mean) while she's here.'

'How can I talk anything over when I don't know what my own mother thinks?'

'If it's her you're worried about, you don't need to be. No, I'm not making this up, either. When we went home last year she spoke so highly of O-Toshi, and asked me all sorts of questions about her. *She* wants O-Toshi for you, you can be sure of that.'

'Maybe she does. I'm tired of all this talk about marrying; proposals here, proposals there—'

'Has another family been on to you then?' asked Suzue, pricking up her ears.

I told her all about the Nakagawas, there being no longer any need for secrecy.

'And what answer have you given them?'

'Refused, of course.'

'Did you? How thankful O-Toshi will be to hear it! That means it's as good as settled between you already.'

'I don't want her to marry me out of gratitude, thank you.'

'Shintaro-san! What's the matter with you today? Can't I say *anything* without your growling at me?'

'We can't let this opportunity slip,' she went on after thinking for a moment. Assuming it was settled as far as O-Toshi and I personally were concerned, she and Seima and Aunt Nakajima would talk Mrs Matsumura round, and she would get her own mother, Aunt Noda, to start formal negotiations, after first making quite sure that my mother was in favour—a general offensive, in fact, with victory guaranteed. 'Everything will work out, I tell you—it's what O-Toshi wants, and that's the main thing. You don't have to be miserable any more. You can't trust a woman's word, did you say? What impudence—as if you knew anything about it! When a woman sets her heart on anything she'll stick to it as stubbornly as any man—more so; that's why so many ghosts are women.'[11]

I couldn't help laughing at this last bit, she brought it out with such a serious air.

'Feeling better at last, are you—I should think so!' said Suzue, sighing with relief and smiling all at once. She called in O-Gin, and soon had me eating a bowlful of rice and spitchcocks. O-Gin sat with us, to my embarrassment at first; we had been talking so loud, she must have overheard every word, but if she had, she was shrewd enough, as you'd expect from an Edoite born and bred, not to give us a hint of her being in the know, and entertained us instead with merry Edo jokes and stories. Suzue, for her part, was no less lively. She told me of the snub Seima's father had administered to the widow Kasamatsu when she had tried, with much show of dignity as 'prospective go-between', to present him with a huge bream:[12] 'No use bringing that here—we loathe the taste of it, all of us. Take it away!', of his summing-up of Mr Kabaya, the Dietman, as having 'nothing but his beard to boast of'; of how awful she had felt when she had burnt the rice black the evening Seima's mother arrived, and was only saved from everlasting disgrace by O-Gin pretending it was *her* fault. 'I didn't know *what* to do, I couldn't even eat it myself!'

'It was a good thing the master could,' laughed O-Gin.

'Good for Seima! A husband's lot must be pretty hard, though, if he has to weep tears of joy over burnt rice whenever his dear wife chooses to cook!'

We all laughed. It wasn't till late that evening that I left the Nodas'.

X.9

Next morning I put on my sandals and mounted Shanks' mare for a five-day tour to Narita in Chiba Prefecture and thereabouts. When I came back at the end of the month, I found waiting for me two postcards from Aunt Nakajima, two letters from Seima, and one from Mr Triangle—all of them asking me to call immediately.

11. i.e. the spirits of women who even after death still cling to what they loved in life, and cannot therefore achieve Buddhahood and the peace of nirvana. Stories of such women are frequent in Japanese folk-lore.
12. A frequent gift on auspicious occasions.

Aunt Nakajima, whose summons I obeyed first, showed me a telegram the moment I got inside her door. It was from Mother, addressed to Mrs Nakajima:

MATSUMURA GIRL BEST POSSIBLE WIFE SHINTARO. CAN YOU ARRANGE. LETTER FOLLOWS.

Mother must have sent it immediately she saw my letter, in the hope of getting things started before Mrs Matsumura left Tokyo. 'The daughter to win,/With the mother begin', or first bring down the horse, as we say, and the rider is yours.

My mother was never out of my thoughts, but at each crisis of my life I was made to realize afresh how precious she was to me, and never more deeply so than now. How was it that she was so alert and quick to act, I wondered admiringly (if a man may say so much of his own mother).

'Your mother being so sensible and straightforward about it encouraged me to make a start while you were away,' Aunt Nakajima began. After a long talk with Seima and Suzue she had approached Mrs Matsumura at once, without waiting for my return. O-Toshi herself had agreed instantly; her mother had raised difficulties at first—we would both be throwing away so much, she complained, myself a straight road to success (she had heard about the Nakagawa girl), O-Toshi the dignity and position of a Dietman's lady right from the start—but eventually sheer numbers won the day. O-Toshi's choice was unequivocal, for one thing; Aunt Nakajima, out of a determination to do all she could for my mother, launched a frontal offensive, inviting Mrs Matsumura to dinner, and keeping up the pressure by calling on her several times at Seima's; Seima and Suzue gave her no rest; even Mrs Ishikawa, to whom she fled as a last refuge, joined the attacking army, till the good lady, driven to 'put her daughter's happiness first, and to recognize the sincerity of Shintaro-san's feelings, and the kindness and goodwill of all concerned', declared that she herself had no further objection, and would do her best to persuade her stepson (though she couldn't help feeling a touch of regret for his sake) and Mr Matsumura to give their consent. Things having progressed thus far, it was felt O-Toshi should accompany her mother home; to which she had agreed without a murmur, in spite of having said previously she wanted to stay on in Tokyo for further study.

Aunt Nakajima was very gay. She had already sent a telegram to my mother announcing her success. 'Stay but a short three days away/You'll find the flowers in full array', as we say of the cherry-blossom: I had never dreamt so much could have happened between my talk with Suzue a week before and this visit to Mrs Nakajima. As I was leaving, Aunt told me of a plan they had for a grand flower-viewing party in two days' time, before O-Toshi and her mother started for home. I was to be there without fail: no running away allowed, or Aunt (as she gleefully insisted) would 'confiscate O-Toshi, and keep her for good!'

Used as he was at the University to tossing words back and forth on such weighty subjects as Philosophy, Truth, Beauty, The Meaning of Life, and therefore in his own estimation tolerably adult, young Mr Kikuchi was as helpless in love now as a three-year-old with something tickling him he doesn't know where—ready to scream one moment, doubled up with happy laughter the next . . . The day before the party I turned out my wicker trunk and paraded up and down in front of the cracked old mirror to study—of all things!—my clothes and deportment. O-Toshi wouldn't mind my usual threadbare state, but it would be a pity to distress my future mother-in-law. It dawned on me at last, though, that if honesty is the best policy, the first and best decoration is simplicity; and on the day itself I set out for the rendezvous at Aunt Nakajima's in my student's uniform, cap on head and stick in hand, as cool—outwardly—as ever.

X.10

Eleven of us—O-Toshi and her mother, Aunt Nakajima, her daughter and little Fujio, Mrs Ishikawa and her little girl Tsu-chan, Seima, Suzue and myself, and a maid—left the Nakajimas' house after lunch for Ueno, and made our way thence via Asakusa to Mukojima, crossing the Sumida River by the Takeya ferry. We had chosen the right time: it was Monday, and rather cloudy into the bargain, so there were few people about, and we had the flowers almost to ourselves.

The embarrassment of having to meet Mrs Matsumura's gaze, and greet her for the first time for four years—the shock of seeing how pale O-Toshi had grown so suddenly! Of my sensations as we strolled down the long embankment under a canopy of blossoms, with a pair of wagging tongues (Aunt Nakajima and Mrs Ishikawa) to match a pair of mutes (O-Toshi and myself)—I will say no more; but one small incident on our way home demands a mention.

We had walked up the east bank of the Sumida as far as Mokubo Temple, on our way home after an early supper at the Uehan restaurant (where I performed no better than at the Matsubara), when a group of ladies appeared from the opposite direction, seemingly on their way to view the blossoms, and walking at a very leisurely pace, despite the fact that everyone else was going home. As we drew nearer—Heavens! who should it be but Mrs Nakagawa, of all people, and (besides two others I didn't know)—yes, the girl with the *shimada* hairdo, O-Ito, or whatever her name was. I was stupefied. But what could I do—here they were abreast of us! Willy-nilly, I stepped aside and bowed to Mrs Nakagawa.

But the lady was too experienced a matron not to be equal to any such occasion. 'Kikuchi-san! it seems so long since we saw you . . . you've been to see the flowers this afternoon?' she enquired, her eyes scanning all eleven of us, and fastening particularly on O-Toshi. 'Your relatives, no doubt? I don't think I have had the pleasure—'

Aunt Nakajima stepped promptly forward. 'Perhaps you will introduce us, Shintaro. Mrs Nakagawa? A pleasure to meet you. Yes, Shintaro here is my nephew; and we are exceedingly grateful for all the kindness you have shown him. Indeed we should have thanked you before.' Thus Aunt Nakajima in her usual powerful voice, oblivious of the rest of the company. O-Ito, though blushing scarlet, was staring at O-Toshi, who blushed as deeply, but returned her gaze. The other two ladies had stepped back a few paces and were whispering to each other.

'Won't you all drop in, Kikuchi-san—just for a cup of tea, nothing special, I assure you—since you're on your way home anyway—'

I was wondering how on earth to answer Mrs Nakagawa's invitation, when Aunt Nakajima announced (how *could* she!) that 'we would gratefully accept, since Mrs Nakagawa was so kind, etc., etc.'

For Kikuchi, embarrassment turned to consternation . . .

Mrs Nakagawa whispered to O-Ito (if that was her name). O-Ito blushed again, bowed, and hurried off with the two ladies down the side of the embankment to the road. By the time the rest of us reached the Nakagawas' villa in Koume after a walk in near-silence (Mrs Nakagawa having joined us, even Fujio and Tsu-chan stopped their chattering, in awe of the stranger) it was dusk, with only the faint light of the moon in a sky swept clean of clouds. In the big room at the villa, the lights were already on; silk cushions had been put out ready for each of us, and even a brazier lighted against the chill of the evening. The daughter received us with great politeness and formality; she must have slipped home by rickshaw to make the preparations.

In the month since my last visit the plum blossom had vanished, and now the cherry trees spread their snowy blossoms above the lake. The scene was poetry itself, with petals drifting gently down to the water at each breath of air like fragments of moonlight. But I could feel no poetry, only a cold sweat, as if I were sitting on a bed of nails. O-Toshi too looked anxious, and O-Ito must have been just as upset: she kept glancing back at O-Toshi, even while she was serving tea and handing round the cakes. Only Seima and Suzue and Mrs Ishikawa were their usual selves. Mrs Matsumura stared in turn at the electric lights, at the decorations, at the garden, at O-Ito, but said not a word; the conversation was left entirely to Aunt Nakajima and Mrs Nakagawa. When Mrs Nakagawa took Aunt Nakajima to another room, as they had 'a little personal matter to discuss', the rest of us all grew so stiff and awkward with each other, I felt my muscles would snap with the tension, but happily Mrs Ishikawa's Edo resourcefulness saved the day; she plunged into a lively dialogue with O-Ito, which eased the agony till Aunt Nakajima reappeared and we could take our leave.

In my relief I practically ran out of the house . . . this 'party' had been every bit as disagreeable as the last—surely there couldn't be any ordeal so painful as a flower-viewing! But this one did help me in two ways. Mrs

Matsumura was much struck with the 'sacrifices' I was making for O-Toshi's sake, for one thing; and secondly, I was neatly released from my entanglement with the Nakagawas. Aunt Nakajima took me aside before we separated, and put her lips to my ear: 'Shin-san! It was drastic treatment, maybe, but I've dealt with that Nakagawa woman. She's got eyes in her head, of course—must have guessed how things were the moment she saw O-Toshi. Anyway, there's one knot cut, and the other tied all the tighter. A happy end to our flower-viewing, wasn't it? I'll sleep sound tonight, I know—and Shin-san, you too can snore in peace for once!'

X.11

Two days after Aunt Nakajima had thus 'dealt with' the Nakagawas, O-Toshi and her mother left for home, and on May 5th[13] I heard from Mother that the negotiations had been successfully completed. O-Toshi, all the parties had finally agreed, was to take the name of Kikuchi ... It couldn't have been easy to mollify Kinji, or to persuade old Mr Matsumura to part with his daughter, and the Dietman and the widow would surely not have given up without a struggle. At seven hundred miles' distance I could only guess at the trouble Mother and Aunt Noda must have been to, and Mrs Matsumura, in her delicate position—and all I could focus on anyway was the single auspicious phrase: Toshiko[14] Matsumura, soon to be Toshiko Kikuchi ...

What happy memories I cherish of that year 1891, the twenty-fourth year of the Emperor Meiji's reign! First there was the good news I have spoken of, arriving on Boys' Festival Day, and then on the fifth of July at Shinbashi Station, I had the joy of welcoming Mother to Tokyo. I was to have gone home, instead of her visiting me; but Mother never having been to the capital, she decided to come—to see the sights, attend my graduation ceremony, and (she insisted) help me to make a start in the world without wasting time on the long trip back to Kyushu. Her cottage she left in the care of her faithful maid, so that if all went well she could stay on and look after me when I set up house. Both Aunt Nakajima and the Nodas invited her very warmly to stay with them, but Mother preferred the freedom of lodgings; so after leaving some of her baggage with the Nakajimas I installed her in a six-mat room on the first floor of my old boarding-house in Yushima.

Of the days that followed I can hardly give an orderly account. Not that there is nothing to write about—quite the reverse. Most vivid still among a flood of images and impressions are Mother's smile under the lamplight at Shinbashi Station, as I saw her again after nearly five years (she might have aged a little, but had mellowed more, I thought; if my eyes weren't

13. The day, appropriately enough, of the Boys' Festival.
14. A more intimate form of the name O-Toshi.

mistaken—though it's not for a son to discuss his mother—there was a new serenity about her, partly the effect of time, no doubt, and partly, perhaps, of Christianity); her small figure among the audience at graduation, stealthily wiping her eye as I walked from the rostrum after giving the Speech of Thanks on behalf of the graduating class; uproarious farewell parties; my name in tiny print in the newspaper, in the list of graduates; the awkward duty of going with Mother to thank Mr Nakagawa for having acted as my guarantor (I would have written to him after Aunt Nakajima administered her 'treatment', to resign any claim upon him; but he had accepted the outcome so gracefully, his attitude to me not changing in the slightest, that I was shamed out of doing so); tears shed with Mother over Komai Sensei's grave in Yanaka Cemetery; the gay little dinner-parties given by Aunt Nakajima and Suzue in honour of Mother and my graduation; and gayest of all, my last goodbye to the Red Gate[15] (I'd decided not to stay on at graduate school) and the hauling of all my bits and pieces on two rickshaws to Mother's lodging.

Most of the lodgers at Shinshichi's had changed in the last three years. The chanters of 'In Edo now I languish'[16], evidently languishing no longer, had found themselves a foothold elsewhere, as had the youth who had tried so hard to get my coat to pawn. Only the medical student survived, still failing his exams, and with his fiancée's photograph still treasured in his pocket; I pitied him sincerely, for the girl's sake, and prayed for the poor fellow's success. But if his lodgers had changed, my good old landlord had not. As friendly as ever, he heard with delight of my graduation, announcing proudly that 'that made three Bachelors from the house of Matsuya.' As a token of his delight and pride he at once produced some saké, which was kind of him, except that when he saw Mother and I didn't touch it he switched to helping himself, till in the end he got quite drunk and bored us both by babbling endlessly to Mother about what a fine, respectable young gentleman her son was, and how he could guarantee my character, morals, etc., etc. It was a relief when his pockmarked lady came in and marched him off (after a goodly scolding), though the welcome he had given us was a rare enough privilege, I dare say—for all it may have smelt a bit of saké—in a city where hardly a soul thinks of anything but getting ahead of his neighbour.

In contrast to the three-mat downstairs room to whose worn-out mats I had once come home exhausted each morning from my delivery round, we were given an upstairs room now, and a six-mat one at that: and my newly-acquired grandeur as a B.A. (though I still squirmed under the title myself) had one unexpected effect in that it guaranteed good service from the landlord and his lady alike. Each morning and evening Mother and I went out walking together, to the envy of some of the students lodging at Shinshichi's, who for lack of the money to travel hadn't seen their mothers for five years or more (these walks took time, as Mother would stop at all the

15. i.e. the University. See note 2, p. 251.   16. See note 5, p. 255.

second-hand furniture shops, to look over old cooking-ranges and braziers and the like); while often we talked on so late into the summer nights that even though we had thought we were barely more than whispering, angry coughs from the rooms on either side would drive us into silence till the morning.

That year, for the first time, I found pleasure in the slow, sticky ordeal of a Tokyo summer.

X.12

Three years of University, so long in anticipation, had slipped by as quick as Lu Sheng's dream[17], and graduate Kikuchi, as he laid aside the student cap he had scarcely begun to wear—or so it seemed—was hard put to it not to be embarrassed by his new status. What had he done in these three years but fill a few notebooks? What had he been taught—*genuinely* taught—but the ABC of his subject? What was the writing he was so proud of but imitation, every word of it? No, he had no right to feel superior, not if he had any sense of shame at all. Kikuchi at the Red Gate, peering into the future—wasn't he like a mountaineer who has just left the first station on the way up Mount Fuji, and stares up, leaning on his staff, at the crags looming above his head? The way till now has been no more than a try-out of his sandals, as he jostled among the noisy picknicking crowds; now he must face the real climb, and sweat it out alone against the heights. Some consolations there are on the road of learning, as on a mountain climb: each upward step extends the view, and the thrill of the struggle grows with its difficulty—like the sweetness in the very salt of the climber's sweat—which he who takes an easier way can never know.

At all events I had finished my three years at Tokyo Imperial University, and was now a first-year man in the greater University of Society. What path forward should I take? No stage of a man's career matters so much as its beginning; stumble at the start, and you'll stumble all the way. I thought long and hard about my future. As a result of the reputation, undeserved and empty glory though it was, that I had acquired at University, a number of unexpected openings came my way. Two that had me in a quandary for a while were an offer of a chance to study abroad and an invitation from Kan Sensei, who was now in Sendai. Two months before my graduation a professor at the University who was also a high official of the Ministry of Education invited me to lunch, and held out a tempting bait—free travel and study abroad, on only one condition: that on returning home I should join the Ministry. The travel part of it was attractive enough, but I knew very well the professor was chiefly intent on building

17. In an ancient Chinese story Lu Sheng was travelling the country in search of wisdom. While asleep one night on a magic pillow he dreamt he had become a wealthy prince—but woke to find his dream had lasted no longer than the time it had taken the innkeeper to boil some millet, and was thereby convinced of the vanity of material wealth and power.

up his influence at the Ministry, without regard to any academic considerations; I detested his dangling public money in front of me simply to put me under a private obligation to himself, and not disposed to end up as a bureaucrat's catspaw, I refused the offer on the spot. Kan Sensei, on the other hand, asked if I wouldn't take the chance of a rest up in Sendai and teach English Literature for a while at the Second National High School—he had already spoken of me privately to the Principal; I had only to say yes, and the arrangements were as good as made.

I felt it best, however, and Mother agreed with me wholeheartedly, that for the next five or six years I should stay in Tokyo, to be ready for any opportunity that might present itself. Kan Sensei's kind offer, therefore, I also turned down, together with one or two other such posts in the provinces (including one at a Middle School in Ehime Prefecture that Mr Kento had recommended me to), and was settling down with Mother in our lodging to live by my pen, in the hope that hack-work would at least keep us in potatoes, when the very thing I wanted turned up—by courtesy of Mr Ando, editor of the *Meiji Review*. This was a part-time job, teaching the outline history of English Literature for ten hours a week at a private college in the north of the city. Not what you'd call a leap to fame, perhaps, especially with it being a private school, and the salary, naturally enough for a fledgling graduate, didn't amount to much. On the other hand, just because it wasn't a state school, there would be no restriction on my freedom outside the work itself; and teaching at that level wouldn't need too much labour on my part, so that I could satisfy the students and still call most of my time my own. After a quick conference with Mother, I accepted, and agreed to start from September.

With my new job settled, it was neither convenient nor economic to stay on any longer at Shinshichi's, and Mother and I tramped around Ushigome Ward every day in search of a place of our own, till we found a little house to rent for five yen a month in Ichigayanaka Street. It wasn't huge, but there were pines and plum-trees and cherry-trees in the garden, and besides an eight-mat and a six-mat room the house boasted a full-size porch and a maid's two-mat room alongside it, not to mention a little four-and-a-half-mat annexe, something like a tea-house, standing by itself at right angles to the house proper, which would make a perfect study, or quiet room for Mother. With the main room facing south, we should be warm in winter and cool in summer. The kitchen, on the other hand, faced north: but if that was a drawback, Mother reckoned that having the well on the shady side more than made up for it, the water was so soft and pure. Nor were the neighbours—a retired gentleman on one side, and an instructor at the Military Academy on the other—likely to be difficult in any way. So we took the place there and then, and moved in towards the end of August. The baggage Mother had left with Aunt Nakajima was sent for, a plate bearing the name SHINTARO KIKUCHI fixed to the gate, a bowl of noodles sent in to our neighbours on each side, as is the custom when one moves, and Mother and I started keeping house together once more—thirteen years after we had last lived in a home we could call our own.

From mid-September I went out every day in *hakama* and high clogs to teach my classes. All my spare time was well filled with reading and study of one kind and another, and with writing articles for the *Meiji Review*; now and again I would draw the water, kick off my clogs and work barefoot in the garden for an hour or two, but otherwise Mother did all the housework. Of which there was plenty—this being for her a home away from home, there was a deal of coming and going to be done just to get in all the pots and pans we needed. Aunt Nakajima and Suzue kept offering to help, but Mother could never be happy with anyone else doing her cleaning and shopping, for every speck of dust and dirt was a personal enemy, and even a pair of fire-tongs she would examine minutely before she bought them, insisting always on what would last, even if it cost a little more. Superintendent of the Kitchen, Mistress of the Household, and Minister of External Affairs—she was all these in our small state, and in her moments off duty would sit busily sewing new kimonos for us both. 'Time you stopped, Mother, you're working too hard!' I would call out sometimes, to which she would answer only, 'Nonsense—as if *this* was hard work!' or if I suggested hiring a maid, 'Wait a bit, dear, wait a bit—later, perhaps.' For my own part, though in the classroom I stood much on my dignity as a new B.A., looking solemn and learned and pulling on imaginary moustaches, the moment I came home I would throw off my *hakama* with a boisterous 'Anything in the larder, Mother?'—a youngster again in spite of myself. Mother didn't mind, though. Quickly she would make the tea and get out the baked sweet potatoes she had ready in the meatsafe, and delicious beyond expression they tasted, as Mother and son sat face to face and exchanged the gossip of the day. Seima was full of admiration for Mother's arrangements when he came to see us. In their home, he would lament, either the house was too small, or it was just that they had packed it too full—there hardly seemed to be a corner to sit down in.

Truly I have never known such happiness as during those weeks. A hundred years in Mother's company, it seemed to me then, would flit by as quickly as a single day. But we were not to have each other to ourselves for long; every hour brought the great change nearer.

X.13

Since she had gone home to Kyushu at cherry-blossom time, my news of O-Toshi came mostly via Seima and Suzue. Mother brought a personal account when she joined me in Tokyo, and even after that, a stream of letters to her from Aunt Noda and Mrs Matsumura kept us pretty well in touch. Every report of O-Toshi, no matter by whom, was cause for pride.

Always fit and well, every day she was busy from morning till night with her sewing and cooking—she herself was hardly allowed into the kitchen nowadays, wrote Mrs Matsumura; Aunt Noda reported how impressed the neighbours were: 'If *that's* what a Tokyo education does for a girl, there's some sense in it after all!' she heard them say admiringly, and a great deal more besides. Every time we spoke of her, Mother fell into a panegyric: 'So intelligent, and yet so gentle and understanding, and with a will of her own, too. I never saw a girl I liked half so much!' To hear one you love praised by one you trust is like holding a jewel to the morning sun: it shines with a double radiance.

Needless to say, O-Toshi and I did not write to each other ourselves. (Once, indeed, Mother had a letter from Mrs Matsumura signed with her name but not in her handwriting. Perhaps she had been ill, and dictated the letter; certainly no one but O-Toshi had written those exquisitely-formed characters, firm yet supple with the grace of a young willow. 'Our affectionate greetings to Shintaro-san' the letter concluded, with Mrs Matsumura's 'signature' immediately after, but the writer's own feeling showed through—as I saw at once, with a rush of tenderness—in the handwriting.) With any communication between us having to be so indirect, if it hadn't been for that evening at Kugenuma the suspense would have been unbearable: as it was, we were sure of each other, and the future was settled, so that there was no need to work myself into agonies of doubt or impatience.

There must have been a deal of discussion about us going on behind the scenes, though, between Mother and the rest—Seima and Suzue, Aunt Nakajima and Mrs Matsumura—for one day Mother asked me out of the blue, 'How would it be if you get married before the end of the year?'

I didn't know what to answer. It would be an early marriage. I was twenty-four by the old method[18] of counting, and O-Toshi eighteen. It was only this summer I had graduated, only last month that I had started as a raw college instructor. With neither position nor property, what was I but a poor student still? I wanted to get a foot on the ladder first, make some sort of reputation, however small, save a little—lay the foundations at any rate, as the world reckons them; so that when we did marry I wouldn't be too poor to give my wife a padded silk kimono, say, and a satin sash, and keep her delicate hands from too early an acquaintance with cracks and blisters. In the West, engagements could last for anything between two and ten years. I wanted to wait another year at least.

But Mother had made up her mind long since. Maybe things were like that in the West, she said, but in Japan a long 'engagement', or whatever they called it abroad, wasn't wise. Marriage wasn't the end but the beginning, so twenty-four wasn't too soon, far from it. Not that position and reputation weren't desirable, but sharing the work and worry of building

18. i.e. by adding one year to one's age each New Year's day, instead of on one's birthday.

up a home from nothing would only make a marriage that much the stronger; and a couple who really understood each other would have no need for extravagance, anyway. No, whatever I might think myself, this I *must* leave to her. So Mother went on, till I was pretty well cornered.

With these first stirrings of events to come, it seemed as if a fragrant mist were rising about me. As a traveller who has glimpsed a mountain or a lake in the hazy distance walks on, thinking how far he has yet to go, till suddenly he finds himself enveloped in that very haze; so 'marriage', that had seemed so remote, was so no longer; already its warm airs swirled around me like the mists of spring. Outwardly my life changed not at all. Up early —help Mother open the shutters—draw the water, maybe—look over my notes for the day's lectures—hurry off to the college, clip-clopping in high clogs—back in the afternoon to read, or write for the *Review*—a walk later, calling in at the *Review* office, perhaps, or at Seima's. Some evenings Asai and two or three other friends would drop in and talk; some I would spend at the University, or at Ueno Library. All as before—save for the soft spring haze overlaid (for me) upon the autumn scene. Believing that a man should keep his head and show himself cool and steady, even indifferent, at such a time, in my own estimation I was as calm as ever. Maybe, though, it was a case of the drunk protesting he's sober.

It was all like a dream, yet the dream was strictly real. Mother was twice as busy now. The Matsumuras and Aunt Noda were constantly writing to her, and she wrote back as often. Seima and Aunt Nakajima were always popping in to discuss something or other with Mother, ignoring me completely. Indeed it could be no dream; for in ten short days from now, O-Toshi and I were to be married.

X.14

The autumn rains gave way to clear, gem-like days. One by one they passed, now quick as lightning, now snail-slow, till a telegram from the Matsumuras announced their departure. Five days later, on October 25th, O-Toshi arrived with her parents at Seima's. The spring mist about me thickened.

Mr and Mrs Matsumura came to call on Mother (while I was out!)— Mother returned the courtesy. On the 27th old Mr Nakajima, our official go-between, put aside for once his Noh texts and drum, and went in full formal dress to Shibuya with our betrothal present. ('What can we give her that's useful?' Mother had asked. A cookery book, I suggested—but Mother only laughed. In the end she decided on a sash of light-brown satin, with a pattern of white chrysanthemums.) Next day Seima, likewise in ceremonial dress, came to deliver the return presents: a roll of *nanakoji* silk and another of plain silk, besides several smaller items. The date of the wedding was fixed for November 3rd, the Emperor's Birthday, and the place, our house in Ushigome, tiny though it was, with nobody but the two families and our closest friends for guests. I was present when all these things were discussed, but only as a formality: Mother, Seima, Aunt Noda and Mrs Matsumura decided everything.

Still I didn't see O-Toshi. But the knowledge that she was in Shibuya, only a mile or two away, and had come to Tokyo this time for good, filled me with inexpressible happiness. Even without seeing her dear voice or hearing the voice I loved, I could feel her presence. Sometimes I longed to steal over to Shibuya and peer through the hedge in the hope of getting a glimpse of her; but mocked myself out of such childish folly. According to Aunt Nakajima, O-Toshi had paled a little, and looked more beautiful than ever. Seima told us how they had had to move everything she had brought with her to the Ishikawas', the house was so crammed already—but what did I care for such trifles, when in less than a week O-Toshi would be truly mine?

I went on with my teaching at the college, and with my reading at home; or pretended to, as if there wasn't a thought in my mind but 'what's so marvellous about a wedding, I'd like to know?' But why were the students at my lectures always smiling? Why, when I tried to read, should each character rise in turn off the page to greet me with a bow and a celebratory dance? Con—gra—tul—a—tions! I heard shouted up and down the street, and ran to the window to find it was the bean-curd man on his afternoon round. A chrysanthemum I was admiring in the garden turned slowly to a human face, smiling and laughing till it was ready to drop from its stalk for joy. Surely they were talking of me, those two sparrows under the eaves, their tiny heads bent confidentially together; suddenly silent as they looked my way, then chattering excitedly once more? More than once, on my way to and from the college, or while out walking, I saw and heard the strangest things, that made me stop to wonder, idiot-like, where I was. Something wrong with me? No: the world was standing on its head, not me! So much greater, then, the need to get on calmly and quietly with my studies. So I concentrated harder than ever on my books—to no purpose. I would put a book down without remembering a word of what I'd read. If I wasn't careful I would spend an hour reading the same line over and over. When I sat down to write my regular article for the *Meiji Review*, I managed the rough draft all right, but who was it sent those characters stalking uninvited across the page—O-Toshi, Toshiko, Toshiko Kikuchi? But why shouldn't I speak her name, at least, when there was nobody to hear, just to see what if sounds like: O-Toshi! I murmured, smiling as a man may when he is alone . . . 'Sir!' said a loud voice directly behind me.

I turned with a jerk. It was the little maid we had hired a couple of days before.

'What is it?'

'Mrs Kikuchi wants you to come for a moment—'

Like a naughty boy expecting a scolding, I went to the six-mat room.

Mother had just finished making me a new *hakama* of Sendai silk. 'Try this on, Shin-san,' she said, smiling, as she bit off the thread she had been using for the last hem. The maid, sitting demurely in the doorway, smiled too. Even the stiff silk *hakama* rustled—in amusement at my folly?

It can't have been this nether world that I lived in during those last few days. Since the mist had closed around me, my senses seemed to function in reverse: small things loomed huge, big things shrunk, the marvellous became ordinary and magic touched the everyday. I walked through the clamorous city as if I were strolling by a quiet brook in spring, and heard voices only where there were none. All harsh, angular objects and forms seemed oval, rounded. My whole being, all feelings, thoughts, fancies, dissolved into a flowing, shapeless mass. Trained and hardened as he thought himself to be, before he could help himself Shintaro Kikuchi was tossed into the furnace—melted in the crucible, till he wondered whether he wasn't going to evaporate altogether.

Fortunately, though, I managed to present some appearance of sanity to the world, and self-consciously, as if to knowing looks from every second, minute, hour and day, approached the mysterious domain of marriage. But while I was all but sleep-walking, Mother worked away, as wideawake and brisk as ever, settling every detail you could think of, till on the day before the wedding not only were all the arrangements complete, but everywhere, inside and out, was so perfectly clean and tidy—corridors gleaming, mats almost slippery from so much sweeping, and the whole garden as neat as if a carpenter had gone over it with a plane—that on this day of all days the maid was left with nothing to do. That evening, under a lamp polished free of every speck of soot and dust, Mother and son sat quietly together, sipping tea but saying little, till late into the night.

X.15

From a dreamless sleep I awoke on the Emperor's Birthday to a perfect autumn morning—my wedding-day. Ignorant as I was of the meaning of marriage, of a husband's duty, I was to be married today—and found myself as reluctant to give up bachelordom as I was impatient for its opposite. I tried hard to think rationally where I stood, to put the past behind me, to bring my mind to some kind of order; but could grasp nothing clearly, nor feel anything but an indescribable freshness, strange and trance-like, as if I had just emerged from a night-long Turkish bath.

After breakfast (I suppose it was breakfast), having nothing more to do, I stepped out, gaily swinging my stick, for a stroll in the neighbourhood. From every house fluttered a Rising Sun; here and there children's voices sang, more magical than ever on this festival day,

> May thy glorious reign
> Last for ages, myriad ages.[19]

I turned off our street to look at some chrysanthemum gardens. The flowers were in their full glory, I think, though I don't remember very clearly.

I came home to find Aunt Nakajima already on the scene, with two maids, and my study (What's this? I nearly cried out, but smiled in time) suddenly invaded by a white pawlonia-wood chest of drawers, a wicker trunk, a portmanteau, a huge bundle in a light-green wrapper, a yellow cotton bag, and a mass of other paraphernalia. This was to be the bride's changing-room, explained Aunt, who had followed me in, and would I kindly keep to the living-room, please?

By the time I had finished lunch (if lunch it was), been to the barber's and had a bath, it was still only two o'clock in the long autumn afternoon. But then, to my surprise and delight, who should appear but Shingo, with whom it was easy to talk the time away. He had business in Tokyo later in the month, but had come early to make sure of being present at the wedding. Apologizing over and over for his mistake in urging me to marry the Nakagawa girl, he brought out a heap of presents for Mother and O-Toshi and me.

The Reverend Shizu arrived soon after Shingo. As he was in Tokyo anyway for a conference of Christian pastors, after talking it over with Mother and the Matsumuras, I had asked him to marry us, the ceremony to be part traditional Japanese and part Christian. Seeing him after so long brought back memories of my dead friend Michitaro: how happy he would have been to be here with us! and for a brief instant I seemed to see among the shadows the lonely figure of O-Fuyu, the girl he was to have married. But only for an instant: the happiness of the day left no room for anything but itself.

The sun goes down; lamps are lit. In Mother's room, with her help, I change into crested kimono, *haori* coat and *hakama*, all of Mother's silk: Mother had bred the worms, unwound the thread from their cocoons, woven the cloth, sent it to Kyoto for dyeing, and sewed every stitch herself. Aunt Nakajima looks on with exclamations of wonder. Blushing, I go to wait in the living-room. The wall-clock strikes six. A swarm of rickshaws clatter outside the gate. I hold my breath. Aunt Nakajima and her husband hurry to the porch; through the single-screen partition I hear voices mingling as everybody talks at once—Aunt Nakajima, Mother, the Matsumuras. The bride is taken straight to my study.

Seima and Mr Ishikawa and Ando from the *Meiji Review*, all smiling broadly, come to greet me where I sit waiting. Cousin Suzue, her hair done up in matronly chignon, mistakes the room for Mother's (she has been sent to fetch something for the bride), exclaiming in surprise as she sees us

---

19. The opening of the Japanese national anthem.

talking; she bows, smiling, to congratulate me, then calls Seima out for a whispered consultation. Seima scratches his head. What can she be saying?

Outside in the street, in the kitchen, in every room, crowds and laughter and congratulatory greetings; chattering voices and lights and colours fill the house like a fountain.

A little later bride and bridegroom are seated side by side facing the alcove in the living-room. In front of us the Reverend Shizu reads from the Bible. Save for the bellflower crest on my kimono, the cords of my *haori*, my neckband and socks, everything I am wearing is black: O-Toshi, save for the delicate cherry-blossom tint of her face and the jet-black of her hair, is a picture of pure white, in the kimono her mother wore at *her* wedding (O-Toshi insisted on this, I am told afterwards), set off by the sash we gave her, with its pattern of chrysanthemums on a fawn ground—but I do not see her: I know only that I am bathed in a dazzling, celestial light.

The Reverend Shizu starts to pray. I sense a bowing of heads behind us, but I hear nothing, see nothing. All that registers is one short passage from the marriage vows, which the Reverend Shizu reads after he has finished praying: '... for richer for poorer, in sickness and in health, to love and to cherish, till death us do part, according to God's holy ordinance.'

The Reverend Shizu gives two copies of the marriage certificate to the Nakajimas, as go-betweens, and one copy each to O-Toshi and myself. We bow to the Reverend Shizu, then to each other, then (at a whisper from Aunt Nakajima) turn and bow to the company. All bow in return.

The ceremony is over. Toshiko Matsumura is Toshiko Kikuchi—for ever.

We were sitting now in the place of honour, with our backs to the alcove, my wife and I (Toshiko had changed into a crêpe kimono of some pale colour), with Mr Matsumura on my right and Mother on Toshiko's left. Mrs Matsumura, Aunt Nakajima and her husband, Seima, Suzue, the Ishikawas, Mr and Mrs Ando, Shingo, the Reverend Shizu, Mrs Nakajima junior (her husband was away at sea. We had invited Mr Kento too, but he sent a messenger with apologies. Aunt Noda, alas, hadn't been able to leave her school) sat in rows down each side of the room. Our maid and O-Gin, who had come over from Shibuya to help, brought in one by one the black lacquer tables with the wedding breakfast, holding each one up high for a moment in the ceremonial way, and set them down before us in turn.

But I did not touch the breakfast—I sat, merely; seeing nothing, hearing nothing, feeling nothing, save only that Toshiko, my wife, was sitting beside me.

The room being too small to accommodate everybody, Shingo and Mrs Nakajima junior had to sit in a part of the adjoining six-mat room (which we had screened off from the rest, to hide the furniture), but happily, so I am told, there was no sense of crowding or confusion. Though we served no saké, the talk and laughter never stopped, so I am told. Seima stood up to read out a telegram from Aunt Noda; old Mr Nakajima, in his element, sang the Noh song *Takasago*[20]; Shingo, his vast bulk making the house seem tinier than it was, lumbered to his feet, all stiff and crinkly in his western suit, and delivered himself of a speech, recalling how he'd known me as a boy way back, and seen in me even then the promise of a brilliant career, together with a deal of reminiscence and prophecies of future glory, all in his uninhibited countryman's style—a speech so fulsome, in fact, that if my ears had been functioning, I'd have died of shame—so I am told. Not to be outdone, Mr Ando told of my first struggling months in the capital, and went on to give a vigorous defence of the writer and his profession; Aunt Nakajima gave me away with an account, which brought loud applause, of my discomfiture when we met the Nakagawas after the flower-viewing party at Mukojima; Mr Ishikawa, as forthcoming and witty as his good lady, had all the company laughing with tales of slips and blunders he had made at the time of *his* wedding—or so I am told. So I am told, I say, for I had no clear idea of what happened till they told me afterwards, nor when I try to cast my mind back can I confirm that the account I was given was true. All I remember through the haze is gay talk and smiling faces, and most clearly of all, the voice of old Mr Matsumura, laughing in huge delight at every small joke and anecdote.

Some three hours later the company broke up in a confusion of leave-taking as animated as the laughter that had greeted the speeches earlier. Soon, after much smiling and many congratulatory bows, they had all gone, and only Mother and my wife and I were left in the eight-mat living-room.

'You must be very tired, Mother?' I said, noticing an unexpectedly serious look on her face.

'Not in the least.' She smiled, but only for a moment. 'Shin-san and O-Toshi-san, would you come with me for a moment, both of you?'

We followed her round the veranda to her own room. Very quietly she folded a small screen that was standing in front of the alcove. On a little table in the alcove itself, already yellowing with age, stood a single framed photograph of my father. Toshiko and I knelt before it with Mother and bowed.

'I have brought them to show you . . . your son and daughter . . .' Mother murmured through her tears. I too wept. Beside me, Toshiko sat with bowed head.

There were no tears but these on that auspicious day.

20. The song of the Twin Pines of Takasago and Suminoe, symbol of lasting married happiness.

EPILOGUE

(1)

A month after the wedding, Mother left for home with Mr and Mrs Matsumura. Toshiko and I tried hard to persuade her to stay on, but her mind was made up: there was so much to clear up at home, she insisted, she must go back, at least for the time being. The real reason, I am sure, was her fear—thinking of Toshiko and me, as always—that she might be in the way, until Toshiko had grown quite used to her new life and surroundings.

The day before she left, as we sat talking in her room, Mother turned to Toshiko.

'From now on the position that was mine in the Kikuchi family is yours; you and Shin-san must decide everything for yourselves, without worrying each time about what I would think. Which reminds me—I've something I want to leave with you, Shin-san and Toshiko-san—' She broke off to take a paper packet from a little box in the cupboard: 'It's not much, four hundred yen in government bonds.' All these years, ever since I ran away from the New School in 1883, Mother had been putting aside, to pay for my education, every sen she had left over from what she earned from her breeding of silkworms and her spinning and weaving. With the interest from the bank and the post office, it had come to more than 500 yen, but she had sent me 50 yen when I was ill, and another 50 to Suzue for her wedding (the expenses of *my* wedding I had met myself, out of the little I had managed to save from the proceeds of my writing). Past misfortune had stripped the house of Kikuchi so bare (said Mother) that all she had to hand on to us, apart from a family-tree, two swords and a few picture-scrolls, was this tiny sum. But if ruin could overtake the wealthiest, it was just as true that a man could pull himself up with nothing to help him but his own efforts. Nothing counted in the end but his own ability and strength of will. 'You've had as hard a time as any, Shin-san, and things won't be easier for a long while yet. But there'll be joy to be had as well as care in fighting your way through.'

Mother was right. If life had been a struggle before my marriage, it was a struggle still, only on a wider front. But just as I had had in Mother, for the first twenty years of life's battle, an ally worth more than any army, so in the ten years since our marriage I have found in Toshiko the most steadfast ally and friend. Truly, though poor in everything else, I have received two of Heaven's best gifts, a wise mother and a loyal wife. Of what I owe to Mother—of how from the day she took me in her arms to comfort me when our family came upon its trouble, she breathed new life into my dull and stubborn being, and for twenty years was a never-failing spring of hope and inspiration and courage—I have given some small account, I hope, in the preceding chapters. Of all that my wife has meant to me since our marriage, of the light and vitality and encouragement she radiates, without which I would never have recovered from many a setback and failure—of her the story remains to be told, though now is not the time.

In the same month that we were married, Toshiko and I drew up a domestic 'constitution' for the House of Kikuchi. It ran as follows:

Article 1. It is prohibited to get into debt, whatever happens; (on the principle that control of a man's purse can mean control of his spirit too)

Article 2. No clothes are to be worn of any material but cotton;

Article 3. Riding in rickshaws is forbidden, except when on urgent business;

Article 4. At least one fifteenth, and when possible one tenth, of all income is to be saved. (Which was exceedingly difficult, with a very small income, and expenses we hadn't budgeted for cropping up only too often. Also, I had now to pay back month by month—though the instalments didn't amount to much in themselves—the scholarship I had had at the University.)

We bound ourselves, in other words, to practise the strictest economy. But 'the poor man sweeps cleanest', as the proverb says, and Toshiko, with her ready imagination, perfect taste, and deft hand, soon brought touches of warmth and beauty to our almost bare little house, planting rose-bushes in a tiny strip of ground in front of my study, and strawberries in the still smaller patch beside the well, mending every tear in our paper screens with paper cut into flower-patterns, and painting morning-glory blossoms on the letter-rack she had made. Besides being marvellously economical, she was always thinking of my comfort and happiness. (Having acquired already, by some mysterious means, an accurate knowledge of all my likes and dislikes, she fed me on all my favourite dishes. If the western saying is true, that the way to capture a man is through his stomach, Toshiko certainly had me at her mercy.) In the intervals of housekeeping she would look up quotations for me, or copy my manuscripts (poring over the Copybooks of Yen Chen-ch'ing to teach herself the formal style of calligraphy, so that her copying shouldn't look too womanish). In everything, indeed, she was my constant helper. But this too is a story I have not the time to tell in full.

My life in the ten years since that autumn of 1891 has been as eventful in in its way as our country's history in the same period. After two years I cut down my teaching to three hours a week. (Principal Katayama had asked me—through my old friend Philosopher Endo, the one who wore his one and only *haori* for five years; he was now pastor of a Christian church in Tokyo—to go back to Kansei College to teach history, and I had had more offers from various High Schools, but had turned them all down.) Mr Ando having given up the editorship to go into business, the *Meiji Review* came pretty much under my control. By good chance I was able to attract more readers than ever before, though most journals were finding it difficult to survive. If the political, social and literary criticism I published was immature, at least it ignored conventional opinion. I could say what I liked, carry any discussion as far as I pleased. The *Review* gave me a chance to speak out as a 'teacher without a school', an unofficial adviser-at-large to the public; a judge without a court, a preacher without a pulpit, a one-man flying-squad for the forces of enlightenment and progress—and to some, at least, the humble name of Kikuchi ceased to be altogether strange. I have published two or three small books, too, and have in my desk a manuscript, as yet unfinished, of a longer one. The study of the Tokugawa period I had begun at the University led me to another absorbing topic: the emergence of a totally new nation from our dying feudal past. The fifty years of transition to twentieth-century Japan, a period of change as turbulent as Niagara, fascinated me with its vast, many-coloured drama. With a boldness that surprised me, I tried my hand at a historical novel—the manuscript I spoke of just now.

Ten years—long enough to determine most men's fate. Of the company that left the University with me to plunge together into society's broad sea, some have disappeared without trace, others have quickly swum through to some island of security. I myself, to be frank, have barely escaped drowning. It's inevitable, I dare say, that a swimmer who ignores the winds and currents should find the going hard, and come in later, maybe, than the rest. Yet we ordinary mortals are so purblind and small in spirit, we cannot see that our lives are but bubbles on the ocean of eternity, that all things, all creatures, are contained within the Creator's hand as they follow their destined cycle of existence. What looks like 'winning' or 'losing' is merely an optical illusion. As little need to envy Egypt and Assyria for having civilized themselves so early, as to lament Japan's misfortune in having come so late upon the scene—for 'the last shall be first, and the first last.' Dancers and spectators alike are actors upon the world's revolving stage. Once let it dawn upon you that the play needs both the star performer and the hack who is good for no better part than that of the village policeman—and what is there left to complain about? So I tell myself: yet whenever I have heard, as I couldn't help but hear, of X's latest promotion in the higher civil service, of the ovation that greeted a public lecture by Y—a doctor of letters now—of Z's position at the Stock Exchange and his groaning coffers, for all my philosophy I have still had a galling sense of being left behind. That I have come thus far without losing my way or weakening in the resolve I made on graduation, is owing to no strength of my own, but to the guiding light of Heaven, and to the inspiration and example of my mother, of my teachers and friends, and of Toshiko, the heart and centre of my family life. But this too is another story.

In due time our family grew, as families will. When our son Shinichiro came, nearly two years after she had gone home, Mother shut up her cottage and joined us in Tokyo. Shizu, our daughter, was born two years later, in the autumn. Three students live with us now, in the six-mat room next to the porch. (The house we are renting at present, though still in Ushigome, is much roomier than the first. There is grass enough in the garden for Shinichiro to practise his somersaults in comfort, and a room upstairs where relatives or friends can stay.)

Looking back over these ten years, I find so much to write about, it would be a pity, perhaps, to say nothing of this later period of my life when I have written so fully of what went before. One day I shall certainly publish a 'Ten Years After', or something of the kind, together with 'A Wife Recalls', Toshiko's account of our married life, which she has somehow found time to put together in the intervals of housework. As it is, my story has run on long enough. But one more event claims a mention—the journey I made a few years ago to my native Tsumagome.

As the name of Shintaro Kikuchi made a modest appearance in the public world, my relatives in Tsumagome (this was long after Uncle Kengo's death) began at last to write to me, with all kinds of enquiries and requests for favours and advice; they asked again and again, too, that I should go down once more and see how the place had changed. Mother and I had agreed I should go for the sixteenth anniversary of Father's death, so that we could have a proper memorial service for him, and I could offer incense and flowers at the tomb on the hillside that held such precious memories; but the outbreak just then of the war with China made the trip impossible. By the spring of 1897, though, things were not so hectic, and at long last I set off with all my family for Kyushu.

It wasn't only from Tsumagome, either, that the suggestion for the visit had come. Seima and his wife and the Matsumuras had been just as insistent. When Seima finished his studies in veterinary science (the year after Toshiko and I were married), he was lucky enough to be offered the post of adviser to the Kyushu Agricultural Testing Station. Leaving Tokyo at once, in no time at all he had bought up Uncle Noda's old estate (very cheaply, thanks to the help he received in the negotiations from the people of the nearby village, who hadn't forgotten their debt to Uncle Noda, and saw a heaven-sent opportunity in Seima's coming) and threw himself into fruit-farming and cattle-raising with a zest he seemed to have inherited from Uncle Noda along with his name. Each year we were presented with tins of butter, of the various kinds of 'jam'—apricot, peach, plum, and many others—Seima was producing, together with photographs of his three chubby offspring. He himself came up to Tokyo now and again, and on every visit would remind us how well the Noda property was looking now—we *must* go and inspect it, and give his parents a chance to see their Tokyo grandchildren too: they were tired of making do with photographs. Aunt Noda was equally insistent.

And then there was Shingo. His coal-mine had continued to prosper; recently (at my suggestion, in connection with a study I was making of labour and social problems) he had introduced a number of new facilities for his workers, and was eager for me to see them in operation. Also, he still had the idea of getting me into the House of Representatives. Already, apparently, he had the agreement of some of the leading citizens of Tsumagome to put me up as a candidate, and though obviously, with my being still in my twenties, there wasn't much prospect of a campaign in the very near future, he wanted to introduce me to the constituency. I knew, of course, that a writer mustn't shut himself up in his study, and that while a seat in the Diet may not be the open sesame some make it out to be, an independent member may be of some small use, provided he can ignore the parties and factions, and think and act purely for the good of the country. On the understanding that the electors would let me follow my conscience in everything I did, and not demand that I put their local interests before those of the nation, I was willing (so I wrote to Shingo) to stand.

So many good reasons for the trip having accumulated, we handed over the house to the care of our student lodgers, and set off at last—Mother, Toshiko, our two children, the maid, and myself—on March 30, 1897, while the dawn mist still hung over the city. After a merry day in the Tokaido train, we stopped off at Kobe for two days (one to enjoy the beaches at Suma and Akashi, and one to revisit Kansei College, where I called on Principal Katayama to apologize for my abrupt departure years before, and was promptly asked to address the whole student body), then took a steamer, to avoid the tedium of the still longer train journey on down to Kyushu.

No matter how often he makes the crossing, who can tire of the Inland Sea in spring? We all went up on deck. Master Shinichiro, or Mr Me, as we nicknamed him from the speed with which he had learnt to say 'Me, me' when he was hardly past his first birthday, wasn't the least bit awed at finding himself on a ship—indeed, it was all I could do to stop him jumping overboard, he wanted so much to catch the gulls floating gracefully on the mirror-like sea; little Shizu lay snug in her mother's arms, sitting up every now and then to feel the sea air on her cheek, till her granny coaxed her over to her own lap. After a while Mother and the maid took the children below. Toshiko and I stayed on, to enjoy the peace of the sea and the mountains. There was no one else on the after-deck, where we were sitting, so we could talk freely: of how eagerly her parents would be waiting; of Seima and Suzue and their new life in the country; of whether we should do some more shopping when the ship put in at Moji, in case we hadn't brought enough presents with us, and of a great many other trivialities which could interest no one but ourselves, till finally we fell silent. An island bright with rape-blossom was falling away astern; we looked back at the pencils of smoke rising from houses we could no longer see, and the white sails skimming along its shore.

'Shintaro!' said Toshiko softly.

'Yes?'

'Do you remember the time I first went up to Tokyo?'

'When I came with you on the boat, with your mother and Suzue? Of course; I remember passing that same island.'

'When Suzue-san—I—' Her voice was almost inaudible.

'Suzue?'

'Suzue-san was so friendly with you, I—I envied her terribly . . .' The lady at my side blushed beneath her matronly chignon. Suddenly I had a vision of a pale girl of thirteen, her hair coiled in the gay 'butterfly' style that young girls wear; she was smiling shyly . . .

Before long we reached Tadotsu in Shikoku. I was leaning on the rail, watching the comings and goings and recalling the day I had brought the unhappy Sone here from Okayama, when a man standing in a lighter that had just come alongside caught my eye; that enormous satchel slung over his shoulder—hadn't I seen that somewhere, and the black cap now turned grey with age? Having first taken off his ancient blue socks, in evident disgust at finding the steps before him less than spotless, he stowed them in his sleeves, and stalked slowly up the gangway. From where I was standing I couldn't see his face, but still the whole figure seemed familiar. Soon we put out to sea again, and I was on my way back to the saloon, when the gentleman of the satchel stepped right in front of me from behind the funnel.

'Mr Nishiuchi!' It was indeed my old benefactor. The beard that walled in half his face had whitened, the lines on his forehead multiplied, but otherwise he had not changed at all. He looked me up and down suspiciously.

'I'm afraid I don't recall—'

It would have been surprising if he had. I had sent him a New Year card every year, but never any photograph, and it was fifteen years since we had met. How he gaped when I told him I was Kikuchi, his messenger boy of so many years ago, whom he had rescued out of the snow that night in the hills above Uwajima! I took him to the after-deck, where we could talk.

He had never married (nor ever would, he said, complaining he was half-senile already). The nephew who was to have been his heir he had disowned instantly when he showed signs of spending his uncle's money instead of sitting on it; his old housekeeper, who called me Shinta-san and drove me frantic with her sardine salad, was still with him—too old to be of any use, but he would keep her, he supposed, till she died, since she had nowhere else to go. The three ferocious dogs, the terror of would-be thieves, were all dead; it was their offspring now who stood sentry over his home. ('Offspring—there you are,' he said sadly, 'if I had a child, I could die in peace; but as it is—') He had been to Osaka for a lawsuit, and now, after a business call in Tadotsu, was going home by way of Hiroshima. Jisa, who had carried me through the snow to Mr Nishiuchi's, (that nagging woman of his had run off with some other man) and the old woman were looking after the house while he was away.

Poor Mr Nishiuchi, well past sixty, yet with so much to do and so little peace of mind; I couldn't help pitying him. He had got entangled some time ago, I gathered, with a villainous character, who had fleeced him eventually of nearly half the fortune he had sweated blood to build. When Nishiuchi finally brought an action, the man bribed the lawyers, so that Nishiuchi could get no one to take the case for him; and now, after losing in two or three lower courts he had gone to the Court of Appeal in Osaka: this was the reason for his present trip.

The law is a closed book to me, but it certainly seemed from what he told me that he had right on his side. Whatever his other faults, and they were many, I knew how incapable he was of telling a lie. I wondered if there was anything I could do to help him—and suddenly remembered my old comrade Asai, now a Bachelor of Laws and one of the most successful young attorneys in Osaka. Nishiuchi brightened a little when I suggested giving him an introduction, then hesitated: he could hardly asked anyone 'so well known', he said. I told him not to worry about the fee, as I would write to Asai explaining everything; and gave him a card with Asai's address and a note 'to introduce my old patron Mr Nishiuchi pencilled on the back.

So, thanks to this unexpected meeting, I was able to pay back a fraction of the debt I owed to my benefactor. Mother added her thanks for all he had done for me, and Toshiko mended the tear her quick eyes had spotted in his old black *haori*. (The children, it's true, didn't take to him. 'Mr Me' was frightened of his beard, and would only shake his head when Mr Nishiuchi tried to coax him to play.) When he went ashore at Ujina, my card locked away under the brass catch of his great satchel, and the handkerchief and towel we had given him as a tiny present for the old housekeeper stowed in his kimono pocket, a gleam of something resembling happiness lit up his withered face.

(3)

From Hiroshima onwards the voyage was uneventful. At Moji one of Shingo's clerks met us on the quay, and after a short rest we took a train on the line that branches southwards from Orio. By nightfall we were at Shingo's.

Of Shingo's ecstasy of joy, of the rush of words and hospitable attentions that overwhelmed us from his lady, the 'warm one from the south', of the volley of songs—*Marching through the Snow, Myriad Ages,*[1] *The Boatmens' Ballad*, and the like—that their troop of children fired off, to the vast

---

1. The national anthem. See p. 350.

astonishment of young Mr Me from Tokyo—of these things I must tell another day. There was so much else—let me just mention the *kakejiku* in the alcove, a painting of Shingo in sandals and peasant breeches, leading his packhorse with a load of charcoal down a mountain track; the 'Precepts for Success', the priest of Ennenji had written out for him on a letter-scroll, now framed and hanging on the wall; the Biblical text 'It is more blessed to give than to receive' that Shingo had once insisted I write for him, this too beautifully framed; Shingo's 'box of valuables', from which he produced the alphabet I had made for him—so proudly!—when I was four or five.

Next day Shingo showed us over his mine. It was fascinating to see the whole complex but orderly process of his business, from the actual mining of the coal to its storing and despatching in trucks to Moji and Wakamatsu, but I was more interested in the clean, airy quarters Shingo had provided for his miners, the big shingle-roofed hut (the People's Club I think he called it), as suitable for sermons as for story-telling and slide-shows; the small but efficient hospital, the Nakamura Savings Bank, which encouraged small savings, and paid half-yearly interest; the evening classes; Shingo's adoption of the eight-hour day, with every Sunday a holiday; the insurance and pension arrangements; the organization of all the miners into five-man groups, giving them a measure of self-government. Several of these schemes Shingo had introduced at my suggestion, and it was good to see them working so well. But any system or organization is dead till a man breathes life into it, and Shingo's achievement in keeping all his projects running so successfully was outstanding. Truly it was amazing how far he had come, by nothing but his own persevering effort, since his packhorse days.

But what delighted me most was the generous way he shared his own success with his workers, in place of the usual capital-labour antagonism. If many of the mine-owners of North Kyushu were undoubtedly far richer than Shingo, none can have been more truly 'paternal' in the best sense of the word. Yet while apparently penalizing himself, with his reduction of working-hours, institution of rest-days, and provision of all kinds of facilities out of his own pocket, the business didn't suffer: little by little he forged ahead of competitors whose only motive was greed. Sheer ability, of course, was his only secret. (There was a disturbing lesson, too—for me—in his success. 'Nothing comes out of a sack but what went in it,' we say; and a man of Shingo's practical bent and determination can not only make himself rich, he can achieve in a day what bookish fellows like myself will dream about and argue over for years.) I congratulated him most sincerely, urging him to go on to make his million and then to lay it out, like Andrew Carnegie, in charitable and philanthropic work. When I lectured (at Shingo's request) to the miners at the 'People's Club', I held him up as a living model of thrift and strenuous work, a reminder too of the need for a man to fix his mind on something higher than the job he earns his living by.

Of the many agreeable experiences we enjoyed during our stay of three days with Shingo, not the least was finding my old friend Sone metamorphosed from the gloomy warder I had talked with in Ishikawajima Prison into Shingo's hardworking and now indispensable assistant, with a family and house of his own. Sadness tempered joy, though, when we met again, for the first time in nearly twenty years, my cousin Yoshi and her mother. Shingo had invited them over specially from Fukuoka. Yoshi looked nearly forty, though in fact she is a year younger than me; only in those firm, almost mannish eyebrows and limpid eyes was there a hint of the girl I said goodbye to at the teahouse on the hill above Tsumagome. But whether from excess of delight at the meeting, so many years overdue, or out of shyness or some private sorrow, she seemed scarcely able to raise her eyes to mine. Her mother, gaunt and weary-looking, whimpered continually of how hard it was that they had had no news of her other daughter, O-Fuji, who had disappeared ten years before—not even a word to say she was still alive—and how dearly she longed to see her girl just once more before her own time came, however low she might have sunk.

Yoshi's husband, Lieutenant Mitsunaga (so I heard later) was a simple soldier, loyal and kind to his wife and mother-in-law, but of no great ability; they were not well off, and what with having to look after the child her sister had abandoned, Yoshi's life must have been hard indeed. Even I, for all my male insensitivity, noticed how pinched they looked, while Toshiko whispered to me afterwards how guilty she had felt to see how well, almost extravagantly dressed our children seemed by comparison, though their clothes could hardly have been more simple. One ray of light there was, though—Kumahiko, Yoshi's own boy of six, whom she had brought with her to show us. He was a bright child, with his mother's steady eyes, and something, by the look of it, of his great-uncle's stubborn nature. Rightly guided, he might one day go far to restore the fortunes of his unhappy family. No man can measure with his own tiny rule the far-ranging purposes of Heaven; but might not this other branch of the Kikuchi, kept alive thus far by my faithful cousin, come in time to a new and brilliant flowering from this young stem? So at least I thought and hoped as I watched Kumahiko, armed with a toy pistol I had just given him, spiritedly chasing Shingo's second son, a much older and brawnier boy. Mother marvelled that a daughter of Uncle Kengo's should be so totally unlike her father. How moving it was to see Yoshi still wearing the comb Mother had given her when we parted, eighteen years before!

Having other visits still to make, we resisted all attempts by the lady of the south to have us stay longer, and left by train on the evening of April 6th, after arranging to meet Shingo again in Tsumagome (my cousin and her mother went straight back to Fukuoka, there being no one there to look after their house: they slipped away quietly, almost shamefacedly, apologizing very humbly to Mother and me before they left that they couldn't come with us and join in the memorial service for Father). Later the same day we arrived in the castle-town, to be welcomed at the station by Mr and Mrs Matsumura, Aunt Noda, Seima and his family—and Seima's step-brother.

(4)

Revisiting after ten years the second home-town of my youth, with its memories of Seizan Sensei, the New School, and Uncle Noda, my greatest joy was finding the two houses of Noda and Matsumura in so flourishing a state. Seima's coming had certainly made the name Noda count once more. His simple sincerity had won him trust from everybody he had to deal with, from the Governor, Assemblymen and officials down to village gaffers and grandmas, and the new Mr Noda was pretty well known already throughout the prefecture. Adviser to the Agricultural Testing Station, President of the Young Men's Association for Industry, Commerce and Agriculture, Founder Member of the Kyushu Agricultural College Promotion Committee, Consultant to the Kyushu Fertiliser Company, Inspector for the Sericulture Council—the list of his titles made it plain how well he had established himself in the community. Suzue supported him loyally in everything. Seima spoke admiringly of her instinct for essentials and practical turn of mind; courteous and kind to all inferiors, like her father before her, she was loved and respected, I was told, both by those who worked for them and by the villagers round about.

Aunt Noda was still living in her school. When she did come to stay with her adopted son, in vacation-time, they got on so well together she never wanted to go back. Seima became so devoted to her, in fact, that his own mother evidently couldn't help feeling a bit jealous, for she had begun to complain in her letters to Toshiko that she feared Suzue was careless to the point of extravagance in her housekeeping, and that Seima ignored everything his own mother and father said and would only listen to his wife, etc., etc. She mellowed, though, when their decision that Seima's second son, Daijiro, should eventually be adopted back into the Matsumura family as its next head provided her with a special focus for her grandmotherly affection. (True, she still worried about the huge meals Suzue gave her children, and even asked me to speak to Seima about it. I suggested, quoting Spencer's *Education* for good measure, that a child's stomach was as reliable a guide as any, so that it was probably just as well to give them as much as they felt they could eat—but to comfort her, agreed that over-eating might be unhealthy, and promised to have a 'serious talk' with the parents.) Mr Matsumura, on the other hand, had always been specially fond of Suzue. In short, relations between the two families were very satisfactory. Even Kinji, prince of bigots, had grown tamer, from the shock of an onslaught from Suzue, apparently, when he had been rash enough to parade his prejudices on the subject of women's education.

The previous owner having made few alterations, the house and grounds were much as they had been in Uncle Noda's time. For Suzue and her mother, the return to their old home must have seemed like a happy awakening from a dream of rootless wandering. The four-mat room I had occupied as Uncle's 'secretary' was now Seima's study, with photographs of Uncle, of Seima's parents, of the Agricultural College in Sapporo, of my own family, looking down from its walls, and the sage words 'Better a born fool than a youthful prodigy' as clear as when I had scribbled them on the plaster by the alcove. The camphor-tree under whose shade Sanjiro Kasamatsu slept away his afternoons, the well by which he and I fought, the cumquat tree by which I stood and nearly cried when Seima left for Tokyo, the persimmon trees whose fruit Cousin Suzue used to bite where it hung—all exactly as before. The estate had been extended, though, and improved in all sort of ways by its new owner.

Early on the morning after our arrival we all went out to Seima's dairy-farm to drink fresh cow's milk, the grownups walking and the children in a donkey-cart with Seima leading the donkey. Piled together in the cart, Seima's children and mine, who till now had known each other only from photographs, soon learnt to be as good friends as their parents; O-Sei, Seima's little girl of seven, and the very image of Suzue, was thrilled with her cousin Shizu, and persuaded Toshiko to let her take her in her arms, while Daiichiro and Daijiro, proudly wearing the red caps we had brought them from Tokyo, broke into a marching song with my small Mr Me. The farm was only about three-quarters of a mile away. It consisted of a single big meadow beside a stream at the foot of a hill, enclosed by a low fence, and with a number of wooden buildings in the west corner. (Managing the farm was the Matsumuras' taciturn but, as I well remembered, quick-footed old servant Mankichi. 'Well!' he said, amazed, when Seima told him who I was, 'the lad's growd a bit!'—a long speech for Mankichi—and started at me wonderingly, as if I couldn't really be that same boy who'd been seasick once in his boat and made such a din, the three of us nearly sank.) Tramping through the morning dew, we saw all round the farm, drank the milk still warm from the milking, and listened while Seima talked about his cows—how this one was a milch cow of pure Australian stock, that a crossbreed for pasturing, a third was already worth so many hundred yen, a fourth was only so many months old—and explained the processes for making butter, condensed milk and cheese, and the economics of maintaining a herd of cattle. He was planning to enlarge the farm, he told us, and build his own slaughterhouse. (Suddenly there was a loud scream from Mr Me, who had been darting about exploring with his cousins. Timidly, after the others had had their turn, he had been stroking the muzzle of an Australian cow that was lying on the grass 'like a house on its side'—when the house moved without warning. Very hasty retreat by scared Mr Me.) As well as cows, Seima kept a few pigs, goats, sheep, and even horses, grazing on his meadow, and a quantity of poultry, both native and imported—ducks, geese, turkey—in an enclosure by a small pond. On the way home from the farm, not far from the house, we saw beehives, and a miniature potato-starch factory in a shed.

Everywhere the new proprietor's steady, painstaking temperament showed in the planned orderliness of his arrangements. Gradually, thanks to scientific management in every detail, Seima was succeeding where Uncle had tried and failed so often. I couldn't help making this comparison, with mingled pleasure and sadness, when we went later that day to visit Uncle's grave. The grave was next to Daiichiro's now, at the highest point of the whole estate—Seima had had it moved from the under the great oak-tree in Yamashita Village the year he bought the property back. We stood by the graveside in silence. It was a glorious day; the larks were singing, our sleeves billowed gently in the spring breeze, and a faint mist hung lazily over all the fields and hills. A mass of fruit-trees—peach, damson, almond, cherry, apple—were in full flower, a gay spread of colour against the terraced wheatfields beyond, while away to our left we could still see the farm we had visited earlier, with Seima's sheep and cows grazing or lying asleep on the grass. I thought of Uncle in his last days, when I had watched by his bedside—how thrilled he must be in his grave to have returned to the estate on which he had spent his dreams, and to see it prospering at last!—and of Aunt's feelings, then and now: grief and pity weighed heavily for a while. In all the wide landscape around us—the acres of green wheat alternating with yellow-flowering colza, the village and its stream, the veiled mountains beyond—nothing had altered, nothing was new, save for the single railway-line winding through the distant haze. (But what of ourselves, the spectators of this unchanging scene?) Here still, indifferent to the years, was the huge rock on which I had sat listening to Cousin Suzue's talk of the capital, a tiny eleven-year old from over the hills: Seima's children and mine were playing at its foot now, and would soon be as old as I had been when we first arrived from Tsumagome.

'Shintaro!' Seima said quietly.

I looked up.

'There's only one thing that spoils it for us here—that you're so far away and we can't see each other more often. Suzue and I have been wondering—couldn't we arrange to meet regularly, in the summer, say? Remember the time we had at Kugenuma?'

'We've had the same idea. Why don't we go swimming every year at Suma or Akashi? You'd find it hard to get away, though, I suppose.'

'The Kobe beaches? That'd still be a bit far for us to go, I'm afraid. Seriously, though, I do have something in mind.' He pointed to a plot of land bordering the property to the west. 'I'm thinking of buying that land —for you to build a house on one day. I know it seems silly to talk of retiring now, but one day you'll come, and we'll be neighbours, in and out of each other's houses, drinking the same milk, breathing the same clean air—till the end comes, and we lie in neighbour graves, as brothers should. Don't you think it's a fine idea?'

We both sighed.

Mother and Aunt Noda were talking quietly in front of the grave. Toshiko sat with Suzue on a boulder a little way away, holding Shizu with one hand and picking a bunch of milk-vetch with the other; Mr Me and his three cousins were happily chasing butterflies round the big rock, stopping now and then to pick wild flowers.

How little time we had left together.

(5)

Two days at the Matsumuras', two days at Seima's—our stay seemed even shorter, there was so much to do. All three families had to be photographed together at the farm, I was invited to speak at Aunt Noda's school, a group of girls she had once taught sewing to came to call on Mother: in the end we stayed longer than we had intended. But it was only a day or so now to the anniversary of Father's death, and we had heard that the Tsumagome folk were expecting us; so we promised Seima and Suzue to spend more time with them on the way back, and started out for Tsumagome before dawn on April 10th, in a little procession of rickshaws.

Six or seven miles out of town the road ran for a while through fields, and the song of larks made harmony with the clattering of our wheels. By now there was a delightful drowsy warmth in the air. As I drank in the scent of the massed colza flowers, suddenly I realized—it was on this very day, in the same month of April, eighteen years ago, that Mother and I had ridden out of Tsumagome on Shingo's faithful horses.

'Shin-san! Notice how much better the road is?' Mother called from the rickshaw in front, which she was sharing with Mr Me. It was true, indeed. The stony, uneven track that had made the horses stumble so often was now a prefectural road, as level as a whetstone.

'I wouldn't have recognized it! Shall I take the boy for a bit?'

'No, he's fast alseep. What about Shizu?'

I looked round.

'She's no trouble—are you, Shizu-chan? Look, there's Granny!' said Toshiko, smiling, from the third rickshaw. Shizu, who was sitting on her mother's lap, a pink bib round her neck, opened wide her big bell-like eyes, and laughingly held out her hands in answer to her granny's nods and cluckings.

We made good time along the road in perfect spring weather, and stopped only for a meal and a rest. The sun was setting, though, when we reached the top of Seven Bend Hill. Mother got down from her rickshaw and took Mr Me by the hand. Together we walked over to Sugi-no-Taira; and there below us in the dusk, like a vision—but so much smaller than I had expected—lay the valley where I was born. The smoke of evening fires rose everywhere; the white gleam of the river was quickly paling, and with it the brilliant yellow of the colza-blossoms; already a few lamps had been lit. Mount Takakura, the sun's last rays lingering on its peak, smiled through gathering clouds. Ah, Mount Takakura! Diminished you must be, to eyes that have seen many of your kind; but no less dear than in childhood days.

Where had they vanished, those eighteen years? There was the cedar-tree to which Shingo had tethered the horses; there, under its shade, the stone Jizo with the faded bib round its neck . . . as if it were only that morning that Mother and I had left the valley.

'Come on, Daddy—do be quick!'

Mr Me's shout woke me from my dream.

I cannot describe all my memories of that visit: the torchlight welcome we found awaiting us at the little teahouse where we had said goodbye to Yoshi, the warm and generous hospitality of our relatives, each one insisting we visit his home, till our voices were hoarse, our necks ached with bowing, and our stomachs turned from eating the same congratulatory dishes at a dozen different houses; the great crowd (including, to our surprise, not only Shingo, but Aunt Noda and Mr and Mrs Matsumura—unknown to us, they had followed us from the castle-town) that came to the memorial service; the times without number the good people thrust scroll and brush into my hands, insisting I write some improving maxim for them to hang up or frame—I resolved to buy a calligraphy copy-book when I got back to Tokyo, and study the art in earnest!—the deluge of questions I was expected to answer, on every conceivable topic from 'The Future of Japan' to 'How to Deal with a Lazy Son,' as if I were a veritable encyclopedia; my speech-making tour of Tsumagome and the outlying villages; the high praise everywhere for Toshiko—'like your Mother grown young again,' said one old granny approvingly, who remembered Mother as a bride; the tears of our faithful O-Ju, as she clung in turn to Mother and to me; our maid's indignant protests, that Mr Me and Shizu were so monopolized by a succession of relatives, she never had time to get near them . . . But here the list must end, so little space remains.

The valley had changed a great deal in eighteen years. A painted bridge spanned Big Stream now; the little thatch-roofed building where I had gone to school had been replaced by a fine big block, just like the great office-buildings the foreigners put up in our cities; the town had acquired a bank, a Tsumagome Club, a factory chimney or two, even a two-storey restaurant—such inroads had sophistication and modernity made even in Tsumagome—with samisen[1] music and the lilt of geisha songs floating from its upper windows. In most of the families to which we were related

---

[1]. A stringed instrument much used to accompany ballads and other popular songs.

the head of the house had long since changed. The persimmon-peeling expert, the old lady with the passion for cats, the chessmaster, these and many others were dead, and their sons in retirement; it was their grandsons who carried the banner now, graduates for the most part of prefectural Middle Schools, or of such Tokyo colleges as Waseda or Keio, and some of their wives had been through Aunt Noda's school. Truly much had changed!

The morning after our arrival in Tsumagome, we all went with O-Ju to Father's grave. O-Ju and our relatives had kept the family burial-ground neat and tidy, but nearly twenty years of wind and rain, inevitably, had turned the pale grey of Father's gravestone almost black. After sweeping the ground clean and sprinkling holy water, we arranged our offerings of *shikimi* flowers, and burnt incense; then all of us, from Mother down to little Shizu, stood in turn before the grave to pray silently to Father's spirit—Mother and I after eighteen years away, Toshiko and the children for the first time. If stones could speak . . . Tears caught me unawares. Mother too had turned away to wipe her eyes.

The old cherry-tree whose branches canopied our little cemetery was all but past its flowering. With every breath of wind, the grave, its stone surround, the incense-burner, and the ground we had swept and swept again so carefully, all disappeared beneath a cloud of falling blossoms. Irises and violets lined the edge of the burial ground. While Mother was telling Toshiko of the earlier generations of Kikuchi who lay buried here, Shinichiro scooped up handfuls of cherry-blossoms to see how far he could blow them, or plucked violets and put them in the vase on Father's grave.

Dimly through the mists of memory I saw a lonely widow and her boy taking their leave of this same grave eighteen years before. I saw Mother standing over me, the glint of her dagger between us . . . My heart overflowed with thankfulness—to Heaven, to my father and to my mother.

'Shin-san!' Mother called to me. She was pointing to a new grave, in a corner of the cemetery where the ground fell away to a lower level. 'Shall we leave flowers here too?'

The grave was Uncle Kengo's. I sighed—Uncle Kengo, the twisted, evil man who had treated us all so cruelly! But the grave puts paid to every debt, alike of enmity and gratitude. Thinking of Cousin Yoshi, who would surely have longed for some such gesture, though she could never have asked us to make it, I sprinkled holy water and laid an offering of flowers at the foot of Uncle Kengo's grave.

Next we visited Ennenji Temple (a young fellow was priest-in-charge now, a graduate of some seminary or other) and the Reverend Saicho's grave. There was the same camellia whose flowers I had picked, to suck their nectar, when I came here as a boy to play, strewing the forecourt now as then with its wealth of blossoms: but the sprightly old priest who had promised not to die till I came back famous, had long since gone to his rest

—and I a long way still from fame. Katsusuke, too, was buried in the temple cemetery; he had died four years before. I stood before his grave, hearing again his parable of the snowball and the sunshine.

Someone from outside the valley—a saké-brewer, like the Kikuchi before him—had bought our old family home when Uncle Kengo died. A teacher at the primary school was living now in the little cottage where Mother and I and O-Ju had spent those first lonely months. The weeping willow in whose shade I used to splash in my tub still dangled its branches over the bamboo fence.

> In my own village I am no longer recognized:
> The children stare, and smile, and question,
> 'Who are you, and where have you come from, old stranger?'[2]

So it seemed when I spoke at the primary school, where once I had sat each day with inky face and hands, and looked down at the small faces staring curiously up at mine.

We stayed in Tsumagome for ten days. The hospitality we received was so lavish and continuous, there was little time for memories, and little energy left after the succession of speeches, visits (with requests everywhere for specimens of my calligraphy), parties (at each of which I had to give a long explanation of why I didn't drink), and changes of lodging; for our relatives invited us in turn. The night before we left, a group of the leading citizens gave a farewell dinner for us at the Tsumagome Club. One after another of my old schoolfriends, one a village headman, another a mayor, a third a member of the Prefectural Assembly, and several others who had achieved no less in different walks of life, rose to make me blush and squirm under their compliments, till at the end of all it was my turn to reply. After thanking the company for the great kindness they had shown us on our return, and rejoicing with them at the valley's prosperity, I spoke of the relationship between the capital and the provinces, using the examples of England and France to show how a nation's true strength lies in its countryside: on the health of the parts depended the vital energy of the whole, and Japan's great need was a combination of 'barbaric' energy and civilizing intellect. I warned my hearers against luxury and softness, and urged upon them the virtues of thrift and hard work. It was the responsibility of our provincial towns and villages, and more particularly of the public-spirited men in every community, to preserve themselves from the corruption of the city, and at the same time to supply our cities unceasingly with the pure blood they needed for regeneration. To end with, I forecast a brilliant future for this little town of my birth, and sat down at last to clamorous applause.

After the party had finished and we had gone home to the house where we were staying, I went out to stroll in the fields for a while. A full moon

---

2. From a poem by the T'ang poet Ho Chih-chang (659–744), on revisiting his native village.

hung over Mount Takakura, bathing all the valley in soft, dreamlike light. I stood and listened. Mountains, fields, villages and sky, all were still; the only sound the murmur of a stream, the louder for the silence of the valley. My life seemed spread out before me like a painted scroll. Is there anything more mysterious than a man's destiny, or more difficult of attainment than his youthful hopes? As a boy I had dreamt of a triumphal return to Tsumagome. Now I had returned, and what triumph could I claim? My resolve, made at the point of Mother's dagger, to recover all Father's land and property, and with it the ancient dignity of our family and ancestors, had not weakened, but even now I was only a wanderer in the distant city, without an acre to my name, and dependent on others even for the care of Father's grave. How fortunate I was, on the other hand, to have come through the trials of these twenty years so fit in mind and body. How fortunate to have a mother still in such good health, and a loving wife and children of my own! There might be no Kikuchi acres in Tsumagome, but I had less tangible assets there in plenty. A group of citizens were eager for me to represent them in the Diet, and a relative had promised to register half his land in my name whenever I needed a local property qualification. In the larger world my name was known a little, I had many friends of like mind. If the Kikuchi tree had all but withered in its native home, the seedling in the capital was showing a bud or two. What could I do but pour out again and again my gratitude to Heaven? And for the future, what else remains but to walk steadfastly, with heartfelt thankfulness for the blessings of thirty years and a prayer as heartfelt for the future, in pursuit of my dreams?

(6)

Dear Reader,

Now that my long story has come to an end, may I trouble you before we part with one last report on how my characters are faring?

The Nodas continue to flourish. They have two more children now, both girls. Aunt Noda's name is known all over Kyushu for her school, which she has run so successfully for fifteen years. Not long ago she was offered the headship of a girls' school in Tokyo, but declined to leave, nor would the parents of her girls have let her go even if she had wanted to. Seima is going to stand for the Diet at the next general election, in succession to my old rival Kabaya; 'Why don't you and I, just the two of us, start a two-man party of our own, and try and knock some sense into both the Seiyukai[3] and the Kenseito!'[3] he has been saying in his letters. If he is still some way from achieving the grand ambition he proclaimed at Kugenuma—of getting everyone from the Kuriles to Formosa to eat as much meat as beancurd—his farm is certainly prospering, though he has been in trouble recently, so he tells me, with fifteen of his milch-cows 'going on strike'—

3. The two leading political parties of the time.

foot-and-mouth disease, in other words. Suzue is agitating for a women's college in Kyushu. Seima has bought up the property next to his, as he promised, and Toshiko and I look forward to the day when we can

> enjoy together the full moon
> as it lights the paths
> in our neighbour gardens:
> share too the delicate green
> of the willow in spring.[4]

The Matsumuras are all well. My father-in-law plans a trip to Osaka next year to see the Exhibition, and says he will be coming on to Tokyo afterwards to see his grandchildren. Even that stiff-neck Kinji is mellowing with the years.

Old Mr Nakajima, who had such a passion for reciting Noh, died last year. 'Now at least he'll have time to breathe!' was one disrespectful comment. Aunt Nakajima is still her old larger-than-lifesize self. 'The race of heroes has died out—all except for you and me,' she complained to Mother not long since. Mr Ishikawa is a Surgeon Major-General by now, attached to a division somewhere up north; as knowledgeable in the art of success as in the science of medicine, he is bound to be made a full Surgeon General before long.

Shingo Nakamura has grown weightier than ever, both physically and in worldly substance. Kaijima, Hiraoka and Miike excepted, his must be the largest coalmine in North Kyushu. Ever since the talk we had when I was down in Kyushu, he has been lecturing everybody he meets about Andrew Carnegie. 'Carnegie Nakamura,' they call him now. Mother told me with a smile how once when he was on a visit to Tokyo he had spoken to her of a house in Azabu that was going for twenty thousand yen; it would 'do just perfect for the young gentleman,' he had said, and offered to buy it for us at once 'if only the young gentleman don't get angry!' The lady from the south continues to thrive. Sone is away in America at the moment, on business for Shingo. Of Mr Kumagae and his lady Kinko I have no news, except that he is no longer teaching at the University.

The Nakagawas wallow in riches as before, only more so. There is talk of the head of the house being made a Baron. O-Ito, or whatever her name was, has been married off to a gentleman with a doctorate in law from the Sorbonne. Kan Sensei has been awarded a doctorate for his thesis on the Comparative Study of Japanese and English Literature. Mr Wilkie Brown has had to resign from Kansei College because of illness, and has gone home to America to recuperate. The Reverend Shizu is in Tokyo now, busy with Christian work among university students, as is my old friend Philosopher Endo. I forgot to mention it in the last chapter, but when we were staying down in Kyushu I went with Seima one day to call on Seizan Sensei. Close on seventy now, but still refusing to wear a coat even in the

4. From a poem by Po Chu-i (772–842).

bitterest winter cold, he was living very quietly in his house among the plum trees. Hardy as he was, though, he had lost too many teeth to be able to manage his old Spartan mixture of millet and rice, and had switched instead to noodlemash. 'Kikuchi, is it now? Grown a bit at last, anyway. Come down to fix yourself a seat in the Diet, I suppose?' was his sardonic greeting. Gradually, though, he thawed, and after half a day of talking over old times he entertained us with a great bowl of the thick yam soup that teacher and students had shared so often seventeen years before. He has very few visitors now apart from Seima, who drops in now and then on account of Sensei's old friendship with Uncle Noda. His wife, the shrivelled little lady who in her kindness would secretly fill my sleeve with Sensei's plums, has been dead five years or more.

Thanks to Lawyer Asai's efforts, Mr Nishiuchi won his appeal. He was so grateful to Asai, he sent him I don't know how many boxes of dried fish and vegetables as well as all his expenses, and even wrote to thank me. Mother is sorry for my benefactor, and wishes she could find him a good wife.

Mr Kento has given up politics. His son Masamichi behaved so outrageously in Tokyo, he was ordered home a year or so ago—he's to be married soon, I hear. O-Fuyu's grandfather, Mr Hachiya, is no more; O-Fuyu herself looks after the house in Matsuyama, holding the fort for her brother while he finishes at law school in the capital. She has had many proposals, but has rejected them all.

Cousin Yoshi writes to Mother now and then from Fukuoka, where she is still living with her family. They are as poor as ever, it seems. To add to her worries, her husband has started drinking, out of resentment and frustration at seeing his friends do so much better than himself. Poor Yoshi!

Which brings me to a very strange twist of events. The winter before last, quite by chance, I had news of my other cousin, O-Fuji. Since her flight from home she had found herself five temporary 'husbands', all of whom had deserted her, and was now living with a sixth in a tenement off Umamichi Street in the Asakusa district of Tokyo. Number six was a policeman—and none other, believe it or not, than my old 'comrade' Sanjiro Kasamatsu. Her mother appealed to me to help them. Eventually, after a deal of consultation, I paid their fare down to Kyushu—Shingo having agreed to give Sanjiro a job—and so O-Fuji's mother was able after all to see her daughter once more. There they remain, thanks to Shingo, a quarrelsome husband and a nagging wife, and with them O-Fuji's son, whom Yoshi looked after for so long. To tell the full history of this branch of our family, Uncle Kengo's branch, would need another book; and a very sad one it would be. Perhaps I may write it some day.

Sanjiro's mother, the widow Kasamatsu, continues to chase madly after straws, wherever she sees or imagines luck beckoning. A pathetic figure, as Mother says.

Ando, one-time editor of the *Meiji Review*, failed after all in his business venture, and has joined us once more on the literary front, this time as editor of the *Churitsu News*. Down in Osaka, Asai is more influential than ever. They say he is getting a lot of support for his independent views on the proposed changes in the criminal law, but I haven't heard detailed news lately. Shinshichi, my old landlord, calls on me sometimes. Of all the many comrades of former days, at Seisan Sensei's, the New School, Kansei College and Tokyo Imperial University, some I have never heard of since, some I run into in the street—to mutual shouts of delight; the names of two I saw in the China casualty lists a few years back. Everybody has had the experience of coming across old friends in unexpected places and unexpected circumstances. Only yesterday I met someone whom I last knew as a brilliant student at the New School: after failing five times in as many different careers, he has sunk now to begging. How hard it is for us to discover our true path in life—and having found it, to pursue it to the end! The happy man is he who finds his life's work early, and is so certain of its rightness for him that he never needs to change. It is painful indeed to hear of so many of the cleverest boys I had known squandering their talent and energies haphazardly in a succession of wild enthusiasms, to end up far lower on the ladder than the less volatile dullards they once despised.

Four more years now the moss has grown on Father's grave back home, on Uncle Noda's grave in my second home, on Komai Sensei's grave in Yanaka, on Michitaro's grave in Uwajima. My family and I are all well and happy. Mother divides her time between fondling her grandchildren and working for the Women's Christian Temperance Union. Toshiko writes whenever she can spare the time; already, she declares triumphantly, she is perfectly capable of producing at the very least a Japanese 'Little Lord Fauntleroy'. Shinichiro is in his third year of primary school, Shizu has started at kindergarten; each morning they go off happily together, though now and again there may be tears. As for myself: I crawl forward still, snail-like, towards such light as I can see, sighing the while that my aim should be so high and my reach so low.

Now at last I have finished. And so, my friends, who have heard me so patiently through this long and dreary tale, Shintaro Kikuchi prays for your health and happiness, as he bids you

FAREWELL

March 1900–March 1901

Originally published in Japanese as Omoide no Ki by
Minyusha, Tokyo in 1901

Published by the Charles E. Tuttle Company, Inc., of Rutland,
Vermont and Tokyo, Japan, with editorial offices at Suido
I-chome, 2-6, Bunkyo-ku, Tokyo, Japan, by special
arrangement with Geroge Allen and Unwin Ltd., London.

English translation © UNESCO 1970

First Tuttle edition published 1971

UNESCO Collection of Representative Works

Japanese Series

This book has been accepted in the Japanese Series of the
Translations Collection of the UNESCO

For Product Safety Concerns and Information please contact our EU representative GPSR@taylorandfrancis.com
Taylor & Francis Verlag GmbH, Kaufingerstraße 24, 80331 München, Germany